Democracy for the Few

Third Edition

Democracy for the Few

Third Edition

Michael Parenti

St. Martin's Press

New York

Library of Congress Catalog Card Number: 79-92301
Copyright © 1980 by St. Martin's Press, Inc.
All Rights Reserved.
Manufactured in the United States of America.
43210
fedcba
For information, write St. Martin's Press, Inc.,
175 Fifth Avenue, New York, N. Y. 10010

TYPOGRAPHY: Murray Fleminger

CLOTH ISBN: 0-312-19356-4
PAPER ISBN: 0-312-19357-2

ILLUSTRATION ACKNOWLEDGMENTS

Page 9: Tony Auth in *The Philadelphia Inquirer*; page 17: Ed Valtman in *The Hartford Times*, Conn./Rothko Cartoons; page 39: drawing by Donald Reilly, © 1974 *The New Yorker* Magazine, Inc.; page 90: B.C. by permission of Johnny Hart and Field Enterprises, Inc.; page 114: copyright 1977 by Herblock in *The Washington Post*; page 118: Margulies/Rothko Cartoons; page 129: Sidney Harris; page 134: by permission of Jules Feiffer, copyright 1977, distributed by Field Newspaper Syndicate; page 151: Sidney Harris; page 191: Sidney Harris; page 206: Sidney Harris; page 227: Konopacki in *The Madison Press Connection*/Rothko Cartoons; page 242: © 1976 by Don Wright, distributed by NYT Special Features Syndicate; page 266: Sidney Harris; page 322: Vadillo in *El Sol de Mexico*/Rothko Cartoons.

To Samuel Hendel and Clara Hendel

Preface to the Third Edition

The study of politics is itself a political act, containing little that is neutral. True, we can all agree on certain "neutral" facts about the structure of government and the like. However, the textbook that does not venture much beyond these minimal descriptions will offend few readers but also will interest few. The truth is that any determined pursuit of how and why things happen as they do draws us into highly controversial subject areas.

Most textbooks pretend to a neutrality they do not really possess. In fact, the standard textbooks are not objective but merely conventional. They depict the status quo and propagate an acceptance of things as they are, fortifying the orthodox notions and myths about American politics while avoiding any serious attempt to explain the injustices and inequities that are the realities of socio-political life.

Democracy for the Few offers an alternative interpretation, one that students are not likely to get in elementary school, high school or most of their college courses, or in the mass media or popular political literature. The book directs critical attention to the existing practices and institutional arrangements of the American political system (who governs, what governs and how?) and critical analysis of the outputs of that system (who gets what?).

I have attempted to blend several approaches. Thus, although the book might be considered an alternative text to the standard works, much attention is given to traditional *political institutions.* The Constitution, Congress, the presidency, the Supreme Court, political parties, elections and the law enforcement system are treated in some detail. However, the presentation is organized within a consistent analytic framework so that the nuts and bolts of the various institutions are seen not just as a collection of incidentals to be memorized for the final examination but as components of a larger system, serving certain interests in specific ways. When the institutional, formalistic features of American government are put into an overall framework that relates them to the realities of political power and interest, they are more likely to be remembered by the student because their function and effect are better understood.

In addition, the book devotes considerable attention to the *historical development* of American politics, particularly in regard to the making of the Constitution and the growing role of government. The major eras of reform are investigated with the intent of developing a more critical understanding of gradualism in American politics.

A major emphasis in this book is placed on the *politico-economic aspects of public policy.* The significance of government, after all, lies not in its structure or symmetry as such, but in what it does. And in describing what government does, I have included a good deal of information not ordinarily found in the standard texts. I have done this because it makes little sense to talk about the "policy process" as something abstracted from its content and substance, and because students are often poorly informed about politico-economic issues. But again, this descriptive information on who gets what, when and how is presented with the intent of drawing the reader to an inquiry, an analysis and an overall synthesis of American political reality.

This third edition contains a great deal of updated information and, I believe, a more highly developed interpretation of such things as the systemic role of the presidency, how Congress operates, the new strength of corporate interest groups, the environmental struggle, and the crisis within the political economy. These issues are likely to be the major ones of the 1980s. Every chapter and almost every page have been reworked with an eye to bringing as much new data to the reader as possible in as clear and readable a way as the limitations of space and talent allow. My hope is that this new edition of the book proves to be as useful a tool for the student and the lay reader as were the earlier ones.

For this third edition I once more enjoyed the conscientious assistance of the staff at St. Martin's Press, including Thomas Broadbent, Ellen Wynn, Michael Weber and especially Bertrand Lummus. It goes without saying that Bert Lummus's professional competence, experience and sly humor were almost always assets.

Bruce Andrews of Fordham University worked over every page of the manuscript of the third edition, doing as superb a job of reviewing as any author might wish. To him I owe a special expression of gratitude.

On short notice Jerome Hanus of American University generously provided me with some expert guidance for one of the chapters. My thanks also go to the many fine people at the Institute for Policy

Studies in Washington, D.C., for making their already crowded facilities and their abundant good will available to me. Gretchen McEvoy, Laurie Wimmer and Nora Lachman also assisted me in various ways, making the eight-month task of writing this revision a lighter and more pleasant one.

The personal inscription remains the same: To Clara and Samuel Hendel, one of the very nicest and best teams in the academic world. Their friendship and support, extending back over many years, have helped me in ways that go beyond the confines of scholarship. In return they have my lasting appreciation. Now into his second or third "retirement," Sam Hendel continues to provide several generations of his former students with the kind of encouragement and guidance we need, and he himself remains an active advocate of the best democratic principles. I hope this book measures up to the standards he has set.

Michael Parenti

Contents

xi

5 **The Growth of Government**   65

Serving Business: The Early Years   66
The "Progressive" Era   68
The New Deal: Reform for Whom?   70

6 **Politics: Who Gets What?**   76

Welfare for the Rich   76
The Pentagon: Billions for Big Brother   81
The Sword and the Dollar: Travels Abroad   88
Taxes: The Unequal Burden   94

7 **Health, Welfare and Environment:
The Leaky Pump**   98

The Poor Get Less   98
"Urban Removal" and the Death of Cities   103
Health and Safety for Nobody   108
On Behalf of Pollution and Radiation   113

8 **Law and Order: The Double Standard**   120

The Protection of Property   121
Criminal Enforcement: Unequal before the Law   124
Police Terror: Who Guards the Guardians?   136

9 **Law and Order:
The Repression of Dissent**   141

The Methods and Victims of Repression   141
Agents of National Insecurity   149
Watergate: "The System Works"—For Itself   156
Mind-Controls for Law and Order   159

Democracy for the Few

Third Edition

1

The Study
of Politics

Who governs in the United States? Whose interests are
served by the American political system? Who gets what, when,
how and why? Who pays and in what ways? These are the questions
investigated in this book. American government as portrayed in
most textbooks bears little resemblance to actual practice. What
many of us were taught in school might be summarized as follows:

1. The United States was founded by persons dedicated to building a nation for the good of all its citizens. A Constitution was
fashioned to limit authority and check abuses of power. Over the
generations it has proven to be a "living document" which,
through reinterpretation and amendment, has served us well.
2. The nation's political leaders, the president and the Congress,
are for the most part responsive to the popular will. The people's
desires are registered through periodic elections, political parties
and a free press. Decisions are made by small groups of persons
within the various circles of government, but these decision-
makers are kept in check by each other's power and by their need
to satisfy the electorate in order to remain in office. The people
do not rule but they select those who do. Thus government decisions are grounded in majority rule—subject to the restraints imposed by the Constitution for the protection of minority rights.
3. The United States is a nation of many different social, economic, ethnic and regional groups, which make varied and competing demands on public officeholders. The role of government

1

is to act as a mediator of these conflicting demands, attempting to formulate policies that benefit the public. Most decisions are compromises that seldom satisfy all interested parties but usually allow for a working consensus; hence every group has a say and no one chronically dominates.

4. These institutional arrangements have given us a government of laws and not of men which, while far from perfect, allows for a fairly high degree of popular participation and a slow but steady advance toward a more prosperous and equitable society.

THE POLITICO-ECONOMIC SYSTEM

In recent years many Americans have begun to question whether the political system works as described above. With the persistence of poverty, unemployment, inflation, overseas interventions, gargantuan military budgets, crises in our transportation, health, educational and welfare systems, environmental devastation, deficient consumer and worker protection, increased taxes, a growing national debt, municipal bankruptcies, urban decay, widespread crime in the streets and in high public places—many persons find it difficult to believe that the best interests of the American people are being served by the existing political system.

The central theme of this book is that our government represents the privileged few rather than the needy many, and that elections, political parties and the right to speak out are seldom effective measures against the influences of corporate wealth. The laws of our polity operate chiefly with undemocratic effect because they are written principally to advance the interests of the haves at the expense of the have-nots and because even if equitable in appearance, they usually are enforced in highly discriminatory ways. Furthermore, it will be argued that this "democracy for the few" is not a product of the venality of officeholders as such but a reflection of how the resources of power are distributed within the entire politico-economic system. The chapters ahead treat various aspects of that system, including the structure of the corporate economy, the distribution of wealth and want, the dominant value system, the outputs and costs of public policy (who benefits, who pays), the role of the mass media, the uses of law and order, militarism and foreign policy, and the functions of voting, elections, political parties, pressure groups, the Constitution, Congress, the presidency, the courts and the federal bureaucracy.

This investigation might be described as holistic; it recognizes, rather than denies, the linkages between various components of the whole politico-economic system. When we study any one part of that system, be it the media or the courts, lobbying or criminal justice, overseas intervention or environmental policy, we will see how that part reflects the nature of the whole and how it serves to maintain the larger system—especially the system's overriding dominant class interests. We will also see that issues and problems are not isolated, unrelated happenings, even though they are usually treated that way by the news media and various political commentators. Rather, they are interrelated, being the causes and effects of each other in direct and indirect ways. This will become more evident as we investigate the actual components of the political system in some detail.

As the term is used here, the "political system" refers to the executive, legislative and judicial institutions of government along with the political parties, elections, laws, lobbyists and private-interest groups that affect public policy. One of my conclusions is that the distinction between "public" and "private" is often an artificial one. Public agencies are heavily under the influence of private-interest groups, and there are private interests, like some defense companies, that depend completely on the public treasure for their profits and survival.

The decisions made by government are called "policy" decisions. One characteristic of policy decisions is that they are seldom, if ever, neutral. They almost always benefit some interests more than others, entailing social costs that are rarely equally distributed. The shaping of a budget, the passage of a piece of legislation and the development of an administrative program are all policy decisions, all *political* decisions, and there is no way to execute them with neutral effect. If the wants of all persons could be automatically satisfied, there would be no need to set priorities and give some interests precedence over others, indeed, no need for policies or politics as the words have just been used.

"Politics" herein refers to the play of forces bearing upon the public decision-making process and the interplay of public and private power, group demands and class interest. The way prisons and mental institutions are run, for instance, is not only an administrative matter but a political one, involving the application of a particular ideology about normality, authority and social control, which is protective of certain interests and suppressive of others.[1]

"Politics" can be used in something other than the interest-group sense. Among socialists, for instance, "politics" signifies not only the

---

1. See the section in chapter 9 entitled "Mind-Controls for Law and Order."

competition among groups within the present system but also the struggle to change the entire politico-economic structure, not only the desire to achieve predefined ends but the struggle to redefine ends by exposing what socialists consider to be the injustices of the capitalist system and by posing alternatives to it.[2]

Along with discussing the political system as such, I will frequently refer to "the politico-economic system." Politics today covers every kind of issue, from abortion to school prayers, but *the bulk of public policy is concerned with economic matters*. The most important document the government produces each year is the budget. Probably the two most vital functions of government are taxing and spending. Certainly they are necessary conditions for everything else it does, whether it be delivering the mail or making war. The very organization of the federal government reflects the close involvement the state has with the economy: thus one finds the departments of Commerce, Labor, Agriculture, Interior, Transportation, and Treasury, and the Federal Trade Commission, the National Labor Relations Board, the Interstate Commerce Commission, the Federal Communications Commission, the Securities and Exchange Commission, and so on. Most of the committees in Congress can be identified according to their economic functions, the most important having to do with taxation and appropriations.

If so much of this study of American government seems concerned with economic matters, it is because that's what government is mostly about. Nor should this relationship be surprising. Politics and economics are but two sides of the same coin. Economics is concerned with the allocation of scarce resources for competing ends, involving conflicts between social classes, and among groups and individuals within classes. Much of politics is a carry-over of this same struggle. Both politics and economics deal with questions affecting the material survival, prosperity and well-being of millions of people; both deal with the first conditions of social life itself.

One of the central propositions of this book is that there exists a close relationship between political power and economic wealth. As

---

2. However, socialists frequently will engage in political struggles for immediate goals, such as agitating against government oppression and U.S. militarism at home and abroad, and supporting progressive causes like environmental protection, human services and labor struggles. They do so because they are interested in alleviating the plight of oppressed people even if only in marginal ways and they wish to contain the ruling powers of the center-right forces as much as possible. Also, through such struggles they seek to heighten political consciousness and to develop ways of fighting the abuses of capitalism. Even when running their own candidates, most socialists see election campaigns primarily as a way of alerting voters to the evasive and deceptive qualities of the major candidates and as a means of creating a dialogue that goes beyond mainstream politics.

the sociologist Robert Lynd once noted, power is no less political because it is economic. By "power" I mean the ability to get what one wants, either by having one's interests prevail in conflicts with others or by preventing others from raising conflicting demands. Power presumes the ability to control the actions and choices of others through favor, fear, fraud or force and to manipulate the social environment to one's advantage. Power belongs to those who possess the resources which enable them to control the behavior of others, such resources as jobs, organization, technology, publicity, media, social legitimacy, expertise, essential goods and services and—the ingredient that often determines the availability of these things—money.

Many political scientists have managed to ignore the relationship between power and wealth, treating the corporate giants, if at all, as if they were but one of a number of interest groups. Most often this evasion is accomplished by labeling any approach which links class, wealth and capitalism to politics as "Marxist." To be sure, Marx saw such a relationship, but so did more conservative theorists like Hobbes, Locke, Adam Smith and, in America, Hamilton, Adams and Madison. Indeed, just about every theorist and practitioner of politics in the seventeenth, eighteenth and early nineteenth centuries saw the linkage between political organization and economic interest, and between state and class, as not only important but *desirable* and essential to the well-being of the polity. "The people who own the country ought to govern it," declared John Jay. A permanent check over the populace should be exercised by "the rich and the well-born," urged Alexander Hamilton.

Unlike most of the theorists before him, Marx was one of the first in the modern era to see the existing relationship between property and power as *un*desirable, and this was his unforgivable sin. Marx wrote during the mid-to-late nineteenth century, when people were becoming increasingly critical of the abuses of industrial capitalism and when those who owned the wealth of society preferred to draw attention away from the relationship between private wealth and public power and toward more "respectable" subjects. The tendency to avoid critical analysis of American capitalism persists to this day among business people, journalists, lawyers and academics.[3]

---

3. See William Appleman Williams, *The Great Evasion* (Chicago: Quadrangle Books, 1964) for an analysis of the way Marxist thought has been stigmatized or ignored by American intellectuals and those who pay their salaries. See also Sidney Fine, *Laissez-Faire and the General-Welfare State* (Ann Arbor: University of Michigan Press, 1964) for a description of capitalist, anti-Marxist orthodoxy in the United States in the late nineteenth century and its control over business, law, economics, university teaching and religion.

UNDERSTANDING "THE SYSTEM"

We hear a great deal of talk about "the system." What is often lacking is any precise investigation of what the system is and what it does or doesn't do. Instead, people will attack "the system" and others will defend it. Some say it does not work and should be changed, overthrown or replaced; others say it does work or in any case, we can't fight it and should work within it. Some argue that the existing system is "the only one we have," the implication being that it is the only one we ever *could* have. Hence some people fear that a breakdown in this system's social order would mean sheer chaos, a breakdown in all social order, an end to society itself, or in any case, a creation of something monstrously worse than the status quo. These fearful notions keep many people not only from entertaining ideas about new social arrangements but also from taking a critical look at existing ones.

Sometimes the complaint is made: "You're good at criticizing the system, but what would you put in its place?" the implication being that unless you have a finished blueprint for a better society, one that is worked out and ready to go, you should refrain from pointing out existing deficiencies and injustices. But this book is predicated on the notion that it is a desirable and necessary function for human beings to examine the society in which they live, possibly as a step toward improving it or even changing it in fundamental ways. The purpose here is to understand what *is* and not to present a detailed yet purely speculative study of what could be. We need not abide by the demand that no diagnosis ever be made of an illness unless the investigator has the perfect prescription. If we were to proceed in that way with problems, medical or social, we would get nowhere.

In any case, suggestions *are* offered in the concluding chapter for an alternative system, one that I consider to be more humane, equitable, just and democratic than the existing one. But since the purpose of this volume is to describe rather than prescribe, these suggestions are perforce schematic and in need of development in a future work. I am hopeful that they may be sufficient to show the reader that things do not always have to be the way they are.

Like so much else in the existing society, political life is replete with deceit, corruption and plunder. Small wonder that many people seek to remove themselves from it. But politics remains very much a part of our lives, whether we want it that way or not. The government plays a crucial role in determining the conditions of our communities, our housing, education, medical care, work, recreation, transportation and natural environment.. As a protector of privilege and a purveyor of power, the state can bestow favors on a select few while sending many off to fight in wars halfway around the world. (It should be added that politics extends beyond the actions of state. Decisions that keep certain matters within "private" systems of power—such as leaving rental costs or health care to the private market—are highly political, having important effects on the distribution of social costs and benefits. Private power is even more inequitable and difficult to evade than public power. However, in this book we will focus on the public realm and how private power bears upon and is served by it.)

In ostrichlike fashion, readers might go "do their own thing," pretending that they have removed themselves from the world of politics and power. They can leave political life alone, but it will not leave them alone. They can escape its noise and its pretensions but not some of its worst effects. One ignores the doings of the state only at one's own risk. Rather than evade controversial questions in the pages ahead, I will pursue certain of them. But my intent is not to provoke controversy for its own sake. Instead, I wish to offer a realistic and long overdue analysis of what is happening in the American polity. If the picture that emerges is neither pretty nor pleasing, this should not be taken as an attack on the United States, for this country and the American people are greater than the abuses perpetrated upon them by those who live for power and profit. To expose these abuses is not to denigrate the nation that is a victim of them. The greatness of a country is to be measured by something more than its military budget, its instruments of dominance and destruction, and its profiteering giant corporations; it can be measured by its ability to create a society free of poverty, racism and sexism and free of domestic and overseas exploitation and social and environmental devastation. Albert Camus once said, "I would like to love my country and justice too." In fact there is no better way to love one's country, no better way to strive for the fulfillment of its greatness, than to entertain critical ideas and engage in the pursuit of social justice at home and abroad.

2

Wealth and Want in the United States

If politics is concerned with who gets what, then we might begin by considering who's already got what. How is wealth distributed and used in the United States? What we discover will tell us something important about the political economy of American capitalism.[1]

WHO OWNS AMERICA?

About one-fifth of one percent of the population, the "super rich," own almost 60 percent of the corporate wealth in this country. Approximately 1.6 percent of the population own 80 percent of all stock, 100 percent of all state and municipal bonds and 88.5 percent of corporate bonds. There are about seventy billionaire families in the United States and over 200,000 millionaires.[2] In just about every

---

1. By "capitalism" I mean that system of production, ownership and consumption found in most Western and Third World countries and Japan which manifests two essential conditions: (1) the means of production, specifically the factories, land, mines, utilities, offices, banks, etc., are under private ownership; (2) their primary function is to make money for those who own them. Terms like "corporate capitalism," and "corporate system" refer herein to modern-day capitalism, a system in which economic power is embodied in a relatively small number of large corporations.

2. Ferdinand Lundberg, *The Rich and the Super-Rich* (New York: Lyle Stuart, 1968), p. 144 ff. Also Robert Lampman, *The Share of Top Wealth-Holders in National Wealth* (Princeton, N.J.: Princeton University Press, 1962). And Richard Parker and David Olsen, "The Economy: Paying the Freight for the Jet Set," *Mother Jones*, August 1977, p. 13.

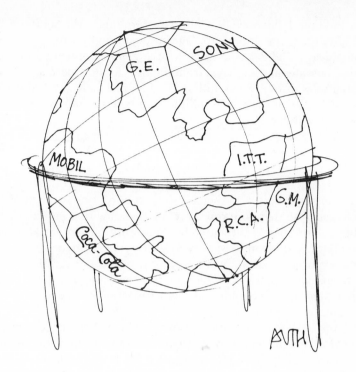

major industry, be it steel, oil, aluminum or automotive, a few giant companies do from 60 to 98 percent of the business. Some two hundred companies account for about 80 percent of all resources used in manufacturing. In 1977 American Telephone and Telegraph (AT&T) alone was worth $86.7 billion. Five New York banks[3] hold a controlling share of stock in three-fourths of the top 324 corporations. Chase Manhattan Bank, controlled by the Rockefellers, is the largest stockholder in CBS, NBC, Union Carbide, General Electric, United Airlines, Eastern Airlines, Safeway Supermarkets and AT&T—to name only a few of its holdings. The wealth of America is not owned by a broadly based middle class. If anything, the trend toward ever greater concentrations of economic power is increasing.[4]

Yet the public is still taught that the economy consists of a wide array of independent producers. We refer to "farmers" as an interest apart from businessmen, at a time when the Bank of America has a

---

3. Chase Manhattan, Morgan Guaranty Trust, Citibank, Bankers Trust and the Bank of New York.

4. See the report released by the Senate Subcommittee on Reports, Accounting and Finances, summarized in *Workers World*, February 17, 1978.

multimillion-dollar stake in California farmlands; the Southern Pacific Railroad is a shipper to "agribusiness" and an owner of vast land acreage; Cal Pak, the world's largest canner of fruits and vegetables, operates at every level from the field to the supermarket with annual sales of over $500 million; and Hunt Foods and Industries, also with sales of over $500 million, has holdings in steel, matches and glass containers.

Many corporations are owned by a wide range of stockholders who, because of their scattered numbers, have little say over the management of their own holdings. From this it has been incorrectly concluded that control of most firms has passed into the hands of corporate managers who themselves own but a tiny segment of the assets and who therefore run their companies with a regard for the public interest that is not shared by their profit-hungry stockholders. Since Berle and Means first portrayed the giant firms as developing "into a purely neutral technocracy," controlled by disinterested managers who allocated resources "on the basis of public policy rather than private cupidity,"[5] many observers have come to treat this fantasy as a reality.

Supposedly the separation of ownership from management has created a benign, service-minded corporation. In fact, the separation of ownership from management is far from complete. Almost one-third of the top 500 corporations in the United States are controlled by one individual or family. Furthermore, many of the "smaller" companies are controlled by the wealthy class in America, including "more than 25,000 family-owned or closely held corporations with assets of more than $1 million which have grown and prospered. . . ."[6] The decline of family capitalism has not led to widespread ownership among the general public. *The diffusion of stock ownership has not cut across class lines but has occurred within the upper class itself.* In an earlier day three families might have owned companies A, B and C respectively, whereas today all three have holdings in all three companies, thereby giving "the upper class an even greater community of interest than they had in the past when they were bitterly involved in protecting their standing by maintaining their individual companies."[7]

Some "family enterprises" are of colossal size. For example, the DuPont family controls eight of the forty largest defense contractors

---

5. A. A. Berle, Jr., and Gardner C. Means, *The Modern Corporation and Private Property* (New York: Harcourt, Brace, 1932), p. 356.
6. F. G. Clark and S. Ramonaczy, *Where the Money Comes From* (New York: Van Nostrand, 1961), p. 42; quoted in G. William Domhoff, *Who Rules America?* (Englewood Cliffs, N.J.: Prentice-Hall, 1967), p. 38.
7. Domhoff, *Who Rules America?*, p. 40.

and grossed over $15 billion in military contracts during the Vietnam war. The DuPonts control ten corporations, each with over $1 billion in assets, including Penn Central, General Motors, Coca-Cola, Boeing and United Brands, along with many smaller firms. Over a million people work for DuPont-controlled firms. The DuPonts serve as trustees in scores of colleges, including some of the country's elite schools. They own about forty manorial estates and private museums in Delaware alone, and, in an attempt to keep the money in the family, have set up thirty-one tax-exempt foundations. The family is frequently the largest contributor to Republican presidential campaigns and has financed and provided leadership for right-wing and antilabor organizations such as the proto-fascist American Liberty League and the American Conservative Union.[8] And in 1976 Pierre DuPont won the governorship of Delaware.

Another powerful family enterprise is that of the Rockefellers. They hold over $300 billion in corporate wealth, extending into just about every industry, in every state of the Union and every nation in the nonsocialist world. The Rockefellers control five of the twelve largest oil companies and four of the largest banks in the world. They have holdings in chemicals, steel, insurance, sugar, coal, copper, tin, computers, utilities, television, radio, publishing, electronics, agribusiness, automobiles, airlines—indeed, in just about every known natural resource or manufactured commodity and service. The Rockefellers finance universities, seminaries, churches, "cultural centers," museums and youth organizations. At one time or another, they or their close associates have occupied the offices of the president, vice-president, secretaries of state, commerce, defense and other cabinet posts, the Federal Reserve Board, the governorships of several states, key positions in the Central Intelligence Agency (CIA), the U.S. Senate and House, and the Council on Foreign Relations.[9]

In companies not directly under family control, the supposedly public-minded managers are large investors in corporate America. Managers award themselves stupendous salaries, stock options, bonuses and other benefits. Thus, despite the decline in the economy and widespread layoffs in various industries, total compensation for top executives rose more than 13 percent in 1977, with the managers of larger firms averaging incomes of $552,000.[10] The executives of

8. Gerald C. Zilg, *DuPont: Behind the Nylon Curtain* (Englewood Cliffs, N.J.: Prentice-Hall, 1974).

9. See Peter Collier and David Horowitz, *The Rockefellers: An American Dynasty* (New York: Holt, Rinehart and Winston, 1976).

10. *Wall Street Journal*, April 18, 1978, and *Daily World*, September 20, 1978.

corporate wealth are almost always wealthy individuals. The interest they have in corporate profits is a direct one. Far from being technocrats whose first dedication is to advance the public welfare, they represent the more active and powerful element of a self-interested owning class.[11] Their power does not rest in their individual holdings but in their corporate positions. "Not great fortunes, but great corporations are the important units of wealth, to which individuals of property are variously attached," C. Wright Mills reminds us. "The corporation is the source of, and the basis of, the continued power and privilege of wealth."[12]

THE PURSUIT OF PROFIT

As the economists Baran and Sweezy write: "The primary objectives of corporate policy—which are at the same time and inevitably the personal objectives of the corporate managers—are . . . strength, rate of growth and size. . . . Profits provide the internal funds for expansion. Profits are the sinew and muscle of strength. . . . As such they become the immediate, unique, unifying, quantitative aim of corporate success."[13] The function of the corporation is not to perform public services or engage in philanthropy but to make as large a profit as possible. The social uses of the product, its effects upon communal life, personal safety, human well-being and the natural environment, win consideration in capitalist production, if at all, only to the extent that they do not violate the profit goals of the corporation.

This relentless pursuit of profit results from something more than just the greed of business people. It is an unavoidable fact of capitalist life that enterprises must expand in order to survive. To stand still amidst growth is to decline, not only relatively but absolutely. Robert Theobald concludes that business firms

> have a special interest in the fastest possible rate of growth, which may not be compatible in the long run with the interests of society. . . . The corporation's profits depend essentially on economic growth and . . . any slowing down in the rate of increase in production tends to cut into

11. For lucid discussions of these points see Ralph Miliband, *The State in Capitalist Society* (New York: Basic Books, 1969), pp. 28–36, and Paul Baran and Paul Sweezy, *Monopoly Capital* (New York: Monthly Review Press, 1968).
12. C. Wright Mills, *The Power Elite* (New York: Oxford University Press, 1956), p. 116.
13. Baran and Sweezy, *Monopoly Capital*, pp. 39–40.

the profits of the firm. The corporation must therefore press for policies that will cause the most rapid rate of growth.[14]

Profits are made by getting workers to produce more in value than they receive in wages. Corporate profit is surplus wealth which must be either distributed to stockholders as dividends or reinvested by the corporation for more profits. As a corporation grows, it must find ways of continuing to grow. It faces the problem of constantly having to devise ways of making more money, of finding new profitable areas of investment for its surplus earnings. Ecologists who worry about the way industry devastates the environment and who dream of a "no-growth capitalism" as the solution, seem not to realize that such a goal is unattainable, for a "no-growth capitalism" is a noninvesting, nonprofit capitalism, which is a contradiction in terms; it is not capitalism at all.

Corporations draw subsidies from the public treasure, rig prices at artificially high levels, impose speedups, layoffs and wage cuts, and move to cheaper labor markets in other countries. In these ways they are often able to increase profits amidst widespread want and unemployment. Business does fine but the people suffer. From 1976 through 1978 there was a 100 percent increase in corporate profits, with giants like GE, RCA, IBM, AT&T and TWA reporting record earnings. In 1978, corporate after-tax profits leaped 25.2 percent. Referring to the earnings made by banks that year, one Wall Street analyst said, "We have simply run out of superlatives."[15]

By cutting labor costs in order to increase profits, corporations also cut into the buying power of the very public that is supposed to buy their commodities.

> Every capitalist's ideal would undoubtedly be to pay his workers as little as possible, while selling products to better-paid workers from other businesses. For the system as a whole, no such solution is possible; the dilemma is basic to capitalism. Wages, a cost of production, must be kept down; wages, a source of consumer spending, must be kept up.[16]

This is one of the contradictions of capitalist economics and one of the causes of its instability.

14. Robert Theobald, *The Challenge of Abundance* (New York: New American Library, 1962), p. 111.

15. Quoted in *American Banker*, July 24, 1978. For reports on corporate earnings see *Wall Street Journal*, October 11, 12, 13, 17, 18 and 19, 1978; also *Business Week*, August 21, 1978; *Washington Post*, March 21, 1979.

16. "Economy in Review," *Dollars and Sense*, March 1976, p. 3.

Recession

The tendency in a capitalist economy is toward the kind of chronic instability caused by overproduction, overinvestment, underconsumption, misuse of productive capacities and labor resources, distorted growth patterns, social dislocation, a glut of nonessential consumer goods and services, and a shortage of essential ones. Production is sometimes cut back, sometimes intensified, in order to maintain profits; prices are raised to compensate for diminished sales; and layoffs and wage cuts are imposed whenever possible. Demand decreases; markets shrink still further; prices are rigged still higher; inventories accumulate; investment opportunities disappear, and the country moves deeper into a recession. This instability is endemic to the system, there having been at least sixteen business cycles within the last hundred years.[17]

Recessions function to keep labor from getting "too aggressive," as well as to weed out the weaker capitalists. In boom times, with nearly full employment, workers are more ready to strike for better contracts. Other jobs are easy to get, and business finds it too costly to remain idle while markets are expanding. Wages are able to cut into profits during good times, but a recession reverses the trend. Business is better able to resist labor demands. A reserve army of unemployed helps to deflate wages. Unions are weakened and often broken; labor contracts offer little in the way of gains, and profits rise faster than wages. A review of the U.S. economy shows big business "coming out ahead of the workers in most areas. The general pattern reveals increased profits, decreased real wages, increased unemployment, higher labor productivity and decreased strike activity."[18]

During recessions, real hardship is experienced by millions, especially in the lower-income brackets. But the very rich, enjoying vast reserves, suffer few personal privations. Indeed, during the recession years of 1974 and 1975, sales of jewelry, antiques, executive apartments, mansions, yachts and Rolls-Royces were booming among upper-class customers.[19] And in business affairs, the economically strong are able to turn the adversity of others into gain for themselves. In the depression of 1875, Morgan, Rockefeller, Gould, Car-

---

17. David M. Gordon, "Recession Is Capitalism as Usual," *New York Times Magazine*, April 27, 1975.

18. Ben Bedell, "Workers Lost Out in 1975," *Guardian*, January 14, 1976, p. 4.

19. See the *New York Times*, February 2, 1975, and the *New York Post*, March 5, 1975. U.S. sales of Rolls-Royce automobiles were up 25 percent in the first quarter of 1976; see *Dollars and Sense*, April 1976, p. 9.

negie, Vanderbilt, Frick and others found ample opportunity to gather control over the broken holdings of smaller competitors, cutting wages, breaking strikes and increasing profits. In more recent depressions, the fortunes of such men as Joseph Kennedy, Howard Hughes and John Paul Getty grew, as did the wealth of the Morgans, Mellons, DuPonts and Rockefellers.

During good times and bad, giant firms rarely go bankrupt. As the steel companies have shown, they can be inefficient and still make profits. While operating at 20 percent below capacity, at a time of high unemployment and price squeeze, U.S. Steel showed a handsome profit growth throughout the 1970s. For the various giants, their position in the industry and their share of the market may change slightly over the years, "but mergers and reorganizations keep the assets and production facilities intact."[20] Even if it is assumed that great profits are the just reward for great risks, in truth there is seldom much risk for the super rich.

Inflation

A major problem of the American economy is inflation. According to mainstream theories, prices fluctuate with economic conditions, going up during times of expansion and down during times of stagnation and recession—as was the case during the Great Depression of the 1930s. Since World War II we have discovered that, be it good times or bad, prosperity or recession, prices move only in an upward direction. The price of goods and services that cost $100 in 1967 almost doubled by 1979. The early months of 1979 showed an inflation rate of over 11 percent, with food, fuel, housing and medical care running well over 12 percent. In the previous year, food prices rose 18.3 percent.[21]

It is often claimed by businesspeople that wage increases are the cause of inflation. In fact, wages have not kept pace with profits. Prices of manufactured goods increased 25 percent faster than labor costs for 1969–1977, causing significantly wider profit margins.[22] In the coal industry, after-tax profits per ton of coal climbed 800 per-

20. Andrew Hacker, *The End of the American Era* (New York: Atheneum, 1970), p. 44.

21. UPI dispatch in the *Morning Union* (Springfield, Mass.), February 24, 1979, and *UAW Washington Report*, August 7, 1978. The average American family spends 70 percent of its income on the four essentials: food, fuel, housing and health care. See *Environmental Action*, November 4, 1978, p. 8.

22. According to a U.S. Commerce Department report cited in *AFL-CIO American Federationist*, March 1978, p. 2.

cent (from 39 cents to $3.25) during the four years of 1974 to early 1978, while miners' wages have risen only 160 percent in the last *twenty* years, and unemployment in the mines has increased drastically.[23] It is not wage demands that cause the upward direction of prices; the "wage-price spiral" has really been a profit-price spiral, and the worker is more the victim than the cause of inflation.

The causes of inflation are not to be found in wage demands so much as in the monopolistic structure of the corporate economy itself. Consider the following:

In almost all major industries, prices are held at artificially high rates, through either deliberate price-fixing or other monopoly practices. In recent years there has been evidence of corporate manipulation of prices in fuel, meat, gasoline and chain-store grocery businesses. One estimate by government officials puts corporate price overcharging at $80 billion a year.[24] Instead of lowering prices when sales drop, the big companies often raise them to compensate for sales losses—as the automotive industry has repeatedly done. The law of supply and demand, which says prices drop during an economic slump, simply does not operate in a market controlled by a few giants.

Wheat shortages in 1972 (supposedly due to the vast amount of wheat sold to the Soviet Union) were used as an excuse for the rise in bread prices. In 1977 a bumper wheat crop brought a surplus which, according to the "free market" principles of supply and demand, should have lowered bread prices; yet the price of bread still rose. According to the U.S. press this was due to the costs and profits of the middlemen—millers, bakers and retailers, all of whom are mistakenly treated as different people. In truth, six grain companies buy 90 percent of the grain and companies like ITT control production from the planting of wheat to the wrapping and selling of bread. The law of supply and demand is thus rewritten according to monopolistic rules: first, the giant companies manipulate the supply, then they demand still higher prices.[25]

---

23. Steve Turner, "Striking Miners Make a Plea In Valley," *Valley Advocate* (Amherst, Mass.), February 22, 1978. Low worker productivity is also cited by management as a cause of inflation, yet studies show that American workers are far more productive than those in most other capitalist nations. See Paul Sweezy and Harry Magdoff, "Productivity Slowdown: A False Alarm," *Monthly Review*, June 1979, pp. 1–12.
24. "The Fix Is In: Price Rigging," *Butcher Workmen*, October 1976.
25. See Bill Del Vecchio, "U.S. Bread Prices Up Despite Overflow Harvest," *Workers World*, July 15, 1977; and Connie Harris, "Administration's Wheat Proposal to Send Bread Prices Up," *Workers World*, September 2, 1977.

The Hartford Times *Ed Valtman '73*

Secondly, prices are rigged at artificially high rates through government subsidies, price supports and limits on production. Thus acreage-reduction programs award billions of dollars to agribusiness for producing nothing—certainly a situation conducive to inflation. When the big companies sell steel, wheat, tobacco, cotton and other products at world prices lower than those inside the United States, the U.S. government makes up the difference with direct giveaway subsidies, enabling the oligopolies not only to compete favorably in foreign markets but to maintain high prices on the domestic market.

A third important cause of inflation is that the U.S. economy is increasingly and disproportionately directed toward nonproductive areas such as:

1. Massive military expenditures designed mostly to protect overseas U.S. investments and right-wing regimes friendly to the multinational corporations (along with a dramatic growth in the domestic police apparatus since the 1960s to control political protest and urban disturbances at home). While creating jobs and distributing billions in income, military and security appropriations produce nothing that would absorb the spending power that is artificially created. Military spending consumes vast amounts of labor and environmental resources but does not produce the things people need in the way of housing, food, fuel and other human services.[26]

---

26. The *Wall Street Journal* notes: "Outlays for defense happen to be a particularly inflation-producing type of federal spending," and the *Journal* quotes one leading conservative economist as saying: "National defense spending makes an already grim inflation picture even grimmer." *Wall Street Journal*, August 30, 1978.

2. Unemployment payments and welfare expenditures to assist the economic victims of capitalism—the poor, the unemployed and others—or at least to provide sufficient palliatives to keep them from becoming too troublesome—in effect, affording them some minimum buying power but little or no opportunity to become productive members of the society.

3. The nonproductive private bureaucracies of big business engaged in extending managerial control over production, finance and distribution, which place increasing numbers of persons in planning, job supervision, banking, bookkeeping, billing, data accumulation, advertising, marketing, consumer surveys and so on.

4. Public bureaucracies to service the activities of giant corporations at home and abroad.[27]

Needs, Productivity and Bigness

One explanation of why our nation's economic problems remain unsolved or actually worsen is that most of society's resources are devoted to other things, to the production of goods and services for private profit. Those who insist that private enterprise can answer our needs seem to overlook the fact that private enterprise has no such interest, at least not when no profit is to be had. The poor may *need* shoes but they offer no market for shoes; there is a market only when need (or want) is coupled with *buying power* to become *demand*. The shoe manufacturer responds to market demand—that is, to a situation in which money can be made—and not to human need no matter how dire it be. When asked by the Citizens' Board what they were doing about the widespread hunger in the United States, numerous food manufacturers responded that the hungry poor were not their responsibility. As one company noted: "If we saw evidence of profitability, we might look into this."[28]

The difference between *need* and *demand* shows up on the international market also. When buying power rather than human need determines how resources are used, then poor nations feed rich ones. Much of the beef, fish and other protein products consumed by North Americans (and their livestock and domestic pets) comes from Peru, Mexico, Panama, India, Costa Rica and other countries where

---

27. See the lively and well-illustrated book *Q. What's Happening to Our Jobs?* (Somerville, Mass.: Popular Economic Press, 1976).

28. Quoted in *Hunger, U.S.A.*, a report by the Citizens' Board of Inquiry into Hunger and Malnutrition in the United States (Boston: Beacon Press, 1968), p. 46.

grave protein shortages exist. These foods find their way to profitable U.S. markets rather than being used to feed the children in these countries who suffer from protein deficiencies. In Guatemala alone, 55,000 children die before the age of five each year because of illnesses connected to malnutrition. Yet the dairy farmers of countries like Guatemala and Costa Rica are converting to more profitable beef cattle for the U.S. market. The children *need* milk, but they lack the pesos, hence there is no market. Under capitalism, money is invested only where money is to be made.

Some defenders of the established system contend that the pursuit of profit is ultimately beneficial to all since the productivity of the corporations creates mass prosperity. This argument overlooks several things: high productivity frequently *detracts* from the common prosperity even while making fortunes for the few, and it not only fails to answer to certain social needs but may create new ones. The coal mining companies in Appalachia, for example, not only failed to mitigate the miseries of the people in that area; they *created* many miseries, swindling the Appalachians out of their land, underpaying them, forcing them to work under inhumane conditions, destroying their countryside and refusing to pay for any social costs resulting from corporate exploits.

Furthermore, an increasing productivity, as measured by a gross national product (GNP) of more than $2 trillion a year, may mean less efficient use of social resources and more waste.[29] As the environmentalist Barry Commoner pointed out, in the last two decades production techniques have been developed which sharply decrease the efficiency of energy use for the sake of profits. Thus the use of leather and steel, which require $.97 and $1.50 worth of oil respectively for the production of $100 worth of goods, has been replaced by the use of plastics, requiring $8.72 worth of oil to produce the same amount of goods.

The *human* value of productivity rests in the social purpose to which it is directed. Is the purpose to plunder the environment without regard to present and future ecological needs, fabricate endless consumer desires, produce shoddy goods that are designed to fall apart quickly, create wasteful high-priced forms of production and service, pander to snobbism and acquisitiveness, squeeze as much

---

29. The GNP is the total value of all the goods and services produced in a given year. Methods of measurement are often arbitrary and imprecise. Important nonmarket services like housework and child-rearing are not counted. And much that *is* counted is of negative social value; thus, highway accidents, which lead to increased auto repairs, wreckage and insurance costs, car sales, and ambulance, hospital and police costs, add quite a bit to the GNP but take a lot out of life.

compulsive toil as possible out of workers while paying them as little as possible—all in order to grab as big a profit as one can? Or is productivity geared to satisfying the communal needs of the populace in an equitable and rational manner? Is it organized to serve essential needs first and superfluous wants last, to care for the natural environment and the health and safety of citizens and workers? Is it organized to maximize the capabilities, responsibilities and participation of its people? Capitalist productivity-for-profit gives little consideration to the latter set of goals. Indeed, what is called productivity, as measured by *quantitative* indices, may actually represent a decline in the *quality* of life—hence the relationship between the increasing quantity of automobiles and the decreasing quality of the air we breathe. Such measurements of "prosperity" offer, at best, a most haphazard accounting of many qualities of social life.

The apologists for capitalism argue that the accumulation of great fortunes is a necessary condition for economic growth, for only the wealthy can provide the huge sums needed for the capitalization of new enterprises. Yet a closer look at many industries, from railroads to atomic energy, suggests that much of the funding has come from the government—that is, from the taxpayer—and most of the growth has come from increased sales to the public—from the pockets of consumers. It is one thing to say that large-scale production requires capital accumulation but something else to presume that the source of accumulation must be the purses of the rich.

In areas of private research, giant corporations leave a good deal of the pioneering work to smaller businesses and individual entrepreneurs, holding back their own investments until money is to be made. Referring to electric appliances, one General Electric vice-president noted: "I know of no original product invention, not even electric shavers or heating pads, made by any of the giant laboratories or corporations. . . . The record of the giants is one of moving in, buying out and absorbing the small creators."[30]

Defenders of the present system claim that big production units are more efficient than smaller ones, a highly questionable contention, for in many instances, huge modern firms tend to become less efficient and more bureaucratized with size, and after a certain point in growth there is a diminishing return in productivity. Moreover, bigness is less the result of technological advance than of profit

---

30. Quoted in Baran and Sweezy, *Monopoly Capital*, p. 49. The record of the biggest oil companies, Exxon and Shell, is strikingly undistinguished in the field of oil exploitation. See Anthony Sampson, "How the Oil Companies Help the Arabs to Keep Prices High," *New York*, September 22, 1975, p. 55.

growth. When the same corporation has holdings in mining, manufacturing, housing, insurance, utilities, amusement parks, publishing and communications, it becomes clear that giantism is not the result of a technological necessity that supposedly brings greater efficiency but the outcome of capital concentration. The search is not for more efficient production but for new areas of investment.

Likewise the concern is not to maintain the well-being of the industry as such, but to extract as large a profit as possible. Ultimately, "efficiency" is not measured by the technical condition of the productive unit but by the return on the investment. One need only recall how railroads, shipping lines, mines, factories and housing complexes have been bought and sold like so many game pieces for the sole purpose of extracting as much profit as possible, often with little regard for maintaining their functional capacity.[31] The long-term survival and capacity of an office, factory, farm, mine, railroad, bus line or newspaper are of less concern to the investor than the margin of profit to be had. If firms sometimes totter on the edge of ruin, to be rescued only by generous infusions of government funds, it is after stockholders have collected millions in high profits. Thus during the years 1967 to 1971, the "depressed" aerospace industry, plagued by climbing costs and layoffs and repeatedly rescued from the brink of insolvency by fat government subsidies, netted for its investors $3 billion in after-tax profits.

The power of the business class is not total, "but as near as it may be said of any human power in modern times, the large businessman controls the exigencies of life under which the community lives."[32] The giant corporations control the rate of technological development and the terms of production; they fix prices and determine the availability of livelihoods; they decide which labor markets to explore and which to abandon; they create new standards of consumption and decide the quality of goods and services; they divide earnings among labor, management and stockholders and donate funds to those political causes they deem worthy of support; they transform the environment itself, devouring its natural resources and poisoning the land, water and air; they command an enormous surplus wealth while helping to create and perpetuate conditions of poverty for millions of people. And they exercise trustee power over religious, recreational, cultural, medical and charitable institutions

31. See the comments in Matthew Josephson, *The Robber Barons* (New York: Harcourt, Brace, 1934), p. 19 and p. 203.

32. Thorstein Veblen, *The Theory of Business Enterprise* (New York: New American Library Edition, n.d.), p. 8. Originally published in 1904.

and over much of the media and the educational system. Describing Standard Oil Company of New Jersey (now Exxon), David Horowitz writes:

> More powerful than many sovereign states, it has 150,000 agents, organizers and hired hands operating 250 suborganizations in more than 50 countries. It is part of an international syndicate which controls the economic lifeblood of half a dozen strategic countries in the underdeveloped world. In itself it is a major political force in the key electoral states of New York, Pennsylvania, New Jersey and Texas, and it has close links with other syndicate members that are major political forces in California, Ohio, Louisiana, Indiana and elsewhere. Its agents and their associates occupied the cabinet post of Secretary of State in the Administrations of Eisenhower, Kennedy and Johnson, and at the same time had influence in the CIA and other foreign-policy-making organizations of government at the highest levels. It has its own intelligence and paramilitary networks, and a fleet of ships larger than the Greek Navy. It is not a secret organization, but it is run by a self-perpetuating oligarchy whose decisions and operations are secret. And these affect directly and significantly, the level of activity of the whole U.S. economy.[33]

THE DISTRIBUTION OF WANT AND MISERY

The United States has been portrayed as a land of prosperity and well-being. But closer scrutiny brings no great cause for celebration. The life expectancy of American men is lower than in eighteen other countries. The infant mortality rate is worse than in thirteen other nations. In eleven countries women have a better chance to live through childbirth than in the United States.[34] More than 22 million Americans have no health insurance and millions have no access to medical care.[35] One out of every four lives in substandard housing.[36] One out of every five American adults is functionally illiterate.[37] Almost 80 million Americans live on incomes estimated as

---

33. David Horowitz, "Social Science or Ideology?" *Social Policy*, 1, September–October 1970, p. 30.

34. Samuel Shapiro *et al.*, *Infant, Prenatal, Maternal and Childhood Mortality in the United States* (Cambridge, Mass.: Harvard University Press, 1968).

35. Report from the Third National Conference on Rural America, in *Guardian*, December 21, 1977.

36. See the report: "The Nation's Housing Needs: 1975–1985," published by the MIT–Harvard Joint Center for Urban Studies, Cambridge, Mass., March 1977.

37. According to a U.S. Office of Education survey; see *Syracuse Post-Standard*, October 30, 1975.

below minimum adequacy by the Department of Labor. About 26 million are designated as living in acute poverty. Of these only 5.4 million get either food stamps or free food. Of the six million school children from rock-bottom poverty families, fewer than two million receive either free or reduced-price school lunches.[38]

Racial minorities suffer disproportionately more in every area of life, be it health care, infant mortality, life expectancy, disability, housing, employment, wages, literacy or whatever. Black people, who compose only about 13 percent of the population, make up something closer to 45 percent of those below the officially designated poverty level. (Statistics like these are usually distorted in a way that underestimates the number of poor, and of Black poor in particular, being based on a national census that drastically undercounts transients, homeless people and those living in crowded ghettos. The Census Bureau reported that the 1970 census had missed counting an estimated 5.3 million people, a disproportionate number being poor and Black.)

Hunger and Poverty

Some Americans believe that those described as "poor" in the United States would be considered fairly well-off in Third World nations.[39] However, the Citizens' Board of Inquiry into Hunger and Malnutrition discovered that in the United States more than 12 million suffer from conditions of malnutrition and hunger comparable to those found in places like Turkey and Pakistan. These conditions, "increasing in severity and extent from year to year," exist in every state in the Union, in rural areas, small towns and large cities.[40]

The Citizens' Board reported that many American infants die within the first two years of life because of starvation. Another study found that the premature-birth rate of the poor in the United States is three times that of middle-income people, and some 50 percent of children from very poor families grow to maturity with impaired learning ability, while 5 percent are born mentally retarded because of prenatal malnourishment.[41] In 1975 a group of scientists at the University of California released a study showing that over *one mil-*

---

38. See *Hunger, U.S.A.*
39. Thus the frenetic Senator S. I. Hayakawa (R.-Calif.) proclaims: "The poor of America are not poor by world standards." See his "Mr. Hayakawa Goes to Washington," *Harper's*, January 1978, p. 43.
40. See *Hunger, U.S.A.*
41. Nick Kotz, *Let Them Eat Promises: The Politics of Hunger in America* (Englewood Cliffs, N.J.: Prentice-Hall, 1969).

lion babies and young children in the nation are suffering brain damage from malnutrition caused by extreme poverty. When malnourished pregnant women are included in the findings, another million babies yet to be born are seriously imperiled.[42] One doctor found "serious malnutrition deficiencies" in almost half the children from poor families in Texas and Louisiana.[43] And a Senate select committee reported that "infectious diarrhea, dehydration, malnutrition and anemia" were typical health conditions among children of the rural poor.[44] In region after region teachers reported that children came to school too hungry to learn and sometimes in such pain that they had to be taken home. Younger children regularly went to bed hungry, never knowing the taste of milk.[45]

Children who live in chronic hunger, according to Dr. Robert Coles, "become tired, petulant, suspicious and finally apathetic." Malnourished four- and five-year-olds, he noted, experience the aches of the body as more than just a physical fact of life. They interpret such misery as a judgment made by the outside world upon them and their families, a judgment that causes them to reflect upon their own worth.

> They ask themselves and others what they have done to be kept from the food they want or what they have done to deserve the pain they seem to feel. . . .
> All one has to do is ask some of these children in Appalachia who have gone north to Chicago and Detroit to draw pictures and see the way they will sometimes put food in the pictures. . . . All one has to do is ask them what they want, to confirm the desires for food and for some kind of medical care for the illnesses that plague them.[46]

The well-known Field Foundation report by a team of doctors investigating rural poverty in 1967 noted:

> In child after child we saw: evidence of vitamin and mineral deficiencies; serious untreated skin infestation and ulcerations; eye and ear diseases, also unattended bone diseases secondary to poor food intake; the prevalence of bacterial and parasitic disease as well as severe anemia, with resulting loss of energy and ability to live a normally active life;

---

42. *New York Times*, November 2, 1975.
43. *New York Times*, April 28, 1970.
44. "Rural Housing Famine," *Progressive*, April 1971, pp. 7–8; see also Homer Bigart, "Hunger in America: Stark Deprivation Haunts a Land of Plenty," *New York Times*, February 16, 1969.
45. *Hunger, U.S.A.*, p. 9.
46. Quoted in *ibid.*, pp. 31–32.

diseases of the heart and lungs—requiring surgery—which have gone undiagnosed and untreated; epileptic and other neurological disorders; severe kidney ailments, that in other children would warrant immediate hospitalization. . . .[47]

In the United States today, there are people living in abandoned cars, tool sheds and shacks who "pick their food out of garbage cans" or out of town dumps.[48] Despite prolonged illness and destitution, many cannot get on welfare, even after repeated tries. Government food programs reach only a small portion of the poor, and often not the neediest. In areas like Detroit, where, according to the mayor's office, 200,000 are starving, hunger has reached epidemic proportions. Fully one-third of the city's residents are eligible for food stamps but only 18 percent are receiving them.[49] And in New York State alone an estimated one million people who are eligible for food stamps are not getting them.[50]

The inflation of recent years has meant additional misery for the poor. As grocery prices soar families with somewhat higher incomes are forced to buy less expensive foods such as beans, rice, grits and flour. The prices on these commodities are then raised still higher by profiteering producers and retailers. (Thus in 1974, the price of dried beans climbed 256 percent and that of rice over 100 percent.) Poor families, already buying the cheapest foods, are hit the hardest as a result. One last response has been an increased human consumption of dog food: an estimated one-third of all dog food sales in low-income area supermarkets goes for human consumption.[51] Among low-income groups "poor diets are increasing in the United States."[52] Even more prosperous Americans are becoming victims of poor nutrition as the food industry, seeking to maximize profits, offers increasing amounts of highly processed, chemicalized, low-nutrition foods. According to a U.S. Senate report, the plethora of junk foods and the paucity of wholesome ones "may be as damaging to the nation's health as the widespread contagious diseases of the early part of the century."[53]

---

47. Quoted in *ibid.*, p. 13.
48. *New York Times*, February 23, 1977.
49. *Workers World*, February 28, 1975.
50. According to six members of the House Subcommittee on Domestic Marketing, reported in *ibid.*, July 1, 1977.
51. John Cook, "Hunger: High Prices Drive Many to Dog Food," *Guardian*, July 3, 1974, p. 3.
52. Survey by the Department of Agriculture, *New York Times*, March 13, 1976.
53. *Guardian*, March 30, 1977; also "The Sugar Mainline," *Village Voice*, August 13, 1979.

Economic want is a common condition among the elderly. Of the almost 30 million Americans who are 65 years or older, more than half live below the poverty level. As many as 50 percent live on diets that fail to provide adequate nutrients.[54] And 27 percent of the White and 36 percent of the Black adults ages 60 and over have a daily intake of less than 1,000 calories—amounting to a slow starvation diet.[55] "We do see regularly those [elderly] who are found dead in their homes who are almost like walking skeletons," noted one county medical examiner in Florida.[56] The elderly are unable to afford needed medical and nursing care or decent housing and transportation that would allow them to maintain normal social relations. They face loneliness and boredom in a market society that treats old people like used cars.[57] Some of them suffer physical abuse, beatings and neglect at the hands of their grown-up children. "With high prices and unemployment," observes one authority on the subject, "some families resent the old person living with them. They consider him just an extra mouth to feed and a nuisance to look after." The mistreatment of elderly parents is "a new social phenomenon with thousands of victims,"[58] a problem that seems to grow as economic conditions worsen.

Unemployment

Unemployment continues to plague millions of Americans. According to *official* statistics, in recent years, anywhere from 6 to 9 percent of the work force has been in need of employment. But this figure includes only persons collecting unemployment insurance or registered as looking for employment. It does not count many whose benefits have run out or who never qualified for benefits, nor those who have given up looking for work, nor part-time or reduced-time workers who need full-time work, nor the tens of thousands of youth thrown into the labor market immediately after leaving school, nor many women who need work but are classified as "housewives," nor the many who join the armed forces because they cannot find employment. A conservative estimate is that 24 million people, one

---

54. *Hunger, U.S.A.*, pp. 9, 24.
55. The Health and Nutrition Examination Survey, 1971–1972, sponsored by the U.S. Department of Health, Education and Welfare, reported in *Workers World*, November 22, 1974. For a statement on poverty and old age, see Sharon R. Curtin, *Nobody Ever Died of Old Age* (Boston: Little, Brown, 1972).
56. *Buffalo Evening News*, October 13, 1974.
57. Millions of elderly "live" on less than $1,000 a year. See John H. Clairborne, "Old Age in Capitalism," *Monthly Review*, November 1972, p. 52.
58. Dr. Erdman Palmore of Duke University, quoted in David Hughes, "Grown-up Children Who Beat Their Aging Parents," *National Enquirer*, June 17, 1975.

worker in four, have been unemployed at some time during each recession year.[59]

The groups that have been hit hardest by unemployment are racial minorities, youths and unskilled workers.[60] Many workers cannot earn enough to support their families. "They work for a living but not for a living wage."[61] The Census Bureau survey of fifty-one urban areas discovered that more than 60 percent of all workers in the inner city could not make enough money to maintain a decent standard of living and 30 percent were earning wages below the poverty level.[62] Almost all farm workers, domestic workers and many unskilled laborers earn poverty wages. Most of the poor have jobs. It is not laziness that keeps them in poverty but the low wages their bosses pay them and the high rents, prices and taxes they have to pay others.

One hears many references to the "affluent workers" of America, of plumbers and construction workers who make more than doctors, and sanitation workers who make more than college professors. Such stories are unfounded. First, it is not clear why sanitation workers should not make more than college professors, since they work harder and at more unpleasant, unhealthy tasks. Second, as a matter of fact, they make substantially less. Even the well-paid "labor aristocracy" of construction workers, given seasonal layoffs and assuming that they can find work at all, average about $12,000 in a good year. The average auto worker, backed by one of the stronger unions and operating in one of the better-paying labor markets, takes home less after years on the assembly line than the young college graduate who enters a management trainee program for the telephone company or the same auto industry. Discussions on "how good labor has it" always focus on these better-paying jobs and ignore the 40 million or more who earn subsistence or poverty-level

59. *Dollars and Sense*, January 1976, p. 10.

60. Official unemployment figures for inner-city Black youths run over 40 percent; see *New York Times*, March 10, 1977. Actual figures may be 60 to 75 percent; see *Chicago Tribune*, February 18, 1979. Because of their concentration in the low-paid service sector of the economy, women have been more successful than men in keeping their jobs during the recession, according to the *New York Times*, March 15, 1977. But women and Blacks are still earning far less than White males, and the Black-White income gap continues to widen; see the U.S. Labor Department report cited in *Valley Advocate* (Amherst, Mass.), October 18, 1978, and *New York Times*, May 8, 1978. Women who move into the better-paying professional and business jobs are mostly from higher-income families or are the well-to-do wives of fairly affluent males. See "Women at Work," *Wall Street Journal*, September 8, 1978.

61. William Spring, Bennett Harrison and Thomas Vietorisz, "Crisis of the Underemployed—In Much of the Inner City 60% Don't Earn Enough for a Decent Standard of Living," *New York Times Magazine*, November 5, 1972.

62. *Ibid.*

wages and who face high injury rates, job insecurity and chronic indebtedness.[63]

There are millions who are obliged to hold down more than one job in order to make a sufficient income. Millions more are compelled by their bosses to work ten- and twelve-hour days for extended periods. Involuntary overtime is a major complaint among automotive, postal, steel, mining, trucking and utilities workers. Owners prefer to impose overtime hours rather than hire more workers, thereby saving on the benefits that must be paid to additional employees.[64] About one out of every four workers puts in more than an eight-hour day because of overtime or an extra job. The result is that the average work week today is no shorter than it was thirty years ago.

From nearly every state and in greater numbers each year, unemployed workers and their families are wandering around the country in the hope of finding work, traveling in all directions— "only to find there are no jobs when they arrive."[65] Mortgage foreclosures in many areas are ten times what they used to be. Unable to keep up payments, many jobless persons abandon their homes and take to the road.

Unemployed workers have resorted to selling their blood in order to feed their families. The father, mother and oldest son of one destitute family, homeless because they could not pay their rent, and denied welfare assistance because they had no permanent address, took to selling weekly pints of plasma until they were rejected because of the low iron content of their blood—a condition caused by malnutrition.[66] A jobless worker ran an advertisement in a Pittsburgh newspaper offering to sell one of his kidneys for $5,000. The Kidney Foundation reported one hundred such offers from persons who "needed money." An unemployed father of five in Georgia offered to sell an eye or a kidney for $10,000.[67]

Social Pathology

With economic hardship there comes an increase in social pathology and human unhappiness. A major study at Johns Hopkins University found that unemployment and recession were bringing a noticeable

63. See for instance Dan Georgakas and Marvin Surkin, *Detroit: I Do Mind Dying* (New York: St. Martin's Press, 1975).

64. Victor Perlo, "Why Bosses Push Overtime," *Daily World*, July 20, 1978.

65. Rod Such, "In Search of Work, Jobless Workers Roam U.S.," *Guardian*, March 26, 1975, p. 3.

66. *Guardian*, April 21, 1976.

67. *New York Daily News*, March 28, 1975; *Ithaca New Times*, February 1, 1976.

rise in illness, alcoholism, homicide and suicide.[68] Over 20,000 Americans take their own lives each year. The suicide rate among youths has tripled in the last two decades, and homicide rates rose 21 percent during the 1970–1974 recession period.[69] As crime increases in both urban and rural areas,[70] so does the prison population. More than half a million people are incarcerated in local, county, state and federal prisons, and each week 300 more go to jail than leave. The United States "is now in the midst of a prison building boom."[71]

An estimated 10 million adults have alcohol problems, the number having doubled in recent years.[72] Heroin addiction doubled during the recession years of 1974–1977; once confined to inner-city youth, the problem has spread throughout the country.[73] One out of six Americans takes tranquilizers regularly.[74] Millions are addicted to amphetamines, barbiturates and other drugs. The pushers are doctors; the suppliers are the drug industry; the profits are stupendous. Almost two million Americans are in mental hospitals—some of which are worse than prisons—and millions more have received psychiatric care.[75] Another 35 million, a preponderant number of them low income, suffer from mental and physical handicaps, many of which could have been corrected with early treatment, or prevented with better living conditions.[76]

Some 28 million women are beaten each year by men, with 4.7 million sustaining serious injury.[77] Nearly two million children, predominantly but not exclusively from low-income families, are brutalized, abused and neglected each year. Child abuse kills more children annually than leukemia, automobile accidents or infectious diseases.[78] In areas of growing unemployment, incidents of child

68. See the study by Dr. M. Harvey Brenner reported in *American Teacher*, January 1977.

69. U.S. Census Bureau, *Statistical Abstracts of the United States: 1974*, 95th ed. (Washington, D.C., 1974), p. 147; *Newsweek*, August 23, 1978; *Moneysworth*, July 21, 1975. Suicide now ranks as the third major cause of death among U.S. youths. The suicide rate for young Black males is twice that of young White males. Herbert Hendin, *Black Suicide* (New York: Basic Books, 1969).

70. *New York Times*, December 27, 1977.

71. *New York Times*, July 2, 1978. From 1976 to 1979, the number of prison inmates increased by more than one-third.

72. *Washington Post*, October 18, 1978; *New York Times*, July 2, 1978.

73. See the report by Ingrid Frank and George Richardson in *Penthouse*, September 1977.

74. *In These Times*, November 8–14, 1978, p. 23.

75. Emotional illness is highly related to conditions of poverty. See the study cited in the *Progressive*, November 1977, p. 13.

76. NBC radio report, May 23, 1977.

77. *Newsweek*, January 30, 1978.

78. *New York Times*, November 21, 1978; Ray Helfer and C. Henry Kempe, *The Battered Child* (Chicago: The University of Chicago Press, 1969); David G. Gill, *Violence Against Children* (Cambridge, Mass: Harvard University Press, 1970).

abuse by jobless fathers have increased dramatically. Child labor is still practiced in the United States. Almost one million children, some as young as seven years, serve as underpaid farm workers, dishwashers, laundry workers and domestics for as long as ten hours a day. Agribusiness is increasingly using child labor in the fields. In some states as much as 75 percent of the commercial farm work is done by children. In Maine, 35 percent of the potato harvest is gathered by more than 15,000 children aged five and older.[79]

The Plight of the Middle American

What of the "middle class"? An amorphous category including everyone from well-paid professionals to thrifty postal employees, the "middle Americans" are said to be economically well-off, increasing in numbers and occupying the comfortable nonmanual jobs of an ever-expanding "service sector." In fact, many jobs classified as "white collar" or "service" are among the lowest-paying, menial occupations. Service workers include such occupations as janitors, typists, waiters, porters, ushers and shoeshine boys. Contrary to myths about "affluent workers," the average annual pay for employees in all occupations, union and nonunion, was $9,843 in 1977, about $6,500 less than the "moderate budget" for a family of four set by the Department of Labor, and $500 less than what the department calls an "austere" budget.[80] Even better-paid employees enjoy a tenuous "prosperity," having nothing to cushion them against loss of earning power through catastrophe, recession, layoffs, wage cuts or simply old age.[81] While they may be earning a comfortable salary, they have virtually no wealth—in a society in which wealth is the only certain measure of security.

A 1977 Gallup poll found that the most pressing problem facing U.S. families was having enough money to meet living expenses. A national sample of Americans were most worried about the high cost of living, inflation and taxes. Other common problems were unemployment, illness, medical costs, educating children and inadequate income for retirement.[82] In recent years the real wages of Americans

---

79. Cassandra Stockburger, "Yes, Child Labor Is Still a Problem," *New York Times*, September 4, 1972, also the U.S. Children's Bureau report cited in the *Guardian*, February 22, 1978.
80. *Denver Post*, April 27, 1977.
81. Andrew Levison, *The Working Class Majority* (New York: Penguin Books, 1974) treats this subject well. See also Arthur Shostak, *Blue Collar Life* (New York: Random House, 1969).
82. Reported in the *Guardian*, August 24, 1977.

have been declining by over 3 percent annually. ("Real wages" are the actual purchasing power of wages after discounting for inflation.)

It is said the the "prosperity" of the United States is widely shared, and incomes are becoming more equal. But recent studies find that the gap between rich and poor has widened over the last twenty-five years. And between 1968 and 1975, there was a marked upward shift in income distribution, with close to $10 billion being redistributed from the bottom three-fifths of American families to the richest one-fifth.[83] The trend toward greater inequality of income continues, with Blacks and poor Whites losing ground, and the newer regions of the country and the suburbs doing better than the rural areas and cities.[84] *Almost one out of every ten Whites and nearly one out of every three Blacks, Puerto Ricans and Chicanos live below the poverty level.*[85]

Many of us have been taught that "America belongs to the people," but in fact almost all Americans are tenants, debtors and hired hands in their own country, working for someone else, paying rent or high interest rates on mortgages, loans and installment purchases to someone else. In these relationships the advantage is on the side of the employers, landlords, manufacturers and banks. The boss hires us to make a profit from our labor; the landlord rents to us so that he can make an income on the rental; the manufacturer sells to us so that he can make more wealth on his product than he put into it; and the bank or loan company extends credit so that it can get back substantially more than it lends.[86]

---

83. Henry S. Reuss, "A Democrat's Critique of Nixonomics," *New York Times Magazine*, July 7, 1974, p. 11; also Congressman Reuss's findings reported in the *Progressive*, July 1977, p. 11.

84. *New York Times*, February 25, 1976; also S. M. Miller and Pamela Roby, *The Future of Inequality* (New York: Basic Books, 1970); and Leonard Ross, "The Myth That Things Are Getting Better," *New York Review of Books*, August 12, 1971, pp. 7–9.

85. The actual number of low-income persons may be drastically underestimated. See earlier comments on p. 23.

86. A basic distinction one might make is between those who own and control the wealth and institutions of the society—the "owning class," or "propertied class"—and those who are dependent on the owning class for their employment, the "working class," which includes not only blue-collar workers but also accountants, clerks, professors and anyone who has a job or is trying to get one. The distinction is blurred somewhat by the range of wealth within both the owning and the working class. Thus while "owners" include both the owners of giant corporations and the proprietors of small grocery stores, the latter control a minuscule portion of the wealth and hardly qualify as part of the *corporate* owning class. Likewise, among the working class are professionals and middle-level executives who in income and life style tend to be identified as "middle class," apart from "ordinary workers." Then there are personages in the entertainment and sports worlds, some lawyers and many doctors who earn such lavish incomes that they invest their surplus wealth and become in part, or eventually in whole, members of the owning class.

By the end of 1978 almost 80 percent of American families were in debt (up dramatically from 54 percent six years earlier), most of these so heavily that they were seriously worried about how to meet their bills. A majority indicated that they had borrowed money not to buy luxuries but to pay for necessities and that they now had to do without essential products and services.[87] And each year Americans go deeper into debt. In 1967 the consumer debt for goods and services amounted to $75 billion. By 1974 it had grown to $200 billion and by 1979, $500 billion. Meanwhile the home-mortgage debt had climbed to over $600 billion.[88] According to one conservative publication, mounting debts "are threatening a financial crackup in more and more families. . . . Excessive debt is engulfing thousands of families."[89] The interest rates charged on most sales (when buying on time) bring more profit to the seller than the price markup, thus constituting a kind of legal usury. As consumers, Americans are also victimized by shoddy, unsafe products, deceptive packaging, swindling sales and numerous other unscrupulous practices.[90]

In sum, the history of the great "affluence" in the United States since World War II is of people becoming increasingly entrapped in a high-production, high-consumption, high-profit system. Millions of Americans live under starvation conditions; millions are desperate for work; millions are afflicted by one or another socioeconomic pathology. Millions live in dilapidated, ill-heated and hazardous domiciles. Millions who identify themselves as middle class live in overpriced, poorly constructed, heavily mortgaged homes or high-rent apartments that consume a large part of their incomes while providing living quarters that are far from satisfactory. Millions are immobilized by inadequate public transportation facilities and have no access to decent recreational areas. At the same time, our rivers are turned into open sewers by the countless tons of raw industrial waste dumped into them, our air made foul, our bodies damaged by environmental pollutants, our forests and wildlife destroyed, our roadsides uglified by commercial enterprise, and our cities are showing serious signs of decay and bankruptcy.

---

87. Harris poll reported in *National Enquirer*, December 5, 1978.
88. Paul M. Sweezy, "Crisis Within the Crisis," *Monthly Review*, December 1978, p. 8; *Newsweek*, January 8, 1979; *Business Week*, October 12, 1974.
89. *U.S. News and World Report*, June 22, 1970; also David Caplovitz, *The Poor Pay More* (New York: Free Press, 1967) for a study of how the poor are victimized as consumers and debtors. The victimization of the poor by insurance companies is treated by Max Apple, "Dreams of Immortality," *Mother Jones*, June 1977, p. 46.
90. See the collection of exposé articles in David Sanford *et al.*, *Hot War on the Consumer* (New York: Pitman, 1969).

It is not enough to denounce the inequities that exist between rich and poor; it is also necessary to understand the connection between them. For it is the way wealth is organized and used which creates most of the existing want. By its very nature, the capitalist system is compelled to exploit the resources and labor of society for the purpose of maximizing profits. It is this operational imperative of the system which creates the imbalances of investment, the neglect of social needs, the privation, wastage and general economic oppression and inequality which bring misery to so many. And, as we shall see in the chapters ahead, it is corporate power which prevents a reordering of our priorities and a move toward a healthier, more equitable society.

I COULDN'T HAVE PUT IT BETTER MYSELF.

3

The American
Way

What kind of a nation is the United States? What are
its predominant values and modes of social organization? Although
our society is composed of over 230 million persons of varying occupational, regional, ethnic and religious backgrounds, there are certain generalizations one can make about its beliefs and institutions—
keeping in mind that these allow for exceptions.

WHO'S ON TOP?

A remarkable but often overlooked feature of American society is
that its industrial, communicational, transportational, educational,
recreational and cultural institutions are controlled by rich business
people. In almost no instance do the workers, the people who contribute the labor and skills essential for production, have any decision-making powers over corporate methods, purposes and profits.[1]
Business control extends into areas beyond the business world. Most
universities and colleges, publishing houses, newspapers, television
and radio stations, professional sports teams, foundations, churches,
private museums, charity organizations and hospitals are organized
as corporations and ruled by self-appointed boards of trustees (or di-

---

1. Richard Barber, *The American Corporation* (New York: E.P. Dutton, 1970);
Richard C. Edwards, Michael Reich and Thomas E. Weisskopf, *The Capitalist System*
(Englewood Cliffs, N.J.: Prentice-Hall, 1972); and Paul Baran and Paul Sweezy, *Mo-
nopoly Capital* (New York: Monthly Review Press, 1968).

34

rectors or regents) composed overwhelmingly of business people. These boards, accountable to no one for their decisions, exercise final and absolute judgment over all institutional matters.[2]

Consider the university: most institutions of higher education are public or private corporations (e.g., the Harvard Corporation, the Yale Corporation) run by boards of trustees with ultimate authority over all matters of capital funding and budget; curriculum, scholarships and tuition; hiring, firing and promotion of faculty and staff; degree awards, student fees, etc. Most of the tasks related to these activities have been delegated to administrators, but the power can be easily recalled by the trustees, and in times of controversy it usually is.[3] These trustees (one of whom is usually the university president) are not elected by students, faculty or staff, although an occasional student or professor may be allowed to sit on the board, usually in a nonvoting capacity. The board members are granted legal control of the property of the institution not because they have claim to any academic experience but because as successful bankers, industrialists, corporate lawyers, realtors and heirs to family wealth, they supposedly have proven themselves to be the responsible leaders of the community.[4]

This, then, is a feature of real significance in any understanding of political power in America: *almost all the social institutions and material resources existing in this society are controlled by non-elected, self-selected, self-perpetuating groups of business people who are accountable to no one but themselves.*

The rest of us make our way through these institutions as employees and clients, performing according to standards set by the

---

2. My book *Power and the Powerless* (New York: St. Martin's Press, 1978) has a more detailed discussion of business power within social and cultural institutions.

3. *Ibid.*, pp. 156–163; also David N. Smith, *Who Rules the Universities?* (New York: Monthly Review Press, 1974); James Ridgeway, *The Closed Corporation* (New York: Random House, 1969).

4. Even if it were true that their guidance might be needed on financial matters, it is never explained why trustees should have ultimate power. They could function as consultants without being accorded executive authority over all matters. In fact, on most technical problems, the trustees themselves rely on advisors and specialists. The argument is made that trustees take the financial risks for the university and therefore should have the authority. In fact, they seldom take on personal financial liabilities. Legal judgments made against their decisions are usually covered by insurance paid out of the university budget. If anything, trustees are likely to profit personally by awarding university contracts to their own firms or the firms of business associates. Another argument for trustee power is that students, faculty and staff compose a transient population and therefore cannot be expected to run the university. But their stay at the university is longer than that of the average trustee, who serves for three years, often does not even live in the same city as the university he or she presides over, and visits it for decision-making meetings, at most, once a month.

ruling oligarchs or their administrative agents. The method of rule exercised over us is hierarchical and nondemocratic. These institutions determine many of our experiences as citizens, students, workers, professionals, consumers, tenants, etc., yet we have no vote, no portion of the ownership and no legal decision-making power within them.

Labor unions provide some collective voice for employees and help limit the abuses of management. Some of the more class-conscious unions have supported progressive legislative measures, taken stands against the Vietnam war and criticized the privileges and powers of big business. It is sometimes said that labor unions have become too powerful and too greedy. In truth, unions seldom can match the material resources that corporations command. During the last thirty years, while the work force has grown substantially, union membership has dropped by over twenty percent and now represents only one out of five workers. Union organizing efforts have declined and unions are losing more and more National Labor Relations Board elections. In the construction trades and various other industries, unions have been systematically shut out and denied contracts by management, so that more and more members are now working at below union wage scales.[5]

Far from being militant and uncompromising, some union leaders take on the boss's perspective, emphasizing labor's common stakes with management and stressing the necessity of maintaining high productivity. They allow their membership little voice in the union. In the worst instances they turn the union organization into a personal bureaucratic empire, misusing funds, padding payrolls and voting munificent salaries for themselves and their cohorts. Union leaders are often described as potentates who preside over vast armies of workers. They are indeed powerful in relation to their own membership, but with management the complacent and corrupt ones tend to be tame junior partners.[6]

In our "democracy," the individual's opportunities for self-governance seem to be limited to those few moments spent in the polling booth—assuming that voting is an act of self-government. Many

---

5. Sidney Lens, "Disorganized Labor," *Nation*, February 24, 1979, p. 207; "Labor's Creaking House," *Newsweek*, December 12, 1977, p. 83 ff.

6. For an account of present-day crime in the teamster's union see Jack Newfield, "This Felon Controls the Most Corrupt Union in New York," *Village Voice*, November 6, 1978, pp. 1, 11–14. For other accounts of the complicity of union leaders with management see *New Politics*, Spring 1970, pp. 15–23; Winter 1972, pp. 22–46; and Winter 1973, pp. 13–29. For a statement on the progressive and worthwhile efforts of unions see Andrew Levison, *The Working-Class Majority* (New York: Penguin Books, 1974).

Americans do not seem terribly upset by this situation. They believe as they were taught, that they are a free people. This belief is held even by many who refuse to voice opinions on controversial issues for fear of jeopardizing their jobs and careers.

The power of business does not stand naked before the public; rather it is enshrouded in a mystique of its own making. In the minds of many, the "free-enterprise system" has become indelibly associated with the symbols of America, Patriotism, Freedom, Democracy, Prosperity and Progress. Today convictions about the virtues of private enterprise and the evils of socialism and communism are widely held among Americans of all classes. Yet we should remember that such beliefs did not emerge full-blown from nowhere, nor do they circulate like disembodied spirits. Rather they have been propagated over the generations by the agencies of a capitalist society, including the media, the professions, the schools, the churches, the politicians and the policymakers.[7]

Courses designed to instill appreciation for our "free-enterprise system," taught by community leaders, businesspeople and economists, are required in high schools in Delaware, Tennessee, Oklahoma, Arizona, Florida and other states. Criticisms of "free enterprise" often are equated with un-Americanism. Capitalism is treated as a necessary condition for political freedom, contraposed as the sole alternative to "communist tyranny." The private-enterprise system, it is taught, creates equality of opportunity, rewards those who show ability and initiative, relegates the parasitic and slothful to the bottom of the ladder, provides a national prosperity that is the envy of other lands, safeguards (through unspecified means) personal civil liberties and political freedom, promises continued progress in the endless proliferation of goods and services and has made America the great, free and beautiful nation it is.

GETTING MORE AND GETTING AHEAD

In the United States many billions of dollars are spent each year to induce people to consume as much as they can and—through installment plans—more than they can afford. The inducements seem to

---

7. See William Preston, Jr., *Aliens and Dissenters* (Cambridge, Mass.: Harvard University Press, 1963); William Appleman Williams, *The Great Evasion* (Chicago: Quadrangle Books, 1964); Michael Parenti, *The Anti-Communist Impulse* (New York: Random House, 1969); Francis X. Sutton *et al.*, *The American Business Creed* (New York: Schocken Books, 1962); Sidney Fine, *Laissez-Faire and the General-Welfare State* (Ann Arbor: University of Michigan Press, 1964); Parenti, *Power and the Powerless*, chapter 11.

work: Americans are a people dedicated to the piling up of goods, services and income. This consumerism is not just a habit but *a way of life*, a measure of one's accomplishment and a proof of one's worth.

For most people life is defined as a series of private goals to be attained through personal means, rather than as collective efforts in pursuit of rewards that might be communally distributed and enjoyed. One should endeavor to "get ahead." Ahead of what? Of others and of one's own present status. This "individualism" is not to be mistaken for freedom to choose moral, political and cultural alternatives of one's own making. Each person is expected to operate "individually" *but in more or less similar ways and similar directions*. Everyone competes against everyone else but for the same goals and with the same values in mind. "Individualism" in the United States refers to *privatization* and the absence of communal forms of production, consumption and recreation. You are an individualist in that you are expected to get what you can for yourself, by yourself, and not to be too troubled by the needs and problems faced by others. This attitude, considered criminal in many societies, is labeled approvingly as "ambition" in our own and is treated as a quality of great social value.

Whether or not this "individualism" allows one to have control over one's own life is another story. The decisions about the quality of the food we eat, the goods we buy, the air we breathe, the prices we pay, the way work tasks are divided and jobs defined, the kinds of transportation, recreation and entertainment we are offered, the opinions and the values fed to us by newspapers, magazines, television and radio, the kind of treatment accorded us in our schools, clinics and hospitals—the controlling decisions concerning the palpable realities of our lives—are made by people other than ourselves. Yet Americans continue to think of themselves as self-reliant individualists. What they seem to be referring to is the privatism and atomization of their social relations and the relative absence of cooperative endeavor.

"We live in an economy of abundance when it comes to producing material goods but in a *society of scarcity* when it comes to creating human relations between people," observes James Boggs.[8] Competitive privatism brings a good deal of loneliness and isolation and few occasions for meaningful community experiences with other human beings. Philip Slater argues that Americans constantly attempt

---

8. James Boggs, "Beyond Malcolm X," *Monthly Review*, December 1977, p. 47 (emphasis in the original).

*"Religious freedom is my immediate goal, but my
long-range plan is to go into real estate."*

Drawing by Donald Reilly; © 1974 The New Yorker Magazine, Inc.

to minimize or deny human interdependence. We seek a private
home, a private country place, a private means of transportation, a
private laundry, private recreation, private lessons, a private garden, etc. Even within the family, each member seeks a separate
room and a separate telephone, television and car when it is economically possible to do so. "We seek more and more privacy,"
Slater notes, "and feel more and more alienated and lonely when we
get it."[9]

The lack of community does not prevent Americans from identifying with larger collective entities, such as a school, a town or the
nation. But even this identification is expressed in terms that are

---

9. Philip Slater, *The Pursuit of Loneliness* (Boston: Beacon Press, 1970), p. 7.

competitive with other schools, towns or nations. In sports, for instance, it is said that the important thing is not who wins but how the game is played; yet whole schools and cities are gripped by joyful frenzy when their team wins a championship. The really important thing is the winning.

The need to be first and foremost extends with special intensity to the nation. We are instructed to love America because it is "the greatest country in the world," the presumption being that if it were not so great it would not be so lovable. America supposedly is great because of its laudable intentions and practices—and its military might. Greatness, then, is a matter not only of virtue but of strength. The superpatriots are usually the most militaristic. Love of country becomes associated with huge military budgets and armed intervention throughout the world. As part of our greatness we need to keep the world safe from revolutionaries who advocate a different kind of social order. The presumption that the United States has a right to police the entire globe rests on the belief that our intentions are honorable, our interests selfless and the outcomes of our actions salutary for other peoples.

In their personal and national egoisms Americans are hardly unique; but the United States is unique in the magnitude of its powers and the effects its actions have on other peoples. For many generations Americans have envisioned mankind developing as an extension of the American experience, enjoying the inspirational example of our political institutions. Our goal has been a world of "law and order" with a decided advantage going to those who define the order and enforce the law—a world respectful of mankind's best interests. That these interests also happen to be identical with the best interests of the United States, as defined by its ruling elites, is no cause for embarrassment, it being understood that less fortunate peoples, if not misled by revolutionaries and if given occasional succor from the happiest, richest, most successful nation in the world, will eventually develop orderly institutions like our own and achieve the blessings of peace and prosperity. Give or take some cultural variations, they will emerge as did America, from the howling wilderness to the machine-fed garden.

This global vision is still with us, but so is the nightmare that always lurked behind it—the fear that others might turn their backs on the American-defined world order and construct competing social systems which propagate values (especially those relating to the use and distribution of wealth) that might somehow undermine our American Way of Life, plunder our treasure, lower our standard of living, and oust us from our position of preeminence. "America," President Nixon warned, "must never become a second-rate power." Only in supremacy do the elites hope to find security. The haves always live in fear that the have-nots will try to equalize things. President Johnson summed it up before a Junior Chamber of Commerce audience: "We own half the trucks in the world. We own almost half of the radios in the world. We own a third of all the electricity. . . ." But the rest of the world wants it for themselves, he added. "Now I would like to see them enjoy the blessings that we enjoy. But don't you help them exchange places with us, because I don't want to be where they are." For many Americans, Johnson was touching the vulgar heart of the matter: keep others from taking what we have.

From their earliest grade school days Americans are taught competitive methods of accomplishment. One's peers are potentially one's enemies; their successes can cause us envy and anxiety, and their failures bring secret feelings of relief. The ability or desire to work collectively with others is much retarded. Competitive efforts are primarily directed against those of the same class or those below, a condition that suits the interests of those at the top. Among the strongest critics of workers who get better wages through collective bargaining and collective action are workers who do not and who complain, like management itself, that their more fortunate brethren are never satisfied. Any unusual success enjoyed by a friend, co-worker or colleague can evoke more jealousy in people than the successes of a multimillionaire on the far-off upper rungs of the social ladder.

Many feel even more competitive toward those defined as their social inferiors: the poor, Blacks, other minorities and women. To be outdone by one's peers is bad enough, but many persons, raised in a sexist, racist, class-chauvinist society and taught to define their self-worth in terms of their superiority over others, find it insufferable to be outdone by their "inferiors." As products of a competitive, acquisitive society, many Americans do not welcome equality; they fear and detest it and have a profound commitment to inequality.

People who have invested much psychic energy and years of toil in maintaining or furthering their positions within the social hierarchy become committed to the hierarchy's preservation. Even those perched on modest rungs of the ladder—the millions of small proprietors, lower-paid semiprofessionals and white-collar workers, often described as "middle Americans," who could have much to gain from a more egalitarian social order—fear that they might be overtaken by those below, making all their toil and sacrifice count for naught.[10]

The hostility they may feel for the welfare poor is felt less intensely toward the welfare rich who receive billions of dollars in government subsidies, tax write-offs and other services. This is mostly because Americans are given little information on how the corporations feed out of the public trough, such subjects being deemed unworthy of treatment by the business-owned media and by mainstream educational institutions. Middle Americans are critical of millionaires who do not pay taxes, but in most respects they tend to see the wealthy as having earned their advantages by effort, intelligence and resourcefulness.

Proximity to the poor is to be avoided, while wealth is something to be attained someday by oneself or one's children—something, in any case, to be admired. Hence the road upward should be kept open with no artificial impediments imposed by the government on those who can advance, while the road behind should not be provided with conveyances for those who wish to catch up effortlessly.

To be sure, Americans have their doubts about the rat race, but they cannot lightly discard the years of effort and sacrifice they have invested in it and shift to another set of values. As Slater notes: "Suburbanites who philosophize over their back fence with complete sincerity about their dog-eat-dog world, and what-is-it-all-for, and you-can't-take-it-with-you, and success-doesn't-make-you-happy-it-gives-you-ulcers-and-a-heart-condition—would be enraged should their children pay serious attention to such a viewpoint."[11]

The American's competitiveness is fortified by a *scarcity psychology* that bears little relation to how much he or she has. There is always more to want and more to get, more to hang on to and more to lose. Thus the highly paid professional feels the pressure of "moreness" as much as the lowly paid blue-collar worker. Economically deprived groups like urban ghetto dwellers, sharecroppers, welfare recipients, female employees and low-income workers are seen as a nuisance and a threat because, like the rest of us, they want more, and more for them might mean less for us. The scarcity psychology, then, leaves us with the feeling that the poor and the racial minorities (our potential competitors) should be kept in their place and away from what we have and want.

A belief in the inferiority of deprived groups is functional for those possessed by a scarcity psychology. Racism, sexism and class

---

10. See Robert Lane, *Political Ideology* (New York: Free Press, 1962), pp. 57–81.
11. Slater, *The Pursuit of Loneliness*, pp. 6–7.

bigotry help us exclude large numbers of people, limiting the field of competitors and justifying in our minds the inequities these groups are made to endure. Having designated them as moral inferiors, we become easily convinced that the hardships they suffer are due to their own deficiencies (lazy poor, dumb Blacks, dirty Mexicans, silly women, etc.). "Those people don't *want* to better themselves," is the comment often made by individuals who then become quite hostile when lower-status groups take actions intended to better themselves. The belief that others are lacking in natural abilities does not seem to free us of the anxiety that they might catch up and even surpass us.

In movies, on television, in grade-school textbooks and in popular fiction, the world is portrayed as a predominantly middle-class place; working-class people are often presented as uncouth, unintelligent and generally undesirable. A TV series like "All in the Family," while supposedly exposing bigotry, practices a bigotry of its own by stereotyping the working-class lead character, Archie Bunker, as a loud-mouthed ignoramus and bully, poking fun at his mispronunciations, life style and physical appearance. Class chauvinism is one of the most widely spread forms of prejudice in American society and one of the least challenged. As one of the characters in Kurt Vonnegut's *Slaughterhouse-Five* observes:

> To quote the American humorist Kim Hubbard, "It ain't no disgrace to be poor, but it might as well be." It is in fact a crime for an American to be poor. . . . Every other nation has folk traditions of men who were poor but extremely wise and virtuous, and therefore more estimable than anyone with power and gold. No such tales are told by the American poor. They mock themselves and glorify their betters. The meanest eating or drinking establishment, owned by a man who is himself poor, is very likely to have a sign on its wall asking this cruel question: "If you're so smart, why ain't you rich?" . . . .
> Americans . . . who have no money blame and blame and blame themselves. This inward blame has been a treasure for the rich and powerful, who have had to do less for their poor, publicly and privately, than any other ruling class since, say, Napoleonic times.[12]

If material success is a measure of one's worth, then the poor are not worth much and society's resources should not be squandered on them. If rich and poor get pretty much what they deserve, then it is self-evident that the poor are not very deserving. If farm workers

---

12. Kurt Vonnegut, Jr., *Slaughterhouse-Five* (New York: Delta, 1969), pp. 111–112.

earn only $2,000 a year, as one prosperous, middle-class person re-marked to me, "Then that's all they must be worth." The competi-tive society has little room for compassion and collective social bet-terment; those who dream of getting ahead and making it to the top have little time for those below.

It would be easy to fault Americans who manifest the above be-lief patterns as people who lack some proper measure of humanity. But what must be remembered about such attitudes is that they evolve as value components of a class society. The value placed on getting ahead, on privatized moreness and material success, on put-ting down others in order to boost oneself is not the outcome of some inborn genetic flaw in the American character. In a society where material wealth is *the key determinant of one's life chances*, and birth, luck, corruption and individuated competition the key means of getting it, then the competitive drive and the desire for material success are not merely symptoms of greed but factors in one's eco-nomic survival, shaping the texture of one's life. When human serv-ices are based on ability to pay, money becomes a matter of life and death. To be poor is to run a higher risk of death, illness, insufficient medical care, malnutrition and job exploitation, and to have a lesser opportunity for education, comfort, mobility, leisure, travel, etc. The desire to "make it," even at the expense of others, is not merely a wrong-headed attitude but a reflection of the actual material condi-tions of capitalist society wherein no one is ever really economically secure except the very affluent.

ARE AMERICANS CONSERVATIVE?

The image of Americans as a nation of acquisitive, competitive, jin-goistic admirers of big money is hardly the whole picture. Many, in-cluding millions of the more conventional minded, have serious questions about the institutions and practices of their society. Polls show that among all groups of Americans there has been a growing feeling of distrust and alienation toward the dominant economic and political elites.[13] One survey found that between 1966 and 1976, public confidence in those who ran the major corporations declined from 55 percent to 16 percent. Confidence in religious, military and other establishment elites showed comparable drops.[14] Fifty-five percent of the respondents in another poll believe that both the Democratic and Republican parties favor big business over the aver-

---

13. Harris survey, *Ithaca* (N.Y.) *Journal*, March 22, 1976.
14. *Ibid.*, see also Harris survey, *Ithaca* (N.Y.) *Journal*, March 25, 1976.

age worker. Forty-one percent want "sweeping changes" in our economy, and only 17 percent are for letting the economy straighten itself out. Most respondents seem open to new and bold experiments in economic matters. Thus a whopping 66 percent would like to work for a company that is owned and controlled by its employees.[15]

Other polls found that by majorities of more than two to one, citizens favor increased government efforts to (a) curb air and water pollution, (b) aid education and (c) help the poor. At the same time they are against increased spending for highways and the space program. By 72 to 20 percent they judge that "too much money is going into wars and defense." By 80 to 13 percent they feel the tax system was set up to favor the rich at the expense of the average person. On almost every major policy issue, the electorate seems to hold attitudes contrary to the policies pursued by corporate and political elites.[16]

A New York Times/CBS survey in 1978 found that the percentage of people who identify as "conservative" and "liberal" remained roughly the same through the 1970s (28 percent conservative, 21 percent liberal), and that by lopsided majorities, both conservatives and liberals favored more public spending on the environment, schooling, medical care, the elderly, employment and job safety. But differences do appear on social and cultural questions, such as legalization of marijuana, abortion, gun control and gay rights.[17] One 1978 survey of college campuses found that, although students were less inclined than in the 1960s to identify themselves as liberal, the spectrum of political ideology was shifting to the left, so what was once "left of center" is now considered "middle of the road."[18] Another campus survey arrived at a somewhat similar conclusion: "There is little evidence to support a 'shift to the right' view. Even conservative students are quite liberal on most issues."[19]

In addition, Americans are becoming more tolerant of cultural and political dissenters. In 1967, by majorities of 60 to 75 percent, respondents declared the following groups "dangerous or harmful to the country": atheists, Black militants, student demonstrators and homosexuals. But by 1973 no majority could be found to label these

15. A Peter Hart poll reported in Mary McGrory's syndicated column, *Ithaca* (N.Y.) *Journal*, September 5, 1975.
16. The *New York Post*, January 8, 1973, and the *Burlington* (Vt.) *Free Press*, April 12, 1973. The large majority willing to "help the poor" were thinking of programs other than welfare. Increased spending for welfare, seen by many as nothing but a handout to loafers, was rejected by two to one.
17. *New York Times*, January 22, 1978; see also "Is America Turning Right?" *Newsweek*, November 7, 1977, p. 34 ff.
18. New York Times/CBS survey, *New York Times*, January 22, 1978.
19. *Daily Hampshire* (Mass.) *Gazette*, July 12, 1978.

groups as harmful. However, lopsided majorities considered the following people dangerous: politicians who engage in secret wiretapping, businessmen who make illegal contributions, generals who conduct secret bombing raids.[20]

In 1972, when the Supreme Court ruled that reporters can be required to reveal their news sources, a Gallup poll found that only about half the public supported reporters' rights to protect their informants. In 1978, a new Gallup poll discovered that by an overwhelming 3 to 1 margin, the public now defended the right of reporters to protect their sources.[21] A Harris poll concluded that substantial majorities of Americans are no longer willing to be stampeded by the kind of fear appeals that characterized past conservative campaigns—such as the "soft on communism," "soft on Blacks" and "soft on crime" issues.[22] And throughout the sixties and seventies, Americans on the whole have been slowly but steadily changing their attitudes in a progressive direction, especially in regard to school busing and integration, housing integration and race relations in general.[23]

In sum, despite the propaganda of the corporations, the political parties, the media and the government—to be explored in the chapters ahead—Americans have not been completely taken in. The disparities between what the established elites profess and what they practice is becoming increasingly apparent to larger numbers of people. Americans are not as conservative, biased and unaware of their own interests as we have been led to believe. If given more truthful information about what is happening and if they could see a way to change things, Americans are likely to move in a progressive direction on most socioeconomic matters—and, indeed, despite everything, they show signs of doing just that.

CONSERVATIVES, LIBERALS, SOCIALISTS AND DEMOCRACY

Political opinion in the United States might be roughly categorized as conservative, liberal and socialist. As just noted, many self-styled "conservatives" are close to liberals on most issues; nevertheless,

20. Harris survey, *New York Times*, January 21, 1974.
21. Reported in *Valley Advocate* (Amherst, Mass.), October 18, 1978.
22. Harris survey, *Chicago Tribune*, January 5, 1975.
23. Reported in *Scientific American*, June 1978; also Harris poll reported in *New York Times*, February 19, 1979; and Gallup polls reported in *Daily World*, August 29, 1978.

there is a conservative ideology shared by most influential socioeconomic elites and many political leaders which is propagated through the business-owned media. The *conservative* ideology supports above all else the system of "free enterprise" and defends the interests of business and property. Conservative leaders believe that most reforms should be resisted. They may recognize that there are some real inequities in society, but these will either take care of themselves or be taken care of over a long period of time in slow and cautious ways or, as with poverty, will always be with us. Conservatives believe that people are poor usually because, as Richard Nixon once noted, they are given to a "welfare ethic rather than a work ethic."

Conservative ideologists are for strong or weak government depending on what interests are being served. They denounce as government "meddling" those policies which appear to move toward an equalization of life chances, income and class, or which attempt to make business more accountable to public authority. But they usually advocate a strong government role in the regulation of private morals, crime control, security surveillance, restrictions on dissent, suppression of leftists and the use of overseas military intervention for purposes of "national defense." They are against all government handouts except defense contracts, corporate subsidies and tax breaks for business and the well-to-do.

Conservative elites say they are for "telling the government to leave the individual alone," yet for them the main component of individual rights is the enjoyment of property rights. Indeed, conservatives cherish private property quite independently of the value placed on individuals, so when the two values conflict, property is often protected in preference to individual life and sometimes at a cost to individual life. In short, conservative opinion leaders put their stock in individual self-advancement, a sound business market, authority, hierarchy, a strong police force, gut patriotism and American military strength. Millions of others who witnessed the bankruptcy of liberal programs that siphoned money from the middle class to the rich in the name of the poor now, not knowing what else to do, oppose big government, centralization, bureaucracy and high taxes—and *call* themselves conservatives.

A *liberal*, like a conservative, accepts the basic structure and value system of the capitalist system but believes that social problems should be rectified by a redirection of government spending and by better regulatory policies. Liberals do not usually see these problems as being interrelated and endemic to the present system. Since they assume that the ills of the politico-economic system are aberrations in the workings of capitalism, they believe that the fault must be with the personages who have gained power. If the right persons finally win office, and with the right combination of will, public awareness and political push, the system will be able to take care of its major crises. Liberals generally support government intervention in the economy in the hope of curbing some of the worst abuses of the economic system and changing "our warped priorities" so that more money will be spent on needed public services and less on private privileges. Yet while liberals call for cuts in "excessive" military spending and advocate protection of individual rights against government suppression and surveillance, and assistance for the poor and needy, in the world of action many liberals vote for huge military budgets, support security and intelligence agencies, and make cuts in human services for the needy.

Some liberals are not overly fond of capitalism, but they like socialism even less. Socialism, in their minds, conjures up stereotyped images of "drabness" and "regimentation," of people waiting in line for shoddy goods wrapped in dull gray packages and of Stalinist purges and labor camps. The liberal's concern seems to be that freedom would be lost or diminished under socialism. (Many liberals believe they are free under the present politico-economic system.) They are also worried about the diminution of their own class and professional privileges and the loss of status they might suffer with the democratization and equalization promised in a socialist society. In this respect, they often resemble conservatives.

In matters of foreign policy, liberals generally have shown themselves as willing as conservatives to contain the spread of socialism in other lands and make the world safe for American corporate investments and markets. Since Vietnam, many liberals have come to think that we should not get involved in suppressing social revolutionary movements in other countries. But whatever their feelings about revolution abroad, most liberals have little tolerance for revolutionary struggle in the United States.

Only a small portion of Americans identify as socialists—although more adhere to views that are close to socialist principles, and socialist opinion has shown a modest but steady growth in recent years.[24] A *socialist* is someone who wants to replace the capitalist system with a system of public and communal ownership and who sees capitalism as the major cause of imperialism, racism and sexism. Socialists are distinguished from liberal reformers in their belief that our social problems cannot be solved within the very sys-

---

24. See, for instance, Paul W. Valentine, "The Coming Out of U.S. Socialists," *Washington Post*, March 25, 1979.

tem that is creating them. Socialists do not believe that *every* human problem at *every* level of existence is caused by capitalism but that many of the most important ones are and that capitalism propagates a kind of culture and social organization that destroys human potentials and guarantees the perpetuation of poverty, racism, pollution and exploitative social relations at home and abroad. Socialists even argue that much of the unhappiness suffered in what are considered purely "interpersonal" experiences relates to the false values and anxieties of an acquisitive, competitive capitalist society.

Socialists believe that American corporate and military expansionism abroad is not the result of "wrong thinking" but the natural outgrowth of profit-oriented capitalism. To the socialist, American foreign policy is not beset by folly and irrationality but has been quite successful in maintaining the status quo and the interests of multinational corporations, crushing social change in countries like Indonesia, Guatemala, the Dominican Republic, Greece, Chile, Brazil and others, and establishing an American financial and military presence throughout much of the world.

Conservatives, liberals and socialists all profess a dedication to "democracy," but tend to mean different things by the term. In this book, *democracy* refers to a system of governance that represents both in *form* and *content* the needs and desires of the ruled. Decision-makers are not to govern for the benefit of the privileged few but for the interests of the many. In other words, their decisions and policies should be of substantive benefit to the populace. The people exercise a measure of control by electing their representatives and by subjecting them to open criticism, the periodic check of elections, and if necessary, recall and removal from office. Besides living without fear of political tyranny, a democratic people should be able to live without fear of want, enjoying freedom from economic, as well as political, oppression. In a real democracy, the material conditions of people's lives should be humane and roughly equal.

Some people have argued that democracy is simply a system of rules for playing the game, which allows some measure of mass participation and government accountability, and that the Constitution is a kind of rule book. One should not try to impose, as a precondition of democracy, particular class relations, economic philosophies or other substantive arrangements on this open-ended game. This argument certainly does reduce democracy to a game. It presumes that formal rules can exist in a meaningful way independently of substantive realities. Whether procedural rights are violated or actually enjoyed, whether one is treated by the law as pariah or prince, depends largely on material realities that extend beyond a written constitution or other formal guarantees of law. The law in its majestic equality, Anatole France once observed, prohibits rich and poor alike from stealing bread and sleeping under the bridges. And in so doing the law becomes something of a farce, a fiction that allows us to speak of "the rights of all" divorced from the class conditions that place the rich above the law and the poor below it. In the absence of certain substantive conditions, legalistic and procedural rights are of little value to millions who have neither the time, money nor opportunity to make a reality of their formal rights.

Take the "right of every citizen to be heard." In its majestic equality, the law allows both the rich and the poor to raise high their political voices: both are free to hire the best-placed lobbyists and Washington lawyers to pressure public officeholders; both are free to shape public opinion by owning a newspaper or television station; and both rich and poor have the right to engage in multimillion-dollar election campaigns in order to pick the right persons for office or win office themselves. But again, this formal political equality is something of a fiction, as we shall see in the pages ahead. Of what good are the rules for those millions who are excluded from the game?

Some people think that if you are free to say what you like, you are living in a democracy. But freedom of speech is not the sum total of democracy, only one of its necessary conditions. A government is not a democracy when it leaves us free to *say* what we want but leaves others free to *do* what they want with our country, our resources, our taxes and our lives. Democracy is not a seminar but a system of power, like any other form of governance. Free speech, like freedom of assembly and freedom of political organization, is meaningful only if it keeps those in power responsible to those over whom power is exercised.

Nor are elections and political party competitions a sure test of democracy. Some two-party or multiparty systems are so thoroughly controlled by like-minded elites that they discourage broad participation and offer policies that serve establishment interests no matter who is elected. In contrast, a one-party system, especially in a newly emerging, social revolutionary country, might actually provide *more* democracy—that is, more popular participation, more meaningful policy debate within the party than occurs between the parties in the other system, and more accountability and responsiveness to the people.

In the chapters ahead, we will take a critical look at our own political system and measure it not according to its undoubted ability to hold elections but by its ability to serve democratic ends. It will be argued that whether a political system is democratic or not depends not only on its procedures but on the *substantive* outputs—that is, the actual material benefits and costs of policy and the kind of social justice or injustice that is propagated. By this view, a government that pursues policies which by design or neglect are so inequitable as to deny people the very conditions of life is not democratic no matter how many competitive elections it holds.

4

A Constitution
for the Few

To help us understand the American political system, we might give attention to its formal structure, the rules under which it operates and the interests it represents, beginning with the Constitution and the men who wrote it.

It is commonly taught that entrepreneurs of earlier times preferred a government that kept its activities to a minimum. In actuality, capitalist theorists and practitioners of the eighteenth and nineteenth centuries were not against a strong state but against state restrictions on business enterprise. They never desired to remove civil authority from economic affairs but to ensure that it worked *for* rather than against the interests of property. If they were for laissez-faire, it was in a highly selective way: they did not want government limiting their trade, controlling their prices or restricting their markets, but not for a moment did they want a weak government as such. Rather they sought one that was actively on their side, and they frequently advocated an *extension* rather than a diminution of state power.

"Civil authority," wrote Adam Smith in 1776, "so far as it is instituted for the security of property, is in reality instituted for the defense of the rich against the poor, or of those who have some property against those who have none at all."[1] Smith, who is above suspi-

---

1. Adam Smith, *An Inquiry into the Nature and Causes of the Wealth of Nations* (Chicago: Encyclopedia Britannica, Inc., 1952), p. 311. A century before Smith, John Locke, in his *Second Treatise of Civil Government*, described one of the central purposes of government as protecting the interests of property.

cion in his dedication to capitalism, argued that as wealth increased in scope, a government would have to perform more extensive services on behalf of the wealthy. "The necessity of civil government," he wrote, "grows up with the acquisition of valuable property."[2] He expected government to "facilitate commerce in general" by maintaining the necessary auxiliaries of trade, transportation and communication and providing for the armed protection of commerce "carried on with barbarous and uncivilized nations."[3]

CLASS POWER IN EARLY AMERICA

Adam Smith's views of the importance of government were shared by men of substance in the late eighteenth century, including those who lived in America. During the period between the Revolution and the Constitution, the rich and the wellborn set the dominant political tone in the United States. Far from keeping a distance between themselves and the state, they were much involved in shaping public affairs.

> Their power was born of place, position, and fortune. They were located at or near the seats of government and they were in direct contact with legislatures and government officers. They influenced and often dominated the local newspapers which voiced the ideas and interests of commerce and identified them with the good of the whole people, the state, and the nation. The published writings of the leaders of the period are almost without exception those of merchants, of their lawyers, or of politicians sympathetic with them.[4]

The United States of 1787 has been described as an "egalitarian" society free from the extremes of want and wealth which characterized the Old World. To be sure, the opulent and corrupt kings and bishops of Europe were not to be found in North America, but there were landed estates and colonial mansions which bespoke a munificence of their own. Although land was abundant compared with Europe, there was no equal opportunity in acquiring it. From the earliest English settlements, men of influence had received vast land grants from the Crown. And through their control of the provincial governments, they had gained possession of the western parts of their states. By 1700 three-fourths of the acreage in New York be-

2. Smith, *Wealth of Nations*, p. 309.
3. *Ibid.*, p. 315 ff.
4. Merrill Jensen, *The New Nation* (New York: Random House, 1950), p. 178.

longed to less than a dozen persons. In the interior of Virginia, seven persons acquired a total of 1,732,000 acres.[5] By 1760 fewer than 500 merchants in five colonial cities controlled most of the trade on the eastern seaboard and themselves owned much land.[6]

Here and there could be found "middle-class" farmers, tavern keepers, distillers and shop owners who, by the standards of the day, might be judged as comfortably situated. But the great bulk of small yeomen, composing about 80 to 85 percent of the White population, were poor freeholders, tenants, squatters, indentured laborers or hired hands. The cities had their poor and their poorhouses, along with their cobblers, weavers, bakers, blacksmiths, peddlers, laborers, clerks and domestics who worked long hours for meager sums.

As of 1787 property qualifications left perhaps more than a third of the White, male population disfranchised. Property qualifications for holding office were so steep that most voters were prevented from qualifying as candidates. In addition, the practice of oral voting, the lack of a secret ballot and an "absence of a real choice among candidates and programs" led to "widespread apathy."[7] As a result, the gentry, merchants and professionals monopolized the important offices. "Who do they represent," Josiah Quincy asked about the South Carolina legislature. "The laborer, the mechanic, the tradesman, the farmer, the husbandman or yeoman? No. The representatives are almost if not wholly rich planters."[8]

The American Constitution was framed by financially successful planters, merchants, lawyers, bankers and creditors, many of them linked by kinship and marriage and by years of service in the Congress, the military or diplomacy. They congregated in Philadelphia in 1787 for the professed purpose of revising the Articles of Confederation and strengthening the powers of the central government. They were impelled by a desire to build a nation and by the explicit intent of doing something about the increasingly insurgent spirit evidenced among poorer people.

The rebellious populace of that day has been portrayed by textbook writers as irresponsible spendthrifts who never paid their debts and who believed in nothing more than timid state governments and inflated paper money. Little has been said about the actual plight of

---

5. Sidney H. Aronson, *Status and Kinship in the Higher Civil Service* (Cambridge, Mass: Harvard University Press, 1964), p. 35.
6. *Ibid.*, p. 41.
7. *Ibid.*, p. 49.
8. Quoted in *ibid.*, p. 49.

the common people, the great bulk of whom lived at a subsistence level. The poorer farmers were burdened by the low prices offered for their crops by merchants and the high costs for merchandised goods. They often bought land at inflated prices, only to see its value collapse and to find themselves unable to meet their mortgage obligations. Their labor and their crops usually were theirs in name only. To survive, they frequently had to borrow money at high interest rates. To meet their debts they mortgaged their future crops and went still deeper into debt. Large numbers were caught in that cycle of rural indebtedness which is the common fate of agrarian peoples in many countries to this day. The underpaid and underemployed artisans and workers (or "mechanics," as they were called) in the towns were not much better off.

During the 1780s the jails were crowded with debtors. Among the people there grew the feeling that the revolution against England had been fought for naught. Angry, armed crowds in several states began blocking foreclosures and sales of seized property and started opening up the jails. They gathered at the county towns to prevent the courts from presiding over debtor cases. In the winter of 1787 farmers in western Massachusetts led by Daniel Shays took up arms. But their rebellion was forcibly put down by the state militia after some ragged skirmishes.

The specter of Shays' Rebellion hovered over the delegates who gathered in Philadelphia three months later, confirming their worst fears about the populace. They were determined that persons of birth and fortune should control the affairs of the nation and check the leveling impulses of that propertyless multitude which composed "the majority faction." "To secure the public good and private rights against the danger of such a faction," wrote James Madison, "and at the same time preserve the spirit and form of popular government is then the great object to which our inquiries are directed." The founders of the Constitution were to agree with Madison when he wrote in *Federalist* No. 10 that "the most common and durable source of factions has been the various and unequal distribution of property. Those who hold and those who are without property have ever formed distinct interests in society." And most of them did not hesitate to construct a strong central government that would ensure their victory in the struggle between these "distinct interests."

The delegates were of the opinion that democracy was "the worst of all political evils," as Elbridge Gerry put it. Both he and Madison warned of "the danger of the leveling spirit." "The people," said Roger Sherman, "should have as little to do as may be about the Government." But it remained for Alexander Hamilton to provide the memorable summation:

> All communities divide themselves into the few and the many. The first are the rich and the well born, the other the mass of the people. The voice of the people has been said to be the voice of God; and however generally this maxim has been quoted and believed, it is not true in fact. The people are turbulent and changing; they seldom judge or determine right. Give therefore to the first class a distinct, permanent share in the government. They will check the unsteadiness of the second and as they cannot receive any advantage by a change, they therefore will ever maintain good government.[9]

CONTAINING THE SPREAD OF DEMOCRACY

The delegates spent many weeks debating their differences, but these were the differences of merchants, slave owners, and manufacturers, a debate of haves versus haves in which each group sought safeguards within the new Constitution for its particular regional or commercial interests. Added to this were the inevitable disagreements that arise over what are the best means of achieving agreed-upon ends. Questions of structure and authority occupied a good deal of the delegates' time: How much representation for the large and small states? How might the legislature be organized? How should the executive be selected? What length of tenure for the different officeholders? But questions of enormous significance, relating to the new government's ability to protect the interests of property, were agreed upon with surprisingly little debate. For on these issues there were no dirt farmers or poor artisans attending the Convention to proffer an opposing viewpoint. The debate between haves and have-nots never took place.

The portions of the Constitution giving the federal government the power to support commerce and protect property were decided upon after amiable deliberation and with remarkable dispatch considering their importance. Thus all of Article I, Section 8 was

---

9. The quotations by Gerry, Madison, Sherman and Hamilton are taken from Max Farrand (ed.), *Records of the Federal Convention* (New Haven: Yale University Press, 1927), vol. 1, *passim*. For further testimony by the delegates and other early leaders, see John C. Miller, *Origins of the American Revolution* (Boston: Little, Brown, 1943), p. 491 ff., and Andrew C. McLaughlin, *A Constitutional History of the United States* (New York: Appleton-Century, 1935), pp. 141–144.

adopted within a few days.[10] This section delegated to Congress the power to

1. Regulate commerce among the states and with foreign nations and Indian tribes
2. Lay and collect taxes and impose duties and tariffs on imports but not on commercial exports
3. Establish a national currency and regulate its value
4. "Borrow Money on the credit of the United States"—a measure of special interest to creditors[11]
5. Fix the standard of weights and measures necessary for trade
6. Protect the value of securities and currency against counterfeiting
7. Establish "uniform Laws on the subject of Bankruptcies throughout the United States"
8. "Pay the Debts and provide for the common Defence and general Welfare of the United States"

Congress was limited to powers specifically delegated to it by the Constitution or implied as "necessary and proper" for the performance of the delegated powers. Over the years, under this "implied power" clause, federal intervention in the private economy grew to an extraordinary magnitude.

Some of the delegates were land speculators who expressed a concern about western holdings; accordingly, Congress was given the "Power to dispose of and make all needful Rules and Regulations respecting the Territory or other Property belonging to the United States. . . ." Some of the delegates speculated in highly inflated and nearly worthless Confederation securities. Under Article VI, all debts incurred by the Confederation were valid against the new government, a provision that allowed speculators to make enormous

---

10. John Bach McMaster, "Framing the Constitution," in his *The Political Depravity of the Founding Fathers* (New York: Farrar, Straus, 1964), p. 137. Originally published in 1896. Farrand refers to the consensus for a strong national government that emerged after the small states had been given equal representation in the Senate. Much of the work that followed "was purely formal" albeit sometimes time-consuming. See Max Farrand, *The Framing of the Constitution of the United States* (New Haven: Yale University Press, 1913), pp. 134–135.

11. The original wording was "borrow money and emit bills." But the latter phrase was deleted after Gouverneur Morris warned that "The Monied interest" would oppose the Constitution if paper notes were not prohibited. There was much strong feeling about this among creditors. In any case, it was assumed that the borrowing power would allow for "safe and proper" public notes should they be necessary. See Farrand, *The Framing of the Constitution*, p. 147.

profits when their securities, bought for a trifling, were honored at face value.[12]

In the interest of merchants and creditors, the states were prohibited from issuing paper money or imposing duties on imports and exports or interfering with the payment of debts by passing any "Law impairing the Obligation of Contracts." The Constitution guaranteed "Full Faith and Credit" in each state "to the Acts, Records, and judicial Proceedings" of other states, thus allowing creditors to pursue their debtors more effectively.

The property interests of slave owners were looked after. To give the slave-owning states a greater influence, three-fifths of the slave population were to be counted when calculating the representation deserved by each state in the lower house. The importation of slaves was allowed to continue until 1808. And under Article IV, slaves who escaped from one state to another had to be delivered up to the original owner upon claim, a provision that was unanimously adopted at the Convention.

The framers believed the states acted with insufficient force against popular uprisings, so Congress was given the task of "organizing, arming, and disciplining the Militia" and calling it forth, among other things, to "suppress Insurrections." In keeping with their desire to contain the majority, the founders inserted "auxiliary precautions" *designed to fragment power without democratizing it*. By separating the executive, legislative and judiciary functions and then providing a system of checks and balances among the various branches—including staggered elections, executive veto, Senate confirmation of appointments and ratification of treaties, and a two-house legislature—the founders hoped to dilute the impact of popular sentiments. In keeping with this goal, they contrived an elaborate and difficult process for amending the Constitution, requiring proposal by two-thirds of both the Senate and the House, and ratification by three-fourths of the state legislatures.[13] To the extent that it existed at all, the majoritarian principle was tightly locked into a system of minority vetoes, making swift and sweeping popular actions nearly impossible.

---

12. The classic study of the economic interests of the founding fathers is Charles A. Beard, *An Economic Interpretation of the Constitution* (New York: Macmillan, 1913). Critiques of Beard have been made by Robert E. Brown, *Charles Beard and the American Constitution* (Princeton, N.J.:Princeton University Press, 1956), and Forrest McDonald, *We the People—The Economic Origins of the Constitution* (Chicago: Chicago University Press, 1958).

13. Amendments could also be proposed through a constitutional convention called by Congress on application of two-thirds of the state legislatures and ratified by conventions in three-fourths of the states.

The propertyless majority, as Madison was to point out in *Federalist* No. 10, must not be allowed to concert in common cause against the established social order.[14] First, it was necessary to prevent a unity of public sentiment by enlarging the polity and then compartmentalizing it into geographically insulated political communities. The larger the nation, the greater the "variety of parties and interests" and the more difficult it would be for a majority to find itself and act in unison. As Madison argued, "A rage for paper money, for an abolition of debts, for an equal division of property, or for any other wicked project will be less apt to pervade the whole body of the Union than a particular member of it. . . ." An uprising of impoverished farmers may threaten Massachusetts at one time and Rhode Island at another, but a national government will be large and varied enough to contain each of these and insulate the rest of the nation from the contamination of rebellion.

Second, not only must the majority be prevented from finding horizontal cohesion, but its vertical force—that is, its upward thrust upon government—should be blunted by interjecting indirect forms of representation. Thus the senators from each state were to be elected by their respective state legislatures. The chief executive was to be selected by an electoral college voted by the people but, as anticipated by the framers, composed of political leaders and men of substance who would gather in their various states and choose a president of their own liking. It was believed that they would be unable to muster a majority for any one candidate, and that the final selection would be left to the House, with each state delegation therein having only one vote.[15] The Supreme Court was to be elected by no one, its justices being appointed to life tenure by the president and confirmed by the Senate. In time, of course, the electoral college proved to be something of a rubber stamp, and the Seventeenth Amendment, adopted in 1913, provided for popular election of the Senate.

---

14. *Federalist* No. 10 can be found in any of the good editions of the *Federalist Papers*. It is one of the most significant essays on American politics ever written. With clarity and economy of language it explains, as do few other short works, how a government may utilize the republican principle to contain the populace and protect the propertied few from the propertyless many, and it confronts, if not solves, the essential question of how government may reconcile the tensions between liberty, authority and dominant class interest. In effect, the Tenth Federalist Paper maps out a method, relevant to this day, of preserving the existing undemocratic class structure under the legitimating cloak of democratic forms.

15. The delegates did expect that George Washington would be overwhelmingly elected the first president, but they anticipated that in subsequent contests the electoral college would seldom be able to decide on one person.

The only portion of government directly elected by the people was the House of Representatives. Many of the delegates would have preferred excluding the public entirely from direct representation: John Mercer observed that he found nothing in the proposed Constitution more objectionable than "the mode of election by the people. The people cannot know and judge of the characters of Candidates. The worst possible choice will be made." Others were concerned that demagogues would ride into office on a populist tide only to pillage the treasury and wreak havoc on all. "The time is not distant," warned Gouverneur Morris, "when this Country will abound with mechanics and manufacturers [industrial workers] who will receive their bread from their employers. Will such men be the secure and faithful Guardians of liberty? . . . Children do not vote. Why? Because they want prudence, because they have no will of their own. The ignorant and dependent can be as little trusted with the public interest."[16]

Several considerations softened the framers' determination to contain democracy. First and most important, the delegates recognized that there were limits to what the states would ratify. They also understood that if the federal government were to have any kind of stability, it must gain some measure of popular acceptance; hence, for all their class biases, they were inclined to "leave something for the people," even if it were only "the *spirit* and *form* of popular government," to recall Madison's words. In addition, some of the delegates feared not only the tyranny of the many but the machinations of the few. It was Madison who reminded his colleagues that in protecting themselves from the multitude, they must not reintroduce a "cabal" or a monarchy, thus erring in the opposite direction. (The specter of monarchy, however, did not frighten the delegates in the same way as did the dread scourge of democracy. The one was linked to the other, it being assumed that the "anarchy and turbulence" of democracy were creating a longing for the security of autocratic rule among certain elements of the gentry—as was the case. Thus in curbing democracy, the founders believed that they also were diminishing the likelihood of what Washington called "the other extreme."[17])

When the delegates agreed to having "the people" elect the lower house, they were referring to a somewhat select portion of the population. Property qualifications disfranchised the poorest White

---

16. Farrand, *Records of the Federal Convention*, vol. 2, p. 200 ff.

17. See Richard Hofstadter, "The Founding Fathers: An Age of Realism," in his *The American Political Tradition and the Men Who Made It* (New York: Knopf, 1948).

males in various states. Half the adult population was denied suffrage because they were women. About one-fourth, both men and women, had no vote because they were held in bondage, and even among Blacks who had gained their legal freedom, in both the North and the South, none was allowed to vote until the passage of the Fourteenth Amendment after the Civil War.

PLOTTERS OR PATRIOTS?

The question of whether the framers of the Constitution were motivated by financial or national interest has been debated ever since Charles Beard published *An Economic Interpretation of the Constitution* in 1913. It was Beard's view that the "founding fathers" were guided by their class interests. Arguing against Beard's thesis are those who believe that the framers were concerned with higher things than just lining their purses and protecting their property. True, they were moneyed men who profited directly from policies initiated under the new Constitution, but they were motivated by a concern for nation-building that went beyond their particular class interests, the argument goes.[18] To paraphrase Justice Holmes, these men invested their belief to make a nation; they did not make a nation because they had invested. "High-mindedness is not impossible to man," Holmes reminds us.

And that is exactly the point: high-mindedness is one of man's most common attributes even when, or especially when, he is pursuing his personal and class interest. The fallacy is to presume that there is a dichotomy between the desire to build a strong nation and the desire to protect property and that the framers could not have been motivated by both. In fact, like most other people, they believed that what was good for themselves was ultimately good for the entire society. Their universal values and their class interests went hand in hand, and to discover the existence of the "higher" sentiment does not eliminate the self-interested one.

Most persons believe in their own virtue. The founders never doubted the nobility of their effort and its importance for the gener-

---

18. For some typical apologistic arguments on behalf of the "founding fathers" see Broadus Mitchell and Louise Pearson Mitchell, *A Biography of the Constitution of the United States* (New York: Oxford University Press, 1964), pp. 46–51, and David G. Smith, *The Convention and the Constitution* (New York: St. Martin's Press, 1965), chapter 3. Smith argues that the framers had not only economic motives but "larger" political objectives, as if the political had no relation to the economic or as if the political objectives were more impelling because they were directed toward a "national interest" rather than self-interest or a class interest.

ations to come. Just as many of them could feel dedicated to the principle of "liberty for all" and at the same time own slaves, so could they serve both their nation and their estates. The point is not that they were devoid of the grander sentiments of nation-building but that *there was nothing in that concept of nation which worked against their class interest and a great deal that worked for it.*

People tend to perceive things in accordance with the position they occupy in the social structure, and that position is largely determined by their class status. Even if we deny that the delegates were motivated by the desire for personal gain that moves others, we cannot dismiss the existence of their class interest. They may not have been solely concerned with getting their own hands in the till, although enough of them did; but they were admittedly preoccupied with defending the propertied few from the propertyless many—for the ultimate benefit of all, as they understood it. "The Constitution," as Staughton Lynd notes, "was the settlement of a revolution. What was at stake for Hamilton, Livingston, and their opponents, was more than speculative windfalls in securities; it was the question, what kind of society would emerge from the revolution when the dust had settled, and on which class the political center of gravity would come to rest."[19]

Finally those who argue that the "founding fathers" were motivated primarily by high-minded objectives consistently overlook the fact that the delegates repeatedly stated their intention to erect a government strong enough to protect the haves from the have-nots. They gave voice to the crassest class prejudices and never found it necessary to disguise the fact—as have latter-day apologists—that their uppermost concern was to diminish popular control and resist all tendencies toward class equalization (or "leveling," as it was called). Their opposition to democracy and their dedication to the propertied and moneyed interests were a matter of openly avowed ideology. Their preoccupation was so pronounced that one delegate did finally complain of hearing too much about how the purpose of government was to protect property. He wanted it noted that the ultimate objective of government was the ennoblement of mankind—a fine sentiment that evoked no opposition from his colleagues as they continued about their business.

19. Staughton Lynd, *Class Conflict, Slavery and the United States Constitution* (Indianapolis: Bobbs-Merrill, 1967), selection in Irwin Unger (ed.), *Beyond Liberalism: The New Left Views American History* (Waltham, Mass.: Xerox College Publishing, 1971), p. 17. For discussions of the class interests behind the American Revolution see Alfred F. Young (ed.), *The American Revolution: Explorations in the History of American Radicalism* (DeKalb, Ill.: Northern Illinois University Press, 1977).

AN ELITIST DOCUMENT

More important than conjecturing about the framers' motives is to look at the Constitution they fashioned, for it tells us a good deal about their objectives. It was and still is largely an elitist document, more concerned with the securing of property interests than with personal liberties. Bills of attainder and ex post facto laws are expressly prohibited, and Article I, Section 9 assures us that "the Privilege of the Writ of Habeas Corpus shall not be suspended, unless when in Cases of Rebellion or Invasion the public Safety may require it," a restriction that leaves authorities with a wide measure of discretion. Other than these few provisions, the Constitution that emerged from the Philadelphia Convention gave no attention to civil liberties.

When Colonel Mason suggested to the Convention that a committee be formed to draft "a Bill of Rights," a task that could be accomplished "in a few hours," the representatives of the various states offered little discussion on the motion and voted unanimously against it. Guarantees of individual rights—including freedom of speech and religion; freedom to assemble peaceably and petition for redress of grievances; the right to keep arms; freedom from unreasonable searches and seizures, from self-incrimination, double jeopardy, cruel and unusual punishment and excessive bail and fines; and the right to a fair and impartial trial and other forms of due process—were tacked on as the first ten amendments (the Bill of Rights) only after the Constitution was ratified and the first Congress and president had been elected.

For the founders, liberty meant something different from democracy; it meant liberty to invest and trade and carry out the matters of business and enjoy the security of property without encroachment by king or populace. The civil liberties designed to give all individuals the right to engage actively in public affairs were of no central concern to the delegates, and, as just noted, were summarily voted down.

The twentieth-century concept of social justice, involving something more than procedural liberties, is afforded no place in our eighteenth-century Constitution. The Constitution says nothing about those conditions of life which have come to be treated by many people as essential human rights—for instance, freedom from hunger, the right to decent housing, medical care and education regardless of ability to pay, the right to gainful employment, safe working conditions, a clean, nontoxic environment. Under the Constitution equality is treated as a *procedural* right without a *substan-*

tive content. Thus "equality of opportunity" means equality of opportunity to move ahead competitively and become unequal to others; it means a chance to get in the game and best others rather than enjoy an equal distribution and use of the resources needed for the maintenance of community life.

If the founders sought to "check power with power," they seemed mostly concerned with restraining mass power, while ensuring the perpetuation of their own class power. They supposedly had a "realistic" opinion of the self-interested and rapacious nature of human beings—readily evidenced when they talked about the common people. Yet they held a remarkably sanguine view of the self-interested impulses of their own class, which they saw as being inhabited by industrious, trustworthy and virtuous men. Recall Hamilton's facile reassurance that the rich will "check the unsteadiness" of the poor and will themselves "ever maintain good government" by being given a "distinct permanent share" in it. Power corrupts others but somehow has the opposite effect on the wellborn.[20]

In sum, the framers laid the foundations for a national government, but it was one that fit the specifications of the propertied class. They wanted protection from popular uprisings, from fiscal uncertainty and irregularities in trade and currency, from trade barriers between states, from economic competition by more powerful foreign governments and from attacks on property and on creditors.[21] The Constitution was consciously designed as a conservative document, elaborately equipped with a system of minority checks and vetoes, making it hard to enact sweeping popular reforms or profound structural changes, and easy for entrenched interests to endure. It provided ample power to build the services and protections of state needed by a growing capitalist class but not the power for a transition of rule to a different class or to the public as a whole. The Constitution was a historically successful undertaking whose effects are still very much with us.

---

20. If the Constitution was so blatantly elitist, how did it manage to win enough popular support for ratification? It did not have a wide measure of support, initially being opposed in most of the states. But the same limitations on the franchise and the same superiority of wealth, leadership, organization, control of the press and control of political office that allowed the rich to monopolize the Philadelphia Convention worked with similar effect in the ratification campaign. Superior wealth also enabled the Federalists to bribe, intimidate and in other ways pressure and discourage opponents of the Constitution. See Jackson Turner Main, *The Anti-Federalists* (Chapel Hill: University of North Carolina Press, 1961).

21. See Hofstadter, "The Founding Fathers. . . ."

5

The Growth of Government

Although the decisions of government are made in the name of the entire society, they rarely benefit everyone. Some portion of the populace, frequently a majority, loses out. What is considered *national* policy is usually the policy of dominant groups strategically located within the political system. The standard textbook view is that American government manifests no consistent class bias. The political system is said to involve a give-and-take among many different groups, "a plurality of interests." What government supposedly does in this pluralistic interplay is act as a regulator of conflict, trying to limit the advantages of the strong and minimize the disadvantages of the weak.

In violation of that notion, I will argue that the existing political system may regulate but it does not equalize, and that its overall effect is to deepen rather than redress the inequities of capitalist society. The political system enjoys no special immunity to the way power resources are distributed in society. It responds primarily, although not exclusively, to the powers and needs of the corporate system. "The business of government is business," President Calvin Coolidge once said. In this chapter we will explore the meaning of that observation, focusing primarily on the "reformist" periods of our history, when government supposedly intervened on behalf of the populace to curb the powers of wealth—specifically the Jacksonian, Progressive and New Deal eras.

65

SERVING BUSINESS: THE EARLY YEARS

The upper-class dominance of public life so characteristic of the founding fathers' generation continued into the nineteenth century. The United States of the early 1800s had an informal but financially powerful aristocracy that controlled "the economic life of the great northeastern cities," and exercised a "vast influence" over the organizational life of the nation.[1] "Amid all the hullabaloo about his alleged dominance in the era, the common man appears to have gotten very little of whatever it was that counted for much," concludes one historian of the period.[2]

During the Jacksonian era, supposedly an "age of egalitarianism," there were more lawyers and bankers occupying top administrative posts than under the Federalist administration of John Adams. President Andrew Jackson's key appointments were drawn overwhelmingly from the ranks of the rich, and his policies regarding trade, finances, state banks and use of government land and resources reflected the interests of that class. Jackson cultivated his "Old Hickory" image, talked a great deal about the virtues of the frontiersmen and the common folk, and for this won their support, but he himself identified with, and in fact *was* a member of the affluent gentry, comfortable in the company of those born to positions of economic, military and political leadership. The fact that Jackson said he would change the social composition of decision-makers and would drive out the money changers led to the mistaken belief that he had actually done so. His attack on the Bank of the United States leaves the misleading impression that he warred against the entire moneyed class. As Aronson notes: "Jackson's followers, who hoped he would democratize the administration, interpreted the small changes that actually took place as major reforms; Jackson's enemies, who feared that he would turn the government over to the mob, regarded the same changes as radical transformations in the social composition of officeholders."[3] Neither group was correct.

The growth of business from local enterprises to large-scale manufacture during the latter half of the nineteenth century was accompanied by a similar growth in governmental activity in the economy. While insisting that the free market worked for all, most

---

1. Edward Pessen, *Riches, Class and Power Before the Civil War* (Lexington, Mass.: D. C. Heath, 1973), p. 278.
2. *Ibid.*, p. 304.
3. Sidney H. Aronson, *Status and Kinship in the Higher Civil Service* (Cambridge, Mass.: Harvard University Press, 1964), p. 160.

businessmen showed little inclination to deliver their own interests to the stern judgments of an untrammeled, competitive economy; instead they resorted to such things as tariffs, public subsidies, land grants, government loans, high-interest bonds, price regulations, contracts, patents, trademarks and other services and protections provided by civil authority.

When government intervened in the economy, it was almost invariably on the side of the strong against the weak. The long hours, low wages, unemployment and hunger that beset great numbers of miners, farmers and laborers failed to enlist the efforts of public officials, but when rebellious workers seized the railroads, as during the depression of 1873, civil authorities were moved to energetic measures on behalf of corporate property, using the militia and then federal troops to crush the railroad strikes. "The industrial barons made a habit of calling soldiers to their assistance; and armories were erected in the principal cities as measures of convenience."[4] Short of having the regular army permanently garrisoned in industrial areas, as was the desire of some owners, government officials took steps "to establish an effective antiradical National Guard."[5]

The high-ranking officials who applied force against workers often were themselves men of wealth. President Cleveland's attorney general, Richard Olney, a millionaire owner of railroad securities, a man of "self-righteous, ruthless, and property-loving nature," used antitrust laws, court injunctions, mass arrests, labor spies, deputy marshals and federal troops against workers and their unions. From the local sheriff and magistrate to the president and Supreme Court, the forces of "law and order" were utilized to suppress the "conspiracy" of labor unions and to serve "the defensive needs of large capitalist enterprises."[6] The very statutes they had declared to be unworkable against the well-known monopolistic and collusive practices of business were now promptly and effectively invoked against "labor combinations."

In the late nineteenth century, the federal government accumulated through tariffs and taxes an enormous budget surplus, most of which it distributed to the wealthy in high-premium bonds. From 1880 to 1890 alone, some $45 million from the public treasury, "collected from the consuming population, and above all from the

---

4. Matthew Josephson, *The Robber Barons* (New York: Harcourt, Brace, 1934), p. 365.

5. William Preston, Jr., *Aliens and Dissenters* (Cambridge, Mass.: Harvard University Press, 1963), p. 24.

6. Matthew Josephson, *The Politicos, 1865–1896* (New York: Harcourt, Brace, 1938), pp. 562, 566.

. . . poor wage earners and farmers," was paid out to big investors.[7] Likewise, a billion acres of land in the public domain, *almost half of the present area of the United States,* was given over to private hands. Josephson describes the government's endeavors to "privatize" the public wealth:

> This benevolent government handed over to its friends or to astute first comers, . . . all those treasures of coal and oil, of copper and gold and iron, the land grants, the terminal sites, the perpetual rights of way—an act of largesse which is still one of the wonders of history. To the new railroad enterprises in addition, great money subsidies totaling many hundreds of millions were given. The Tariff Act of 1864 was in itself a sheltering wall of subsidies; and to aid further the new heavy industries and manufactures, an Immigration Act allowing contract labor to be imported freely was quickly enacted; a national banking system was perfected. . . . Having conferred these vast rights and controls, the . . . government would preserve them, as Conklin termed it, so as to "curb the many who would do to the few as they would not have the few do to them."[8]

For all its activities on behalf of business, the government did exercise a kind of laissez-faire in certain areas, giving little attention to unemployment, education and the spoliation of natural resources. Left to the fate of the "free market" were the millions crowded into squalid tenements, the children who worked ten- and twelve-hour days in unsanitary, unsafe factories, and the farmers who were the indebted victims of merchants and bankers.

THE "PROGRESSIVE" ERA

By the turn of the century, government was to play a still more active role in helping large firms extend their hold over the economy. Contrary to the view that the giant trusts controlled everything, price competition with smaller companies in 1900 was vigorous enough to cut seriously into the profits of industries like iron and steel, copper, agricultural machinery, automobile and telephone.[9] Suffering from an inability to regulate prices, expand profits, limit

---

7. Allan Nevins, *Grover Cleveland: A Study in Courage* (New York: Dodd, Mead, 1932), p. 279, quoted in Josephson, *The Robber Barons,* p. 395.

8. Josephson, *The Robber Barons,* p. 52.

9. Gabriel Kolko marshals a great deal of evidence to support this conclusion; see his *The Triumph of Conservatism* (Chicago: Quadrangle Books, 1967), chapters 1 and 2.

competitors and free themselves from the "vexatious" laws of state and local governments, big business began demanding greater economic intervention by the national government. Such intervention would be dominated by the large corporations and would be designed to protect them from the competitive threat of smaller firms. As the utilities magnate Samuel Insull said, it was better to "help shape the right kind of regulation than to have the wrong kind forced upon [us]."[10]

During the 1900–1916 period, known as the Progressive Era, federal regulations in meat packing, food and drugs, banking, timber and mining were initiated at the insistence of the strongest corporations within these industries. The overall effect of regulation was to raise prices and profits for the large producers, tighten their control over markets and weed out smaller competitors.

Of the several White House occupants during the Progressive Era, Teddy Roosevelt might be considered most representative of the period. Hailed by many as a "trust-buster," Roosevelt actually was hostile toward unionists and reformers. Toward business he manifested bluster but virtually no bite. His major legislative proposals reflected the desires of corporation interests. Like other presidents before and since, he enjoyed close relations with big businessmen and invited them into his administration. His occasional verbal attacks against the "malefactors of great wealth" were largely ceremonial, doing little to challenge industry's control of legislators and the courts.[11]

What was true of Roosevelt held equally for Taft and Wilson, the other two presidents of the Progressive Era. Neither "had a distinct consciousness of any fundamental conflict between their political goals and those of business."[12] Wilson railed against the corrupt political machines and like Roosevelt, presented himself as a "trust-buster," but his campaign funds came from a few rich contributors, most notably the copper magnate Cleveland Dodge. Wilson wrote his first inaugural speech on Dodge's yacht, conferred regularly with Dodge and other associates of Morgan and Rockefeller, and brought numerous businessmen into his administration.[13] In his Latin American interventions and his implementation of the Federal Reserve Act and the Federal Trade Commission Act, Wilson, the "liberal

---

10. See James Weinstein, *The Corporate Ideal in the Liberal State* (Boston: Beacon Press, 1968), p. 87.
11. Patrick Renshaw, *The Wobblies* (Garden City, N.Y.: Doubleday, 1968), p. 24.
12. Kolko, *The Triumph of Conservatism*, p. 281.
13. Frank Harris Blighton, *Woodrow Wilson and Co.* (New York: Fox Printing House, 1916).

Democrat," showed himself as responsive to business as any of the previous Republicans. "Progressivism was not the triumph of small business over the trusts, as has often been suggested, but the victory of big businesses in achieving the rationalization of the economy that only the federal government could provide."[14]

With the advent of World War I, relations between industry and government grew still closer. Sectors of the economy were converted to war production along lines proposed by business leaders—many of whom now headed the government agencies in charge of defense mobilization.[15] The police and military were used without hesitation against workers. Strikes were now treated as seditious interference with war production. Federal troops raided and ransacked headquarters of the Industrial Workers of the World and imprisoned large numbers of workers suspected of socialist sympathies. Nor did things improve during the postwar "Red scare," as the federal government resorted to mass arrests, deportations, political trials and congressional investigations to suppress anticapitalist ideas.[16]

During the "normalcy" of the 1920s, prosperity was supposedly within everyone's grasp; stock speculations and other get-rich-quick schemes abounded. Not since the Gilded Age of the robber barons had the more vulgar manifestations of capitalist culture enjoyed such an uncritical reception. But there were millions of lower-income people who remained untouched by the postwar prosperity, and with the depression of 1929, their ranks were soon joined by millions more.

THE NEW DEAL: REFORM FOR WHOM?

The New Deal era of the 1930s is commonly believed to have been a period of great transformation on behalf of "the forgotten man," but the definitive history of who got what during the 1930s has still to be

---

14. Kolko, *The Triumph of Conservatism*, pp. 283–284. The period between 1900 and 1916 is called the Progressive Era because of the flurry of muckraking against big-business abuses, the occasional trust-busting and the municipal and state electoral reforms which introduced such things as the long ballot, the referendum and recall, and the nonpartisan election. The era was "progressive" more in tone than substance.

15. Paul A. C. Koistinen, "The 'Industrial-Military Complex' in Historical Perspective: The Inter War Years," *Journal of American History*, 56, March 1970, reprinted in Irwin Unger (ed.), *Beyond Liberalism: The New Left Views American History* (Waltham, Mass.: Xerox College Publishing, 1971), pp. 228–229.

16. See Preston, *Aliens and Dissenters, passim*.

written.[17] From what we know, the central dedication of the Franklin Roosevelt administration was to *business recovery* rather than to *social reform*. The federal government sought to revivify the economy through a system of subsidies, credits and supports, applying price and market regulatory methods of a kind advocated by industry. Hence, when an early version of the National Recovery Act (NRA)—allowing firms to limit production and fix prices—was opposed by corporation spokesmen, the Roosevelt administration withdrew it and substituted the approved business version.[18] The effect of the NRA was to injure small business and contribute to the concentration of American industry.[19] In attempting to spur production by financing private investments, the government in effect funneled huge sums from the public treasure into the hands of the moneyed few: in nine years the Reconstruction Finance Corporation alone lent $15 billion to business. As long as such measures were aimed at price and production recovery, they were popular with much of the business community, though of little help to low- and middle-income people.

The local charity arrangements of the early 1930s, almost unchanged from colonial times, were hopelessly inadequate. Faced with mass unrest, the federal government instituted a relief program which eased some of the hunger and starvation and—more importantly from the perspective of business—limited the instances of violent protest and radicalization. But as the New Deal moved toward measures that threatened to compete with private enterprises and undermine low wage structures, businessmen withdrew their support and became openly hostile. While infuriating Roosevelt, who saw himself as trying to rescue the capitalist system, business opposition probably enhanced his reformist image in the public mind.

The enormous disparity between the New Deal's popular image and its actual accomplishments remains one of the unappreciated as-

17. The standard works on the period are often quite detailed yet lacking in any analysis of the class distributions of inputs and outputs. Only a few American historians describe how the Roosevelt administration serviced the corporate class while reserving its best rhetoric for the common man: see Paul K. Conkin, *The New Deal* (New York: Crowell, 1967); also Barton J. Bernstein, "The New Deal: The Conservative Achievements of Liberal Reform," in Barton J. Bernstein (ed.), *Towards a New Past* (New York: Pantheon, 1963); and Brad Wiley, "Historians and the New Deal," a pamphlet published by the Radical Education Project, Ann Arbor, Michigan, n.d. A good critical treatment of welfare and relief policies under the New Deal can be found in Frances Fox Piven and Richard A. Cloward, *Regulating the Poor* (New York: Pantheon Books, 1971), chapters 2 and 3.

18. Piven and Cloward, *Regulating the Poor*, p. 72. Also Basil Rauch, The *History of the New Deal, 1933–1938* (New York: Creative Age Press, 1944), pp. 70–71.

19. Bernstein, "The New Deal . . ." p. 269.

pects of the Roosevelt era. To cite specifics: the Civilian Conservation Corps provided jobs at subsistence wages for 250,000 out of 15 million unemployed persons. At its peak, the Works Progress Administration (WPA) reached about one in four unemployed, often with work of unstable duration and wages below the already inadequate ones of private industry. Of the 12 million workers in interstate commerce who were earning less than forty cents an hour, only about a half-million were reached by the minimum wage law. The Social Security Act of 1935 made retirement benefits payable only in 1942 and thereafter, covering but half the population and providing no medical insurance and no protection against illness before retirement. Similarly, old-age and unemployment insurance applied solely to those who had enjoyed sustained employment in select occupations. Implementation was left to the states, which were free to set whatever restrictive conditions they chose. And social welfare programs were regressively funded through payroll deductions and sales taxes.

The federal housing program stimulated private construction, with subsidies to construction firms and middle-class buyers and protection for mortgage bankers through the loan insurance program—all of little benefit to the many millions of ill-housed poor.

Like so many other of its programs, the New Deal's efforts in agriculture primarily benefited the large producers through a series of price supports and production cutbacks, while riding "roughshod over the most destitute."[20] Thus many tenant farmers and sharecroppers were evicted when federal acreage rental programs took land out of cultivation.[21] The fate of the Roosevelt administration's "land reform" efforts was a familiar one. In rural areas the government began buying up land and redistributing it to the destitute. Some ten thousand families were resettled in 152 projects, but even this limited effort was too much for conservatives in Congress, who managed to stop land distribution. Indigent farmers who wanted to buy land now had to apply for government guaranteed private loans, leaving poor Whites with little chance—and poor Blacks with even less chance—of favored treatment when it came to securing credit.[22]

---

20. Piven and Cloward, *Regulating the Poor*, p. 76; and Bernstein, "The New Deal . . ." pp. 269–270.

21. By February 1935, 733,000 farm families were on the relief rolls, a rise of 75 percent in sixteen months under the New Deal's agricultural program. The lot of the small farmer did not noticeably improve under Roosevelt and frequently worsened.

22. See Ben H. Bagdikian, "A Forgotten New Deal Experiment in Land Reform," *I. F. Stone Weekly*, July 31, 1967, p. 3. See also Conkin, *The New Deal*, chapter 3; Piven and Cloward, *Regulating the Poor*, chapters 2 and 3.

Piven and Cloward argue that it was not the misery of millions which brought government aid—since misery had prevailed for years before—but the continued threat of acute political unrest. That government programs were markedly inadequate for the needs of the destitute seemed less important than that they achieved a high visibility and did much to dilute public discontent. Once the threat of political unrest and violence subsided, federal relief was actually cut back: in 1936–1937 WPA rolls were reduced by over half and the emergency relief program was slashed, leaving many families with neither work nor relief, reducing them to a destitution worse than any they had known since the 1929 crash. "Large numbers of people were put off the rolls and thrust into a labor market still glutted with unemployed. But with stability restored, the continued suffering of these millions had little political force."[23]

At the same time, organized labor gained a new legitimacy, but on terms highly functional to the corporate system. Labor leaders, including most of those who had earned reputations as "militants," were dedicated to maintaining the capitalist system. In 1935 John L. Lewis warned that "the dangerous state of affairs" might lead to "class consciousness" and "revolution as well"; he pledged that his own union was "doing everything in their power to make the system work and thereby avoid it."[24] Men like Lewis, William Green and Sidney Hillman cooperated closely with management in introducing speed-up methods into production, limiting strikes and maintaining a "disciplined" labor force. The Congress of Industrial Organizations' (CIO) dedication, as Hillman noted, was not to changing "the competitive system" but to trying "to make the system workable."[25] Many owners relied on CIO leaders to keep a "production-minded" control over the workers, utilizing the good will of the union for management's purposes. To the very poor and the many millions of unemployed, the unions offered no help, giving little support to relief programs or to the wider problems of economic change.

The Roosevelt administration's tax policies provide another instance of the disparity between image and performance. New Deal taxation was virtually a continuation of the Hoover administration's program. Business firms avoided many taxes during the depression by taking advantage of various loopholes.[26] The 1935 tax law "did

---

23. Piven and Cloward, *Regulating the Poor*, p. 46.
24. Quoted in Ronald Radosh, "The Corporate Ideology of American Labor Leaders from Gompers to Hillman," *Studies on the Left*, 6, November–December 1966, reprinted in Unger, *Beyond Liberalism*, p. 226.
25. *Ibid.*, p. 224.
26. Conkin, *The New Deal*, p. 67 and *passim*.

not drain wealth from higher-income groups, and the top one percent even increased their shares during the New Deal years."[27] When taxes were increased to pay for U.S. military spending in World War II, some of the additional load fell on the upper-income brackets, but the major burden was taken up by those of more modest means, who had never before been subjected to income taxes. "Thus, the ironic fact is that the extension of the income tax to middle- and low-income classes was the only original aspect of the New Deal tax policy."[28]

In sum, the New Deal introduced some new social-welfare legislation, extended the opportunities for collective bargaining and created a number of worthwhile public-works projects. Yet the Roosevelt era was hardly a triumph for the "forgotten man." Of the New Deal's "three Rs," relief, recovery and reform, it can be said that *relief* was markedly insufficient for meeting the suffering of the times and, in any case, was rather harshly curtailed after the 1936 electoral victory; that attempts at *recovery* focused on business and achieved little until the advent of war spending; and that *reform,* of the kind that might have ended the maldistribution and class abuses of the capitalist political economy, was rarely attempted.[29]

As with class reform, so with race reform. In regard to school desegregation, open housing, fair employment practices, voting rights for Blacks and antilynch laws, the New Deal did nothing. Blacks were excluded from jobs in the Civilian Conservation Corps, received less than their proportional share of public assistance, and under the NRA were frequently paid wages below the legal minimum.[30] The Resettlement Administration, headed by Rexford Tugwell, was probably the only New Deal agency to support equal benefits for Blacks. According to Conkin, it was one of the most honest and class-conscious of New Deal agencies. Eventually antagonizing powerful economic interests, it was abolished by Congress.

By 1940, the last year of peace, the government had poured enough money into the economy to spur production to something close to predepression levels. Yet the number of ill-clothed, ill-fed and ill-housed showed no substantial decrease. Unemployment was over 9 million, almost as high as in 1933, and the national income

---

27. Bernstein, "The New Deal . . ." p. 275.
28. Gabriel Kolko, *Wealth and Power in America* (New York: Praeger, 1962), p. 31.
29. Conkin, *The New Deal,* pp. 65–66.
30. Bernstein, "The New Deal . . ." pp. 278–279.

was still lower than in 1929. One historian of the period offers this conclusion:

> The New Deal failed to solve the problem of depression, it failed to raise the impoverished, it failed to redistribute income, it failed to extend equality and generally countenanced racial discrimination and segregation. It failed generally to make business more responsible to the social welfare or to threaten business's pre-eminent political power. In this sense, the New Deal, despite the shifts in tone and spirit from the earlier decade, was profoundly conservative and continuous with the 1920s.[31]

Looking back at the 1930s, erstwhile New Dealer Robert M. Hutchins offers some criticisms that are strikingly at odds with the popular notion of the New Deal as a dynamic, reformist period:

> It does not seem possible that there was ever another decade like the thirties, distinguished by the air of stupefication, not to say petrification, that hung over us. We were and remained prisoners of our illusions. . . .
> We entered the thirties with a free-wheeling and autonomous economy and with no suspicion that there could be anything wrong with such a system or that it could ever come to an end. . . .
> Why wasn't there a revolution? . . . [Because] everyone believed in the received ideas. The 13 million men on the bread line cherished these convictions just as deeply as did those . . . who sold their own stock short. It is a great tribute to the power of the American educational system that nobody had any other ideas.
> After eight years of "recovery," nobody—including the Federal Government—had anything to show for it but deficits. The emergency did not end. The Depression would not lift. . . . As the war got closer . . . we made the adjustment easily, for the idea of unbalancing the budget to kill people was more familiar to us than the idea of unbalancing it to save the lives of fellow citizens. When the war came, it was sound to do what had been unsound in the years before.[32]

Only by entering the war and remaining thereafter on a war economy was the United States able to maintain a shaky "prosperity."

---

31. *Ibid.*, pp. 264–265.
32. Robert M. Hutchins, "In the Thirties, We Were Prisoners of Our Illusions, Are We Prisoners in the Sixties?" *New York Times Magazine*, September 8, 1968, pp. 44–59, *passim.*

6

Politics: Who Gets What?

In the successive administrations since the New Deal, be they Democratic or Republican, the government's use of public resources on behalf of private gain has never faltered. If anything, it has grown in scope. What follows is a sampling of the ways that government has operated in recent years in the service of powerful interests.[1]

WELFARE FOR THE RICH

In any given year the U.S. Treasury distributes some $25 billion in direct subsidies or benefit-in-kind subsidies to manufacturing, shipping, aviation, communication, mining, timber, agriculture and other enterprises. For example, anywhere from $7 billion to $9 billion a year is allocated, mostly to agribusiness firms, to limit acreage production and buy up crop surpluses. The effect is to keep prices and profits high while subsidizing an expansion of giant corporate farms at the expense of family farms. (About 2,000 family farms go under each year.) Among those who receive agricultural

---

1. A good source on this subject is *The Economics of Federal Subsidy Programs* prepared by the Joint Economic Committee (Washington, D.C.: U.S. Government Printing Office, 1972). Also Morton Mintz and Jerry S. Cohen, *Power Inc.*, (New York: Viking Press, 1976); Grant McConnell, *Private Power and American Democracy* (New York: Knopf, 1966) and the numerous studies cited therein; William Proxmire, *Uncle Sam: The Last of the Bigtime Spenders* (New York: Simon and Schuster, 1972).

subsidies are oil companies, some state universities, a bowling alley in Dallas, a municipal airport in Nebraska, a radio station in Ohio, a mental hospital in Alabama and even the Queen of England (who got $68,000 for not producing anything on her plantation in Mississippi).[2]

The federal government gives away in direct subsidy payments about $1 billion a year to the shipping industry, millions to the sugar industry and hundreds of millions to private aviation facilities used mostly by a few thousand executives and well-to-do flying enthusiasts. The costs of one quarter of all U.S. fertilizer exports are financed by the federal government (while the profits remain with the exporters), as are exports of iron, steel, railroad equipment, rice, textiles, tobacco, petroleum, chemicals, automobiles and other products. In 1976 Congress voted to spend over $6 billion to subsidize railroads, thus ensuring high dividends to stockholders and big bank creditors who in turn allow railroads to continue to deteriorate.[3]

The Protection Racket

The government provides hundreds of millions of dollars to cushion the financial losses suffered by cattle ranchers, airlines, shoe manufacturers, ski resorts and even banks. The most intriguing case of compensation involves corporations like DuPont, General Motors, Ford, Exxon and ITT, which owned factories in enemy countries during World War II and produced everything from tanks to synthetic fuels for the Axis war effort. GM executives like Alfred P. Sloan, Jr., served on the board of directors of GM-owned firms in Nazi Germany throughout the war. ITT produced direction finders in American plants to protect Allied convoys at sea, while manufacturing in its German plants bombers that wreaked havoc on the same Allied convoys. After the war, rather than being prosecuted for trading with the enemy, ITT collected $27 million from the U.S. government for war damages inflicted on its German plants by

---

2. *New York Times*, July 11, 1973; see Senator John Williams's comments as reported in the *Philadelphia Inquirer*, July 11, 1967; also Edward Higbee, *Farms and Farmers in an Urban Age* (New York: Twentieth Century Fund, 1963), p. 139 ff.; William Robbins, "Farm Policy Helps Make the Rural Rich Richer," *New York Times*, April 5, 1970; Larry Casolino, "This Land Is Their Land," *Ramparts*, July 1972, pp. 31–36; *Washington Post*, March 27, 1978.

3. Blessed with such bounty from the public treasure, the railroads in question stripped themselves of their own cash assets of over $9 million and distributed the money to their stockholders in what was one of the highest dividend payments in New York Stock Exchange history. See *Workers World*, March 12, 1976.

Allied bombings. GM and Ford subsidiaries built the bulk of Nazi Germany's heavy trucks, which served as "the backbone of the German Army transportation system." GM collected more than $33 million in compensation for damages to its war plants in enemy territories. Ford and other multinational corporations collected lesser sums.[4]

Along with its subsidies, grants and credits, the government serves the business class by maintaining prices at noncompetitive, monopolistic levels in "regulated" areas of the economy at an estimated annual cost of $80 billion to American consumers.[5] The government engages in preferential enforcement—or nonenforcement—of regulatory standards, as when the FCC sets an "allowed rate of return" for the telephone company and then ignores it, enabling American Telephone and Telegraph to overcharge customers by a staggering half-billion dollars each year on interstate long distance calls.[6]

Private electric utilities offer another illustration of the advantages of government "regulation." Utilities are nonrisk enterprises whose expenses are virtually guaranteed by the government. They never go bankrupt; they pay high dividends to their shareholders and give their managers handsome salaries and stock options. Their rates are set so as to allow them a net income as high as 15 to 25 percent, which explains why private utility rates are sometimes more than two, three or four times those of publicly-owned ones.[7]

The federal government gives private corporations the use and sometimes ownership of new technologies developed at public expense. Nuclear energy, electronics, aeronautics, space communication, mineral exploration, computer systems—much of the basic re-

---

4. The information and quotation come from documents declassified in 1974. See Bradford Snell, "GM and the Nazis," *Ramparts*, June 1974, pp. 14–16; "Memo from COPE" (AFL-CIO report), August 30, 1973; Thomas De Baggio, "The Unholy Alliance," *Penthouse*, May 1976, pp. 74–91. Some of the war plants were spared from American bombing because they were owned by big corporations. Thus while Cologne was leveled by saturation bombing, its Ford plant, providing military trucks for the Nazi Army, was untouched—and used by German workers as an air-raid shelter. Ford collected $1 million for some broken windows and the plant was back in operation a short time after the U.S. Army entered Cologne. See eyewitness correspondence by E. F. Patterson, *Ramparts*, August 1974, p. 8.

5. See, for instance, the regulation of trucking and railroad rates by the ICC, *New York Times*, March 2, 1975.

6. Frye Gaillard, "Trouble on the Line," *Progressive*, February 1978, p. 31. The author cites a Federal Communications Commission study.

7. See Lee Metcalf and Vic Reinemer, *Overcharge* (New York: McKay, 1967); also Richard Morgan, Tom Riesenberg and Michael Troutman, *Taking Charge: A New Look at Public Power* (Washington, D.C.: Environmental Action Foundation, 1978).

search and development work in these and other fields is done for the benefit of private firms at a cost of many billions of dollars to the taxpayer. For instance, through its political influence in the White House and Congress, AT&T managed to have the entire satellite communications system ("Comsat") put under its control in 1962—after U.S. taxpayers had put up the initial $20 billion to develop it. Then AT&T decided not to extend the benefits of Comsat to its U.S. customers, the reason being that billions of dollars worth of the company's equipment would have become obsolete overnight if satellites were put into use within the United States. The big savings for long-distance customers would have meant huge losses for AT&T owners. In order to preserve its obsolete but highly profitable investment, AT&T withheld satellite service from the very U.S. public that had financed it.[8]

As in olden days, government continues to give away, lease or sell at bargain rates the national forests, grasslands, wildlife preserves and other public lands containing priceless timber, minerals, oil and water and recreational resources—with little consideration for environmental values or for desires other than those of the favored corporations.[9] For instance, several major petroleum companies leased acreage in Alaska for oil exploration, paying a sum of $12 million for leases worth upwards of $2 *billion*. In a subsequent oil-lease auction, the companies paid the government $900 million for lands that are expected to be worth some $50 billion within a decade.[10]

Each year the government distributes more than $26 billion in research and development grants mostly to big corporations, which are permitted to keep the patents developed at taxpayer expense and to charge taxpayers exorbitant prices when the inventions are marketed.[11] The government pays out many billions in unnecessarily high interest rates, and permits billions of government dollars to re-

---

8. Steve Babson and Nancy Brigham, "Why Do We Spend So Much Money?" *Liberation*, September/October 1973, p. 19.
9. See James Ridgeway, *The Politics of Ecology* (New York: E. P. Dutton, 1970); also The Ralph Nader Study Group Report, *The Water Lords* (New York: Grossman, 1971), James M. Fallows, project director; The Ralph Nader Study Group Report, *The Vanishing Air* (New York: Grossman, 1970), John C. Esposito and Larry J. Silverman, project directors.
10. Barry Weisberg, "Ecology of Oil: Raping Alaska," in Editors of *Ramparts* (eds.), *Eco-Catastrophe* (San Francisco: Canfield Press, 1970), p. 107 and p. 109.
11. Three-fifths of the technical research done in this country is funded by the government; three-fourths is controlled by the corporations. See Harry Braverman, *Labor and Monopoly Capital* (New York: Monthly Review Press, 1975), p. 166 *fn*; also "Double Jeopardy," *Progressive*, February 1978, p. 8.

main on deposit in banks without collecting interest. It tolerates overcharging by firms doing business with the government, as well as tax favoritism and monopoly practices.[12] The government awards highly favorable contracts and provides emergency funding to ensure the survival and continued profits of armaments companies; it furnishes big business with risk-free capital, long-term credits and tariff protections and provides lowered tax assessments and cost write-offs amounting to many billions of dollars yearly; it makes available to defense industries many billions of dollars worth of government-owned land, buildings, machinery and materials, thereby in part "saving them the job of financing their own investments";[13] and it applies the antitrust laws in a manner so lackadaisical as to make them inconsequential.

The Deficit Spender

One of the ways that government keeps business profits high is by spending more than it collects in taxes, a process known as "deficit spending." The government subsidizes business costs, compensates for business losses, purchases billions of dollars worth of corporate goods and services, yet cuts business taxes. As economists Huberman and Sweezy remarked: "It is hardly surprising that businessmen are so enthusiastic about *this* kind of deficit spending. Boiled down to essentials it amounts simply to using the borrowing power of the federal government to subsidize corporate profits."[14]

The image of conservatives holding the line against the wild spenders in Washington is a false one, for conservative leaders have been among the wildest spenders. In its first four years, the Nixon administration produced budget deficits amounting to $73.8 billion. President Ford's budget deficit for the fiscal year of 1976 alone was $51.8 billion. With deficit spending, corporate profits grow but so does the national debt. In 1979, the Carter administration's budget added $37.4 billion to a national debt that came to over $800 billion.

As government spends more than it collects, it must borrow money from those who have it by floating risk-free, high-interest bonds. Ordinary citizens can buy nonmarketable government bonds

---

12. See Senator Russell Long's comments quoted in Richard Harris, "Annals of Politics: A Fundamental Hoax," *New Yorker*, August 7, 1971, p. 53.

13. Sidney Lens, *The Military-Industrial Complex* (Philadelphia: United Church Press, 1970), p. 8.

14. Leo Huberman and Paul Sweezy, "The Kennedy-Johnson Boom," *Monthly Review*, February 1965, reprinted in Marvin Gettleman and David Mermelstein (eds.), *The Great Society Reader* (New York: Random House, 1967), p. 103.

of modest denomination through various payroll savings plans, but most federal bonds are held by banks and very rich individuals and come in nothing smaller than $5,000 denominations. As the government continues to borrow money, the national debt increases, and so does the interest paid on it to the very rich. This interest payment represents another huge subsidy to the wealthy and is one of the largest single items in the federal budget each year: in 1980, it was over $45 billion, *a sum more than twice the amount spent on federal welfare payments to the poor.* The bulk of this money, drawn from the salaried and wage-earning public, constitutes a reverse redistribution of income, a manifestation of what one writer called the "trickle up theory" of income.[15]

The overall effect of federal fiscal policies has been to diminish the buying power of the wage earner, a buying power that was considered one of the causes of inflation, without stopping the inflation itself or diminishing the unemployment. However, the government's intent is not to achieve full employment but to ensure business profits, it being presumed that high profits will eventually bring high employment, a presumption held more firmly by those who make the profits than by those looking for jobs.

In any case, as noted earlier, from business's standpoint, recession is not without its compensations, since it acts as a check on wages, though not on prices, and guarantees a pool of unemployed, cheap labor. Recessions allow the giant corporations to tighten their hold on the market by taking over weakened smaller firms, thereby emerging all the stronger for the next boom.[16] Such phrases as "cooling off the economy" and "weeding out the overgrowth" are metaphors used effortlessly by those who do not suffer the chilling effects of the cooling and who in fact do the weeding. When it is said that the goal of government and business is a sound, stable economy, it must be asked: Sound and stable by whose definition? For whose interests and at whose expense?

THE PENTAGON: BILLIONS FOR BIG BROTHER

As measured by the federal budget, government's greatest devotion is to the military establishment. The Department of Defense (commonly known as the Pentagon) is the largest, richest, most powerful

---

15. Robert Fitch, "Selling the Debt," *Ramparts*, April 1972, p. 20.
16. R. D. Corwin and Lois Gray, "Of Republicans and Recessions," *Social Policy*, 2, November–December 1971, p. 43.

unit of government. Its budget, estimated at over $125 billion in 1980, continues to grow in leaps, increasing at a rate far exceeding the rate of inflation—regardless of whether there is war or peace. The Pentagon projects a military build-up in the 1980s costing about $1.5 trillion, proportionately far more than the $2 trillion spent on armaments and wars from 1945 to 1980. (It is estimated that each person in the United States works the equivalent of five years to pay for U.S. military expenses.[17])

The Pentagon repeatedly conjures up the specter of Soviet military supremacy in order to maintain its hold over the public purse. In 1956 the American public was alerted to a dangerous "bomber gap"; in 1960 it was a "missile gap," and in 1967 an "antiballistic missile gap." In each instance it was subsequently discovered that no such gap existed and that U.S. capabilities were superior to the Soviet Union's. But these revelations came only after multibillion-dollar allocations for bomber, missile and ABM programs had been voted by Congress. In 1975 the Department of Defense announced that it was falling behind the Russians in the development of "multiple independently targeted nuclear warheads" (MIRVs). In fact, as one military analyst noted, "The U.S. has had MIRVs for years. It has hundreds of them ready to use while the Soviets are just getting them."[18]

From 1977 through 1980, television reports and scare articles began appearing in the business-owned media describing how the Soviet Union had moved far ahead of the United States in armaments and was thereby posing a threat to Western Europe.[19] The Pentagon and its political and corporate supporters called for multibillion-dollar increases in conventional weapons to strengthen NATO and match the Soviet "build-up"—even though, as Senator Proxmire pointed out, the Soviet arms build-up was almost entirely on its China border.[20]

---

17. Harold Freeman, "On Consuming the Surplus," *Progressive*, February 1977, p. 20. For an overall critique on the military establishment see Richard F. Kaufman, *The War Profiteers* (New York: Bobbs-Merrill, 1971); also Seymour Melman, *Pentagon Capitalism* (New York: McGraw-Hill, 1970); Seymour Melman, *The Permanent War Economy* (New York: Simon and Schuster, 1974); Adam Yarmolinsky, *The Military Establishment* (New York: Harper & Row, 1973); David Horowitz (ed.), *Corporations and The Cold War* (New York: Monthly Review Press, 1969).

18. James McCartney writing in the *Philadelphia Inquirer*, quoted in Richard E. Ward, "War Budget $100 Billion: What Detente?" *Guardian*, March 5, 1975, p. 3.

19. See *New York Times*, January 15, 1978.

20. See Proxmire's letter to the *New York Times*, January 30, 1979. The ultimate build-up against a nonexistent threat occurred in 1969, when the Chinese did not possess a single missile that could hit the U.S. mainland. Yet President Lyndon Johnson was pressured by the Pentagon and several large corporations into ordering a $5 billion

The leading beneficiaries of defense contracts, the large corporations, have helped propagate the military's cause with skillful lobbying and mass advertising that stresses the importance of keeping America "strong." And as private industry became the supporter of defense preparedness, military men spoke more openly about the blessings of free enterprise and the "American Way of Life." With 90 percent of the contracts awarded with no competitive bidding, relations between corporate and military personnel became an all-important determinant of who got what. Senior military officers and civilian Pentagon officials who promoted the right corporate contracts looked forward to early retirement and to entrance into high-paying corporate jobs.[21]

As a result of the overall military-industrial partnership, enormous portions of American purchasing power have been siphoned off by the government through taxation and channeled into the major corporations, with the twenty-five largest contractors receiving over half the prime contracts for weapons production, thereby further centralizing corporate wealth in America.[22]

Profitable Waste

Waste and duplication are a standard part of the Pentagon's operations. Thus, the Army allocated $1.5 billion to develop a heavy-lift helicopter—even though it already had heavy-lift helicopters—while the Navy was building an almost identical one. At the cost of many hundreds of millions of dollars, the Air Force and the Navy simultaneously developed sophisticated airborne warning systems.[23] A coalition of Congressmen discovered on one occasion that the Pentagon was unable to locate where half its procurement budget, a sum of $20 billion, was being spent, the money having gone to corporate subcontractors of whom no record was kept by the Defense Depart-

---

antimissile system that had no purpose except to shoot down China's nonexistent trans-Pacific missiles. See Jack Anderson, "Military Fraud and Waste Cited," *Washington Post*, January 5, 1979.

21. See for instance, Wendell Rawls, Jr., "Ex-Pentagon Aide Joins Hughes Aircraft to Oversee Missile He Promoted," *New York Times*, February 15, 1977; also William Hoffman, "Vietnam: The Bloody Get-Rich-Quick Business of War," *Gallery*, November 1978, p. 42. In recent years, a total of eighty high-ranking Pentagon officials, including generals and admirals, have been implicated in various bribe scandals involving favored treatment for military contractors. Not one of the officers has been discharged from the service, and none of the companies, such as Rockwell, Raytheon or Northrop, has been prosecuted or penalized. See *Workers World*, April 23, 1976; also Jack Anderson's column, *Ithaca* (N.Y.) *Journal*, December 20, 1975.

22. *Wall Street Journal*, October 30, 1978.

23. *New York Times*, July 4, 1969.

ment.[24] It was also discovered that Pentagon officials had lost track of up to $30 billion in weapons and other military equipment intended for foreign orders.[25]

The General Accounting Office (GAO) published a detailed report showing that the defense budget was regularly padded by an estimated $3 billion to $5.7 billion to ensure against congressional cuts.[26] Meanwhile, the Pentagon hands out huge sums to defense companies to compensate for losses and mismanagement and to save them from bankruptcy. Lockheed Corporation alone received a $1-billion loan guarantee from the federal government to keep it solvent.[27]

That certain firms suffer losses does not mean that defense is a high-risk, low-profit industry. *Sales* profits may appear low, but since most of the costs are paid by the government, profits on the company's actual investments are usually astronomical.[28]

Many items in the defense budget end up costing far more than the original bid. Often firms do not explain their cost overruns, even when requested to do so by the government. The C5A transport plane eventually cost $2 *billion* more than the original $1 billion contract. A study by the Brookings Institution concluded that "virtually all large military contracts . . . ultimately involved costs in excess of original contractual estimates of from 300 to 700 percent."[29] In one decade, at least sixty-eight such weapons systems were abandoned as unworkable.

The rewards for all this waste and inefficiency have been high. In 1978 the GAO revealed that profits before taxes—and the big corporations pay almost no taxes—were 56.1 percent for defense contractors, while one company made a profit of 240 percent.[30] Two highly regarded scientists demonstrated after a painstaking study

24. *New York Times*, May 23, 1977.
25. See the report in *Business Week*, July 24, 1978.
26. *New York Times*, February 4, 1976; *New York Times*, February 8, 1971.
27. The grant is known in the Pentagon as an "amendment without consideration," meaning money given without assurance of getting anything in return. See A. Ernest Fitzgerald, *The High Priests of Waste* (New York: Norton, 1972); also *New York Times*, April 30, 1973.
28. See the discussions in Kaufman, *The War Profiteers*, *passim*.
29. Cited in Lens, *The Military-Industrial Complex*, chapter 1. A 1979 report by the GAO found that fifty-five major weapons systems, totaling some $210 billion, have suffered a 70 percent increase over their initial estimates. William Flannery, "Pentagon Spending," *New York Times*, February 27, 1979.
30. Hoffman, "Vietnam: The Bloody Get-Rich-Quick Business of War," p. 43. After these kinds of revelations by the GAO, a House committee launched an investigation— not of the Pentagon but of the GAO. See also James Barron, "Bad Weapons Never Die: Onward and Upward with the GBU-15," *Nation*, January 27, 1979.

that the defense budget could be cut by 40 percent with no loss in military capability.[31]

Armaments and the Economy

It is not enough to condemn the waste and profligacy of the Pentagon; we must also try to understand its function in the existing capitalist society. For the millions of taxpayers who are deprived of essential domestic services because the military budget devours such a large chunk of the public treasure, defense spending is wasteful. But for the industrial empire that has grown rich and immense by servicing the U.S. military, defense spending is wonderful. First, the taxpayers' money underwrites all the risks and most of the costs of weapons development and sales. Unlike automobile manufacturers who must worry about selling the cars they produce, the weapons manufacturer has a contracted market complete with cost-overrun guarantees. Second, with noncompetitive bids on defense contracts, a company can submit an inflated price and get the contract. Indeed, the *higher* the negotiated contract, the *more* welcome it is, since both the contractor and the military are sympathetic to the largest possible operation.[32] Third, the defense industry is the most lucrative business there is, with profits being many times higher than in the private consumer market. Fourth, the armaments market does not compete with the consumer market, for it creates a whole new area of demand and investment. Military products have a brief life span, becoming technologically obsolete not long after they come off the production line. Technical changes suggested by the corporate producer or by the military buyer or by fearful and often imaginative references to Soviet advances in weaponry create a built-in obsolescence and an endless demand for newer, more sophisticated and more expensive weapons systems. So it is that the military budget continues to expand. Its growth is a perfectly functional, desirable arrangement for the big corporations.

Taking into account the multiplier effect of a dollar spent and the network of subsidiary services that feed on the defense dollar, possibly a fifth of all economic activity in the United States is dependent on military expenditures. In 1974 Defense Secretary James Schlesinger defended a last minute $1 billion increase in the military budget on the grounds that it would provide a stimulus to a lagging

---

31. See the comments by Philip Morrison and Paul F. Walker in the October 1978 issue of *Scientific American*.
32. Freeman, "On Consuming the Surplus," p. 21.

domestic economy. He thereby acknowledged that Pentagon spending was dictated, as the *Times* noted, "in part by domestic fiscal considerations and not strictly by military requirements."[33]

Some people have defended military spending because it provides jobs. So do the heroin, prostitution, pornography and advertising industries. The millions of highway accidents each year provide employment for wreckers, repairmen and hospital workers. The cigarette industry provides jobs, but that is no reason to encourage cigarette consumption. There are many useful and needed things that our labor and resources might be expended on, but these do not include the capacity to blow up the world a hundred times over or to produce mountains of obsolete, death-dealing weapons.

Measured by the number of jobs created, military appropriations are not the most efficient job provider. The Public Interest Research Group in Michigan, in a depth study, found that arms spending creates fewer jobs per billion dollars than any other government spending except the space program. U.S. workers could reap almost 1.25 million extra jobs each year if money poured into the Defense Department were devoted to nonmilitary purposes.[34]

The long-range effect of military spending on the economy has been deleterious. The Pentagon has been the largest user of capital and technology in the United States since World War II, and this has placed serious restrictions on resources available for civilian use, making it difficult for productivity in the civilian sector to keep up with production costs. In addition, the annual injection into the economy of over $100 billion in defense spending raises demand in the civilian sector without providing a comparable increase in the supply of civilian goods and services. The result is inflation. During the Vietnam war years of 1965 to 1969, the inflation rate more than tripled. As Richard Barnet noted, a country which spends billions to support a defense establishment of five million persons who produce nothing, and which spends billions on machines that make nothing is not on the road to prosperity.[35]

As prices soared, foreign competitors were able to capture greater shares of the American market with their less expensive goods, as happened with automobiles, electronic products, steel products and consumer items like shoes and cameras.[36] Military

33. *New York Times*, February 27, 1974.
34. The report is summarized in the *Guardian*, March 1, 1978; earlier findings of the Michigan research group appear in the *Progressive*, April 1976, p. 11.
35. Richard J. Barnet, "Challenging the Myths of National Security," *New York Times Magazine*, April 1, 1979.
36. Seymour Melman, "Beating 'Swords' into Subways," *New York Times Magazine*, November 19, 1978, p. 48.

spending has not brought prosperity but an increasing impoverishment of the civilian sector. The people of New York City, for instance, pay more money in taxes to the Pentagon than to New York City. So we have the spectacle of the military feasting on billions while day-care centers, schools, hospitals, and nursing homes are closed down for want of funds. One Main Battle Tank, costing $1 million, could pay for the special national milk program for children which Congress abolished in a recent economizing effort. The cost overruns on forty-five weapons systems (just the overruns, not the costs themselves), amounting to $38 billion, could pay for a water-pollution abatement program for the entire nation. The $11 billion proposed for the B-1 bomber could provide decent housing for millions of low-income Americans.[37]

The Military Culture

Of the many agencies engaged in propagandizing the public, none is more active than the Pentagon.[38] The armed services currently compose the strongest lobby in Washington, exerting more influence over Congress than that body exerts over the Defense Department. That it happens to be a federal offense to use the taxpayers' money to propagandize taxpayers seems not to have deterred the military. The Pentagon spends many millions a year on exhibitions, films, books, magazines and brochures, recruitment tours to schools and a flood of press releases which, publicized as "news reports" and "news events" in thousands of newspapers and magazines and on radio and television shows, propagate the military's view of the world without identifying the military as their source.[39]

The influence of our military state is heavily felt in the academic community. Many institutions of higher education draw anywhere from 10 to 80 percent of their budgets from government sources. Two of the top 100 defense contractors are universities: in 1977 Johns Hopkins received $117,740,000 in military funds, while the Massachusetts Institute of Technology (MIT) was awarded $108,872,000. At least ninety universities and colleges have been researching problems of counterinsurgency, command-control systems, defoliation techniques, internal security and antiriot strat-

---

37. Melman, *The Permanent War Economy;* also Hoffman, "Vietnam: The Bloody Get-Rich-Quick Business of War," p. 43.

38. See J. William Fulbright, *The Pentagon Propaganda Machine* (New York: Vintage, 1971); Lens gives a description of the public-relations efforts of the Pentagon in his *The Military-Industrial Complex.*

39. Fred C. Cook, "The Juggernaut," *Nation,* October 28, 1961, p. 286; also Lens, *The Military-Industrial Complex,* chapter 5.

egies, population-relocation methods and seismic and magnetic detection systems. Dr. A. J. Hill, a weapons researcher at MIT, noted: "Our job is not to advance knowledge but to advance the military."[40]

Many social scientists have joined programs financed by the military, including psychological, sociological, economic and political studies devoted to counterrevolutionary techniques and the manipulation of opinion at home and abroad. In hundreds of conferences and in thousands of brochures, articles and books written by members of the intellectual community who are in the pay of the government, military propaganda is lent an aura of academic objectivity. Casting a shadow on their own integrity as scholars and teachers, such intellectuals transmit to an unsuspecting public the military view of reality and the Pentagon's sense of its own indispensability.

The proliferation of Pentagon-financed "independent" corporations such as RAND and the Hudson Institute—the "think tanks" that solve technical military problems for a fee—testifies to the growing role played by the nonmilitary person. Progressively less able to provide the brainpower for all their needs, the armed services simply buy up such human resources from the universities, corporations and planning institutions. The staggering fact is that over two-thirds of all the technical research in America is consumed by the military.

If we define "military state" as any polity that devotes a major portion of its public resources to purposes of war, then the United States is a military state, the biggest in history. Contrary to the conventional view, a civilian constitutional government is as capable of becoming a militarist power as is a dictatorship. The political system of a nation is of less importance in determining its military capacity than is the level of its industry and wealth, the intensity of its anxiety about domestic and foreign enemies and the scope of its overseas investments and ambitions.

THE SWORD AND THE DOLLAR: TRAVELS ABROAD

The postwar growth of American corporations has been stupendous, but problems come with such success. Enormous surplus profits remain after operational expenses are paid and even after the $28 bil-

---

40. Quoted in Bert Cochran, *The War System* (New York: Macmillan, 1965), p. 307.

lion in yearly dividends is distributed—chiefly to the wealthiest 1 or 2 percent of America's families. The remaining undistributed profits must be invested somewhere. As noted earlier, the growth in profits intensifies the search for new profit-yielding opportunities which, in turn, create more profit surplus and a still more strenuous pursuit of investment (i.e., profit) opportunities. In a word, profit abundance and profit hunger are but two sides of the same coin. Overseas investments—especially in underdeveloped countries—become increasingly attractive because of the cheap native labor, the high investment return, the absence of corporate taxes, the marketing of products at monopoly prices and the opportunity to invest a surplus capital which—if invested at home—would only glut the domestic market and depress the profit rate, and—if invested in other industrialized nations—would bring a lower return.[41]

The federal government performs overseas two major functions for capitalism, roughly the same ones it performs at home: first, it subsidizes and finances corporate foreign investments with sums amounting to many billions yearly; and second, it provides a military force to protect private investments and capitalist social orders from revolutionary change. Consider each of these in turn:

1. The U.S. government spends $6 billion to $8 billion yearly on a multibillion-dollar foreign aid program ostensibly designed to help poorer nations help themselves but which actually helps "the United States maintain a position of influence and control around the world," as President John Kennedy proudly noted.[42] American aid is allocated to Third World countries usually on the condition that it be used to buy American goods at American prices, to be transported in American ships. The highways, roads, ports, dams and utilities constructed in foreign lands with U.S. government funds are planned around the needs of American-owned factories, mines, oil fields, refineries and plantations. Abroad, as at home, the U.S. taxpayer pays for the "social overhead capital" needed to service the multinational corporations.

The U.S. government finances overseas loans and investments and subsidizes business exports. The government compensates corporate investors for losses due to war, revolution, insurrection or confiscation by a foreign government, and refuses aid to any country which nationalizes without compensation assets owned by U.S.

41. See Harry Magdoff, *The Age of Imperialism* (New York: Monthly Review Press, 1969); also Magdoff's *Imperialism: From the Colonial Age to the Present* (New York: Monthly Review Press, 1978).

42. Quoted in Teresa Hayter, *Aid as Imperialism* (Baltimore: Penguin Books, 1971).

firms. U.S. funds were given to Latin American governments for the purpose of having them expropriate *unprofitable* U.S. firms at *above-market prices.* "In turn, U.S. corporations used the funds procured to invest in more profitable activities. . . ."[43]

Many persons wonder why the gap between rich and poor nations grows wider despite the increase in Third World investments. The answer is that the gap widens *because* of such investments. Unless we assume that multinational corporations are philanthropic undertakings, it is clear that investments have the ultimate purpose of *extracting* wealth from poorer nations. Between 1950 and 1972, U.S. corporations showed a $50 billion overseas investment outflow and a $99 billion profit influx.[44] In Chile alone over the last several decades, U.S. copper companies extracted $3.8 billion in profits, leaving in their wake devastated mining lands and impoverished communities.

U.S. aid allows multinationals to exploit the recipient country's labor, monopolize its resources, control its politics and influence its tastes, markets and technical needs so that dependency on American

43. James Petras, "U.S. Business and Foreign Policy," *New Politics,* 6, Fall 1967, reprinted in Michael Parenti (ed.), *Trends and Tragedies in American Foreign Policy* (Boston: Little, Brown, 1971), p. 98.

44. Paul Sweezy, "Growing Wealth, Declining Power," *Monthly Review,* March 1974, pp. 6–7.

products continues well after the aid program has ceased.[45] The effect of foreign aid and private U.S. investment is to dislocate the economy of the poorer country, retarding its productive capacity by limiting it to a few specialized extractive industries like oil, timber, tin, copper and rubber or cash crops like sugar, coffee, cocoa, cotton or tobacco. The labor and resources of the land are mobilized to fit the interests of U.S. corporations rather than the needs of the populace. The result is low wages, high illiteracy and chronic poverty. In a country like Guatemala, while U.S. corporations own three-fourths of the arable land and extract enormous profits, the rural population has a smaller per capita food supply today than during the Mayan civilization.[46]

U.S. aid and corporate investments leave Third World countries deeply indebted to U.S. banks. Like addicts, debtor nations become hooked on U.S. credit to remain solvent, borrowing increasingly larger sums at high interest rates to pay off an ever-growing debt, the temporary relief of each new loan only creating a heavier debt obligation for the future. Some Third World nations devote the major part of their export earnings to paying off their multibillion-dollar debts to American banks.[47]

2. The growth of American capitalism from a weak domestic position to a dominant international one has been accompanied by a similar growth in American military interventionism. Sometimes the sword has rushed in to protect the dollar, and sometimes the dollar has rushed in to enjoy the advantages won by the sword. To safeguard the ever-expanding U.S. corporate empire, the United States government has had to embark on a global counterrevolutionary strategy, suppressing insurgent peasant and worker movements throughout Asia, Africa and Latin America. But the interests of the corporate elites never stand naked; rather they are wrapped in the flag and coated with patriotic appearances. Knowing that the American people would never agree to sending their sons to fight wars in far-off lands in order to protect the profits of Gulf Oil and

45. Magdoff, *Age of Imperialism*, p. 129 ff; also "The U.S. Foreign Aid Program," *Dollars and Sense*, March 1979, p. 8.

46. For a more detailed look at the effects of overseas corporate investments and government aid, see Paul Baran and Paul Sweezy, *Monopoly Capital* (New York: Monthly Review Press, 1968), pp. 186–207; and James Petras, *Critical Perspectives on Imperialism and Social Class in the Third World* (New York: Monthly Review Press, 1978).

47. Jonathan Aronson and Elliot Stein, Jr., "Bankers Milk the Third World," *Progressive*, October 1977, pp. 49–51; Isabel Letelier and Michael Moffitt, "Human Rights, Economic Aid and Private Banks" (Issue Paper, Institute for Policy Studies, Washington, D.C., 1978).

General Motors,[48] the corporate elites and their political spokesmen play upon popular fears, telling us that our "national security" necessitates American intervention wherever a colonial order is threatened by a popular uprising seeking to establish a socialist economic system.

Our policymakers claim they are defending democracy from communism in Asia, Africa and Latin America. But closer examination shows they are defending the capitalist world from social change—even if the change be peaceful, orderly and democratic. Guatemala in 1954 and Chile in 1973 are two cases in point. In both countries popularly elected governments began instituting progressive changes for the benefit of the more destitute classes and began to nationalize or threatened to nationalize U.S. corporate holdings. And in both countries, the United States was instrumental in overthrowing these governments and instituting right-wing fascist regimes that accommodated U.S. investors and ruthlessly repressed the peasants and workers. Similarly, in countries like Greece, the Philippines, Indonesia, East Timor and in at least ten Latin American nations over the past fifteen years, popular governments have been overthrown by military oligarchs—largely trained and financed by the Pentagon and the CIA—who prove themselves friendly to the investment interests of American capitalism.

For all their talk about "human rights," U.S. government leaders have been propagating fascist regimes throughout the world, using assassination squads, torture and terror to support the allies of the corporate world order.[49] In countries like Chile, the Philippines, Zaire, Thailand and South Korea, strikes have been outlawed, unions destroyed, wages cut back, and dissidents murdered. Illiteracy, poverty and hunger are the lot of the many, while wealth and power accumulate in the hands of a few rulers who prove themselves cooperative friends of the multinational corporations.

This policy of containing social change in order to make the world safe for capitalism has had its serious setbacks. In recent years successful national liberation movements in Vietnam, Cambodia, Laos, Guinea-Bissau, Mozambique and Angola have vanquished

---

48. A Harris poll in 1975 found that the American people opposed sending U.S. troops to aid countries under attack. If North Korea invaded South Korea, 65 percent of the respondents opposed and 14 percent favored sending troops. If China invaded Taiwan, 59 percent opposed and 17 percent supported sending troops. The only country Americans supported (by a 77 to 12 percent margin) sending troops to in case of invasion was Canada. See *Burlington* (Vt.) *Free Press*, March 25, 1975.

49. See Ernest Volkman and John Cummings "The White Hand," *Penthouse*, June 1979, pp. 72–79, for a discussion of CIA-trained killers and torturers in Latin America.

U.S. or U.S.-backed forces and have instituted popular socialist governments in their respective nations. But if military-corporate America lost the war in Indochina, it was not from want of trying. The United States government, under the leadership of Democratic and Republican administrations, spent $150 billion and more than ten years prosecuting the Indochina war, dropping almost 8 million tons of bombs, 18 million gallons of chemical defoliants and nearly 400,000 tons of napalm. The Vietnamese, Laotian and Cambodian countrysides were desolated by saturation bombings; several million Vietnamese, Cambodians and Laotians were killed, millions more were maimed or wounded and almost 10 million were left homeless; 55,000 Americans lost their lives and hundreds of thousands more were wounded or permanently disabled. But the war did bring benefits to a tiny segment of the American population: corporate defense contractors like DuPont and ITT.[50]

If we define "imperialism" as that relationship in which one country dominates, through use of economic and military power, the land, labor, resources, finances and politics of another country, then the United States is the greatest imperialist power in history. The American empire is of a magnitude never before equaled. More than 1.5 million American military personnel are stationed in 119 countries. The United States maintains 429 major military bases and 2,972 lesser bases in thirty countries, covering some 4,000 square miles and costing over $5 billion a year. The military has some 8,500 strategic nuclear weapons and 22,000 tactical ones deployed throughout the world. The U.S. Navy deploys a fleet larger in total tonnage than all the other navies of the world combined, consisting of missile cruisers, nuclear submarines, nuclear aircraft carriers, destroyers and spy ships which sail every ocean and make port on every continent. Two million native troops and large contingents of native police, under the command of various military juntas, have been trained, equipped and financed by the United States and assisted by U.S. counterinsurgency forces, their purpose being not to defend these countries from outside invasion but to protect capital investments and the ruling oligarchs from the dangers of domestic insurgency.

With 5 percent of the earth's population, the United States expends one-third of the total world cost of war. Two-thirds of the federal budget (that is, the discretionary portion, not obligated by so-

---

50. The top ten defense firms grossed $11.6 billion in contracts during the Vietnam war years of 1965–1970. See Hoffman, "Vietnam: The Bloody Get-Rich-Quick Business of War," p. 42.

cial security, veterans' benefits, etc.) is spent on war preparation. Despite a nuclear "overkill" capacity that can destroy the entire world more than twenty-five times over, the U.S. nuclear arsenal continues to grow at the rate of three H-bombs each day. Since World War II, probably more than $80 billion in U.S. military aid has been given to some eighty nations.[51]

This American global expansionism demands costly government expenditures. But, as Veblen pointed out long ago, "the costs are not paid out of business gains, but out of the industry of the rest of the people.'[52] The profits of empire flow into private hands, while the growing military and overhead costs are socialized and carried by the taxpayer.

This is not to say that U.S. expansionism has been impelled by purely material motives, but that various other considerations—such as national security and patriotism—are defined in a way that serves the material interests of a particular class. Indeed, much of what passes for "the national interest" in capitalist America, not surprisingly, has been defined from the perspective of a capitalist social order. "A serious and explicit purpose of our foreign policy," President Eisenhower observed in 1953, "[is] the encouragement of a hospitable climate for investment in foreign nations.[53] Since American "security" is supposedly dependent on American power, and such power depends in part on American wealth (i.e., a "sound economy," "secure markets," "essential raw materials," etc.), then policies which are fashioned to expand U.S. corporate wealth abroad are presumed to be in the national interest. Thus we avoid any question as to whose interests are benefited by military-industrial global expansionism, at whose cost, and in pursuance of whose particular definition of "security" and "national interest."

TAXES: THE UNEQUAL BURDEN

Massive federal spending requires massive taxes. Who pays for all the billions spent? Our tax structure is thought to burden the rich more than the poor. In truth the tax load falls more heavily on those

51. No one knows precisely how much goes for military aid. Congress exercises no effective oversight over the program. See "Curbing Arms Aid," Progressive, April 1971, p. 7.

52. Thorstein Veblen, Theory of Business Enterprise (New York: New American Library Edition, n.d.), p. 217.

53. New York Times, February 3, 1953, quoted in Magdoff, The Age of Imperialism, p. 126.

least able to pay. Taking into account all local, state and federal sales and excise taxes, social security taxes, and income taxes, we find that lower-income people pay a higher percentage of their earnings than do upper-income persons, while generally getting less for what they pay. Kolko has shown that families earning under $4,000 together contribute substantially more in federal taxes than the government spends "on what by the most generous definition may be called 'welfare.' "[54]

The wealthier the person, the greater the opportunities to enjoy nontaxable income from capital gains, expense accounts, tax-free municipal and state bonds, stock options and various kinds of business and professional deductions.[55] For the very rich, almost any investment can be turned into a tax shelter. Herds of cattle, baseball teams, orange groves and office buildings can provide depreciation and maintenance write-offs during the time they are not producing income. Imaginary income that did not come in can be claimed as a loss so that one can make a substantial real earning yet show a loss and enjoy a hefty tax deduction. In 1976, 182 millionaires paid no income taxes at all. Billionaires like H. L. Hunt and J. Paul Getty, with annual incomes of $50 million and $100 million respectively, paid only a few thousand dollars a year. In contrast, a New York City dishwasher who earns $4,800 pays $1,213 in federal, state and city income taxes plus another $200 in sales taxes, or the equivalent of four months' salary.[56]

It has been argued that if the rich were more heavily taxed this would make no appreciable difference in total federal revenues, since wealthy people are so few in number. In fact, families with incomes of $100,000 and above—about one-third of one percent of the population—receive tax preferences of more than $11 billion annually.[57] And there are the many billions which rich corporations fail to pay. Companies like Chase Manhattan Bank, AT&T, Ford Motor Company, U.S. Steel, Exxon and Texas Gulf pay little or no

54. Gabriel Kolko, *Wealth and Power in America* (New York: Praeger, 1962), p. 39. The same inequality exists in regard to property taxes: the richer the family the lower the percentage of property taxes paid. See Thomas Bodenheimer, "The Poverty of the State," *Monthly Review*, November 1972, pp. 13–14.

55. A Senate study in 1978 found that almost half of all tax breaks go to those with incomes over $30,000—about 5 percent of all taxpayers. For critiques of our tax structure see Philip Stern, *The Rape of the Taxpayer* (New York: Random House, 1973); Herman P. Miller, *Rich Man, Poor Man* (New York: Crowell, 1971); Joseph Pechman, *Federal Tax Policy* (Washington, D.C.: Brookings Institution, 1966).

56. See Stern, *Rape of the Taxpayer*; also *Workers World*, April 15, 1977.

57. See the estimates reported by Erwin Knoll, "It's Only Money," *Progressive*, March 1972, p. 25.

taxes each year. In fact, if the top one hundred corporations were taxed at the same rate as the average middle-income family, there would be enough revenue for all federal expenditures on behalf of the poor, education, housing, environmental protection, medical care and much more.[58]

While the share of federal revenues coming from individual taxpayers has been rising, the portion paid by corporations has dropped from 50 percent in 1945 to 14 percent in 1979. Nor do these tax cuts act as a spur to new investments, since most of the tax deductions are taken against investments that would have been made anyway. And past experience shows that tax windfalls to big companies neither ease unemployment nor trickle down to wage earners, but certainly do their share in feeding inflation and fattening profits.[59]

While corporations claim they need still more tax benefits in order to have sufficient capital for investment, the truth is that "major producers are engulfed by a massive cash flow and are casting about for interesting diversions for their money."[60] In 1977 the oil industry's cash flow amounted to more than $30 billion. Its return on invested capital jumped 30 percent, amounting to $10.7 billion after taxes. There was no capital shortage and there were more profits than ever. Yet the following year, Congress passed a tax law that cut corporate taxes by yet another $3.7 billion and capital gains by $2.2 billion.[61]

Some corporations, like the private utilities, not only fail to pay their fair share but also pocket most of the tax dollars charged to their customers. In 1975, the largest utilities collected taxes on their monthly billings to customers, but by taking advantage of write-offs, they were able to keep the lion's share, $1.5 billion, for them-

---

58. It is estimated that in an average year anywhere from $77 billion to $91 billion is lost to the federal government in the form of tax preferences and write-offs, the largest share going to the business community. See *New York Times*, March 2, 1975, and *Workers World*, April 15, 1977.

59. Paul Rosenstiel, "How Business Profits from Inflation," *Nation*, March 17, 1979, pp. 270–273.

60. See the letter by the New Jersey Department of Energy Commissioner in the *New York Times*, June 1, 1978.

61. Some business enterprises—specifically those owned by religious organizations—are altogether free of tax obligations. The billions collected by churches from Sunday collection plates, bingo games, wills and bequests and from investments in housing, real estate, publishing, liquor, dairy farms, armaments, television, radio, etc., go untouched by taxes and are exempt by law from audit and disclosure. As churches accumulate more property, the tax base shrinks and the tax burden increases for wage earners and small-property owners. See Martin Larson and Stanley Lowell, *The Religious Empire* (Washington: Robert B. Luce, 1976).

selves.[62] In addition, an estimated 350,000 companies are illegally withholding Social Security and income taxes from their employees' paychecks and then pocketing the money. Few of these delinquent firms have been prosecuted by the Internal Revenue Service (IRS).[63]

The activities of the IRS reflect the same class bias that permeates the rest of government. The agency is more likely to audit the itemized returns of lower- than upper-income persons.[64] With the giant corporations the IRS is downright lackadaisical; thus its failure to audit AT&T properly cost about $3 billion in lost revenue.[65]

To summarize the major points in this chapter: the outputs of the political system, as manifested by the services, subsidies, prices, protections, taxes, leases, credits and market quotas established by public authority, affect the various areas of business enterprise and socioeconomic life mostly to benefit those who own the wealth of the nation and at the expense of the working populace. In almost every area of enterprise, government has provided business with unsurpassed opportunities for nonrisk investments, gainful inefficiency, monopolistic pricing, lucrative contracts and huge profits. Government feeds capital surplus through a process of deficit spending, offers an endless market in the defense, space and nuclear industries, and provides for the financial aid, global expansion and military protection of modern multinational corporations. From ranchers to resort owners, from doctors to bankers, from auto makers to missile makers, there prevails a welfarism for the rich of such stupendous magnitude as to make us marvel at the big businessman's audacity in preaching the virtues of self-reliance and private initiative whenever lesser forms of public assistance threaten to reach hands other than his own.

---

62. *Progressive*, February 1977, p. 6. One year, Con Edison charged its customers almost $100 million in federal taxes and paid only $100,000 of that sum to the government.

63. *Moneysworth*, October 13, 1975.

64. *New York Times*, November 17, 1975.

65. See the report by Taxation with Representation, a citizens interest lobby, April 1978, p. 3.

7

Health, Welfare and Environment: The Leaky Pump

As we have seen, government plays a major role in maintaining the corporate economy through a multibillion-dollar system of subsidies, supports, write-offs and regulations. In addition, government must take care that the worst abuses of the politico-economic system do not incite large portions of the population and lead to a disruption of the system itself. With a concern for easing popular discontent and restiveness, and faced with the inability of business to meet the human needs of the populace, government embarks upon a series of programs ostensibly designed to assist the poor and the ordinary working people. Although widely publicized, such programs are gravely inadequate and appear rather feeble when measured against the massive giveaways discussed in the previous chapter. Of a proposed $532 billion budget in 1980, not more than $30 billion was for human services, including education, housing, welfare and job programs. And of this sum, only a relatively small amount will reach those most in need.

THE POOR GET LESS

During the 1960s large sums were allocated for a "war on poverty" that brought no noticeable betterment to millions living in destitution, nor to millions of others who, although technically above the poverty level, were still burdened by low wages, high taxes, debts, inflation and lack of job security.[1] After studying antipoverty programs in a dozen cities, one observer noted that extensive funds were appropriated "in the name of the poor . . . without direct concern for, or serious attempts at, involvement of the poor."[2]

What is true of the inner cities is equally true of rural America. During the 1960s, $7 billion was invested by federal, state and local governments in the Appalachia region, yet the bulk of the poor "remain largely untouched" by the expenditures.[3] Some Office of Economic Opportunity officials complained that the poverty program was "chiefly a boon for the rich and for the entrenched political interests," specifically Appalachia's suburban and town "Main Streeters"—merchants, bankers, coal-industry leaders, civic boosters and road contractors.[4]

One study shows that federal transfer payments, such as Social Security, workmen's compensation, unemployment benefits and veteran's disability compensation, distribute $7 billion more to people earning above $10,000 than to those below, with a person under the $5,000 income level receiving only a third of the share available to someone in the $25–50,000 bracket.[5] Social Security, better described as "social insecurity," condemns most elderly to a life of poverty, providing benefits for aged individuals averaging several thousand dollars below the poverty level.

While conservatives complain about "welfare chiselers," the truth is that half of the more than eleven million people on welfare in the late 1970s were children, 13 percent were mothers without means of support, 37 percent were aged, disabled or blind, less than 1 percent were able-bodied men, and about 55 percent are White. Large numbers of welfare recipients suffer from poor diet, insufficient clothing, overcrowded housing, chronic illnesses and inadequate or nonexistent medical care. Approximately one-fourth of all

1. See Richard Parker, *The Myth of the Middle Class* (New York: Liveright, 1972).
2. The social psychologist, Kenneth B. Clark, quoted in the *New York Times*, November 9, 1969.
3. *New York Times*, November 29, 1970.
4. *Ibid.*
5. Taylor Branch, "The Screwing of the Average Man. Government Subsidies: Who Gets the $63 Billion?" *Washington Monthly*, March 1972, p. 22. Branch drew from a study by the Brookings Institution; Joe Harris, "Facts on Social Security," *Daily World*, December 7, 1978. About 20 million retired or disabled persons receive Social Security benefits averaging about $250 a month. The regressive quality of Social Security funding should be noted. A corporate executive with a $200,000 salary pays no more Social Security tax than one of his accountants who earns $15,000 and only a little more than the janitor who cleans his office and makes $6,500. Those in the lowest paying jobs who are too poor to pay income taxes must still pay Social Security.

welfare children, ages five to fourteen, have never seen a dentist; at least half suffer from malnutrition.[6]

Unlike the industrialists and bankers who enjoy federal handouts, welfare recipients are closely policed by officialdom. The greater portion of the $10 billion or so spent yearly on welfare (Aid to Families with Dependent Children) goes for administrative oversight and for hunting fraud.[7] In many states, the number of recipients has been reduced by administrative fiat even as needs have increased. The evidence is mounting that the real "welfare chiselers" are the agencies that deny needy applicants their benefits, intentionally using bureaucratic inefficiency, unnecessary delays and complicated procedures as a means of discouraging the poor and minimizing costs.[8] One welfare expert estimates that, under the present program, for every two people receiving support, there are between two and three entitled to assistance who do not get it, not including those who receive payments smaller than they legally deserve.[9]

Millions of poor Americans receive no assistance at all. They find themselves too young for Social Security or not covered by it, too old for Aid for Dependent Children, not disabled enough for Aid to the Totally Disabled, not covered by unemployment benefits, eligible for food stamps but without money to buy them, often eligible for welfare but unable to collect it. Other services to low-income people, however paltry, have been cut in recent years, including slashes in aid to the handicapped and in day-care and child-nutrition programs.

Most federal assistance programs do little for the have-nots. The following are only a few examples:

1. Under the federal school lunch program, most lunches are distributed to middle-class children rather than to the poor.

---

6. See data published by Children's March for Survival in the *New York Times*, March 19, 1972; also the Department of Labor study reported in the *New York Times*, August 7, 1978; also the *Boston Globe*, March 6, 1977.

7. A typical example is California's Alameda County, where to administer $16 million in payments some $28 million was spent, out of which $7 million was used to hunt "fraud." *Guardian*, January 18, 1978.

8. *New York Times*, December 12, 1977; *Guardian*, May 3, 1976.

9. David Steinberg, "Life Under the Plague," *Activist*, 7, Fall 1966, p. 20. See also Homar Bigart, "Hunger in America: Stark Deprivation Haunts a Land of Plenty," *New York Times*, February 16, 1969. For detailed accounts of the inhumane effects of welfare programs, see Paul Jacobs, *Prelude to Riot* (New York: Random House, 1966); James J. Graham, *The Enemies of the Poor* (New York: Random House, 1970), chapters 1–4; and Gilbert Y. Steiner, *Social Insecurity* (Chicago: Rand McNally, 1966).

Food programs reach only about 18 percent of the indigent. The very poor are least likely to benefit from food programs because they have insufficient funds to pay for them.[10] Since the programs are under the jurisdiction of a Department of Agriculture primarily dedicated to serving large agricultural producers, children often are fed whatever tends to accumulate in farm surplus programs, mostly white flour, white sugar and other low-nutrient products, their diets being more "a result of economic policies rather than the types of food they really need," according to two nutrition experts.[11]

2. As with lunch so with breakfast. Some 14 million low-income children are eligible for the school breakfast program; yet the great majority of schools in poor areas do not have the program, while upper-income schools do. Thus, the upper-class prestigious Phillips Exeter Academy offers the breakfasts while Mississippi's schools—which have a 90 percent eligibility rate—do not.[12]

3. Most of the sums intended for the education of underprivileged school children have been used to perpetuate racially segregated unequal facilities in both North and South. The main beneficiaries have been middle- and upper-income schools and the "textbook publishers and professional producers of education hardware," who have sold millions of dollars worth of their products to the schools under the federal program.[13] State aid is supposed to counterbalance the great inequities between rich and poor school districts, but most states dispense money through matching funds, giving larger sums to upper-income districts and smaller sums to lower-income districts and thereby doing little to lessen inequities and much to intensify them.[14]

4. The same pattern can be found in higher education, where the main beneficiaries of public aid have been in the upper-income brackets. Thus the students who attended the University of California in the mid-1960s and received an average subsidy of about $5,000 were mostly upper and upper-middle class, while lower-middle or working-class students were concentrated in the

10. *Hunger, U.S.A.*, a report by the Citizens' Board of Inquiry into Hunger and Malnutrition in the United States (Boston: Beacon Press, 1968).

11. Dr. Michael Latham and Dr. Jean Mayer testifying before a Senate subcommittee, *New York Times*, December 18, 1968.

12. *Guardian*, October 26, 1977.

13. See the study done by the NAACP and the Washington Research Project, reported in the *Chicago Sun-Times*, November 9, 1969; also *Champaign-Urbana* (Ill.) *Courier*, January 12, 1971; *Workers World*, March 3, 1978.

14. John Coons, William Clune and Stephan Sugarman, *Private Wealth and Public Education* (Cambridge, Mass.: Harvard University Press, 1970).

California junior colleges, where the per capita subsidy was only about $1,000.[15] Educational opportunities are limited according to one's ability to pay rather than one's ability to learn. The children of the sharecropper, the migrant worker and the ghetto poor still have little chance of getting an advanced education. About 200,000 working-class persons graduating from high school each year will not go to college because they lack the money. The student financial-aid programs mostly benefit the middle and upper-middle class students who do go to college.[16]

5. Publicly funded "educational research" is frequently little more than publicly supported commercial research in disguise. Federal and state monies help finance the schools of business, law, agriculture and technology that provide expensively trained personnel, specialized consultations, research skills and various other services to the large firms in these respective fields.

6. The multibillion-dollar federal manpower programs have been described as a "business bonanza" for the corporations that run the training programs at considerable profit to themselves while generating few jobs for the unemployed.[17] Companies like General Electric, IBM, Philco and AT&T have won lucrative contracts to operate urban training centers for the poor and for community volunteers.

7. Generally there has been a major shift from aid to the poor "to aid for more middle-class Americans in the suburbs and smaller towns."[18] Spending programs supposedly intended for the inner-city needy have given "power to the powerful and peanuts to the poor,"[19] being used for such things as a tennis complex in an affluent neighborhood in Little Rock, Arkansas, a convention hall and parking garage in Spartanburg, South Carolina, and a golf course in Alhambra, California.[20] The Farmers Home Administration, a federal agency ostensibly concerned with the

---

15. W. Lee Hansen and Burton A. Weisbord, *Benefits, Costs and Finance of Public Education* (Chicago: Markham, 1969).

16. *Chronicle of Higher Education*, September 25, 1978, p. 3.

17. The training of people for jobs presumes the existence of the jobs. The training programs do nothing to answer the unemployed's first need, which is the creation of a faster expanding job market. On the shortcomings of one program, see Ivar Berg and Marcia Freedman, "The Job Corps: A Business Bonanza," *Christianity and Crisis*, May 31, 1965, pp. 115–119.

18. *New York Times*, September 26, 1975.

19. Ian Menzies, "Money for Poor Going to Suburbs," *Boston Globe*, September 29, 1976.

20. *Ibid.* Generally, the federal government spends more money in rich counties than in poor ones. See *Guardian*, October 5, 1977, and *New York Times*, February 3, 1978.

problems of rural America, provided multimillion-dollar funds for the construction of over five hundred private golf courses.[21]

"URBAN REMOVAL" AND
THE DEATH OF CITIES

American cities are among the prime victims of the profit system. Consider the housing crisis and the problem of urban decay. By conservative estimates, one out of every five Americans lives in a substandard domicile lacking adequate plumbing, heat, electricity and space. Millions of people suffer from overcrowding or pay so much rent that they have insufficient income left for food, medical care and clothing.[22] While new housing is beyond the means of 75 to 85 percent of the nation's families,[23] lavish assistance has been provided for upper-income homeowners in the form of low-cost federal guaranteed credit, income-tax deductions and other subsidies amounting to more than $5 billion a year. The wealthiest fifth of the population receives easily twice as much in housing subsidies as the poorest fifth.[24] As the *New York Times* reports, "the bulk of urban aid from Washington is targeted not at still festering poverty sections but at . . . well-to-do neighborhoods . . . and suburbs."[25]

The scarcity of decent homes allows landlords to charge exorbitant rents. In places like New York City, landlords take ownership of a building and milk it ruthlessly, paying neither the real estate taxes, mortgage payments nor fuel bills, permitting violations to pile up without making repairs, but at the same time collecting rents from the tenants. The landlord eventually abandons the building in a ruined condition and disappears with thousands of dollars in excess of the initial investment. Yet there exists no federal or state law which makes such conduct criminal. "The economics of ghetto housing ensures that bad housing is profitable and that good housing cannot be maintained."[26]

21. *National Enquirer*, February 21, 1971.

22. *America's Housing Needs 1970–1980* (a report by the Joint Center for Urban Studies, Cambridge, 1977).

23. *Ibid.*; also the study by the Department of Housing and Urban Development reported in the *Progressive*, May 1976.

24. William Proxmire, *Uncle Sam: The Last of the Bigtime Spenders* (New York: Simon and Schuster, 1972), pp. 196–197.

25. *New York Times*, April 19, 1976.

26. William K. Tabb, *The Political Economy of the Black Ghetto* (New York: Norton, 1970), pp. 13–14; also *New York Times*, June 25, 1976.

The billions spent by the Department of Housing and Urban Development (HUD) supposedly to aid the poor have failed to do so because these funds have been channeled into the private sector of the economy, a sector that operates in response to the profit interests of developers, banks and speculators and therefore *has no functional capacity to provide homes for people who cannot afford market prices.* In a vain attempt to make the private profit system work for public needs, the government opens the door to manipulation and profiteering. Speculators buy up large numbers of old houses, apply cosmetic improvements, then get an inflated appraisal of the property's worth, often at several times its actual market value. Incredibly enough, HUD has no practice of actual inspection of these properties, and decrepit structures are routinely certified as "up to standard." The houses are then sold to low-income families with a federal guarantee covering the mortgage. Once they take possession, the families find their homes to be in unlivable condition. Unable to afford the major repairs, they eventually abandon the houses. At this point HUD is obliged to pay off the mortgage holders at the inflated value and take possession of the home.[27] Speculators have made an average profit of over 100 percent on HUD-guaranteed houses, according to Justice Department investigators.[28] Defaults on HUD mortgages have created hundreds of thousands of abandoned domiciles in our cities and have been a major factor in the spread of urban blight.

Housing developments built with federal assistance are often rented to low-income people for a year or two in order to qualify for the federal funds, then renovated or sold to other private owners who, not held to the original contract, can turn the units into high-market rentals. Many already sound houses are rehabilitated with federal funds so that landlords can then drive out the poorer residents and get higher rents.

At first glance we are confronted with a seemingly senseless state of affairs: HUD leaves blocks and blocks of burned-out shells standing while using funds to tear up and renovate inhabited, well-constructed buildings. Such a policy is irrational when measured against human and social needs, but the imperatives of the housing industry have less to do with *community* needs than with the *market* and *profit* needs of banks and developers. It is these latter considerations that guide the funding. In this sense, HUD's policy successfully

---

27. G. C. Thelen, Jr., "Homes for the Poor: The Well-Insured Swindle," *Nation*, June 26, 1972, pp. 814–816.
28. *Guardian*, June 16, 1976.

serves the existing corporate political economy on its own terms and does not, and can not, transform it into a force for social reconstruction.

Urban renewal is better described as "urban removal." By the power of eminent domain, the municipal or state government is able to do for realty investors and corporations what they could not do for themselves—namely, forcibly buy large tracts of residential areas from reluctant small owners and small businessmen, or from "far-sighted" speculators who, armed with inside information, buy up land in the "condemned" area for quick resale to the city at substantial profit. Then the city sells this land, often at less than the market value, to big developers, underwriting all investment risks on their behalf. The losses suffered by the municipality in such transactions are usually made up by federal funds and constitute another multibillion-dollar public subsidy to private capital.[29]

The chairman of the president's National Commission on Urban Problems, former Senator Paul Douglas, concluded that "Government action through urban renewal, highway programs, demolition on public housing sites, code enforcement and other programs has destroyed more housing for the poor than government at all levels has built for them."[30] Blacks, Chicanos, Native Americans, Chinese and other racial minorities occupy a disproportionate share of the nation's bad housing. According to one Senate report: "From 1960 to 1968, the percentage of non-whites occupying substandard housing actually increased from 22 to 33 percent."[31] Nor was that trend reversed in the 1970s.

The transportation system provides another example of how public resources are used to benefit the haves at the expense of the have-nots. The largest federal outlays are for highways—of little use to the millions of very poor, elderly and others who cannot afford automobiles. Another 20 percent of transportation expenditures goes to airlines, while the smallest portion is given to mass transit systems.[32] Thus relatively high-income air travelers are sumptuously subsidized while the low-income areas, "where the greatest number

29. See Paul Baran and Paul Sweezy, *Monopoly Capital* (New York: Monthly Review Press, 1968), pp. 289–300; also Edward C. Higbee, *The Squeeze: Cities Without Space* (New York: Morrow, 1960).

30. Quoted in Michael Harrington, "The Betrayal of the Poor," *Atlantic*, January 1970, p. 72. See also *New York Times*, July 17, 1968.

31. Senate Committee on Nutrition and Human Needs, quoted in "Rural Housing Famine," *Progressive*, April 1971, p. 8.

32. Robert S. Benson and Harold Wolman (eds.), *Counterbudget, A Blueprint for Changing National Priorities 1971–1976* (New York: Praeger, 1971), p. 157.

of persons suffer from the most severe problems deriving from transportation," including pollution, congestion and sheer lack of service, receive the least support.[33]

As mass transit systems decline, a growing reliance is placed on the automobile—leading to a further decline in public transportation. The social costs of the automobile are staggering. About 50,000 people are killed on the highways each year and hundreds of thousands more are injured and maimed. More than 60 percent of the land of most U.S. cities is taken up by the movement, storage and servicing of automobiles.[34] Homes, schools, churches, recreational areas and whole neighborhoods, particularly in working-class communities, are razed to make way for highways. The single greatest cause of air pollution in urban areas is the automobile: its carbon monoxide exhaust now claims over a thousand lives a year, and deaths from emphysema, a related lung disease, have been increasing drastically.[35] As the number of cars grows, so do the revenues from the gasoline tax that are put into the Highway Trust Fund. As more superhighways are built with these accumulated billions, the carnage, environmental devastation and—just as significantly—the profits of the oil, auto, trucking, tire, cement, construction, motel and other businesses increase. At the same time the mass-transit systems—the most efficient, cleanest and safest form of transporting large numbers of people—fall into further decay.

Most of the municipal transit systems are funded by deficit spending, with bond issues that are sold to wealthy individuals, banks and business firms. In any one year, these transit systems pay out millions of dollars in interest to wealthy bondholders, while they themselves come close to bankruptcy, being forced to lay off workers, cut services and raise fares.[36] Much of what is called "public ownership" in transportation is really privately bonded, with tax-free, risk-free dividends going to the rich, while the costs are paid by taxpayers.

---

33. *Ibid.*; also *Environmental Action*, November 4, 1978, p. 15.
34. According to the Highway Action Coalition, a public-interest group in Washington, D.C., as reported in Renee Blakkan, "Profits Clog the Highways," *Guardian*, November 29, 1972.
35. *Ibid.*
36. A good example is the Chicago Transit Authority, which has a history of purchasing highly inflated bonds to buy up bankrupt private transit companies, after the companies have been milked by their investors. (The New York City subway system came under municipal ownership in the same way.) About $300 million will eventually be returned to bondholders who originally paid $138 million, a 220 percent profit from a "public, nonprofit" transit authority. See *Workers World*, April 5, 1974, and September 26, 1975.

What is true of municipal transit systems is true of cities in general. Like the Third World debtor nations discussed in the previous chapter, cities are the victims of private "aid" and investment. Unable to meet the expenses of servicing the business community and satisfying minimal public needs, the cities borrow huge sums from banks and rich individuals at high dividend rates. With each bond issue a city goes deeper into debt. Speaking of New York City, Jack Newfield observed, "The banks acted like a drug dealer, and the city became a junkie. The banks made a pusher's profits, and the city got addicted."[37] New York City pays out more than 20 percent of its annual budget to service its debt. The further the city falls into debt, the greater the bargaining power of the banks to exact ever higher interest rates for each successive loan. In 1975 New York City faced bankruptcy when it could not sell a half-billion-dollar bond issue needed to pay off earlier debts that had fallen due. The city was put in receivership by large creditors, led by David Rockefeller, who eventually formed the Emergency Finance Control Board to exercise final approval authority over all city expenditures. The bankers bought billions of dollars worth of high-interest bonds—bonds that were virtually default-proof because they were backed by city taxes.[38]

In addition, most large municipalities pay much more in federal taxes than they receive in federal funds. This situation, plus an ever increasing debt burden, has a devastating impact on their economies. To "rescue" the cities from their plight, the federal government and the banks had a plan, first applied to New York and later to be used against other major urban centers: drastically cut services to the people. New York closed down day-care and drug-rehabilitation centers, health clinics, every venereal disease clinic, senior citizen centers and summer park services for children; 43,000 city employees, including hospital workers, sanitation workers, firemen and teachers, were laid off; hundreds of millions in new taxes were introduced; free tuition at City University was abolished and the subway fare was raised. Yet in the midst of all this austerity, the city granted $276 million in tax deductions to big landlords, and spent $100 million to renovate Yankee Stadium for the benefit of its rich owners.[39]

---

37. Jack Newfield, "Who Killed New York City?" *New Politics*, 11, Winter 1976, pp. 34–38.

38. See the report "New York and the Crisis of Our Cities," published by the New American Movement, Chicago, *circa* 1978.

39. *Ibid.*; also Newfield, "Who Killed New York City?" and *New York Times*, May 26, 1976.

At present, every indicator suggests that the urban crisis will deepen. The cities are caught in the squeeze of a capitalist system working its inexorable effect. The juxtaposition of private wealth and public poverty so frequently found in the United States is no mere curiosity. The two go together and reinforce each other. The profit imperatives of the private sector create maldistribution, want and social dislocation. Confronted with these problems, the government works through the same private sector that is creating them, thereby doing little to prevent, and sometimes much to augment, the process of social disintegration.[40]

HEALTH AND SAFETY FOR NOBODY

Consumer protection is another area in which government efforts seem designed to advance the interests of private producers at the expense of the public. Adulterated products, contaminated foods, unsafe additives, false advertising, overpricing, planned obsolescence and shoddy and dangerous commodities are common evils of the consumer market.[41] The Food and Drug Administration (FDA) tests but 1 percent of the millions of yearly shipments of drugs and foods that are marketed, yet issues reassuring pronouncements on the safety of numerous products whose long-range, or even immediate, effects are highly suspect. One study found that the FDA approved drugs for public use on the basis of "inaccurate and unreliable" data supplied by the drug industry itself.[42]

Drug companies spend $1 billion a year to promote sales—three times more than they spend on research and development. Physicians admit that drug salespeople, who know almost nothing about medicine, are their first source on the uses of new drugs.[43] The

---

40. Thus, after visiting areas of the South Bronx that had been plundered and then abandoned by private capital and were suffering a major deterioration in housing, transportation, job opportunities, sanitation disposal, pest control and public health and morale, President Carter could think of nothing better than to propose $10 billion in guaranteed federal loans to be disbursed by banks to private enterprises that looked like "good credit risks" in declining urban communities.

41. David Sanford (ed.), *Hot War on the Consumer* (New York: Putnam, 1969).

42. Report by the GAO in the *Guardian*, June 15, 1977. Hundreds of hair dyes, cosmetics and drugs marketed for years without benefit of FDA testing have been linked to cancer and birth defects. *New York Times*, July 22, 1973, and March 18, 1975; and Susan Sloane, "An Update on Food Hazards," *The Real Paper* (Boston), February 12, 1977, pp. 3–4, 7.

43. Amanda Spake, "The Pushers," *Progressive*, April 1976, p. 18.

World Health Organization reports that one out of four people who die in hospitals is killed by drugs and that this is probably because physicians are unfamiliar with the dangers of the new drugs they freely prescribe.[44]

FDA's claim that it has not enough staff to police the food, drug and cosmetics industries has not prevented its agents from spending much time investigating, prosecuting and stigmatizing as "faddists" those health food innovators whose ideas about nutrition and medicine are critical of established drug and food enterprises.[45]

Given the way health care is organized, money often makes the difference between life and death. Many sick people die simply because they are poor and cannot afford medical assistance. Millions live in areas where treatment is unavailable except for substantial fees. Almost all Americans, including those who can afford to pay their doctor's bills, have fallen prey to a rapacious medical industry. Doctors' fees have more than doubled in recent years, and hospital bills have been rising five times faster than the overall cost of living; yet it is almost universally agreed that people are not receiving better care, only more expensive care, and in some areas the quality of care has deteriorated.[46]

Doctors organize their practices as would any private entrepreneur, incorporating themselves to avoid taxes, selling a service to customers who are charged what the market will bear. Physicians have cheated Medicaid and Medicare of hundreds of millions of dollars by consistently overcharging for services and tests, by fraud-

---

44. See Irving Oyle, *The Healing Mind* (New York: Pocket Books, 1976), p. 20 ff. and citations therein. According to a Senate Subcommittee on Health about 30,000 die each year from adverse reactions to medical drugs. Other studies place the toll as high as 100,000; see Bernard Winter, M.D., "Health Care: The Problem is Profits," *Progressive*, October 1977, p. 16. The medical profession is being increasingly criticized for its excessive and often ignorant reliance on drugs and its hostility toward alternative forms of treatment, including homeopathic, osteopathic and naturopathic methods. For a critique of the beliefs and practices of the medical profession see the essays in John Ehrenreich (ed.), *The Cultural Crisis of Modern Medicine* (New York: Monthly Review Press, 1978).

45. Omar V. Garrison, *The Dictocrats' Attack on Health Foods and Vitamins* (New York: Arco Publishing, 1971); Estes Kefauver, *In A Few Hands* (New York: Pantheon Books, 1965); and Richard Harris, *The Real Voice* (New York: Macmillan, 1964).

46. "Doctors' Incomes Are Still Going Up—And Up," *New York Times*, March 26, 1978; also *Washington Post*, January 9, 10 and 11, 1979. Another area of medical care that has been turned into an exploitative enterprise is the nursing-home business, a highly profitable industry that is guilty of widespread mistreatment of the elderly. See Mary Adelaide Mendelson, *Tender Loving Greed* (New York: Knopf, 1974); also Linda Horn and Elma Griesel, *Nursing Homes: A Citizen's Guide to Action* (Philadelphia: Nursing Homes, 1978).

ulent billing for nonexistent patients or for services not rendered, by charging for unneeded treatments and hospital admissions[47] and— most unforgivably of all—by performing unnecessary surgery. An estimated two million unnecessary operations are performed yearly, costing about $4 billion and leading to the death of some 10,000 patients and an undetermined number of disabilities.[48]

The conditions Senator Edward Kennedy found during his Senate investigation of health care were the same throughout the nation: people denied emergency treatment because they could not show proof of ability to pay, others ejected from hospitals in the midst of an illness because they were out of funds, still others bankrupted by medical bills despite supposedly "comprehensive" insurance coverage, many who were victims of surgery done for the sole purpose of profiting the physicians, many who suffered injury and death in hospitals that were below minimal federal standards of cleanliness, safety and staff.[49]

Health care will continue to worsen no matter how many more billions are spent on it. As with agriculture, housing and transportation, medical care is organized as a private enterprise; not surprisingly, then, its purpose is to make a profit for those who control it.

Just as our defense budget has little to do with actually defending the United States, so our health budget has little to do with restoring, and much less with maintaining, the health of the American people. It is, rather, a costly and wasteful mechanism for funneling money to a sprawling medical industry that encompasses not only physicians and hospitals but equipment manufacturers, pharmaceutical corporations, banks and insurance companies, real estate developers and construction

---

47. *New York Times*, June 25, 1976, and April 16, 1978; *National Enquirer*, January 30, 1979. A Ralph Nader task group estimates that surgeons overcharge about $3 billion a year. The group found differences of as much as $1,560 for the same surgical procedures in the Washington, D.C. area. *Washington Post*, March 30, 1979; see also Marcia Millman, *The Unkindest Cut: Life in the Backrooms of Medicine* (New York: William Morrow, 1976).

48. *New York Times*, January 26, 1976; also the report of the House Subcommittee on Interstate and Foreign Commerce in the *Guardian*, January 10, 1979. The likelihood of surgery bears a curious relationship to the availability of medical insurance. And perhaps the uninsured are not the most unfortunate: reductions in elective surgery during a doctors' strike in Los Angeles, led to a significant drop in the death rate. *Washington Post*, January 11, 1979, and March 27, 1979.

49. Edward Kennedy, *In Critical Condition: The Crisis in America's Health Care* (New York: Simon and Schuster, 1972); also *Washington Post*, April 13, 1979; Barbara and John Ehrenreich, *The American Health Empire* (New York: Vintage, 1970); Robert R. Alford, *Health Care Politics* (Chicago: University of Chicago Press, 1975); Richard Kunnes, M.D., *Your Money or Your Life* (New York: Dodd, Mead, 1975).

combines. The impulse that drives this industry is the impulse that drives every industry—the maximization of profit.[50]

As past efforts have shown, unless the service itself is reorganized on a nonprofit basis, additional monies poured into the medical system will only lead to more profits for the few, not better services for the many.

One cannot talk about the health of America without mentioning the awesome problem of occupational safety. Every year 16,000 workers are killed on the job. Another 100,000 die prematurely from work-related diseases, such as black lung, brown lung and cancer, and still another 390,000 become seriously ill from work diseases each year.[51] At least one out of every four workers suffers from occupationally connected diseases.[52] The daily casualties suffered by working people are many times higher than what Americans sustained during the Vietnam war, yet no one is organizing mass protests against this industrial slaughter. Much of the reason is that the public remains poorly informed about the carnage of the work place—given the business-owned media's reticence about the subject.

It may be that industrial production will always carry some kind of risk, but the present rate of attrition can be largely ascribed to inadequate safety standards, speed-ups and lax enforcement of safety codes.[53] Thus almost all coal mine accidents could be avoided if proper safety measures were taken. Work conditions in U.S. mines are among the worst in the world. In Poland, the world's second largest exporter of coal, accidents are "rare," according to the *New York Times*, because of elaborate safety measures. This same emphasis on worker safety is found in other noncapitalist countries.[54]

On the infrequent occasions that government officials get around to acting on violations, the penalties against employers are

50. Winter, "Health Care: The Problem is Profit."

51. Dorothy McGhee, "Workplace Hazards: No Women Need Apply," *Progressive*, October 1977, p. 22.

52. Jeanne M. Stellman and Susan M. Daum, *Work Is Dangerous to Your Health* (New York: Pantheon, 1973); Rachel Scott, *Muscle and Blood* (New York: E. P. Dutton, 1974). For a well-documented historical and analytic survey see Daniel M. Berman, *Death on the Job* (New York: Monthly Review Press, 1978); also *New York Times*, April 28, 1975, and May 12, 1976; *Progressive*, May 1976, p. 7.

53. The federal government fails to protect the health and safety of its own employees as well as those working for industry; see the *New York Times*, June 22, 1978.

54. *New York Times*, October 26, 1974; see also the report of a West Virginia miner who visited the Soviet Union, *United Mine Workers Journal*, November 1, 1974.

somewhat laughable. When six workers at a Gulf refinery were killed due to company negligence, the fine was $600. After eight people were killed by gas seepage from a faulty Atlantic Richfield well, federal investigators fined the firm $550. With yearly profits of over $3 billion, Exxon was fined $1200 for safety violations that led to the death of three workers and the serious injury of twelve others.[55]

The absence of worker safety is the result of something more than just "negligence" on the part of business and government. The overbearing imperative of the capitalist economy is to maximize profits. One way of doing this is by cutting the substantial costs of maintaining safe conditions. Money spent not on production for profit but on safety for the worker is money spent primarily in the worker's interest rather than the owner's. A major determinant of how much industry expends on safety measures is how much it will save when it reduces injury. Low-wage workers are less expensive to "damage"—that is, the amount of production lost is less than when a highly skilled, better-paid worker is·disabled. Hence, in those industries where it is cheaper to replace the injured worker than to make safety changes, injury rates tend to be higher.[56] Consider the testimony of a farm worker (among the lowest paid of unskilled laborers) about conditions on a big commercial farm in California:

> I began to see how everything was so wrong. When growers can have an intricate watering system to irrigate their crops but they can't have running water inside the houses of workers. Veterinarians tend to the needs of domestic animals but they can't have medical care for the workers. They can have land subsidies for the growers but they can't have adequate unemployment compensation for the workers. They treat him like a farm implement. In fact, they treat their implements better and their domestic animals better.
>
> . . . Stoop labor is very hard on a person. Tuberculosis is high. And now because of the pesticides, we have many respiratory diseases. The University of California at Davis has government experiments with pesticides and chemicals, to get a bigger crop each year. They haven't any regard as to what safety precautions are needed.[57]

---

55. *Guardian*, January 14, 1976; *Workers World*, February 10, 1978; also Joseph A. Page and Mary-Win O'Brien, *Bitter Wages* (New York: Grossman, 1973). Over 80 percent of the violations filed by federal inspectors lead to no penalties at all; see "Your Job May Be Hazardous to Your Health," *Dollars and Sense*, February 1976, p. 11.

56. See the study by labor economist Robert S. Smith, reported in the *New Haven Register*, December 22, 1972.

57. Farm worker quoted in Studs Terkel, *Working* (New York: Pantheon, 1972), p. 12.

To condemn government for doing so little for the have-nots and so much for the haves and to urge it to change its ways is to presume that government *can* act differently in the existing politico-economic context, that it can respond to the dictates of social justice rather than to the realities of power and interest, and that it can allocate its resources for the community needs of the populace and ignore or even violate the overriding systemic needs of the corporate economy. The actual political methods that business employs to keep government subservient to its interests will be explored further in the chapters to come.

ON BEHALF OF POLLUTION AND RADIATION

Like sin itself, pollution is regularly denounced but vigorously practiced. Strip mining and deforestation by coal and timber companies continue to bring ruination to millions of acres. For the sake of short-term profits, the ecological balance of our rivers and seas is being systematically destroyed by industrial wastes, overfishing and tanker accidents and offshore drillings that spill about 1.3 billion gallons of oil into the waters each year. Agribusiness sprays tons of poisonous herbicides and pesticides directly onto our pastures, croplands and orchards—with little control exercised by any government agency. Industry introduces some one thousand new chemicals into the marketplace annually, adding to the 70,000 already there, almost none of which is covered by safety regulations.[58] Over 1 billion pounds of chemicals are released into the environment *each day,* causing one government study to conclude that the air we breathe, the water we drink and the food we eat are now perhaps the leading cause of death in the United States.[59]

Consider also the newly discovered dangers of ground pollution. Some 92 billion pounds of toxic chemical wastes, produced yearly by the manufacturers of plastics, pesticides, herbicides and other such

58. For a general critique of what is happening to our environment see James Ridgeway, *The Politics of Ecology* (New York: E. P. Dutton, 1970); also the reports of the Cousteau Society (New York, 1978); *New York Times*, July 31, 1975, January 2, and January 5, 1977 for accounts on pesticides and oil spillage; Bartle Bull, " 'Harvesting' the National Forests," *Village Voice*, August 17, 1972; Dorothy McGhee, "The Secret Killers," *Progressive*, August 1977, p. 26.

59. Summarized in Dennis Schaal, "Environmental Nightmare—No Longer a Dream," *Guardian*, September 13, 1978, p. 6. Evidence is accumulating that the carcinogens introduced by humans into the environment could be the cause of almost all cancer. See the *Ithaca* (N.Y.) *Journal*, January 24, 1976.

"COULD YOU HURRY AND FIND A CURE FOR CANCER? THAT WOULD BE SO MUCH EASIER THAN PREVENTION"

----copyright 1977 by Herblock in The Washington Post

commodities, are buried in makeshift sites—only to leach over wide areas and contaminate billions of gallons of ground water.[60] Whole residential areas, such as the Love Canal neighborhood in Niagara County, New York, have suffered contamination as the underground toxins percolate into homes and play areas, causing a startling number of birth defects, miscarriages, headaches, sores, liver and kidney abnormalities and instances of epilepsy and cancer. At least 51,000 sites across the country pose serious health hazards to surrounding communities, farmlands and livestock.

60. Michael E. Brown, "Love Canal, U.S.A.," *New York Times Magazine*, January 21, 1979, pp. 23, 38–44; also *New York Times*, November 22, 1978; *Wall Street Journal*, May 22, 1979.

Then there is kepone, an insecticide more poisonous than DDT, destroying a multibillion-dollar fishing and seafood industry after being dumped into the James River and Chesapeake Bay by Allied Chemical, putting 3,000 people out of work and threatening premature death to hundreds of contaminated workers and their families; there is dioxin, one of the deadliest of all chemicals, used as a defoliant in Vietnam and as an herbicide in the United States, sprayed on American pasture lands and national forests, even used as a weed killer in residential areas and as an additive in certain laundry solutions, causing birth deformity, miscarriage and cancer; there are carcinogenic plastic wrappings and other vinyl chloride products, carbon dioxide, sulfate and nitrate emissions, microwave radiation, lead and mercury poisoning, PCB, DES, carcinogenic mothers' milk, and carcinogenic dyes, cosmetics and hair sprays. The picture that emerges is of the nearly ubiquitous contamination of our rural, urban and household environments.[61]

One of the reasons pollution continues unabated is because it is profitable for the pollutors. Production costs are cheaper when industrial wastes can be dumped into the air, water and ground. Rather than instituting costly controls and safety tests of products, industry passes the social and human costs to the public in the form of ecological devastation, illness and death.

Enforcement of pollution laws is so rare as to be newsworthy, and the penalties so minor as to be farcical. After the first oil spillage at Santa Barbara, the petroleum companies were charged with 343 violations of the Fish and Game code; upon conviction, each company was fined the grand sum of $500. A little-publicized provision of the Pesticide Control Act even makes pollution a money-making venture for some industries, allowing the government to compensate—at retail prices—the producers of pesticides for financial losses suffered if their products are ordered off the market as unsafe. One congressman observed: "This measure may set a precedent for the Government to pay compensation to private enterprise every time a legitimate Government action taken in the public interest results in a loss of profit for the business community."[62]

---

61. One of the earliest and most influential of environmental exposes was Rachel Carson, *Silent Spring* (New York: Houghton-Mifflin, 1962); see also *New York Times*, July 31, 1975. For evidence of a more recent menace see Paul Brodeur, *The Zapping of America: Microwaves, Their Deadly Risk and the Cover-Up* (New York: Norton, 1977); *New York Times*, December 27, 1977, and May 6, 1977; Daniel Zwerdling, "Chemical Catastrophes," *Progressive*, February 1977, pp. 15–18.

62. Richard D. Lyons, "Pesticide Compensation Bill Seen Costing Billions," *New York Times*, October 15, 1972. Increased use of pesticides often *causes* serious infestations of pests by eliminating their natural enemies and creating generations of insects

The approach taken by state, local and federal government in regard to pollution, like the approach taken in most other problem areas, hews closely to three principles: (1) the forms of public control must never compete or interfere with the basic profit interests of private investment—that is to say, the solutions to pollution must be accommodated to the capitalist production system; (2) in keeping with the above requirement, the costs of pollution control are to be borne by the public rather than by the producers; and (3) the companies that pollute the most will get the most. Thus the larger the company's profits, the greater is its pollution subsidy under the 1969 Tax Reform Act. This measure is in pursuance of a certain perverse logic: big profits are made by big producers, and big production generally means big pollution, which, in turn, demands big cleanup subsidies and big tax credits. In sum, the polluter is rewarded rather than punished.[63]

Not yet mentioned is probably the greatest menace of all: nuclear power. A major accident at a nuclear reactor site could kill as many as half a million people and contaminate an area the size of California—and there have been some frightfully close calls.[64] Public attention has focused mostly on the familiar commercial light-water reactors and has overlooked the far more dangerous liquid-metal-cooled, fast-neutron, breeder reactor employed by the military.[65] Breakdowns causing contaminating leakages are common occurrences, and the plants themselves are so hazardous that insurance companies refuse to handle them.[66]

---

that are ever more resistant to chemical controls and that require still heavier dosages. In the last thirty years, pesticide use in the United States has increased twelvefold and crop losses to insects have almost doubled. See Robert Van Den Bosch, *The Pesticide Conspiracy* (Garden City, N.Y.: Doubleday, 1978). Some commercial farms have begun to realize the self-destructive effects and the enormous expense of pesticides and are turning to organic methods of pest control. See "Food and Agriculture," *East West*, March 1978, p. 12.

63. Barry Weisberg, *Beyond Repair: The Ecology of Capitalism* (Boston: Beacon Press, 1972); Barry Commoner, *The Politics of Energy* (New York: Knopf, 1979), and his *The Closing Circle* (New York: Bantam, 1972).

64. There have been near disasters involving reactors in Idaho Falls, Detroit, Hanford (Washington) and Brown's Ferry (Alabama). The more recent accident at Three Mile Island (Pennsylvania) was distinctive in that it received national press coverage. See *Washington Post*, April 8, 1979, and subsequent editions; also John G. Fuller, *We Almost Lost Detroit* (New York: T. Y. Crowell, 1976); Ralph Nader and John Abbotts, *The Menace of Atomic Energy*, rev. ed. (New York: W. W. Norton, 1979), pp. 94–96; Michio Kaku, "Countdown to Meltdown," *Seven Days*, March 30, 1979, pp. 20–21.

65. Kaku, "Countdown to Meltdown." The military and noncommercial research reactors account for half of all radioactive waste.

66. John W. Gofman and Arthur R. Tamplin, *Poisoned Power* (New York: Signet, 1971); Anna Gyorgy *et al.*, *No Nukes* (Boston: South End Press, 1979), p. 99ff.

Perhaps as dangerous as a catastrophic accident is the radiation emitted into the environment by the mining, milling, refinement, storage and shipment of various nuclear materials and wastes. In addition, the emissions resulting from the daily operations of nuclear plants are far in excess of "permissible" levels established by the Nuclear Regulatory Commission (NRC).[67] No one has ever demonstrated that there *is* such a thing as a "permissible" level of radioactive leakage. The best scientific evidence indicates that *any* amount of emission can have a damaging effect on health and genetic structure.[68] High rates of cancer have been found among persons residing close to nuclear plants. Persons living within thirteen miles of the nuclear arms plant in Rocky Flats, Colorado, had cancer rates that were 40 to 140 percent higher (depending on the type of cancer) than the national average.[69]

Nuclear wastes, some of which remain radioactive for 250,000 years, are building up in the soil and in the silt of rivers. The nuclear industry has no long-term technology for safe waste disposal. At the Hanford, Washington, nuclear dump, more than half a million gallons of radioactive liquids leaked from the storage tanks into the ground water and the Columbia River. Millions of other gallons of corrosive, contaminated wastes are buried at sites throughout the country in tanks that have a life expectancy of less than fifteen years.[70]

Nuclear energy is the most expensive and least efficient large-scale method of producing electricity.[71] Then why do the corporations continue to promote it? The nuclear industry is dominated by a few giants who draw billions from the federal treasury for atomic production and research and for uranium price supports. The nuclear industry, like the defense industry, is largely a government-subsidized market for the profit of private suppliers. The more expensive things get, the more the contractors rake in. Furthermore, utilities are allowed only a fixed rate of profit on their capital investments. In costing much more than fossil fuel or hydroelectric power,

---

67. An official of the NRC, Walter Jordan, complained that the NRC has underestimated the effects of radiation from mining and milling of uranium by 100,000 times; see Gyorgy *et al.*, *No Nukes*, p. 24 and *passim.*

68. Nader and Abbotts, *Menace of Atomic Energy*, pp. 72–81.

69. *New York Times*, April 10, 1979.

70. *Nucleus* (a report to Union of Concerned Scientists Sponsors), August 1978; also report from Natural Resources Defense Council, July 1978; *New York Times*, July 12, 1978.

71. "Nuclear Power Costs More and More," *Dollars and Sense*, April 1976, pp. 4–5; Nader and Abbotts, *Menace of Atomic Energy*, *passim; Guardian*, January 3, 1979.

"GENTLEMAN, IF GOD HAD INTENDED MAN TO USE THE SUN AS A SOURCE OF ENERGY, WE WOULD HAVE HELD A CONTROLLING INTEREST IN IT"

nuclear plants raise the amount of capital in the rate base and allow the utilities a higher return in abolute dollars.[72]

The federal government has served as a faithful tool of the nuclear industry, spending millions to publicize the false notions that nuclear energy is safe and cheap, and repeatedly suppressing findings by its own scientists that demonstrate the contrary.[73] The devotion to nuclear power and profits is such that the government spends almost nothing on alternate fuel sources such as solar, geothermal and tidal energies. Much of the federal money for solar energy development has gone to Westinghouse and General Electric, the two major nuclear reactor builders, who, not surprisingly, announced that solar energy technology is not yet commercially viable—although hundreds of thousands of people around the world are already relying on solar heating devices.[74]

In the energy field as elsewhere we discover the basic contradictions between our human values and our economic system: the social need to conserve energy and use it in rational ways as opposed to the

---

72. Nader and Abbotts, *Menace of Atomic Energy*, pp. 262–263; also Allen Hershkowitz's correspondence in the *Nation*, April 14, 1979.

73. *New York Times*, November 10, 1974; Gofman and Tamplin, *Poisoned Power*, p. 103ff; Gyorgy *et al.*, *No Nukes*, pp. 92–94. The government repeatedly covered up or failed to publicize the hazardous and even lethal effects of atomic bomb tests; *Washington Post*, March 2, 1979; Pam Solo and Mike Jendrzejczyk, "Radiation Roulette in Nevada," *Nation*, June 2, 1979, pp. 631–632.

74. Gyorgy *et al.*, *No Nukes*, pp. 225–295; John Berger, "Let the Sun Shine In," *Progressive*, February 1977, pp. 43–46.

corporate need to get people to consume expensive forms of energy in greater quantities in order to maximize profits; the human need for safe, clean energy sources versus the corporate need for profitable energy markets, no matter how destructive and lethal they may be.

To conclude this chapter: a large part of the domestic budget appears to be spent on worthwhile things, and indeed *some* of these monies get to the have-nots; *some* school lunches, child-care centers and rehabilitation programs help the needy. But the methods of spending—through private producers in a capitalist economy—most often bring great costs to the taxpayer, fat profits to the corporate few, and little benefit to the people. The government's programs in housing, health, transportation, urban development, energy and ecology do not achieve the goals we would want because they are not designed to. Their purpose is not to pursue the public interest and fulfill human needs but to satisfy the profit needs of a few giant producers, thereby fulfilling the capitalist dictum: "To them that have shall be given. From them that have not shall be taken even what little they have."

8

Law and Order: The Double Standard

For all its neglect of human welfare, the government does expend many billions each year for social programs, the great bulk of which is concentrated in a few things like Social Security, Medicaid, Medicare and welfare payments to the poor. (The other human services programs, while vast in number, remain, by federal standards, minuscule in size and funding.) The primary function of these expenditures is to ameliorate the conditions of want—so as to take the edge off popular discontent and avoid civil riot and other more serious challenges to the existing politico-economic system. But government does not rely solely upon social welfare programs to keep people quiescent. There are sterner measures. Besides the carrot, there is the stick. Behind the welfare bureaucracy, there stand the police, courts and prisons.

No system of law operates in a vacuum with equal effect upon all. The distribution of protections and punishments is neither random nor equitable, being more a reflection of the way politico-economic power is distributed than of any abstract principle of justice. Since we have been taught to think of the law as an institution serving the entire community and to view its representatives—from the traffic cop to the Supreme Court justice—as guardians of our rights, it is discomforting to discover that laws are often written and enforced in the most tawdry racist, class and sexist ways.

THE PROTECTION OF PROPERTY

Far from being a neutral instrument, the law belongs to those who write it and use it—primarily those who control the resources of society. It is no accident that in most conflicts between the propertied and the propertyless, the law intervenes on the side of the former. The protection of property is deemed tantamount to the protection of society itself and of benefit to all citizens, presumably even the propertyless. Those who equate the interests of property with the "common interest" seldom distinguish between (a) large corporate property used for the production of profit and (b) consumer-use possessions like homes and personal articles. Most political conflicts are concerned with the distribution and use of (a), not (b).

The law's intimate relationship to property can be seen in the curriculum of the average law school: one learns corporate law, tax law, insurance law, torts and damages and realty law chiefly from the perspective of those who own the property. Owners, trustees and landlords have "rights," but workers, students, consumers and tenants have troublesome "demands." In most instances, crime is defined by law as something which the have-nots commit against the haves. Under the property law, management may call in the police to lock out workers, but workers cannot call in the police to drive out management. University trustees may bring in the police to suppress striking students, but students cannot call on the police to control unresponsive trustees. Landlords can have the police evict rent-striking tenants, but tenants cannot demand that police evict rent-gouging landlords. The landlord's rights are usually automatically upheld by the courts, the burden being on the tenant to prove violations. Low-income residents soon learn that laws dealing with the collection of rents, eviction of tenants and protection of property are swiftly enforceable, while those dealing with flagrant violations of building and safety codes, rent overcharging and the protection of people go unenforced.[1]

The biases written into the law, which reflect the one-sided and often unjust property relations of the society, are compounded by the way the law is enforced. Even when the letter of the law is on their side, the poor have little else working for them. Although they are in greatest need of legal protection, they are least likely to seek redress of grievances through the courts, having neither the time nor

---

1. Stuart S. Nagel, "The Poor, Also, Want Law and Order," *Chicago Daily Law Bulletin*, April 26, 1968.

money. And when they find themselves embroiled in court cases, it is almost always at the initiative of the bill collector, merchant, or landlord, who regularly use the courts as a means of asserting their property interests.[2]

The law does little to protect us from business crime even though it is socially more damaging than most working-class crime, since it involves the health, safety and earnings of millions of workers and consumers. Ralph Nader estimated that each year orange juice companies steal more money from the American public by watering down their product than bank robbers steal from banks.[3] White-collar crimes like embezzlement, fraud, commercial theft and business-related arson cost over $40 billion a year, according to U.S. Chamber of Commerce estimates, or ten times the value of property-related street crimes like robbery, burglary and auto theft. This figure excludes the cost of antitrust violations, which may add as much as $160 billion.[4] Fraud in federal aid programs costs an additional $12 billion or more; the bulk of this sum does not go to the "poor persons receiving the benefits, but [to] relatively well-to-do doctors, pharmacists and businessmen who have contracted with the Government to provide services and then set out to defraud it intentionally and systematically."[5]

The criminality of corporations, Sutherland concludes, is persistent, "like that of professional thieves."[6] Looking at seventy of the largest corporations in the United States, he found that in several decades they had been convicted of an average of ten criminal violations each (a figure that greatly underestimates the actual amount of crime, since most violations go unchallenged). Any ordinary citizen with such a conviction record would be judged an "habitual offender" deserving of heavy punishment. Yet the guilty companies were provided with special stipulations, desist orders, injunctions and negotiated settlements or were let off with light penalties.

Often companies are not even obliged to appear in court. They can file "consent decrees" which, in effect, say that the firm has

---

2. For a further discussion of the relationship between property and power see my *Power and the Powerless* (New York: St. Martin's Press, 1978).

3. "Nader Report: Consumers Lose Billions to Invisible Bilk," *Crime and the Law* (Washington, D.C.: Congressional Quarterly, 1971), p. 21.

4. See statement by Rep. John Conyers (D.-Mich.) in the *Guardian*, December 20, 1978, p. 8; also *New York Times*, May 23, 1977.

5. *New York Times*, April 16, 1978.

6. Edwin Sutherland, *White Collar Crime* (New York: Holt, Rinehart and Winston, 1949), pp. 210–222. Sutherland found that three-fourths of all banks were violating the banking laws. See also Sarah Carey, "America's Respectable Crime Problem," *Washington Monthly*, April 1971; and Robert Heilbroner *et al.*, *In the Name of Profit* (New York: Warner Books, 1972).

done nothing wrong and promises never to do it again. Then the government's files are made confidential and all the evidence against the company is locked away. Persons seeking damages in civil suits must try to uncover the evidence on their own. Wealthy corporate criminals are separated administratively from low-income offenders, facing "a far gentler disciplinary system composed of inspectors, hearing examiners, boards and commissions. . . . For the affluent, the loopholes are so abundant that it takes determination to avoid them."[7]

Nonenforcement of the law is common in such areas as price fixing, restraint of trade, tax evasion, environmental and consumer protection, child labor and minimum wages. The antitrust laws, supposedly intended to restrict the unfair practices of large firms, have snared almost no businessmen in the eighty-five years of their existence. From 1890 to 1946 only seven were sentenced to prison, and all seven had their sentences suspended. In the early 1960s some thirty electrical firm executives were found guilty of conspiracies to fix prices; twenty-three were given suspended sentences, and seven served thirty days. The triple damage payments which the firms had to pay their customers, however, were ruled to be tax-deductible business expenses by the IRS. In effect, the government picked up the costs—another case of the taxpayers being punished for the crimes of the corporations.

The law leans consistently in the direction of business. To break strikes, and unions, the courts can impose injunctions and massive fines. A federal district judge imposed a $5 million fine on the United Mine Workers for failing to contain a wildcat strike by its rank and file, and a teamster local was fined $5.8 million for a wildcat strike. In contrast, the maximum fine for a violation of the Sherman Anti-Trust Act is $50,000, a figure not likely to terrorize Wall Street.[8]

A study of the New York State court system found that persons who committed crimes like burglary, theft and small-time drug dealing received harsher sentences than persons convicted of securities fraud, kickbacks, bribery and embezzlement.[9] One judge imposed a small fine on a stockbroker who had made $20 million

---

7. Senator Philip Hart, "Swindling and Knavery, Inc.," *Playboy*, August 1972, p. 156.

8. *New York Times*, September 2, 1975; *Guardian*, June 14, 1978.

9. *Guardian*, October 18, 1972. Seventy-one percent of persons convicted of auto theft go to jail for an average of three years, while only 16 percent of those convicted of securities fraud—involving sums many times greater than the worth of any car—are jailed, for an average term of 1.7 years. Whitney North Seymour, Jr., *Why Justice Fails* (New York: Morrow, 1973).

through illegal stock manipulations and, on the same day, sentenced an unemployed Black to one year in jail for stealing a $100 television set from a truck shipment.[10] When a low-income, five-time petty offender stole $73, a Dallas court gave him 1,000 years in prison.[11] And a New Orleans judge gave a four-time petty offender life imprisonment for possession of a stolen television set.[12] In contrast, the notorious Dr. Bernard Bergman, convicted of swindling millions of dollars in the nursing home business, was sentenced to four months. And two wealthy contractors, who received $1.2 million in phony government contracts for work they never did, were ordered to pay $5,000 in fines and to give 200 hours of "community service."[13]

Relations between the judiciary and the business community may be described as close and loyal. In 1958, twenty-nine oil companies were indicted for fixing prices and creating artificial scarcity. The evidence compiled by the Justice Department was detailed and devastating, including letters and testimony from various company executives. But Federal Judge Royce Savage dismissed the case as based on "hearsay," without bothering to hear the defense. A year later Savage became a top executive at Gulf Oil, one of the twenty-nine companies.[14]

Judges and top government officials are usually drawn from the same social strata as businessmen; indeed, most judges have wide-ranging financial connections and are reluctant to treat businessmen as they would "common" criminals, feeling sure that mild penalties and admonitions are enough to get these respectable gentlemen to abide by the law.[15]

CRIMINAL ENFORCEMENT: UNEQUAL BEFORE THE LAW

Looking at the criminal law enforcement process, we find that various racial, sexual, political and class factors—external to any actual criminal behavior—help determine the kind of treatment accorded an individual from the time of arrest to the time of imprisonment.

---

10. Leonard Downie, Jr., *Justice Denied* (New York: Praeger, 1971).

11. Gary Cartwright, "The Tin-Star State," *Esquire*, February 1971, p. 100.

12. Bob Pratt, "How One U.S. City Has Slashed Its Crime Rate," *National Enquirer*, June 8, 1976.

13. *Washington Post*, May 30, 1979. For a discussion of the biases of the judicial process see Herbert Jacob, *Justice in America*, 2nd ed. (Boston: Little, Brown, 1972).

14. Burton H. Wolfe, "The Judge Who Saved the Oil Companies," *San Francisco Bay Guardian*, January 9–16, 1975. Fifteen years later Savage appeared as a key figure involved in Gulf's illegal political contributions.

15. Sutherland, *White Collar Crime, passim*.

Arrest ✎

An arrest is not only the first step in the enforcement process, it is often a punishment in itself, leading to incarceration, legal expenses, psychological intimidation and sometimes severe physical abuse and loss of job. Of the 7.5 million people arrested in 1969 for all crimes, excluding traffic offenses, more than 1.3 million were never prosecuted or charged, and 2.2 million were acquitted or had the charges against them dismissed, according to the FBI Uniform Crime Report. The large number of arrests without charges or conviction, especially of ghetto residents and antiwar demonstrators, suggests that frequently the purpose of arrest is not to convict but to intimidate and immobilize. Police have the power to jail anyone for up to two or sometimes three days without pressing charges, and once charged, a suspect can have a "hold" placed on him by the district attorney or some other law official and be kept in prison until trial time.

The class and racial prejudices of the society and the police can be a crucial determinant of who gets arrested and who does not. "If you are stopped by the cops for weaving boozily through late-night traffic, you will be far wiser to be a Congressman in a large new car than an unemployed hod carrier in a 1950 Chevrolet with one fender missing."[16] A study of 1,700 persons weighted toward the upper-income brackets found that 91 percent admitted (after being guaranteed anonymity) to having committed at least one felony or serious misdemeanor including car theft and burglary. None had ever been arrested.[17] The notion that crime is the special practice of the poor is false. What *is* true is that the poor—especially among the racial minorities—are more likely to suffer the consequences for their criminal actions than the well-to-do.

Charges

The kind of charges brought against an arrested person may depend on the kind of person he is. Members of rich and influential families and persons who occupy high positions are often able to hush up an embarrassing arrest and avoid being charged.[18] Every arrest situa-

---

16. Russell Baker's column, *New York Times*, September 14, 1974.

17. Jessica Mitford, *Kind and Usual Punishment: The Prison Business* (New York: Vintage, 1974). The *victims* of street crime are overwhelmingly poor people, particularly inner city Blacks and Hispanics, according to a Law Enforcement Assistance Administration study discussed in the *Guardian*, June 7, 1978.

18. The former lobbyist Robert Winter-Berger gives an interesting account of his successful efforts to cover up the arrest of a U.S. senator in a bar in New York; see his *The Washington Pay-Off* (New York: Dell, 1972), pp. 82–84.

tion has enough ambiguity to allow authorities some discretion in determining charges. Whether a situation is treated as "disorderly conduct" or "mob action," whether it be "aggravated battery" or "attempted murder," depends somewhat on the judgment of the law enforcers, both police and prosecutors, and their feelings about the suspect.

A factor sometimes determining the seriousness of the charges is the degree of injury *sustained*, not inflicted, by the individual during the course of his arrest. Police are inclined to bring heavier charges against someone they have badly beaten—if only to justify the beating and further punish the "offender." The beating itself is likely to be taken as evidence of guilt. "I cannot believe a state trooper would hit anyone for no reason," announced one judge in a trial involving a college professor who had been repeatedly clubbed by troopers while participating in an antiwar demonstration.[19] "In the eyes of the police," a civil liberties lawyer argues, "arrest is practically tantamount to guilt, and the police will supply the allegations necessary for conviction; the courts are treated as a mere adjunct to their purpose."[20]

Bail and Legal Defense

After being charged and booked, the suspect is held in jail to await arraignment. At arraignment the judge has the option of doing anything from releasing the defendant on his own recognizance to imposing a bail high enough to keep him in jail until his trial date— which might come a couple of years later—as was the fate of numerous Black Panthers[21] arrested and held on bonds of $100,000 and $200,000. Even if found innocent—as was the case of the New York and New Haven Panthers—the defendant will have suffered the immense costs and anxieties of a trial and an extended imprisonment. This "preventive detention," commonly employed against large numbers of persons rounded up during urban disturbances, allows the state to incarcerate and punish people without having to convict anyone of any crime.[22]

---

19. Michael Parenti, "Repression in Academia: A Report from the Field," *Politics and Society*, 1, August 1971, pp. 527–537.

20. Paul Chevigny, *Police Power* (New York: Pantheon, 1969), pp. 276–277.

21. The Black Panthers are a Black leftist group that advocated socialist revolution during the late 1960s and early 1970s.

22. See Jerome Skolnik, "Judicial Response in Crisis," in Theodore Becker and Vernon Murray (eds.), *Government Lawlessness in America* (New York: Oxford University Press, 1971), p. 162.

"Recognizance" would be most helpful to those unable to afford bail, but it is usually granted to "respectable" middle-class persons and seldom to indigents. One study found that in state cases 73 percent of all indigents were denied pre-trial release as opposed to 21 percent of nonindigents.[23] Most of the people held in all county and municipal jails have been convicted of no crime but are awaiting either a trial or hearing.[24] Pre-trial detention makes it almost impossible for the poor to assist their attorneys in the preparation of an adequate defense. Brought into court directly from jail, a defendant is more likely to be convicted and more likely to be sentenced to a longer term than someone who has been free on bail and whose lawyer can point to his "rehabilitation" and law-abiding life since the original arrest.[25] Poor people also are more likely to be persuaded to plead guilty to reduced charges ("plea bargaining").[26] Ninety percent of all defendants plead guilty without a trial; of the other 10 percent, more than half are convicted of something. This statistic hardly fits with the image of "coddled" criminals and "soft-hearted" courts propagated by the get-tough advocates.

Lawyers, Juries and Judges

Like medical service, legal service in our society best serves those who can pay for it. The man who has the $100,000 for top legal assistance experiences a different treatment from the law than the poor person with a court-appointed lawyer who will have little time for the defendant, sometimes seeing him for the first time on the day of his trial. Being mostly of White middle-class background, the "Public Defenders" often share the same prejudices about their non-White, poor clients as do police, prosecutors, judges, juries and probation officers, a factor that can further influence their efforts. Most indigents, especially in the lower courts, are deprived even of this token representation, being encouraged by judges to waive their right to counsel.

---

23. Stuart S. Nagel, "Disparities in Criminal Procedure," *UCLA Law Review*, 14, August 1967, pp. 1272–1305.

24. 1970 National Census, statistics reproduced in *Crime and the Law*, p. 12.

25. Ralph Blumenfeld, "The Courts: Endless Crisis," *New York Post*, May 15, 1973. See also Stuart Nagel, "The Tipped Scales of American Justice," *Transaction*, 3, May–June 1966, pp. 3–9; and Nagel's "Disparities in Criminal Procedure."

26. Contrary to the belief that plea bargaining gives the criminal an easy way out, most defendents end up with sentences as severe as any they would have received had they stood trial; so finds a Washington, D.C., study of street-crime convictions. *Morning Union* (Springfield, Mass.), August 21, 1978.

In most states, prospective jurors are chosen from voter registration rolls or county tax lists, which underrepresent racial minorities, women, the propertyless—and even more so, young persons and low-income people. Officials do not pick randomly but usually choose a jury pool from street lists and neighborhoods they favor. Since most officials are White males over fifty, it is not surprising that jury pools are greatly overrepresented by middle-aged and elderly White males—the very ones most likely to believe the police and least likely to credit the testimony of young persons and minorities. Women are often granted exemptions without even requesting them, and, in some counties, college students seem to be "automatically disqualified."[27] The few cultural or political "deviants" who might get called for jury duty are usually weeded out at selection time by the peremptory challenges of the prosecutor.

As portrayed in the media, judges are distinguished-looking persons possessed of a wise and commanding air, calming courtroom passions with measured admonitions, showing fear and favor toward none, yet capable of a certain compassion for the accused. Turning from Hollywood to reality, we discover that judges are often arrogant, corrupt, self-inflated persons. After observing courtroom procedures for two years, the investigative journalist Jack Newfield concluded that along with "personal venality" many judges were marked "by cruelty, stupidity, bias against the poor, short tempers or total insensitivity to civil liberties."[28] Investigations by a special prosecutor in 1975–1976 in New York found widespread sale of judgeships to moneyed persons. Once on the bench, these individuals commonly sold "not guilty" verdicts to rich businessmen, crime-syndicate bosses and corrupt politicians brought before them.[29]

A study of state courts found that judges were more inclined to send poorly educated persons to prison and less likely to give them

---

27. See Tom Lesser and Bill Newman, "Cross-Examining the Jury System," *Valley Advocate* (Amherst, Mass.), March 9, 1977, p. 2, *Buffalo Courier Express*, March 29, 1974, and *Spectrum* (Buffalo, N.Y.), April 1, 1974, for reports on jury-pool selection in Western Massachusetts and Erie County, New York. Persons called for jury duty have been subjected to secret background checks by IRS agents as U.S. prosecutors have sought to exclude those with "antigovernment biases." *New York Times*, April 19, 1976.

28. Jack Newfield, "The Next 10 Worst Judges," *Village Voice*, September 26, 1974, p. 5. For an exposé of venality on the bench see Charles Ashman, *The Finest Judges Money Can Buy* (Los Angeles: Nash, 1973). For an inside view of the widespread corruption of police, judges and lawyers see the personal account of a professional criminal: Bruce Jackson, *Outside the Law: A Thief's Primer* (New York: E. P. Dutton, 1972).

29. The special prosecutor, Maurice Nadjari, launched 500 investigations, got 79 convictions and 296 indictments against judges and other officials. His efforts proved so troublesome to the powers that be that he was eventually fired by Governor Carey.

*"The opportunity to be fair and just
is rewarding—but what I especially like
is taking the law into my own hands."*

suspended sentences or probation than better educated and better-income persons convicted of the same crimes.[30] A study of courts in Seattle, Washington, found that persons who convey the appearance of a middle-class status are treated as more worthy of leniency by judges than those who by dress or attitude do not seem to value

---

30. Nagel, "Disparities in Criminal Procedure."

"the same things which the court values."³¹ One federal judge observes that his colleagues are "likely to read thick briefs, hear oral arguments, and then take days or weeks to decide who breached a contract for the delivery of onions"—such are the efforts devoted to business cases—but when dealing with criminal charges against a common defendant, "the same judge will read a pre-sentence report, perhaps talk to a probation officer, hear a few minutes of pleas for mercy—invest, in sum, less than an hour in all—before imposing a sentence of 10 years in prison."³²

Like police, many judges are inclined to see any defendant who enters their court as guilty of something. One observer of New York City courts concluded: "Favoritism to the prosecution is the rule among most judges here. . . ."³³ Judges not only identify with the prosecutor, they frequently *are* former prosecutors, having made their way to the bench via the office of district attorney or state attorney or the Justice Department. The image we have in our heads of an orderly, even-handed, dignified system of justice does not coincide with the picture drawn by Newfield:

> Routinely, lives are ruined and families broken by 30-second decisions. Some judges quit work at 2:00 P.M. to play golf, while some 8,000 men and women presumed innocent under the Constitution wait months for trials in the city's overcrowded detention jails. Other judges have tantrums on the bench and call defendants "animals" and "scum." Cops pay court attendants ("bridgemen") $5 to call their cases first. Legal Aid lawyers defend 50 poor clients a day with not a second for preparation. The bail system lets bondsmen buy freedom for the rich and well-connected. Clerks sell advance word on court assignments and decisions. Civil cases almost always get decided in favor of the landlord or businessman, or city agency.³⁴

Penalties and Prisons

Echoing a favorite conservative theme, President Nixon once complained of "softheaded judges" who showed more concern for "the rights of convicted criminals" than for innocent victims.³⁵ But an

---

31. For a report on the study see Ray Bloomberg, "Court Justice Tied to Middle-Class Values," *Quaker Service Bulletin*, 54, Spring 1973, p. 8. This study found poverty to be a bigger factor in court bias than race. Nagel finds the same, although he allows that there is much overlap.
32. Marvin E. Frankel, *Criminal Sentences: Law Without Order* (New York: Hill and Wang, 1973).
33. Ralph Blumenfeld, "The Courts: Endless Crisis," *New York Post*, May 15, 1973.
34. Jack Newfield, "New York's Ten Worst Judges," *New York*, October 1972, p. 32.
35. See the response by Marvin E. Frankel, "An Opinion by One of Those Softheaded Judges," *New York Times Magazine*, May 13, 1973, p. 41. In his book *Crim-*

American Bar Association study found that, far from coddling criminals, American jurists imposed much severer sentences than their opposite numbers in Western European countries. Sentences of over five years for felony convictions are rare in Europe but common in the United States,[36] where jail terms sometimes have an eighteenth-century quality about them. In Norfolk, Virginia, a man received ten years for stealing eighty-seven cents; in Detroit, a Black youth was found guilty of stealing seven dollars and given three to ten years; a youth in Louisiana got fifty years for selling a few ounces of marijuana, and another got forty years in Virginia for doing the same.[37]

In contrast, a major heroin dealer, with previous arrests and important mob connections, was given a conditional discharge. A big-time racketeer had felony charges against him dismissed by a compassionate judge known for his stern rulings against hippies and Blacks. A detective with gangland connections, caught dealing in heroin, was convicted of a misdemeanor and given a suspended sentence. "What criminal cases reveal . . . is that there is one law for the poor, another for the organized criminal with the expensive name lawyers."[38]

Consider how the law was applied in these cases:

1. A White, unemployed migrant farm worker, Thomas Boronson, and his family were eating one meager meal each day from money earned by selling their blood. Boronson and a friend, Lonnie Davis, took over a welfare office in a desperate attempt to get the several hundred dollars owed to the Boronson family. The youngest of Boronson's six children was a sick infant who had been denied medical care by local doctors because the family could not afford to pay. Boronson and Davis were arrested and convicted of kidnapping, assault and robbery, even though the welfare workers refused to press charges. They were sentenced to nine and seven years respectively.[39]

---

inal Sentences, Judge Frankel describes judges as "arbitrary, cruel and lawless" in the ways they determine sentences.

36. Frankel, "An Opinion by One of Those Softheaded Judges."

37. *Washington Star*, April 29 and April 30, 1975. While the penalties against pot smokers has eased in some states, the FBI revealed that 441,000 persons were arrested on marijuana charges in 1977, a considerable increase over previous years. *New Age*, March 1978, p. 24.

38. Herbert Mitgang, "The Storefront Lawyer Helps the Poor," *New York Times Magazine*, November 10, 1968. The leniency and neglect with which the big and influential mobsters are treated by the law might help explain why organized crime continues to be a growth industry. See Jonathan Kwitny, *Vicious Circles: The Mafia in the Marketplace* (New York: Norton, 1979).

39. *Guardian*, May 26, 1976.

2. A Black student, Philip Allen, joined a small crowd watching a drunk smash a store window. When the police arrived, they jumped Allen with drawn pistols, according to witnesses. The police claim that Allen, who is 5′ 3″ and weighs 135 pounds, overpowered several of them, seized one of their guns, shot three of them—killing one—without leaving any fingerprints on the gun and then was captured by the other two. No witnesses saw Allen holding a gun at any time. The police most likely shot each other in the scuffle. Allen was convicted and given a life sentence.[40]

3. A bus carrying Black children was attacked by a mob of Whites, some of whom were armed. According to the bus driver, a gun was fired from the crowd; it missed the bus but killed a White youth. When the Black students were forced out of the bus and to their knees by police, one of them, Gary Tyler (age fifteen at the time), was arrested for "interfering with an officer" when he objected to the deputy sheriff's putting a gun to the heads of Black students. The police "found" a gun in the bus, but it curiously turned out to be a police revolver with no fingerprints. Tyler was charged with murder, convicted by an all-White jury, and sentenced to die in the electric chair. The prosecution's case rested entirely on two witnesses, both of whom later recanted their testimony, charging that police had coerced them into fingering Tyler. The police had threatened to take one witness's child away from her and charge her as an accessory to the murder. The judge refused to grant a new trial.[41]

Those convicted of crimes must then face our "correctional institutions." American prisons are overcrowded, filthy, unhealthy places, breeding crime, violence, rape and mental and physical degradation.[42] Prisoners who protest the inhumane conditions are likely to be subjected to extreme forms of harassment and retribution. (At Atmore and Holman prisons in Alabama, forty-five of the inmates who organized for better prison conditions were indicted on charges. In a year and a half, five of the leaders had been either

40. Communiqué from the Philip Allen Defense Committee of the First Unitarian Church, Los Angeles, California, April 1976.

41. *Workers World*, May 21, 1976. Tyler's death sentence was commuted to life imprisonment. He has exhausted all appeals and is serving his time. For a general critique of the problem of justice for Blacks, see Haywood Burns, "Can a Black Man Get a Fair Trial in This Country?" *New York Times Magazine*, July 12, 1970, pp. 5, 38–46. See also the case of Earl Charles in Marc Levinson, "Like a Checker on a Checkerboard," *Nation*, December 16, 1978.

42. Mitford, *Kind and Usual Punishment*; also Alan Dershowitz, "Let the Punishment Fit the Crime," *New York Times Magazine*, December 28, 1975.

shot, hanged or beaten to death while handcuffed—by prison guards.[43]) Eighty percent of all inmates are Black, Chicano, Puerto Rican, Native American and Asian. Blacks tend to get substantially longer prison terms than Whites convicted of the same crimes, even when the Black is a first-time offender and the White a second- or third-time offender.[44]

During times of economic hardship, the state has to operate more repressively than usual against the have-nots. Not surprisingly, then, in these times of recession, the severest of all punishments—the death penalty—seems to be making a comeback. Numerous arguments have been posed against the death penalty, such as:

1. There are no data to support the idea that it is a deterrent to capital crimes.

2. It leaves no room for redress should the wrong person be convicted and executed—in effect, it assumes the infallibility of the enforcement process.

3. The state should not commit premeditated institutionalized murder.[45]

4. The death penalty has been applied almost exclusively against the poor and racial minorities, most usually in rape and murder cases involving a Black offender and a White victim.[46] "I don't know of a wealthy person ever executed in the United States," observes a former longtime warden of San Quentin prison.[47]

The death penalty is also arbitrarily applied. There are child-killers and cold-blooded "contract" murderers who are paroled after doing ten or fifteen years of a life sentence, while one teenage boy received a death sentence for the sale of heroin that led to the purchaser's accidental demise by overdose, and a woman in Georgia is on death row for a murder her husband committed; she was convicted of being a co-conspirator, which she vehemently denies.[48]

---

43. Walt Shepperd, "Alabama's State Prison System: Unfit for the Shelter of Animals," *Ithaca* (N.Y.) *New Times*, February 1, 1976.
44. Frank L. Morris, "Black Political Consciousness in Northern State Prisons," paper presented at the National Conference of Black Political Scientists, New Orleans, May 1973; also *Denver Post*, May 1, 1977.
45. For selections of pro and con arguments see Hugo Adam Bedau (ed.), *The Death Penalty in America*, 2nd ed. (Chicago: Aldine, 1967).
46. See the study by the Southern Poverty Law Center reported in the *Guardian*, March 10, 1976; also the study by sociologists William Bowers and Glenn Pierce discussed in Peter Ross Range, "Will He Be the First?" *New York Times Magazine*, March 11, 1979, p. 78.
47. Clinton Duffy quoted in Range, "Will He Be the First?" p. 78.
48. *Ibid.*

To sum up what might be said about criminal enforcement: poor and working-class persons, the uneducated and the racial minorities are more likely to be arrested, less likely to be released on bail, more likely to be induced to plead guilty, more likely to go without a pre-trial hearing even though entitled to one, less likely to have a jury trial if tried, more likely to be convicted and receive a harsh sentence and less likely to receive probation or a suspended sentence than are mobsters, businessmen and other upper- and middle-class Whites. "The rich have little reason to fear the system and the poor have little reason to respect it."[49]

Women of upper-class social background are more likely to receive favored treatment at the hands of the law than are low-income or impoverished people of either sex, and in most kinds of cases White women receive better consideration than Black men. But race and class aside, women suffer legal injustices of their own.[50] Most laws against prostitution, for example, are either written or enforced so as to place all the guilt on the prostitute and none on her male clients. In some states wives still have not achieved equality with their husbands in regard to consent in contracts and handling of property. As victims of rape, women often receive little justice in the courts, it frequently being assumed by police, attorneys, judges and jurors that the rape victim "was asking for it" (an assumption that is far less likely to be made if the alleged rapist is Black). Women in prison are subjected to sexual abuse from male guards, sheriffs and jail trustees. In one women's prison in Alabama there were eight births in one year, most of them the result of sexual as-

---

49. Hart, "Swindling and Knavery, Inc.," p. 162.
50. Karen De Crow, *Sexual Justice* (New York: Random House, 1974).

saults by male guards.[51] In many states there still exists a host of female "juvenile crimes," such as going into a bar, getting pregnant, fighting with parents, running away from home and staying out late at night, that are not crimes and should be taken off the books but which are used to incarcerate many young and spirited women.

Every year thousands of women are hospitalized because of repeated beatings from their spouses. It is a crime to assault anyone, yet the law is seldom enforced against husbands who batter their wives. The law also has yet to prove effective in breaking down discriminatory employment and wage practices or protecting women from sexual harassment on the job. And women who have agitated for equal pay, prison reform, day care, lesbian rights and legalized abortion have been the object of FBI and CIA surveillance.[52]

As with Blacks, the poor and women, so with homosexuals: the oppression practiced in the wider society is reflected and reinforced in the law and the courts. Thus when gay people go to court to contest the discrimination they suffer in housing and employment, they are most likely to find that the rights of property take precedence over the rights of people, and the doctrine of equal protection under the law does not apply to them. Such was the case in Dade County, Florida, where an antigay campaign led by singer Anita Bryant led to the rescinding of a gay rights housing ordinance. Gay rights organizers have been beaten and arrested by law officers in Detroit, Houston, Seattle and elsewhere. In thirty-six states gay love is still punished under "sodomy" or "unnatural acts" laws, and two people who love each other but are of the same sex find themselves treated as criminals or "perverts" to be hustled off to jail or a mental institution for "treatment" and "cure." In 1976 the Supreme Court ruled that states may prosecute and imprison people committing homosexual acts even when both parties are consenting adults and the act occurs in private. And in 1978 the Court upheld lower-court decisions that a teacher could be fired for no other reason than being a homosexual.[53]

Gays have been barred from sensitive government jobs on the highly dubious assumption that their homosexuality is indicative of personal instability and leaves them open to corruption or blackmail, making them poor security risks. Both female and male gays

---

51. *Workers World*, March 5, 1976.
52. Letty Cottin Pogrebin, "The FBI Was Watching You," *Ms.*, June 1977, pp. 37–44.
53. *Doe* v. *Commonwealth's Attorney*, 425 U.S. 901 (1976); also *Gish* v. *Board of Education of Paramus, N.J.*, 434 U.S. 879 (1978); and *Gaylord* v. *Tacoma School District*, 434 U.S. 879 (1978).

have been discharged from the armed services for no other reason than that they were homosexuals. Lesbian mothers have been denied custody of their children on the grounds that their sexual preferences made them unfit parents.[54] Gay bars are frequently raided by police or closed down by municipal authorities and gay individuals often are "cruised" by undercover police, posing as fellow gays, whose intent is to entice and entrap them, an undertaking that some law officers perform with an enthusiasm that seems to involve something more than the call of duty.

POLICE TERROR: WHO GUARDS THE GUARDIANS?

No discussion of law and order would be complete without some mention of America's only legally armed minority: the police. Despite cutbacks in city budgets, police work is among the fastest growing occupations in the United States and law enforcement represents the largest budget item of many municipalities. Yet the urban crime rate continues to rise, and "there is less resistance, official or otherwise to organized-crime enterprise now than at any other time. . . ."[55]

If the police have been unsuccessful in the "war against crime," they have not been idle in their war against workers, poor people, youth, racial minorities and other elements that might prove troublesome to the interests of property and propriety. The police are like an occupying army patrolling the exploited and hostile low-income areas, keeping the sullen population in line with large doses of terror. Each year in almost every city in the nation scores of unarmed persons, mostly low-income non-Whites, are brutalized or killed by the police. Studies[56] show that Blacks, Chicanos, Puerto Ricans and low-income Whites have many more personal encounters

54. Glifford Guy Gibson and Mary Jo Risher, *By Her Own Admission: A Lesbian Mother's Fight to Keep Her Son* (Garden City, N.Y.: Doubleday, 1977).

55. Thomas Plate, "The Pin-Striped, Pencil-Packing Modern Mafia," *Penthouse*, June 1977, p. 28; *New York Times*, March 30, 1976. For an insider's view of the corruption and incompetence of the police in their war against crime see Peter Maas, *Serpico* (New York: Bantam, 1974).

56. David H. Bayley and Harold Mendelsohn, *Minorities and the Police* (New York: Free Press, 1971), p. 122; Paul Jacobs, *Prelude to Riot* (New York: Random House, 1968), pp. 29–30. In one year in Houston fourteen Chicanos—all unarmed—were murdered by the police under highly questionable circumstances, and in Los Angeles twenty-eight people, mostly unarmed Blacks and Chicanos, were shot to death by police. *Guardian*, November 2, 1977, and February 22, 1978.

with police brutality than middle-class White "respectables." Consider these instances:

A Black man is forced to lie face down in a Detroit motel and a policeman cold-bloodedly pumps a bullet into his head.
In Cambridge, Massachusetts, a White working-class youth is beaten to death by police in a paddy wagon.
A 12-year-old Chicano boy in Dallas, arrested as a burglary suspect, is shot through the head while sitting handcuffed in a patrol car.
A 10-year-old Black boy walking with his foster father in Queens, New York, is killed by a plainclothes policeman who leaps from his unmarked car without identifying himself, shouts "Hey niggers!" and opens fire.
A White hippie, finding his home surrounded by armed, unidentified men in Humboldt County, California (who turn out to be county police and narcotics agents raiding the wrong place), flees in terror out the back door and is shot dead.
A Black shellshocked Vietnam veteran is killed by two police on a Houston street as he reaches into his pocket to take out a Bible.
A New York policeman shoots a 22-year-old Black student who is standing with his hands in the air and then plants a toy pistol next to his body.
A Black youth attempting to retrieve a basketball in a schoolyard is shot through the head by Chicago police.
A Chicano youth in Houston is taken to a secluded spot by police, beaten until unconscious, then thrown into a bayou to drown.[57]

A study of police in three major cities found that all the victims of brutality had one thing in common: they were from low-income groups.[58] Sometimes it is enough just to be Black—even if middle class. Take the case of Carl Newland, a Black 48-year-old accountant who happened to be walking by a newsstand that had just been robbed. He was roughed up by the police, then brought before the newsstand clerk, who emphatically denied he was the stickup man.

57. For accounts of these and similar incidents see John Hersey, *The Algiers Motel Incident* (New York: Knopf, 1968); Murray Kempton, "The Harlem Policeman," in Becker and Murray (eds.), *Government Lawlessness in America*, pp. 47–49; Joe Eszterhas, "Death in the Wilderness," *Rolling Stone*, May 24, 1973, pp. 28–34, 44–54; also the weekly issues of the *Guardian*, *Workers World*, the *Militant* and the *Daily World*.
58. Albert J. Reiss, "How Much 'Police Brutality' Is There?" *Transaction*, July/August 1967, reprinted in Stephen M. David and Paul E. Peterson, *Urban Politics and Public Policy* (New York: Praeger, 1973), p. 282.

Nevertheless, because of his "belligerent attitude" he was taken to jail, and, according to statements by several prisoners, repeatedly and severely beaten by the police. He died in his cell that night.[59]

Few of the law officers involved in these kinds of cases have ever been indicted for murder. Most have been exonerated by review boards despite the highly incriminating testimony of eyewitnesses. A few have been suspended from the force, and a few have been tried for "justifiable homicide" or "manslaughter" and acquitted or given light sentences.[60] One White officer, who had held a young Black boy with one hand and shot him with the other, was awarded tax-free disability pay of $1,000 a month for the rest of his life because of the "trauma" he supposedly suffered after murdering the boy.[61] After shooting an unarmed 15-year-old boy, another officer was acquitted because of "temporary insanity" caused by a "rare form of epilepsy"—so rare that medical specialists have never heard of it. His first and last "seizure" came at the instant of the shooting, and he was released from a mental institution shortly after his trial because doctors could find nothing wrong with him.[62] In Mobile, Alabama, a grand jury investigation of police terror concluded that "police department command personnel not only accepted but encouraged such behavior," a finding that could be applied to any number of departments in the nation.[63]

Police frequently ally themselves with unlawful elements whose prejudices they share. In various places Black homeowners, terrorized by White mobs and arsonists, have been unable to secure protection from law agents or, worse still, have themselves been subjected to police attack. To describe only one of many such incidents: when a Black home was attacked by a mob in East Boston, the police did nothing to stop the attack and instead broke into the home and

---

59. *Workers World*, June 4, 1976. See also the account of the police murder of Brooklyn Black community leader Arthur Miller, *Workers World*, November 3, 1978. Atrocities like these are reported weekly in publications like the *Guardian* and *Workers World* but seldom in the business-owned press.

60. Sara Blackburn (ed.), *White Justice* (New York: Harper & Row, 1972). For recent instances see *Guardian*, March 9, 1977, June 7, 1978, and May 30, 1979; *New York Times*, March 15, 1977, and March 29, 1978; *Workers World*, March 10, 1978; *Daily World*, October 18, 1978.

61. *Workers World*, February 7, 1975.

62. *New York Times*, December 1, 1977.

63. *Guardian*, May 19, 1976. For similar findings in regard to Newark, Houston and Philadelphia see the *New York Times*, March 2, 1975, and April 15, 1979; *Newsweek*, July 4, 1977. In New York, fifty-nine police officers admitted taking bribes from gangsters and racketeers "in lieu of taking proper police action." None were suspended, dismissed or demoted. All were merely given fines. *New York Times*, July 1, 1978.

arrested the resident and seven visitors for "loud and abusive language." Witnesses for the defense, including a priest, a lawyer and a local resident, testified that the defendants had acted peacefully at all times. Nevertheless, the eight received jail sentences of six to eight months.[64]

The history of the labor movement in the United States reveals a similar pattern of police harassment and violence. From the earliest days of industrial conflict to today, agents of the law have sided with the propertied and powerful, either looking the other way or actively cooperating when goons and vigilantes attacked workers, union headquarters and pickets.[65] In recent years throughout the country, police in riot gear have attacked striking construction workers and farm workers, truckers and miners, arresting and badly injuring hundreds. Many workers have been imprisoned for ignoring court injunctions against strikes and pickets. In Harlan County, Kentucky, a striking coal miner was shot to death by a scab, as was a farm worker in Texas; and in Elwood, Indiana, within a period of a few months, seven strikers were shot by company goons. In all these instances police apprehended no one.[66]

The law and its enforcement agents do many worthwhile things. Many laws are intended to enhance public safety and individual security. The police sometimes protect life and limb, direct traffic, administer first aid, assist in times of community emergency and perform other vital social services with commendable dedication and courage. But aside from this desirable *social service* function, the police and the law serve a *class control* function—that is, they protect those who rule from the protests and confrontations of those who are ruled. And they protect the interests of property from those who would challenge the inequities of the system. The profiteering corporate managers, plundering slumlords, swindling merchants, racist school boards, self-enriching doctors, special-interest legislators and others who contribute so much to the scarcity, misery and anger that lead to individual crimes or mass riots leave the dirty work of subduing these outbursts to the police. When the police charge picket lines—beating, gassing and occasionally shooting

64. *Workers World*, October 17 and November 14, 1975; March 5, 1976. For other instances of this kind of treatment, see the *Guardian*, April 14, 1976; *Workers World*, April 18 and June 20, 1975.

65. Jeremy Brecher, *Strike!* (Greenwich, Conn.: Fawcett, 1974).

66. *Workers World*, July 29, 1977. For an excellent historical and systemic analysis of the class function of the police see *The Iron Fist and the Velvet Glove, An Analysis of the U.S. Police*, 2nd ed., written and published by the Center for Research on Criminal Justice (Berkeley, California, 1977).

workers—they usually are operating with a court injunction which allows them to exert force in order to protect the interests of the corporate owners.

When police commit acts of brutality against slum dwellers, they are doing what serves the existing politico-economic system; they are waging war against the troublesome have-nots. In doing so, they confront dangers, threats and social miseries of a kind most of us can only imagine. They deal with the waste products of an affluent, competitive corporate society: the corpse in the street, the back-alley mugger, the pimps and child molesters, the winos, heroin pushers and psychopaths, the unemployed, ill-fed and ill-housed, the desperate and the defeated. As someone once said, the slums are not the problem, they are the *solution*; they are the way capitalism deals with the surplus people of a market economy. And for all they cost the taxpayer in crime, police, arson and welfare, the slums remain a source of profit for certain speculators, investors, realtors, big merchants and others. But they do present problems of violence and social pathology that need to be contained. And that is the job of the police: to sweep protest, riot and poverty under the rug—even if it takes a club or gun. Repressive acts by police are not the aberrant behavior of a few psychotics in uniform but the outgrowth of the kind of class-control function that law officers perform and rulers insist upon—which explains why the police are able to get away with murder.

9

Law and Order: The Repression of Dissent

Among those whom the law treats repressively are persons who oppose capitalism and advocate alternative social orders. Since capitalism is considered an essential component of Americanism and democracy, anticapitalists are treated as antidemocratic, unAmerican and a subversive threat to the "national security," and thus fair game for repression. As repression gathers momentum, it is directed not only against communists but against anyone who shows an active interest in progressive causes. Under the guise of defending democracy, security agencies deny dissenters their democratic rights and move the nation closer to a police state.

THE METHODS AND VICTIMS OF REPRESSION

When directed toward social reform, the law usually proves too weak for effective change. But when mobilized against political dissenters, the resources of the law appear boundless, and enforcement is pursued with a punitive vigor that itself becomes lawless. Dissident groups have had their telephones tapped, their offices raided, their records and funds stolen by law officers, their members threatened, maligned, intimidated, beaten, murdered, or arrested on trumped-up charges, held on exorbitant bail, subjected to costly, time-consuming trials which, whether won or lost, paralyze their leadership, exhaust their funds and consume their energies. With

141

POLITICAL PRISONER

these kinds of attacks, the government's message comes across loud and clear: people are not as free as they think. They may organize against government policies, but their public utterances and private behavior will be watched by one or more of the many security agencies. And if they persist, they run the risk of being struck down by police violence or devoured by the repressive legal mechanism of the state. The law is a weapon used against people who want to change the class and racial relations of the society.[1]

Consider some specific cases: the Black socialist Martin Sostre, long an opponent of heroin traffic in the ghetto, was convicted and sentenced to 30 years for dealing in heroin—on the sole testimony of a convict who was released from prison after appearing against Sostre and who subsequently admitted in a sworn statement that his testimony had been fabricated. The trial judge refused to believe his recantation. Sostre served nine years, mostly in solitary confinement and was subjected to sadistic treatment at the hands of prison authorities. After much protest from progressive and humanitarian groups, the governor of New York granted Sostre amnesty.[2]

Then there was George Jackson. Sentenced as a youth to a long, indeterminate prison term for a relatively minor crime, Jackson became radicalized while in the penitentiary. He began organizing inmates and writing books about his revolutionary creed—efforts which won public attention.[3] For this he was placed in solitary for long periods, repeatedly beaten and eventually shot dead by guards. At the trial of the surviving Soledad brothers, the defense produced an undercover FBI agent who described the elaborate and successful plans of the police to kill Jackson during what was to appear as an "escape attempt."[4]

Frank Shuford, a Black community activist and a socialist in Santa Ana, California, was organizing young people to oppose poverty, bad schools, drug pushers and police complicity with the drug

1. Note how the law was used against the antiwar movement; see Jessica Mitford, *The Trial of Doctor Spock* (New York: Knopf, 1969); and Jason Epstein, *The Great Conspiracy Trial* (New York: Vintage, 1971).

2. *New York Times*, December 25, 1975.

3. See George Jackson, *Soledad Brother: The Prison Letters of George Jackson* (New York: Bantam, 1970); also Eric Mann, *Comrade George: An Investigation into the Life, Political Thought and Assassination of George Jackson* (New York: Harper & Row, 1974).

4. *Guardian*, April 21, 1976. The agent told of his experiences as an undercover provocateur in a book: see Citizens Research and Investigation Committee and Louis Tackwood, *Glass House Tapes* (New York: Avon, 1973); also Mann's examination of Jackson's murder in *Comrade George*.

traffic. It was after his campaign against the drug traffic began to show success that he was arrested for the shooting of two store clerks, although at the time of the crime Shuford was home with family and friends. One clerk could not identify him as the gunman and the other offered contradictory and uncertain statements. No material evidence was presented against him. The first trial ended in a hung jury. (Meanwhile the community youth organization he had started to deal with drugs, breakfast programs, jobs and tutoring had become demoralized and had fallen apart.) At his second trial Shuford was branded a "revolutionary troublemaker" by the prosecution. His own lawyer conducted a strangely lackadaisical defense, neglecting to object to any of the district attorney's tactics, and then himself was appointed a district attorney immediately after Shuford was found guilty by an all-White jury and sentenced to thirty years. In prison Shuford was drugged, beaten, denied medical care and scheduled for a lobotomy. Only community pressure on his behalf prevented the operation from taking place.[5]

When a White mob invaded the Black community in Wilmington, North Carolina, in 1971, setting fire to several buildings, police did nothing to stop them. But a year later, in connection with those same fires, the Reverend Ben Chavis, along with eight other Black community activists and one White woman organizer, were arrested on charges of arson. (Chavis had been previously arrested on seventy-eight separate trumped-up charges over a three-year period and acquitted on all.) On the first day of the trial, faced with a jury of ten Blacks and two Whites, the prosecutor developed a sudden "stomach pain." Instead of calling a recess for a few days, the judge declared a mistrial. At the second trial a jury of ten Whites and two Blacks found the "Wilmington Ten" guilty on the testimony of three persons, including two who were themselves facing long jail terms for an unrelated crime. Chavis was sentenced to 34 years, while the others received sentences of 29 to 34 years.[6]

The guardians of the law are quick to use unlawfully violent measures in the repression of dissent. This account of a police attack

---

5. *Guardian,* September 24, 1975; also Shuford Defense Committee *Newsletter,* January 1978.

6. Buffy Spencer, "North Carolina: Laboratory for Racism and Repression," *Outfront* (Amherst, Mass.), August 1976, p. 9. All three prosecution witnesses eventually repudiated their testimony. As of 1979, nine of the Wilmington Ten were out on parole, but Chavis was still in prison. Cases like the above few examples indicate that almost any political activist, especially if he or she is non-White, risks confrontations with the law.

against a peace demonstration in New York in 1969 is typical of incidents that occur throughout the United States during political protests and labor conflicts:

> A number of policemen came charging into the crowd, many, but not all, with their clubs in hand raised to the levels of their heads. . . . I saw other people being beaten. Some were arrested and others were not. It appeared to me that the police were just beating people at random with no clear indication that the people they were attacking had committed an illegal act. I saw none of the people being attacked fight back or attempt to hit the police. Most attempted to protect themselves by covering their heads or tried to run.[7]

Witness this assault on an antiwar protester:

> At least four times that soldier hit her with all his force, then as she lay covering her head with her arms, thrust his club swordlike between her hands onto her face. . . . She twisted her body so we could see her face. But there was no face there: all we saw were some raw skin and blood. We couldn't even see if she was crying—her eyes had filled with the blood pouring down her head. She vomited, and that too was blood. Then they rushed her away.[8]

The police have killed many unarmed people participating in collective protest actions. Of the one hundred or so murders of persons associated with the civil rights movement during the 1960s, almost all were committed by police and White vigilantes. Few of the murderers were caught; none was convicted of murder. From 1968 to 1971 local police stormed into and wrecked Black Panther headquarters in more than ten cities, stealing thousands of dollars in funds and arresting, beating and shooting the occupants in well-planned, unprovoked attacks. More than forty Panthers were killed by police in the period, including Chicago leader Fred Hampton, who was shot while asleep in his bed. More than three hundred were arrested and many were imprisoned for long periods without bail.[9]

7. Quoted in Peggy Kerry, "The Scene in the Streets," in Theodore Becker and Vernon Murray (eds.), *Government Lawlessness in America* (New York: Oxford University Press, 1971), p. 61.
8. Eyewitness testimony by Harvey Mayes, *New York Times*, December 3, 1967. Descriptions of brutality at the Pentagon were not carried in the *Times* or other newspapers. Mayes's account, along with numerous others, appeared in a full-page paid advertisement.
9. For the FBI's role in instigating and assisting in the police attacks see *Chicago Tribune*, April 20, 1976, and June 12, 1976.

In Orangeburg, South Carolina, three Black students were killed and twenty-seven wounded when police fired into a peaceful campus demonstration. No guns were seen or found among the students, and many of the victims had been shot in the back while fleeing.[10] During a nonviolent demonstration at Southern University in Louisiana, two unarmed Black students were killed by police. In antidraft and anti-ROTC demonstrations in 1970, unarmed Black students at Jackson State were murdered by police. At Kent State University in Ohio, four White students were murdered and two maimed by National Guardsmen. In the latter two instances, the evidence gathered by government agencies clearly indicated that the lives of the law enforcement officers and Guardsmen were never in danger and that the men who did the shooting got together after the event and agreed to tell investigators the false story that their lives had been in danger. In both cases, state grand juries refused to indict the murderers but did indict demonstrators, including several who had been wounded.[11]

The list of killings could go on, but the pattern remains the same: law enforcement agents have used lethal weapons against antiwar activists, ghetto protesters, rebellious prisoners and political radicals, none of whom were armed, a few of whom were reported to be hurling rocks or making "obscene gestures." In almost every instance, an "impartial investigation" by the very authorities responsible for the killings exonerated the uniformed murderers and their administrative chiefs. The few killers who are indicted are seldom convicted.

Political dissenters in the military are often meted out harsh treatment; they have been denied access to radical publications, confined to quarters, subjected to racial insults, physically threatened, given the least desirable assignments, framed on trumped-up charges, courtmartialed and incarcerated in the stockade.[12]

---

10. *New York Times*, December 12, 1968; also Jack Nelson and Jack Bass, *The Orangeburg Massacre* (New York: World, 1969). A federal grand jury refused to indict any of the highway patrolmen involved in the action.

11. I. F. Stone, "Fabricated Evidence in the Kent State Killings," *New York Review of Books*, December 3, 1970, p. 28. After much public pressure, the Justice Department indicted the Guardsmen involved in the Kent State killings. However, the judge threw the case out, arguing that the prosecution had proven excessive and unjustified force had been used but had not shown that the Guardsmen had acted with premeditation. *New York Times*, November 9, 1974. Guardsmen who admitted to having lied under oath in earlier grand jury investigations were never tried for perjury. See Peter Davies, "Kent State Questions," *New York Times*, May 4, 1976; see also *New York Times*, May 7, 1978.

12. See Robert Sherrill, *Military Justice Is to Justice as Military Music Is to Music* (New York: Harper & Row, 1970). In contrast, American Nazis in the U.S. Army are

146 / *Democracy for the Few*

Similarly, persons who organize and develop a political consciousness in prison do so at the risk of their lives. The rebellion at New York's Attica State Penitentiary in 1971 against inhumane conditions revealed the murderous force of the state. Asserting that the uprising was the work of "revolutionaries," Governor Nelson Rockefeller ordered an armed assault by troopers. Blasting their way into the prison yard, the troopers killed thirty-four inmates and nine prison guards who were being held as hostages and wounded more than a hundred other inmates. Not a single gun was found among the prisoners. A Special Commission on Attica declared the assault to be "the bloodiest attack by Americans on Americans" since the 1890 U.S. Army massacre of Indians at Wounded Knee.[13]

Among those singled out for special oppression have been members of the American Indian Movement (AIM), a group that has persistently challenged the injustices accorded Native Americans. The case of Russel Means, AIM leader, is instructive. Within a five-year period, Means was pistol whipped by a sheriff while getting out of a car; assaulted and arrested by tactical squad police because, as a spectator in court, he refused to stand when the judge entered, then convicted of "rioting" and sentenced to four years because of the courtroom incident; faced with four other trials with sentences threatened of more than 111 years; shot in the back by a police agent while a candidate for election on an Indian reservation; shot again as he rode in a car, the sniper's bullet grazing his forehead; arrested and charged with murder after visiting a bar to buy a six-pack of beer—even though the dying victim told police that Means had not been in the bar when the shooting occurred; and forced out of a house he was visiting by unidentified armed men who shot and wounded him and another AIM activist "at close range in an execution attempt," as one witness put it. While serving the four years for the courtroom incident, Means was again the target of an unsuccessful assassination attempt, being stabbed close to the heart by a White inmate.[14]

---

treated well. One Army spokesman explains that Army regulations do not prohibit any soldier from joining the Nazi party and wearing the Nazi uniform when off duty. *New York Daily News*, October 26, 1977. (Army regulations, however, do provide up to five years in prison and $10,000 fine for any soldier who joins a union.)

13. Annette T. Rubinstein, "Attica Now," *Monthly Review*, January 1976, pp. 12–20.

14. *Workers World*, July 4, 1975, May 14, 1976, February 9, 1979; *News and Observer* (Raleigh, N.C.), July 17, 1975; *Guardian*, April 14, 1976. Numerous other Native American activists have been subjected to similar harassments, attacks and imprisonments. See *Workers World*, March 14, 1975; *Guardian*, March 3, 1976; *Seven Days*, April 11, 1977. Another AIM member, Dick Marshall, was convicted in the same bar-

Along with the club and the gun, the state has more subtle instruments of oppression. One of these is the grand jury. Supposedly, grand juries are groups of citizens who weigh prosecution evidence to see whether there are sufficient grounds for a trial. Intended to protect the innocent from unjustifiable prosecution, the grand jury has been turned into its very opposite, usually doing what the prosecutor wants.[15] A common device is to grant a witness immunity from prosecution. The Fifth Amendment right against self-incrimination ceases to apply, and if one refuses to testify, one can be imprisoned for contempt. The upshot is to turn anyone into an involuntary informer regarding any conversation or activity to which she or he has been privy. The grand jury is often used to carry out "fishing expeditions" against dissenters in the hope of turning up unexpected violations of law and to intimidate persons engaged in political activities and jail those who refuse to cooperate. Within three years the Justice Department ran more than one hundred grand juries in over eighty cities. People have been required to appear without benefit of counsel and without being told the nature of the investigation. They can be forced to answer any question about political ideas and associations with friends, neighbors or relatives—or face up to eighteen months in prison for refusing to do so.

Socialists and other dissenters also encounter oppression within the "private sector" of society. Employment opportunities, job tenure, and professional certification may depend on how well one conforms to the sociopolitical attitudes of those who control the jobs. Employees who agitate for better working conditions or enunciate unpopular political opinions risk loss of job. Professionals who take unpopular stands, such as doctors who show themselves sympathetic to socialized medicine, may suffer professional censure. At most universities, students seldom get the opportunity to investigate the world from an anticapitalist perspective, since the bulk of their readings and almost all their instructors are either ignorant of or hostile to socialist perspectives. Socialist faculty members often find their contracts not renewed. At Dartmouth College, a dozen radical faculty members regularly met for lunch, but within three years the contracts of all but one had been terminated—a dramatic but

---

room shooting involving Means by an all-White jury on the basis of testimony by an FBI informer and several witnesses who have since changed their testimony. Marshall had accompanied Means into the bar; the shooting victim had not identified him as the attacker. He is serving a life sentence at hard labor.

15. John Conyers, Jr., "Grand Juries: The American Inquisition," *Ramparts*, August/September 1975, p. 15; also Marvin Frankel and Gary Naftalis, *The Grand Jury* (New York: Hill and Wang, 1977).

not unique example of the quiet purge conducted on campuses throughout the nation.[16]

Our government also protects us from ideas imported from abroad. In recent years scores of Marxist scholars, novelists, artists and union leaders have been denied visas and prevented from entering the United States to participate in cultural events and conferences to which they had been invited by private groups. Also banned by the McCarran-Walter Act are aliens who are "anarchists" or advocates of the "economic and global doctrines of communism."[17]

When the U.S. ambassador to the United Nations, Andrew Young, a Black man, remarked that "there are hundreds, perhaps, thousands of political prisoners in the United States," American politicians and news commentators whipped themselves into a frenzy of indignation.[18] President Carter quickly silenced his ambassador. Carter's widely heralded "campaign for human rights," directed mostly at political violations in the Soviet Union and other communist countries, had not for a moment been intended to bring critical attention to police-state repressions within the United States. The official view, still propagated by public officials and news media alike, is that in a democracy like the United States there is no such thing as a political prisoner.

In truth, considering only widely known cases, there has been a long history of American political prisoners: Eugene Debs and many hundreds of other socialists and radical IWW organizers were imprisoned during the First World War and in the Palmer raids immediately afterward. Then there were Sacco and Vanzetti, the anarchists executed for a crime they did not commit, and the mass arrests of socialists and pacifists who opposed both World War II and the Korean war, plus the scores of others jailed under the Smith Act, or for refusing to cooperate with congressional witch hunts during the McCarthy era. At the time of Ambassador Young's remark in 1978, at least several hundred persons were incarcerated because of their

---

16. For summaries of repressive actions on campus see Michael Miles, "The Triumph of Reaction," *Change, The Magazine of Higher Learning*, 4, Winter 1972-1973, p. 34; J. David Colfax, "Repression and Academic Radicalism," *New Politics*, 10, Spring 1973, pp. 14-27; and Michael E. Brown, "Academic Freedom in the State's University: The Ollman Case as a Problem for Theory and Practice," *New Political Science*, I, Spring 1979, pp. 30–46.

17. Many thousands are prevented from visiting or emigrating to the United States each year because of these restrictions. John Rosenberg, "The Chaos of Immigration Policy," *Nation*, September 2, 1978; *New York Times*, March 10, 1977; *Progressive*, November 1977.

18. Peter Biskind, "Political Prisoners U.S.A.," *Seven Days*, September 8, 1978, p. 22. Young added that he considered himself a political prisoner ten years before when he was arrested during a civil rights demonstration.

political activities—including some twenty-five members of the Black Liberation Army; almost fifty AIM leaders; a smaller number of surviving Black Panthers; a dozen Republic of New Africa persons (a radical Black separatist group); about twenty anti-Vietnam war resisters—including the Camp Pendleton 14; scores of Chicano, Black, and Puerto Rican community activists, nationalists and radicals, and a lesser number of White ones; and dozens of prison inmates who had been given additional sentences for their work with prisoners' rights groups.[19] Contrary to the image cultivated by officialdom, political prisoners are as American as apple pie.

AGENTS OF NATIONAL INSECURITY

At least twenty well-financed federal agencies (of which the FBI and the CIA are only the best publicized) and hundreds of state and local police units actively engage in the surveillance, infiltration, entrapment, disruption and suppression of dissenting groups.[20] The Army employs an estimated 1,200 agents for *domestic* spying. Counterinsurgency methods developed by the government for use in other lands are applied at home to combat civil disturbances caused by racial minorities, student radicals and striking workers. The Army has contingency plans enabling it "to strike concurrently at rioters in as many as 25 major cities."[21] The Justice Department's Law Enforcement Assistance Administration has poured more than $10 billion into research and law enforcement hardware for state and local police, providing such things as electronic sensors, wall-penetration surveillance radar, voice-print equipment, night-vision devices, command and control systems, television street surveillance systems, SWAT squad assault training and riot equipment, and so forth.[22] The unrestricted adoption of surveillance technology by police moved one Rand Corporation engineer to speculate that "we could easily end up with the most effective, oppressive police state ever created."[23]

---

19. See *ibid.*, pp. 24–25, for a partial list.
20. See Frank Donner, "The Theory and Practice of American Political Intelligence," *New York Review of Books*, April 22, 1971, p. 27. A good collection of studies of government repression is Theodore Becker and Vernon Murray (eds.), *Government Lawlessness in America* (New York: Oxford University Press, 1971). See also Michael Parenti, "Creeping Fascism," *Society*, 9, June 1972, pp. 4-8.
21. *New York Times*, March 5, 1972.
22. Les L. Gapay, "Pork Barrel for Police," *Progressive*, March 1972, pp. 33–36; "Deadly Force," *Valley Advocate* (Amherst, Mass.), June 14, 1978, pp. 10, 17–19.
23. Quoted in Robert Barkan, "New Police Technology," *Guardian*, February 2, 1972.

In urban areas where organized crime and corruption are rife, police units have devoted more time to radicals and politically conscious minority members than to mobsters or violent lawbreakers. According to Illinois Police Superintendent James McGuire, there are more police throughout the country "on political intelligence assignments than are engaged in fighting organized crime."[24]

Files stolen from a Media, Pennsylvania, FBI office in 1971 and subsequently published revealed that a great portion of FBI work in the mid-Atlantic region during the 1960s was directed against Black militants, White radicals and antiwar organizers. Relatively little attention was being given to organized crime.

As long as street gangs confine their activities to rape, robbery and burglary within the inner-city communities, they have relatively little trouble from the police. But should these gangs become radicalized, as did the Devils Disciples and the Young Lords in Chicago and New York, they become the objects of intensive police intimidation and attack. Here we might understand one reason why law officers cannot win the "war against crime"—they are not engaged in it, being too busy protecting us from the Red Menace.

The intelligence business is a massive enterprise. Government agencies expend approximately $10 billion each year on intelligence at home and abroad. This is, at best, a rough estimate, since Congress has no exact idea how much money organizations like the CIA are spending or for what purposes.[25] Over a billion dossiers are kept on individuals suspected of harboring unorthodox political views. Data on political dissenters are shared by federal, state and local intelligence units and are sometimes fed to the press and to employers, landlords and others who might have opportunity to harass the persons under surveillance.[26]

"Justice," as the late FBI chief J. Edgar Hoover said in a 1970 television interview, "is merely incidental to law and order. It's a part of law and order but not the whole of it." Indeed, the whole of it,

---

24. Quoted in Donner, "The Theory and Practice of American Political Intelligence," p. 28 *fn*. Some of these units, which became less active after the antiwar movement ended, are being reactivated to deal with the growing antinuclear movement and with the possible growth in "terrorist" organizations.

25. See the excerpts from the report of the House Select Committee investigating the CIA, published in the *Village Voice*, February 16, 1976. The CIA officials questioned by the Committee refused to state the size of their budget.

26. *New York Times*, October 3, 1975. A Senate subcommittee revealed that federal agencies maintained a total of 858 data banks containing about 1.25 billion files on individuals, mostly of a political nature; Martin Michaelson, "Freedom of Information: Up Against the Stone Wall," *Nation*, May 21, 1977, p. 617. In addition, private dossier companies maintain secret files on over 100 million Americans; James B. Rule, *Private Lives and Public Surveillance* (New York: Schocken, 1974).

the indispensable goal of law and order, Mr. Hoover made clear on many occasions, is the preservation of the American socioeconomic status quo. In pursuance of that goal, the FBI has conducted hundreds of illegal burglaries against dissident individuals and organizations, stealing private files, letters and documents, while repeatedly denying any knowledge of such crimes.[27] As the *New York Times* noted: "Radical groups in the United States have complained for years that they were being harassed illegally by the Federal Bureau of Investigation and it now turns out that they were right."[28] FBI agents have infiltrated leftist organizations and liberal

---

27. *New York Times*, September 26, 1975, March 29 and June 24, 1976. FBI agents continued their illegal break-ins even after being ordered to stop by FBI Director Kelley; *New York Times*, August 11, 1976.

28. *New York Times*, November 24, 1974; also William M. Kunstler, "FBI Letters: Writers of the Purple Page," *Nation*, December 30, 1978, pp. 721, 735–740.

ones, including the Southern Christian Leadership Conference and Americans for Democratic Action, with the intent of sabotaging their operations. Undercover agents have fomented ideological divisiveness among political groups, instigated violent conflict between rival Black militant groups and planted false information identifying prominent members of political organizations as federal agents.[29]

The FBI collected secret dossiers, conducted wiretaps and carried out physical surveillance of White House political opponents, journalists, congressmen and members of congressional staffs. The Bureau infiltrated and spied on several labor unions in an attempt to brand them as "communist controlled."[30] At a time when organized crime was expanding its operations in New Jersey, FBI officers in that state were working at fever pitch, planting false information and in other ways attempting to drive a scoutmaster from his job, their reason being that he might contaminate young minds because his wife was a socialist.[31] The FBI keeps a "security index," a list of 15,000 persons, mostly members of leftist groups, who are slated for arrest and detention in case of a "national emergency." Although the law authorizing this practice was declared unconstitutional, the Bureau still maintains the detention list—despite statements to the contrary by its director.[32]

In contrast to the way they treat the left, the FBI and the police have given a free hand to or have actually assisted right-wing extremists. Thus the Bureau provided information and encouragement to organizations like the Minutemen and the John Birch Society in their harassment campaigns against progressive groups. In San Diego, the FBI created and financed a crypto-fascist outfit called the Secret Army Organization (SAO), whose members were heavily armed with automatic weapons and explosives. All SAO activities, ranging from burglary and mail theft to bombings, kidnapping, as-

---

29. *New York Times*, November 24, 1974, January 29, 1975, September 4, 1976, and November 22, 1977; *Chicago Tribune*, February 5, 1976. Documents released under the Freedom of Information Act reveal an FBI campaign of harassment against Puerto Rican independence groups, *New York Times*, November 22, 1977; and William Lichtenstein and David Wimhurst, "Red Alert in Puerto Rico," *Nation*, June 30, 1979, pp.780–782.
30. *New York Times*, February 24, 1975. The FBI used more than a dozen of its agents to break a Teamsters strike in San Francisco; *Guardian*, July 5, 1978. On the Bureau's surveillance of journalists and congressmen see *New York Times*, December 4, 1975.
31. *New York Times*, March 23, 1975.
32. *New York Times*, August 3 and October 25, 1975. For information on political surveillance and repression consult issues of *The Public Eye* (P.O. Box 3278, Washington, D.C.).

sassination plots and attempted murder, were conducted under the supervision of the FBI.[33] Bureau agents infiltrated the Ku Klux Klan and took part in numerous acts of racist terrorism and violence, including the killing of a civil rights activist. According to the sworn testimony of one undercover informer, the FBI rarely acted to head off violent Klan attacks against Blacks and civil rights workers despite advance notice.[34]

Supposedly it is the left's propensity for violence that brings it into confrontations with the law: more truthfully, it is the left's propensity for challenging the established interests. Violence as such has never bothered the FBI or the police; it depends on who is using it against whom. To note a few of many such instances: in 1973, the Center for Cuban Studies in New York City was shattered by a bomb. Right-wing Cuban exile groups had repeatedly threatened to blow up the center, but the FBI made no arrests. In 1974, when two Chicano socialists were killed by bombs planted in their respective cars, the FBI made no arrests. A powerful bomb wrecked the offices of several progressive and civil libertarian groups in New York, injuring three people; the police made only a perfunctory investigation.

When a young Cuban-American, who led an organization seeking normalized relations between the United States and Cuba, was murdered in San Juan, Puerto Rico (right-wing Cuban exiles had frequently threatened his life), the police and FBI took no action.[35] The Unidos Bookstore in the East Los Angeles Chicano community was bombed twice. A group calling itself the provisional wing of the American Nazi party publicly claimed credit for the first attack, but the police failed to arrest anyone. A progressive bookstore in Venice, California, was the target of a fire bomb. Police arrived a half hour after being called. No arrests were made.[36]

The largest army of domestic political spies is not in the FBI but in the local police "red squads" operating throughout the country; 250 of these political intelligence units belong to the federally

---

33. *San Francisco Examiner*, January 11, 1976.
34. *New York Times*, December 3, 1975; *Workers World*, December 12, 1975. On government and police involvement with the KKK see Patsy Sims, *The Klan* (New York: Stein and Day, 1978).
35. *Miami Herald*, May 3, 1979.
36. For an account of these incidents see the *Guardian*, December 12, 1973, March 12 and May 21, 1975. Hundreds of Nazi war criminals live unmolested by the law in the United States. Federal law agencies have done little to extradite them and much to protect them from the investigations of others; some of these criminals have been active in anticommunist causes and may have even worked for U.S. intelligence; see Howard Blum, *Wanted: The Search for Nazis in America* (New York: Quadrangle, 1977).

funded Law Enforcement Intelligence Unit, through which they exchange dossiers and other information. Investigations of red squads in cities like Detroit, Chicago, New York, Washington, D.C., Indianapolis and Baltimore reveal the same dismal record of unlawful burglaries and wiretapping, infiltration of groups engaged in no illegal activity, aid to right-wing terrorist organizations and attacks against the left.[37]

Local, state and federal police closely collaborate with spies, secret agents and security forces employed by giant corporations. There are one million police in the United States, only half of whom are sworn to uphold the law; the rest are hired by moneyed interests to protect moneyed interests and are engaged in the surveillance and harassment of organized labor, peace, environmental, minority and civil liberties groups and individuals who might be troublesome to business interests.[38]

The Central Intelligence Agency matches the FBI and the red squads in its readiness to violate the rights of Americans. The CIA's legal mandate is to act as an overseas intelligence-gathering agency. It is prohibited from engaging in domestic spying. Nevertheless the Agency has been heavily involved in extensive domestic intelligence work, including wiretapping and break-ins, and has collected dossiers on Americans involved in protest activities.[39] In addition,

1. For twenty years the CIA opened the mail of private citizens. Agency officials knew it was illegal and took measures to conceal it. (When the FBI found out about the program, it became an active participant.)

2. The CIA infiltrated the campaign organizations of congressional candidates and admitted to maintaining surveillance on members of Congress.

---

37. Among the sinister organizations that the Chicago police "Red Squad" has kept under surveillance are the World Council of Churches, the Chicago Ethical and Humanist Society, and the Parents-Teachers Association (yes, the PTA); see the *Progressive*, April 1977; also the interview with ACLU investigator Linda Valentino in *People*, June 11, 1979, pp. 89–94, for similar findings on the Los Angeles police; and the *Guardian*, March 30, 1977, for a report on Michigan state police.

38. See the report published by the American Friends Service Committee, *The Police Threat to Political Liberties* (Washington, D.C., 1979); also George O'Toole, *The Private Sector: Rent-a-Cops, Private Spies and the Police-Industrial Complex* (New York: W. W. Norton, 1978; Jim Hougan, *Spooks: The Haunting of America—the Private Use of Secret Agents* (New York: William Morrow, 1978).

39. David Wise, *The American Police State* (New York: Random House, 1976); also Victor Marchetti and John D. Marks, *The CIA and the Cult of Intelligence* (New York: Knopf, 1974); Morton Halperin *et al.*, *The Lawless State* (New York: Penguin, 1976).

3. It has given sums of money to private corporations but has refused to disclose the purpose of such payments. The Agency also owns a complex of insurance companies whose profits are secretly invested in private securities.

4. The CIA has conducted electronic and physical surveillance of newspaper reporters to find out their sources of information concerning government practices. It has infiltrated various news services, and at least forty overseas American correspondents are in its pay.

5. The CIA has worked closely with the notorious foreign intelligence agencies of Chile, South Korea and Iran (under the Shah's regime), allowing them to terrorize, burglarize, kidnap and even murder exiles from these countries residing in the United States.[40]

6. The CIA assiduously propagates its cold war, counterinsurgency view of the world in the groves of academe, maintaining relations with academics on more than one hundred campuses, keeping hundreds of professors on its payroll, conducting its own summer-intern and scholar-in-residence programs, and having hundreds of its agents openly participating in academic conferences.[41]

The CIA has infiltrated student, labor, scientific and peace groups, has secretly financed the writings of "independent" scholars, and has subsidized publishing houses and periodicals. The Center for International Studies at MIT was financed in large part by the CIA as were research programs on mind-control drugs conducted at leading universities throughout the country.[42] Numerous police departments around the country have received training in surveillance, detection and counterinsurgency from the CIA, despite the law's prohibition against domestic activity.

It has even been revealed that the White House and the Treasury and Commerce departments were infiltrated by CIA agents, that the Agency was involved in the Southeast Asia heroin trade, that it had used notorious mobsters to assist in CIA assassination plots, and

---

40. *New York Times*, June 4, 1977; *Chicago Daily News*, May 3, 1977; John D. Hanrahan, "Foreign Agents in Our Midst," *Progressive*, November 1977, pp. 31–35; Jeffrey Stein, "The Letelier-Moffitt Mystery," *Progressive*, November 1977, pp. 36–38.
41. *New York Times*, July 1, 1977, and May 9, 1978.
42. John D. Marks, *The Search for the Manchurian Candidate* (New York: Times Books, 1979). The CIA spent over $25 million experimenting with mind-control drugs, often on unsuspecting persons, and was responsible for the death of at least one government employee.

that it retained a stockpile of poisonous gas despite a previous presidential order to destroy it.[43]

The CIA's crimes against the peoples of other nations are too numerous to record here in any detail. In various Latin American countries, the Agency has used military force, terror and sabotage to bring down democratically elected governments and install reactionary dictatorships friendly to American corporate interests. It has infiltrated and fractured the trade-union movements of other nations. It has funded and trained secret armies, torture squads, death squads and "destabilization" campaigns.[44] It has been involved in the assassination of labor, peasant and student leaders in various states. And it has meddled in the electoral processes of other nations, financing conservative parties and various reactionary movements.[45] The net effect of these activities has not been to defend democracy but to make the world safe for the multinational corporations—often at the expense of democracy.

WATERGATE: "THE SYSTEM WORKS" —FOR ITSELF

In June 1972, a group consisting mostly of ex-CIA agents, some of whom were associated with President Nixon's campaign staff, were caught breaking into the Democratic party headquarters in the Watergate building in Washington. Subsequent investigations revealed that the burglary was only a small part of an extensive campaign involving political espionage, electoral sabotage, wiretapping, illegal entry, theft of private records, destruction of campaign finance records, illegal use of funds, perjury, conspiracy to obstruct justice and other such acts, planned and directed by members of Nixon's campaign staff and White House staff and directly implicating the president himself. Testimony by persons close to the president alleged

---

43. *New York Times*, June 11 and 20, 1975, July 9 and 10, 1975, April 13, 28 and 29, 1976, August 2, 1977; also Alfred W. McCoy, *The Politics of Heroin in Southeast Asia* (New York: Harper & Row, 1973).

44. Jesse Leaf, an ex-CIA agent active in Iran, reported that CIA officials were involved in instructing the Shah's secret police on torture techniques. The CIA torture seminars, he said, "were based on German torture techniques from World War II" and the torture project was "all paid for by the U.S.A.," *New York Times*, January 7, 1979.

45. See Philip Agee, *Inside the Company: CIA Diary* (London: Allen Lane, 1975); Philip Agee, Louis Wolf et al., *Dirty Work: The CIA in Western Europe* (Secaucus, N.J.: Lyle Stuart, 1979). For a film on the illegal and violent methods of the CIA, FBI and other security agencies see "The Intelligence Network," by the Campaign for Political Rights (Washington, D.C., 1979).

that Nixon withheld evidence of a break-in at the office of Daniel Ellsberg's psychiatrist and may have even ordered it, that he tampered with the judge presiding over the "Pentagon Papers" trial of Ellsberg and Russo by offering him the directorship of the FBI while the trial was still in progress, that he failed to respond to warnings from his acting FBI Director, Patrick Gray, who informed him of cover-up efforts by high-placed members of the White House staff, and that he himself had engaged in cover-up activities.

Nixon denied the charges made against him, and there the matter might have stood: the president's word against those of several underlings. Most likely Nixon would have survived in office, albeit as a weakened president. But then it was discovered that tapes of all Oval Office conversations had been maintained, and these revealed that Nixon had known all along about the Watergate cover-up, had been engaging in cover-up activities and had been lying to the public. In August 1974, facing impeachment proceedings in the House of Representatives, Nixon resigned from office. Vice-President Gerald Ford succeeded to the presidency and promptly pardoned Nixon.

Other high-placed persons found guilty in the Watergate affair, such as Herbert Kalmbach, Jeb Magruder and John Dean, were given light sentences. Former Attorney General Richard Kleindienst, who committed perjury before a Senate committee regarding his role in related matters, was allowed to plead guilty to a misdemeanor count of "failing to testify fully," was given a thirty-day suspended sentence and a $100 fine—and won praise from the judge for being an outstanding public servant.

Not long after Nixon retired with his presidential pardon and a yearly $55,000 pension, many opinion makers were announcing with satisfaction that the "the system worked." Apparently they believed the tapes would be there again next time. But how did the system work? It was not only Nixon and his aides who attempted to limit the Watergate crisis to save their necks; Congress and even the press, which is credited with exposing the scandal, played a part in downplaying Watergate, first by not making any investigation for half a year after the break-in, then by emphasizing Nixon's personal role and defining the events in narrow ways. The press and Congress focused on Nixon's failure to pay his income taxes, his personal corruption in appropriating funds for his estate, his use of illegal campaign funds and his attempts at cover-up. Little attention was given to the president's repeated violations of the Constitution, his unlawful and genocidal bombing of Cambodia, his role in the assassination of foreign leaders, his unlawful campaign to destroy radical groups, his use of political sabotage and denial of civil rights to leftists and others, and the unlawful cover-up role played by the entire intelligence community, including the FBI and CIA.

In addition, Congress and the press used Watergate to legitimate the system by treating it as a unique and unprecedented instance of government lawlessness. In fact, for more than half a century the same illegal and clandestine tactics have been and continue to be employed against political heretics. What shocked the establishment politicians was that in this instance the crimes were committed against a segment of the establishment itself—specifically, the Democratic party and mass-media newsmen. (The White House's use of such activities was consistent with Nixon's claim that he had the "inherent executive power" under the Constitution to commit even criminal acts when impelled by considerations of national security. And "national security" seemingly embraced every conceivable area of political activity.[46])

Rather than taking steps to prevent future Watergates, Congress and President Ford initiated measures to ensure that a Watergate *exposure* would not happen again. Political leaders seemed to want not only to ignore the abuses of power that brought on the crisis but to ratify them into law. Thus Ford proposed, and Congress considered, bills that would make it a crime for anyone in government to give the public and the press access to classified information. The problem of the abuse of power is solved to the satisfaction of those in power by making sure no one ever again discovers the abuses. There would continue to be Watergates, but there would be no more Watergate scandals.

The response of congressional leaders to the attempted takeover of the nation by the executive branch has been to increase the power of the executive branch; their response to being completely deceived has been to increase government secrecy; and their response to the dangers of a secret police has been to issue the secret police a license for even wider action. Unable and unwilling to stop police-state crimes, Congress seemed prepared to make them legal.

Nor is the trend likely to reverse itself without a great deal of popular agitation and mass protest. As economic conditions worsen and popular discontent deepens, the necessity for tighter controls becomes more urgent. Unable to satisfy the needs of the people, the establishment must suppress or neutralize growing pressures for change. The increasing repression denotes a weakness, rather than

---

46. Nixon reiterated this position in a television interview with David Frost, May 19, 1977: "When the President does it, that means that it is not illegal."

strength, of the existing politico-economic system, for it is a manifestation of the declining popularity of the dominant interests, and of the growing need to rule by fear and force.

It is difficult to have a "nice" repression. If it is the unenviable task of police to keep a lid on the anger and frustration of the victims of economic, racial and political oppression—a task assigned to them by those in power—then criminal acts by law officers inevitably occur. If it is the job of law officers to suppress radical political ideas and organizations and keep surveillance on every imagined political "troublemaker," then it is not long before the police, the FBI, the CIA, Army Intelligence and other such units begin to see the Constitution as little more than an obstacle to be circumvented or brushed aside. Before long, the state's security forces become a law unto themselves.

By now, it should be apparent that what is called "law and order" is a system of authority and interest that does not and usually *cannot* operate with equitable effect. The laws are themselves *political* rulings and judgments, the outcome of a legislative process that is most responsive to the pressures of the politically stronger, as we shall see. Rather than being neutral judgments, laws are the embodiment of past political victories and therefore favor the interests of the victors. The law is inevitably an outgrowth of the established order which produced it, and by its nature it serves the established interests far better than the unestablished ones. When discussing law and order, then, it is imperative to ask *whose* law and *whose* order we are talking about. While the courts, the security forces and the lawmakers claim to be protecting order as such, they really are protecting a particular kind of order, one that sustains the self-appointed, self-perpetuating oligarchs who rule most of our economic, technological, educational and social institutions.

MIND-CONTROLS FOR LAW AND ORDER

In their never-ending campaign to control behavior that is unacceptable to the existing order, authorities have moved beyond the clubs, bullets and eavesdropping devices of the police and are resorting to such things as electroshock, electrode implantations, mind-destroying drugs and psychosurgery. Since the established powers presume that the present social system is a virtuous one, it follows that those who are prone to violent or disruptive behavior, or who show themselves to be manifestly disturbed about the conditions under which they live, must be suffering from *inner* malfunctionings which can best be treated by various mind-controls. Not only are political and social deviants defined as insane, but sanity itself has a political definition. The sane person is the obedient one who lives in peace and goes to war on cue from his leaders, is not too much troubled by the inhumanities committed against people, is capable of fitting himself into one of the mindless job slots in a profit-oriented hierarchical organization, and does not challenge the established rules and conventional wisdom. If it happens that he actually has been victimized by class conditions—if, for instance, he has been raised in poverty, has received no education, has been repeatedly discriminated against because of his race, cannot find decent housing or employment, and sees his children go hungry and his family and his life falling apart—then he must be able to handle these distresses without resorting to aggressive and troublesome behavior or other such "abnormalities." Most individuals treated by mind-control methods are selected because of their socially deviant and "disturbed" (i.e., disturbing) attitudes and behavior.

What is called sanity or insanity, normal or abnormal, in many cases is a *political* judgment made by privileged medical professionals and other institutional authorities loyal to the status quo. Seldom do they manifest any awareness of the class, racial, sexual and political biases influencing their supposedly scientific diagnoses. Their eagerness to work with law enforcement authorities reflects the ideological presumption under which they operate. Since they accept the present politico-economic system as a good one, then anything that increases its ability to control dissident and unhappy persons—whose rebellion is rarely thought of as a justifiable response to an unjust social system—is also seen as good.[47]

Among the mind-control methods employed, probably the most inhumane is psychosurgery, better known as lobotomy, an operation that modifies behavior by destroying brain cells. Between 600 to 1,000 brain-altering operations are reported in the nation each year, with an unknown number going unreported. Advertised as a cure for anger, anxiety, depression, homosexuality, espousal of unpopular political opinions and refusal to take orders, psychosurgery has been used on rebellious prison inmates, old people, mental patients, incarcerated political dissenters, "hyperactive" children and, most

---

47. One scientist financed by the government has experimented on mental patients, producing placid persons with electrode implants in the brain; see Jose M. Delgado, *Physical Control of the Mind: Toward a Psychocivilized Society* (New York: Harper & Row, 1969).

commonly, women. In most cases, drastic personality changes result: individuals become compliant, robotized, emotionally dulled, less able to cope with new situations and show a striking deterioration in memory and intelligence.[48] One leading psychosurgeon noted that lobotomized men find it difficult to get a decent job and lobotomized women find it easier doing routine housework.[49]

Psychosurgeons at the Harvard Medical School received funds from the Law Enforcement Assistance Administration to study the possibilities of using "corrective treatment" on "violent slum dwellers" who participate in ghetto uprisings. Of painful interest is the case of a 27-year-old Black man arrested in one of the very slum riots that so disturbed the Harvard lobotomists. He was declared unfit for trial and committed to a mental hospital. But his psychiatrist found that much of his mental trouble stemmed from head injuries suffered when police beat him after he was arrested. Proving a difficult patient, he was lobotomized.[50]

There are many weapons in the arsenal of the American mind-control state. Some 200,000 people each year are subjected to electroshock treatment, which has an injurious effect on the brain and the nervous system. From 6 to 8 million Americans a year are treated—mostly with drugs—by the multibillion-dollar mental-health industry, and at least 5,000 patients are killed each year by their treatment.[51] Over 30 million Americans annually are given psychoactive drugs, including the 2 million nonhospitalized persons who take the powerful tranquilizers Thorazine and Stelazine, "sometimes called chemical straitjackets," and of these two million more than a third are poor or Black or both.[52]

Prison inmates who are proponents of revolutionary or Black nationalist ideas or who have engaged in organizing protests among fellow inmates have been singled out for mind-control programs.

---

48. Lani Silver *et al.*, "Surgery to the Rescue," *Progressive*, December 1977, p. 23; "Violence upon the Brain" unpublished monograph by the Greater Boston Medical Committee for Human Rights, n.d.

49. Dr. Walter Freeman quoted in *Liberation*, July/August 1976, p. 39. A congressionally authorized commission endorsed psychosurgery, changing its status from "experimental" to "therapeutic," thus making it easier to bypass legal protections for prisoners and mental patients; Silver *et al.*, "Surgery to the Rescue."

50. "Behavior Control: Psychosurgery Widespread," *Guardian*, April 28, 1976.

51. Bruce J. Ennis, *Prisoners of Psychiatry* (New York: Avon Books, 1972); Philip Brown (ed.), *Radical Psychology* (New York: Harper & Row, 1973); Peter Schrag, "Mind Control," *Playboy*, May 1978, pp. 136–138, 175–178.

52. Schrag, "Mind Control," p. 138. There is evidence that the more powerful mind-control drugs cause serious physical and cerebral disabilities; Susan Abrams, "Mass. Court Probes Meaning of Patient's Rights," *Valley Advocate* (Amherst, Mass.), January 11, 1978.

Prisoners like the socialist Stephen Kessler, charged with disrupting a federal penitentiary by "promoting racial unity, collectivizing the inmate population, attempting to secure legislative inquiries . . . into prison conditions and being involved with outside radical groups," are placed in "behavior modification" units to be subjected to mind-altering drugs, beatings, forced rectal searches, prolonged shackling, isolation and other tortures.[53] In the words of one Oklahoma prisoner: "As long as prisoners confine themselves to gambling, shooting dope, running loan rackets and killing each other, everything is fine. Let them pick up a book on Marx's theory of dialectical materialism and they are immediately branded a communist agitator and locked in solitary confinement."[54]

In a class-action suit against the behavior-modification program in Marion Federal Penitentiary, Warden Ralph Aron testified: "It [the program] is necessary because of the revolutionary attitudes acting throughout our country." Asked by one of the inmates' lawyers, "Is the control unit used to control prisoners with revolutionary attitudes and tactics?" Aron replied: "That is correct."[55]

Behavior-modification programs use several approaches. One technique is to put the prisoner in solitary confinement under excruciating conditions of filth, cold, insufficient food and sensory deprivation and make piecemeal improvements in each of these conditions as a reward if he develops the kind of attitude and behavior patterns desired by the authorities. The conversion must be a "sincere" one and inmates are forced to make repeated and ever more heartfelt confessions of their "criminal and destructive attitudes." "Reformed" prisoners are then forced to harass, oversee and inform upon their fellow inmates and engage in marathon sessions to help break other prisoners. Those who refuse to cooperate are once more subjected to behavior-modification torture themselves.[56]

Another method is "aversion therapy." By the use of electric shock, a prisoner is made to associate pain with whatever the authorities consider bad. In Vacaville, California, inmates accused of homosexuality are shown erotic gay films and shocked whenever a polygraph indicates the prisoner is sexually aroused. Drugs which

---

53. *New York Times*, February 20, 1974; *Guardian*, January 21, 1976.

54. Letter from Chuck Stotts, inmate in Oklahoma State Prison, *Liberation*, February 1975, p. 5.

55. Phyllis Roa, correspondence in *New York Review of Books*, March 9, 1978. See also Marion Brothers News Report (St. Louis, Mo.), Summer 1978, which quotes U.S. District Judge James Foreman as noting that the behavior-modification control unit had been used against prison critics and inmates who were "philosophical and economic dissidents." See his decision in *Bono* v. *Saxbe*.

56. Mark Kleiman, "Drugs Replace Clubs in Nation's Prisons," *Guardian*, May 29, 1974.

induce a death panic by paralyzing one's breathing for a couple of minutes are sometimes used.[57] A group of prisoners in one behavior-modification program wrote: "Anyone who has spent any amount of time in [Dannemora State Hospital] must know at least one person who was sent for punishment, and returned with the mind of a vegetable or moron if he returned at all."[58] Eddie Sanches, who became a socialist while in prison, wrote from the behavior-modification unit at the federal penitentiary in Marion, Illinois: "Since I've been confined here on and off since 1971, I've personally seen over two dozen men driven insane. . . . Others have been driven to suicide or attempts at suicide."[59]

More than a million children are kept in orphanages, reformatories and adult prisons. Most have been arrested for minor transgressions or have committed no crime at all and are jailed without due process. Ninety percent of the children brought into juvenile court are impoverished and of those incarcerated, a majority are Black or some other minority. Many are subjected to beatings, sexual assault, prolonged solitary confinement, mind-control drugs and in some cases psychosurgery.[60]

"Hyperkinetic" or "hyperactive" children in local schools run some of the same risks. Coming to school hungry, physically ill, and under emotional stress from growing up in impoverished, unhappy home and neighborhood conditions, low-income children are regularly treated with powerful mind-control drugs "whose safety has never been documented and whose efficacy has never been proved."[61] Among the ninety-nine symptoms of hyperactivity or "minimal brain dysfunction" listed by the "experts" are such questionable categories as: awkwardness, slowness in finishing work, foot-tapping, wriggling, insistent questioning, interest in sexual matters and "spotty or patchy" intellectual defects.[62] Nearly a mil-

---

57. Joel Meyers, "Electrode Torture and Starvation: Legal 'Therapy' in U.S. Prisons," *Workers World*, May 25, 1973, p. 6.

58. Letter by Dannemora inmates Chester Gibson, Isaac Richards, Felix Huerta, Che Avada, Juke Elmore, Makau-Chuh Champelle in *Workers World*, May 25, 1973, p. 15.

59. Letter to *Workers World*, November 15, 1974; also *Workers World*, May 20, 1977.

60. Thomas Cottle, *Children in Jail* (Boston: Beacon Press, 1977); Kenneth Wooden, *Weeping in the Playtime of Others* (New York: McGraw-Hill, 1976).

61. "Minimal Brain Dysfunction (MBD): Social Strategy or Disease?" report by the Medical Committee for Human Rights, New York, n.d.

62. Peter Schrag and Diane Divoky, *The Myth of the Hyperactive Child* (New York: Pantheon, 1975). Much hyperactivity in children has recently been traced to artificial flavorings and colorings in foods. Often hyperactivity disappears miraculously when children leave school, suggesting that school is not just the setting but the cause of nervousness in many children.

lion youngsters are treated with drugs, at a yearly profit of many millions for the drug industry and with side effects like weight loss, growth retardation and acute psychosis for the children.[63]

Other kinds of medical aggression perpetrated against poor people, especially racial minorities, include the sterilization of women without their knowledge or consent. One of every four Native American women of childbearing age is sterilized.[64] One of every three women in Puerto Rico has been sterilized, most of them involuntarily. In Los Angeles and parts of the Southwest, Chicana women have been forcibly sterilized without their consent. And in parts of North Carolina and South Carolina, Black girls whose mothers are on welfare are routinely sterilized when they turn fifteen.[65] While the federal government is limiting funding for Medicaid abortions and thus depriving low-income women of access to medically safe abortions, the government continues to fund the costs for permanent sterilization operations for low-income people.[66]

Of the institutions devoted to repression and control, none is more pernicious than the mental hospital. There are almost twice as many people in mental institutions as in prisons, and 90 percent of them are confined involuntarily—incarcerated on the testimony of hostile relatives, school authorities, social workers, employers or police. Many are brought in for having committed sexually deviant or other taboo acts, including using marijuana; others are confined for their culturally and politically unorthodox beliefs and practices. Legal protections for mental patients are often nonexistent. Commitment can come without benefit of investigation, counsel, trial or other procedural safeguards, and is based on "medical" considerations that betray a marked class and racial bias.[67] A worker in a New York mental hospital reports:

> One Black woman was admitted . . . because she began screaming at the landlord who had come to evict her and her several children . . . . The Bureau of Child Welfare took her children. This upset her even

---

63. Cottle, *Children in Jail*; and Wooden, *Weeping in the Playtime of Others*.
64. Evidence of massive involuntary sterilization of American Indians was unearthed by a GAO study; see the report in *East West Journal*, March 1977, p. 10.
65. For these and other instances see Claudia Dreifus, "Sterilizing the Poor," *Progressive*, December 1975, pp. 13–18; *Guardian*, June 11, 1975, and July 12, 1978; *New York Times*, June 28 and August 1, 1973.
66. *Valley Advocate* (Amherst, Mass.), February 28, 1979.
67. See Bruce J. Ennis, "Mental Commitment," *Civil Liberties*, October 1969, p. 3; Thomas Szasz, *Law, Liberty and Psychiatry* (New York: Macmillan, 1963); Seymour Halleck, *The Politics of Therapy* (New York: Science House, 1971); Ronald Leifer, *In the Name of Mental Health* (New York: Science House, 1969).

more. She came to the Admissions Committee, crying, hysterical and angry. Obviously a "paranoid schizophrenic. . . ." The comfortable middle-class psychiatrist said so, and after all he *knows*. . . .

Patients [upon release] are often secured jobs working for companies which pay them considerably less than other workers. Social workers advise the patient not to join unions and "make trouble" or they will be returned to the hospital.[68]

Almost all mental patients are forced to take mind-altering drugs—which have damaging side effects to health. In California alone, over a five-year period, 1,600 mental patients died in state hospitals from neglect, drug overuse or other mistreatments.[69] In some of the worst institutions, inmates are forced to live naked in barren cells without bed or toilet. Many are subjected to the sadistic sport of the guards. Some who are quite rational when they first arrive eventually begin to deteriorate. Presumed insane (guilty) by virtue of their presence in the institution, they find it impossible to prove their sanity (innocence). The very protests they make against their oppression are taken as symptoms of illness. One reporter records these impressions of his visit to a mental hospital:

We walked on down the hall. The guide told me about one 60-year-old inmate who had been in since the age of 7. His offense: running away from home. . . . This was the section for killers, I had been told, so I asked what [one] thin man had done.

"He painted a horse. . . . It was in a field. A live horse. He was drunk and somebody bet him he couldn't make a horse look like a zebra, I think, so he painted it and they put him here. For being drunk, probably."

"How long has he been in?"

"Thirty-seven years. By the time they got around to letting him out he really was crazy. . . . For his own good we just can't let him go out of here."[70]

---

68. "Mental Hospitals and the Poor," *Workers World*, December 25, 1970, p. 7. The author is identified only as a "woman worker" within the hospital. For the horrifying story of how an independent-minded, leftist Hollywood actress was railroaded into an asylum, tormented, raped, drugged, electroshocked and finally lobotomized into submission, see William Arnold, *Frances Farmer: Shadowland* (New York: McGraw-Hill, 1978).

69. Findings of a California state commission, reported in the *Guardian*, February 16, 1977. See also the documentary film "Hurry Tomorrow" about a California state mental hospital (distributed by Tricontinental Film Center, New York and Berkeley, Calif.); also Frederic Wiseman's documentary on a Massachusetts state mental hospital, "Titicut Follies."

70. Bruce Jackson, "Our Prisons Are Criminal," *New York Times Magazine*, September 22, 1973, pp. 54, 57.

Police, judges, FBI and CIA agents, surveillance technicians, psychosurgeons, drug-pushing school authorities, prison guards and the attendants in mental institutions all have one thing in common: they work to make the world safe for those on top by exercising arbitrary power over those below—all in the name of peace and security, normality and well-being, law and order.

10

The Mass Media: By the Few for the Many

Much of what is called "culture" does not evolve innocently and haphazardly but consists of values and practices that are cultivated by the dominant interests of society. These values and practices are functional for maintaining the existing politico-economic system of power and property.[1] Those who adhere to conformist beliefs and behavior are more likely to win approval, advancement and material reward within the established institutions than politically unorthodox and radical persons. The rewards and punishments for conformity and nonconformity are distributed by the dominant socializing institutions—the family, community, school, college, church, firm, profession, government, police and courts. Their influence extends not only to the broad contours of our behavior but to the very images in our head. Most of the larger organizations of society, as noted earlier, are controlled by wealthy interests and are dedicated to propagating the myths of the established corporate order, censoring information that does not fit the accepted view of reality, while feeding us information and impressions that do.

Playing a strategic role in all this are the mass media of newspapers, magazines, movies, radio and television. They select most of the information and misinformation that help us define sociopolit-

---

1. For an analysis of how social institutions function as agents of political socialization and class control see Michael Parenti, *Power and the Powerless* (New York: St. Martin's Press, 1978).

ical reality. Almost all the political life we experience is through the media. How we view issues—indeed, what we even define as an issue or event—what we see and hear and what we do *not* see and hear are greatly determined by those who control the mass media. By enlarging our vision through technology, we have actually surrendered control over much of our own sensory experience.[2]

The control the media exercise is of a most insidious kind, giving every appearance of being independent and objective. And most of us, even those who are often critical of news distortions, are inclined to accept what we see, hear or read in the media, or at least we find ourselves letting the media decide what are the important topics and personalities that will occupy our minds.

It is argued that the media are not a crucial factor in political life: one can point to the many Democratic presidents who won elections despite the overwhelming endorsement of their Republican opponents by the press. But despite a low rate of editorial endorsement, Democratic candidates manage to buy political advertisements and receive coverage during their campaigns, unlike socialist candidates, who receive almost no exposure and almost no votes. The argument also overlooks the subtler, more persistent role played by the media in defining the scope of respectable political discourse, channeling public attention in certain directions and determining—in ways that are essentially supportive of the existing socioeconomic structure—what *is* political reality.

It is said that a free and independent press is a necessary condition for democracy, and it is frequently assumed that the United States is endowed with such a press. While the news in "totalitarian" nations is controlled, we Americans supposedly have access to a wide range of competing sources. In reality, the controls exerted over the media in the United States, while more subtle and less severe than in some other countries, leave us with a press that is far from "free" by any definition of the word.

HE WHO PAYS THE PIPER

Who controls the mass media? Five New York banks (Chase Manhattan, Morgan Guaranty Trust, Citibank, Bankers Trust and the Bank of New York) own controlling shares in the three national tele-

---

2. Robert Cirino, *Don't Blame the People* (New York: Vintage, 1972), pp. 30–31. Cirino's book is a well-documented study of how the news media censor and distort the news. For a study of how the corporations control the media see Herbert I. Schiller, *The Mind Managers* (Boston: Beacon Press, 1973).

vision and radio networks (NBC, CBS, ABC) and are powerful shareowners of the *New York Times, Time,* Columbia Pictures and Twentieth Century–Fox. These banks have representatives on the boards of the three networks and control all network fiduciary and debt-financing functions. The networks themselves exercise a controlling interest over publishing houses, film companies and recording companies. They own television stations located in key urban areas, reaching a lion's share of the national audience.[3]

Of the "independent" stations, 80 percent are network affiliates. Practically the only shows these "independents" produce are the local evening newscasts, the rest of their time being devoted to network programs. Most of the remaining "independents" are affiliated with NET, the "educational" network, which receives almost all its money from the Ford Foundation (controlled largely by the Morgan and Rockefeller banks) and a few allied foundations. The Foundation picks NET's board of directors and reserves the right to inspect every program produced with Ford money.

Newspapers show the same pattern of ownership with most of the large-circulation dailies owned by chains like Newhouse, Knight-Ridder and Gannett. The trend in ownership concentration continues unabated, as the large chains buy not only independent papers but also other chains. Less than 4 percent of American cities have competing newspapers under separate ownership; and in cities where there is a "choice," the newspapers offer little variety in editorial policy, being mostly mainstream conservative. Most of the "independents" rely on the wire services and big-circulation papers for syndicated columnists and for national and international coverage. Like television stations, they are independent more in name than content.[4]

Although declining in number, newspapers are doing quite well as business ventures. Through mergers, packaged news service and staff cutting, the larger conglomerates gross many billions of dollars. The same is true of television. In 1979, the three networks were expected to earn $4 billion from advertising revenues.[5] Like most of corporate America, control of the media is principally in the hands

---

3. See Peter Brosnan, "Who Owns the Networks?" *Nation,* November 25, 1978, pp. 561, 577–579. Brosnan notes that "an incredible 77.29% of ABC common stock is held by a tight circle of financial institutions, comprising less than 1% of all ABC stockholders."

4. *New York Times,* February 15, 1977; James Aronson, *Packaging the News* (New York: International Publishers, 1971).

5. Desmond Smith, "Mining the Golden Spectrum," *Nation,* May 26, 1979, p. 595. The radio industry shows a similar pattern of high profits; *New York Times,* December 12, 1977.

of the Morgan and Rockefeller financial empires. And like other businesses, the media corporations are diversified and multinational, controlling film, television and radio outlets throughout Latin America, Asia and the Middle East—as well as Europe and North America.[6] In recent years, independent publishing houses have been bought up by the giant corporations who place a great emphasis on mass-market books and profits; thus, Bobbs-Merrill is owned by ITT, Simon & Schuster by Gulf & Western, and Putnam by MCA. "Is it beyond belief that most of the books in the racks a few years hence may be chosen for you, like television programs, by Mobil, Exxon and the rest?"[7]

The primary function of the media is not to keep the public informed but, like any business, to make money for their owners, a goal seldom coinciding with the need for a vigilant, democratic press. This is not to imply that those who control the media are indifferent to its political content. Quite the contrary: the influence of big-business ownership is reflected in its political content. The media are given over to trivialized "features" and gossip items. Coverage of national and local affairs is usually scant, superficial and oriented toward "events" and "personalities," consisting of a few short "headline" stories and a number of mildly conservative or simply banal commentaries and editorials.[8] As one group of scholars noted after a study: "Protection against government is now not enough to guarantee that a [person] who has something to say shall have a chance to say it. The owners and managers of the press determine which person, which facts, which version of the facts, and which ideas shall reach the public."[9]

Unions have few opportunities in the business-owned media to present programs on the needs and struggles of labor, but corporations, led by the oil companies, underwrite an estimated 75 percent of prime-time shows—both on public and commercial television— "from which they derive enormous public relations benefits."[10]

The business-owned media have little to say about the relationship of the capitalist system to pollution, bad housing, poverty and

---

6. Herbert Schiller, *Mass Communication and American Empire* (New York: Augustus Kelley, Publishers, 1969); and Schiller's *Communication and Cultural Domination* (New York: Pantheon, 1978).

7. Leonard C. Lewin, "Publishing Goes Multinational," *Nation*, May 13, 1978; also *New York Times*, May 18, 1977.

8. For a critique of local news shows see Ron Powers, *The Newscasters* (New York: St. Martin's Press, 1977).

9. Report by the Commission on Freedom of the Press, quoted in Cirino, *Don't Blame the People*, p. 47.

10. J. Foley, "Public TV: Who Does It Serve?" *Guardian*, April 11, 1979.

inflation, the relations between political and business leaders, and the role of the multinational corporations in shaping American interventionist policy abroad. No positive exposure is given to the socialist alternatives emerging throughout the Third World or the socialist critique of capitalism at home.

Many interesting documentaries made by independent film producers, dealing with racism, women's oppression, nuclear energy, conditions in prisons and mental hospitals, labor struggles, poverty, the FBI and U.S. imperialism, reveal a side of reality highly critical of the established order. Few of them have been shown in commercial movie houses or on the major television networks. A documentary on nuclear power, "Paul Jacobs and the Nuclear Gang," was not shown on many PBS affiliates because of pressure from the nuclear industry. A film, "The Battle of Chile," was deemed too controversial (that is, too radical) for public television and of course was never even considered for commercial stations. A documentary on the Vietnam war, "Hearts and Minds," won an Academy award, yet its producer, Columbia Pictures, refused to give it mass circulation and its director had trouble getting financial backing for another film. And a documentary on the working and living conditions of farm workers was not shown on Florida educational television after a few powerful orange growers interceded.[11]

Journalists, columnists and telecasters who occasionally report facts troublesome to the established interests have had their copy censored by superiors. Relying on institutional authorities for much of their information, newspersons are disinclined to be critical of these sources. A police reporter learns to see local crime from the perspective of the police and prosecution. News reports on business developments rely mostly on business and allow little space for the views of organized labor or consumers. Reports about State Department or Pentagon policies rely heavily on State Department and Pentagon releases. Media coverage of the space program uncritically accepts the government's claims about the program's desirability and seldom gives exposure to the arguments made against such costly ventures. In general, most of what is reported as "news" is nothing more than the transmission of official views to an unsuspecting public.

Far from being vigilant critics, most newspersons share the counterrevolutionary, anticommunist assumptions and vocabulary of

---

11. Ralph Nader in the *Washington Star*, March 17, 1979; also the *Progressive*, July 1977, p. 11; Andrew Kopkind, "Hollywood Politics: Hearts, Minds and Money," *Ramparts*, August/September 1975, p. 46; Lynora Williams, "Public TV Suppresses 'Black Britannica,'" *Guardian*, August 30, 1978.

the ruling class that employs them.[12] For years the press has propagated support for cold war policies and attitudes, including hatred and fear of the Soviet Union and of socialism, and support for the domestic witch hunting and red-baiting that culminated in McCarthyism, loyalty oaths, the Korean war and U.S. involvement in Southeast Asia.

Consider how the Vietnam war was covered. From 1945 to 1954 the United States spent several billions of dollars supporting a ruthless French colonialism in Vietnam, but the American public was never informed of this. In the following decade the United States assumed full responsibility for the maintenance of the South Vietnam right-wing dictatorship, but the public neither read nor heard a word of debate in the media about this major policy commitment. In 1965 the United States began a massive buildup of ground forces in Vietnam, but Americans were told that the troops were merely a small support force. The *New York Times* and other major news agencies knew the real nature of the buildup but felt it was in the "national interest" to keep this information from the public.[13] Reporters who covered the Vietnam war were expected to "get on the team"—that is, to share the military's view of the war and its progress—and most of them did. From at least 1965 on, American forces engaged in massive destruction of the Vietnamese countryside, resorting to indiscriminate saturation bombings, defoliation, free-fire zones, and the wholesale killing of civilians. Yet it took years before these facts became widely known. Stories by journalists describing how American soldiers slaughtered hundreds of defenseless women, children and old people in the village of My Lai were turned down by the wire services, several national magazines and news weeklies, one network and major newspapers in New York and Boston.[14]

Throughout the Vietnam war, the insurgent forces were described as the "enemy," although it was never explained why they deserved to be so considered. Reporters who pride themselves on their objectivity saw cities "fall" to the "enemy" when they could

---

12. To give one example among many: the PBS evening radio news show "All Things Considered," on February 22, 1979, described Yugoslavia and Romania as Soviet "satellites," even though Romania was in serious conflict with the Soviet Union regarding use of its troops in the Warsaw Pact and various other foreign policy issues, and even though Yugoslavia had been taking an independent line on domestic and foreign policy for thirty years. The news media never refer to Britain, South Korea or Guatemala as "U.S. satellites." See also James Aronson, *The Press and the Cold War* (Boston: Beacon Press, 1973); Michael Parenti, *The Anti-Communist Impulse* (New York: Random House, 1970).

13. Robert Cirino, *Power to Persuade* (New York: Bantam, 1974), p. 63.

14. More than a year and a half after My Lai, the story was finally broken by Dispatch News Service. See Cirino, *Power to Persuade*, pp. 61–62.

have as easily viewed them as "liberated," or merely changing polit-ical hands.[15] Communists "nibbled" and "gobbled" territory and en-gaged in "terror" attacks, but the war of terror waged by U.S. forces was never labeled as such. During April 1975, as insurgent forces achieved a final victory in Vietnam, the U.S. public was bombarded with stories of refugees fleeing from the "invading communists." But a story buried in the back pages of the *New York Times* noted that most refugees reported they were fleeing because they feared the re-turn of U.S. bombings or they simply wanted to get away from the fighting. Almost none mentioned fear or hatred of communism as a cause for flight.[16] Yet the media continued to give the American public a contrary impression. During this period the press talked constantly of the impending "blood baths" that would supposedly occur when the communists took over in Vietnam, Cambodia and Laos. Subsequent reports by Westerners who remained in these countries revealed that the massacres never materialized. But this fact also was buried in the back pages of newspapers, if reported at all.[17]

Within a couple of years after the Indochina war, the U.S. press began to circulate stories of mass atrocities in Cambodia, claiming that the poorly equipped Khmer Rouge, numbering not more than 35,000 cadres, seized by mysteriously wanton impulses, had some-how managed to slaughter one, two, three or sometimes even four million of their eight million compatriots. How they accomplished this feat was never explained. A series of photographs, purportedly showing grisly executions in Cambodia but declared by U.S. State Department intelligence sources to be fake pictures taken in Thai-land, were nevertheless widely circulated in major publications like *Time, Newsweek* and the *Washington Post*.[18] The press made no mention of the dreadful destruction of life, land and property, the forced urbanization and the starvation caused by the massive U.S. saturation bombings of Cambodia.[19]

---

15. Andrew Kopkind, "The Press at War," *Ramparts*, August/September 1975, p. 37.
16. *New York Times*, March 26, 1975.
17. See *Newsweek*, August 18, 1975; and *Time*, February 16, 1976.
18. Douglas Foster, "$20,000 Profit on Faked Photo," *Pacific Sun*, February 24–March 2, 1978, p. 15. For a balanced eyewitness account of events in Cambodia, by two Southeast Asian specialists, see George C. Hildebrand and Gareth Porter, *Cambodia: Starvation and Revolution* (New York: Monthly Review Press, 1976). In Cambodia, as in every revolution including our own, there were violent acts of retri-bution committed, but the scope of these has never been reliably documented.
19. Hildebrand and Porter, *Cambodia: Starvation and Revolution*. For accounts of similar U.S. mass destruction in Vietnam and Laos see Noam Chomsky, "After Pink-ville," *New York Review of Books*, January 1, 1970; reprinted in Michael Parenti (ed.),

The U.S. media ignored the slaughter by the right-wing Indonesian military of some 500,000 Indonesians, just as it ignored the genocidal campaign waged by this same military in East Timor and the massive repression, torture and murder of progressives in Uruguay, Argentina, Paraguay, Brazil, Zaire, the Philippines and other U.S.-supported procorporate regimes.[20] For twenty-five years, the Shah of Iran, a friend of the U.S. oil companies and a product of the CIA, maimed and murdered tens of thousands of dissident workers, students, peasants and intellectuals. For the most part, the U.S. press ignored these terrible happenings and portrayed Iran as a citadel of stability and the Shah as an enlightened modernizer. Then when a popular revolution overthrew the Shah and executed several hundred of his henchmen, including numerous secret-police torturers, the press suddenly became acutely concerned, giving front-page play to the executions and talking about the "repression" and "cruelty" of the revolution. Habitually, the business-owned press treats the atrocities of U.S.-supported right-wing regimes with benign neglect while casting a stern, self-righteous eye on the popular revolutions that challenge such regimes.[21] Generally the U.S. media defames leftist movements and governments and supports those reactionary governments that are clients of the multinational corporations.[22] The view from the newsroom is essentially the view from the Pentagon and the CIA, which in turn is the view from the boardrooms of Exxon and ITT.

The workings of the capitalist political economy remain another area uncharted by the news media. The need to invest surplus capital; the falling rate of profit; the drive toward profit maximization; the tendency toward instability, recession, inflation and underemployment—these and other such problems are treated scantily, if at

Trends and Tragedies in American Foreign Policy (Boston: Little, Brown, 1971), pp. 190–213.

20. After twelve years of ignoring the Indonesian genocide, the *Times* quoted in its back pages the Indonesian chief of security, Admiral Sudomo, as proudly announcing that "500,000 Communists" were killed after the right-wing takeover in 1965; *New York Times*, December 21, 1977. See also Noam Chomsky, "East Timor: The Press Cover-Up," *Inquiry*, February 19, 1979; Jon Steinberg, "The Battle for Zaire," *Seven Days*, June 16, 1978, pp. 18–20.

21. Even nonrevolutionary democratic governments are treated poorly by the press if they have socialist leanings; see Roger Morris, "Through the Looking Glass in Chile: Coverage of Allende's Regime," *Columbia Journalism Review* (November/December 1974), pp. 15–26; John C. Leggett *et al.*, *Allende, His Exit and Our "Times"* (monograph, Livingston College, Rutgers University, New Jersey, 1978).

22. For a critique of how the U.S. press distorted the news about the leftist movement in Portugal, see Michael Parenti, "Portugal and the Press," *Progressive*, December 1975, pp. 43–45.

all, by newspersons and commentators who have neither the knowledge nor the permission to make critical analyses of multinational corporatism. Instead, economic adversity is ascribed to innocent and unavoidable causes, such as "hard times." One television commentator put it this way: "Inflation is the culprit and in inflation everyone is guilty."[23]

There are few progressive and no socialist commentators in the mass media. In contrast, reactionaries, militarists and ultrarightist elements have a multimillion-dollar yearly propaganda budget donated by business firms and public utilities, and each week across the country they make over 17,000 television and radio broadcasts— with much of the air time freely donated by sympathetic station owners.[24]

On the infrequent occasions when liberals muster enough money to buy broadcasting time or newspaper space, they still may be denied access to the media. Liberal commentators have been refused radio spots even when they had sponsors who would pay. A group of scientists, politicians and celebrities opposing the Pentagon's anti-ballistic missile program was denied a half hour on television by all three major networks despite the fact that they had the required $250,000 to buy time. On various occasions the *New York Times* would not sell space to citizens' groups that wanted to run advertisements against the war tax or against the purchase of U.S. Savings Bonds. A *Times* executive turned down the advertisement against bonds because he judged it not to be in the "best interests of the country."[25]

Denied access to the media, the political left has attempted to get its message across through little magazines and radical newspapers, but these suffer chronic financial difficulties and harassments from police and rightist vigilantes. This has been the fate of radical publications in Cambridge, Massachusetts; Atlanta, Georgia; San Diego, California; and Urbana, Illinois.[26] Student newspapers in junior and senior high schools and even in colleges are regularly censored and restricted when daring to treat controversial topics.[27]

---

23. Garner Ted Armstrong, "Channel Nine News," Ithaca, N.Y., February 11, 1976.

24. Report by In the Public Interest with statistics by Group Research Inc., Washington, D.C., n.d.

25. Cirino, *Don't Blame the People*, pp. 90, 302.

26. Aronson, *Packaging the News*, pp. 67–69.

27. Karen De Witt, "School Press, With More Articles on Controversial Topics, Is Under Increasing Attack," *New York Times*, May 6, 1979.

THE POLITICS OF ENTERTAINMENT

While the entertainment sector of the media, as opposed to the news sector, supposedly has nothing to do with politics, entertainment programs in fact undergo a rigorous political censorship. Shows that treat controversial antiestablishment subjects have trouble getting sponsors and network time.[28] Songs containing references to drugs, prison conditions, junk foods, the draft and opposition to U.S. military interventions have been cut from entertainment shows.[29] When David Susskind submitted five thousand names of people he wished to have appear on his talk show to the advertising agency that represented his sponsor, a third of the candidates were rejected because of their political viewpoints. The censorship code used by Proctor and Gamble for shows it sponsored stated in part: "Members of the armed forces must not be cast as villains. If there is any attack on American custom, it must be rebutted completely on the same show."[30]

While political critiques are censored out of entertainment shows, there is plenty of politics of another sort. In soap operas and situation comedies, adventure programs and detective stories, comic strips and children's cartoon shows, conventional American values are preached and practiced.[31] In the media world, adversities are caused by ill-willed individuals rather than by the economic and social system in which they live, and problems are solved by individual effort within the system rather than collective effort against it. Demonstrators, radicals, revolutionaries and foreign agents are seen as menacing our land, and the military and police as protecting it. In an episode of "Kojak" on CBS, the tough cop was pitted against a terrorist Puerto Rican organization whose members were characterized as violent fanatics and assassins. The organization's name was "El Comite," the same as a Puerto Rican group founded in 1970 and committed to socialism. Shortly after the show was aired, the ever-alert FBI began a series of harassing raids on the homes of real-life members of El Comite.[32] Thus life imitates art.

---

28. Eric Barnouw, *The Television Writer* (New York: Hill and Wang, 1962), p. 27.
29. See Cirino, *Don't Blame the People*, pp. 305–306, for various examples.
30. Murray Schumach, *The Face on the Cutting Room Floor*, quoted in *ibid.*, pp. 303–304.
31. See Rose Goldsen, *Television, The Product Is You* (New York: McGraw-Hill, 1977) for an excellent treatment.
32. " 'Kojak' Attacks El Comite on CBS," *New American Movement*, February 1975.

In the world of Hollywood and television, establishment figures like judges, businessmen, doctors and police are fair and competent—never on the take, never on the make, never corrupt, bigoted or oppressive. Or, if there *are* a few bad ones, they are soon set straight by their more principled colleagues. Various kinds of aggressive behavior are indulged in and even glorified. Conflicts are resolved by generous applications of violence. Nefarious violence is met with righteous violence, although it is often difficult to distinguish the two. The brutal and sometimes criminal behavior of law officers is portrayed sympathetically as one of those gutsy realities of life. One study of "cop and crime" shows found that police actions habitually violate the constitutional rights of individuals. ". . . The message communicated is that evil may be subdued by state-sponsored illegality."[33] The profound importance of the concept of due process is lost as TV police carry out illegal searches and break-ins, coerce suspects into confessing, and regularly use homicidal violence against suspected criminals in shoot-em-up endings. Violence on television and in Hollywood films is omnipresent, often linked to sex, money, dominance, self-aggrandizement and other attributes that represent "manliness" in the male-chauvinist, capitalist American culture.[34]

In the media, women appear primarily in supportive roles as housewives, secretaries and girlfriends. They usually are incapable of initiating actions of their own; they get into difficulties from which they must be extricated by their men. When not treated as weak and scatterbrained, women are likely to be portrayed as devious, dehumanized sex objects, the ornaments of male egoism. In media advertisements, women seem exclusively concerned with getting a fluffy glow shampooed into their hair, waxing "their" floors, making yummy coffee for hubby, getting Johnny's clothes snowy white,

---

33. Stephen Arons and Ethan Katsh, "How TV Cops Flout the Law," *Saturday Review*, March 19, 1977, pp. 11–18.
34. The typical hour of TV network programing contains 7.43 violent episodes. Forty people are murdered every week; the wounded and assaulted are too numerous to contemplate. Saturday morning television, expressly designed for children, averages one violent act every three-and-a-half minutes. See Media Action Project findings reported in the *Guardian*, October 15, 1975; also *Liberation*, July/August 1976, p. 39; and Joseph J. Seldin, "The Saturday Morning Massacre," *Progressive*, September 1974, pp. 50–52. Studies show that adults become more belligerent after large doses of TV violence and more fearful of racial minorities, cities and criminal attack. See Richard Saltus, "The Research Shows Cop Shows Make Us Violent," *Leisure*, February 21, 1976, p. 22; George Gerbner's report in *Psychology Today*, April 1976, finds that heavy TV viewers are more convinced that more police repression is needed to control crime.

and in other ways serving as mindless, cheery handmaidens. Of late there have been a few programs featuring women as lawyers, police and other such lead characters, but even these women still play predominantly sexist roles, operating in an exclusively male-defined world devoid of feminist values and oblivious to the oppressions of women.

Responding to the public outcry against television violence, the networks have adopted new program strategies, substituting sexiness and sexism for murder and mayhem, "replacing gunplay with foreplay," or sometimes combining the two, as in shows like "Charlie's Angels," in which the sexy female investigators catch crooks with alternative doses of seduction and karate.[35] Television's hard sell of soft pornography creates new opportunities to exploit women in the same old sexist ways.

Perhaps most repugnant of all is daytime television, consisting largely of two types of programs. There are soap operas that portray a White, middle-class world of young professionals who spend most of their waking hours wrestling with a never-ending succession of personal crises in a world devoid of politico-economic oppression and social injustice. (Rape, alcoholism, unemployment and wife-battering make their appearance but always as personal rather than social problems.) And then there are quiz shows in which contestants are encouraged to divest themselves of every shred of dignity and privacy in a greedy and sometimes frenetic effort to win money or a new refrigerator or some other such material prize.

Of late there have been a number of what have been called "quality programs," dramatizations or series like "Lou Grant" or "Kaz" and a few movies, which have touched on important sociopolitical issues in essentially evasive ways. While sometimes directing our attention to questions of injustice and oppression, these shows fall short of any kind of systemic critique. Having little to say about economic power, capitalism, class structure and other such issues that would horrify sponsors and networks, "quality programs" are mostly engaged in packaging "modishness and the cosmetics of rebellion."[36]

The mass media are also the White media. For years Blacks and other racial minorities were allowed no appearance on television or radio except in such shows as "Amos 'n' Andy," which specialized in

---

35. Tim Patterson, "TV Substitutes More Sexism for Violence," *Guardian*, July 6, 1977; James Wolcott, "The American Girls Exploit Their Assets," *Village Voice*, October 9, 1978.

36. The phrase is Marcus Raskin's; see his *Being and Doing* (Boston: Beacon Press, 1971), p. 152.

Negro dialect stereotypes, or "Beulah," the Black maid in a White family "who looked as though she'd been taken off a package of pancake mix."[37] More recently, Blacks have been appearing in TV commercials living in make-believe integrated suburbs, in "superstud" detective movie roles and in comedy series like "Sanford and Son," an updated, slicker version of "Amos 'n' Andy." Of the some sixty lead and supporting performers in twenty-one new television shows in the 1978-1979 season, two were Black and one was Puerto Rican. Minorities do make frequent appearances in cop shows—as crooks, pimps, informers or persons in need of assistance from White professionals.[38] What is missing is any treatment of life as it is lived by the great mass of ordinary Black, Chicano and other minority peoples in rural areas and urban ghettos. The few programs about Blacks are created by middle-class Whites who are guided by their own stereotyped notions of how minorities live and feel.[39]

As mentioned earlier, working-class people in general, be they White, Black, Chicano or whatever, have little representation in the entertainment media except as uncouth, ignorant persons, hoodlums, buffoons, servants and other such stock characters. The tribulations of working-class people in this society—their struggle to make ends meet, the specter of unemployment, the lack of decent recreational facilities, the machinations of unscrupulous merchants and landlords, the loss of pensions and seniority, the battles for unionization and union reform, the dirty, noisy, mindless, dangerous, alienating quality of industrial work, the abuses suffered at the hands of bosses, the lives wrecked and cut short by work-connected injury and disease—these realities and others relating to class struggle and class exploitation are given no dramatic treatment in the business-owned media.

One-fifth of all television time is taken up with commercials that often characterize people as loudmouthed imbeciles whose problems are solved when they encounter the right medication, cosmetic,

37. Bob Ray Sanders, "Black Stereotypes on TV: 25 Years of 'Amos 'n' Andy,'" *New American Movement*, February 1975, p. 9.

38. Of the nine Blacks portrayed in one year of episodes of "Hawaii Five-O," a detective adventure show, five were pimps, two prostitutes and two students. The eleven Hawaiians and Polynesians in the show included two pimps, two assassins and three mobsters—according to a study by the U.S. Civil Rights Commission, which charged the television industry with perpetuating racial and sexual stereotypes; see *New York Post*, August 16, 1977.

39. The same is true of the White ethnic minorities; see Randall M. Miller (ed.), *Ethnic Images in American Film and Television* (Philadelphia: Balch Institute, 1978); Michael Parenti, "The Media Are the Mafia: Italian-American Images and the Ethnic Struggle," *Monthly Review*, March 1979, pp. 20-26.

cleanser or gadget. In this way industry confines the social imagination and cultural experience of millions, teaching people to define their needs and life styles (and those of hubby, wifey and baby) according to the profit dictates of the commodity market.[40]

Not all air time is given to commercial gain. The Federal Communications Commission (FCC) requires that broadcasters devote about 3 percent of air time, worth a half-billion dollars, to public-service announcements. Like the free space donated by newspapers and magazines, this free time is monopolized by the Advertising Council, a group composed of representatives from the networks, national magazines, advertising agencies and big corporations. No public-interest groups are represented. While supposedly "nonpolitical," the Council's "public service" commercials laud the blessings of free enterprise and urge viewers to buy U.S. Savings Bonds. With little regard for the truth, the ads tell us that business is "doing its job" in hiring veterans, minorities and the poor. Workers are exhorted to take pride in their work and produce more for their employers—but nothing is said about employers paying more to their workers. The ads blame pollution on everyone (but not on industry) and focus on littering as the major environmental problem. Unemployment is a matter of better "job training." In general, social and political problems are reduced to individual failings or evaded altogether, and the air time that could be used by conservationists, labor, consumer and other public-interest groups has been preempted by an Advertising Council which passes off its one-sided ads as noncontroversial and nonpartisan.[41]

REPRESSING THE PRESS

On those rare occasions when the news media expose the murky side of official doings, they are likely to encounter serious discouragements from public authorities. Government officeholders are inclined to treat news that places them in an unfavorable light as "slanted" and exert pressure on reporters to present the "accurate" and "objective" (that is, uncritical and supportive) viewpoint. More than any other public figure in recent years, former Vice-President Spiro Agnew repeatedly launched attacks upon the press. Agnew

---

40. For a provocative study of how advertising has been used to create the kind of consumerism needed by capitalism, see Stuart Ewen, *Captains of Consciousness* (New York: McGraw-Hill, 1976).

41. Bruce Howard, "The Advertising Council: Selling Lies," *Ramparts*, December/January 1974–1975, pp. 25–32.

said nothing about the press's monopoly structure but criticized its occasional willingness to air facts and commentaries critical of the White House, a tendency that was certain evidence in his mind of a "liberal" bias and lack of "responsibility." This kind of attack by Agnew allowed the media to appear as liberal defenders of free speech against government censorship, instead of supporters of the established order as they more commonly have been.[42]

The federal government has used the FBI to harass and arrest newspersons who persist in writing troublesome news reports;[43] and the Justice Department won a Supreme Court decision requiring reporters to disclose their information sources to grand jury investigators, in effect, reducing the press to an investigative arm of the courts and the prosecution—the very officialdom over whom it is supposed to act as a watchdog. Dozens of reporters have since been jailed or threatened with long prison terms on the basis of that decision.[44] On repeated occasions the government has subpoenaed documents, films, tapes and other materials used by news media. Such interference imposes a "chilling effect" on the press, an inclination to think twice before reporting something, a propensity—already evident in news reports—to slide over the more troublesome and damning aspects of a story and censor oneself in order to avoid censorship by those in power. One might recall how the president of CBS offered to cooperate more closely on news stories about the White House in return for government assistance in quashing a congressional contempt citation against CBS for its mildly critical documentary about the Pentagon.[45]

Most American presidents and other top officials have attempted to control or slant the news, winning the cooperation of the press in killing "sensitive" stories and planting favorable ones. Members of the press knew that our government was flying U-2 planes over Soviet territory; they knew that our government was planning an invasion of Cuba at the Bay of Pigs; they knew that there were facts about the Tonkin Bay incident in Vietnam which differed from the official version; they knew that the United States was engaged in a massive, prolonged saturation bombing of Cambodia. But in each instance they chose to act "responsibly" by not informing the American public. "The old blather about 'responsibility' to keep secrets

---

42. See Cirino, *Don't Blame the People*; William E. Porter, *Assault On the Media* (Ann Arbor: University of Michigan Press, 1977).
43. Porter, *Assault On the Media*.
44. *United States* v. *Caldwell*, 33 L. Ed. 2d 626 (1972); also *New York Times*, September 4, 1976, and November 19, 1978.
45. *Ithaca* (N.Y.) *New Times*, January 18, 1976.

instead of exposing abuses has begun to creep back into press parlance," complained columnist Jack Anderson.[46] "Journalistic responsibility" should mean the unearthing of true and significant information. But the "responsibility" demanded by government officials and often agreed to by the press means the opposite, the burying of some piece of information precisely because it is troublesomely true and significant.

The relationship between the CIA and much of the press offers another example of how the media have been anything but independent of the official viewpoint. More than four hundred American journalists, including nationally syndicated columnists, have carried out secret assignments for the CIA over the last three decades. Publishers and top executives from the networks, news services and leading newspapers and magazines have actively cooperated with the Agency.[47] The CIA has had two principal objectives in developing its media network. One is to provide a cover for hundreds of operatives and to use journalists as operatives to gather intelligence and do espionage throughout the world. The other is to manipulate the news so as to create a climate of opinion supportive of the government's policy objectives.

From what has been said so far it should be clear that one cannot talk about a "free press" apart from the economic and political realities that determine who owns and controls the media. Freedom of speech means not only the right to hear both sides of a story (Republican and Democratic) but the right to hear *all* sides. It means not only the right to *hear* but the right to *be heard*, to talk back to those in government and in the network offices and newsrooms, something few of us can do at present.

There is no such thing as unbiased news. All reports and analyses are selective and inferential to some inescapable degree—all the more reason to provide a wider ideological spectrum of opinions and not let one bias predominate. If in fact we do consider censorship to be a loathsome danger to our freedom, then we should not overlook the fact that the media are *already* heavily censored by those who own and control them. Creative, imaginative, progressive, socialist, antiimperialist, communalist, anarchist, radical feminist, Third World and working-class themes are consistently programmed out

---

46. Quoted in *Ramparts*, July 1975, p. 8.
47. *New York Times*, December 25, 26 and 27, 1977; Carl Bernstein, "The CIA and the Media," *Rolling Stone*, October 20, 1977. The FBI also used news media to plant damaging stories; see Joe Trento and Dave Roman, "The Spies Who Came in From the Newsroom," *Penthouse*, August 1977, pp. 45–50.

of the media, while violent, competitive, sexist, authoritarian, trivial, tasteless, individuated, privatized, consumeristic, capitalist, racist, progovernment themes are programmed in. The very process of selection allows the cultural and political biases and class interests of the selector to operate as a censor. Some measure of ideological heterodoxy could be achieved if public law required all newspapers and broadcasting stations to allot substantial portions of space and time to a diverse array of political opinion, including the most radical and revolutionary. But given the interests the law serves, this is not a likely development.

Ultimately the only protection against monopoly control of the media is ownership by community people themselves, with legally enforceable provisions allowing for the maximum participation of conflicting views. As A. J. Liebling once said, freedom of the press is guaranteed only to those who own the presses. In Europe some suggestive developments have taken place: the staffs of various newspapers and magazines like *Der Stern* in Germany and *Le Figaro* in France have used strikes to achieve greater editorial control of the publications they help produce. And *Le Monde's* management agreed to give its staff a 40 percent share in the profits and a large share in managerial decisions, including the right to block any future sale of the paper.[48]

While they point to alternative forms of property control, these developments are themselves not likely to transform the property relations of a capitalist society and its mass media. With few exceptions, those who own the newspapers and networks will not relinquish their hold over private investments and public information. Ordinary citizens will have no real access to the media until they come to exercise direct community control over the material resources that could give them such access, an achievement that would take a different kind of economic and social system than the one we have. In the meantime, Americans should have no illusions about the "free press" they are said to enjoy.

---

48. Aronson, *Packaging the News*, p. 99.

11

The Sound and the Fury: Elections, Parties and Voters

As noted earlier, most institutions in America are ruled by self-appointed, self-perpetuating business elites who are answerable to no one. Presumably the same cannot be said of *government*, since a necessary condition of our political system is the regular election of those who govern, the purpose being to hold officeholders accountable to the people who elect them. Whether or not the electoral process keeps government responsive to public needs is a question to be treated here.

THE HARVESTING OF VOTES

The harvesting of votes is the task of the political parties. The job has gone to persons who have enjoyed a class and ethnic familiarity with the common voters and who have been sufficiently occupied by the pursuit of office and patronage to remain untroubled by questions of social justice. Alan Altshuler describes the machine politicians:

> Though they distributed favors widely, they concentrated power tightly. Though their little favors went to little men, the big favors went to land speculators, public utility franchise holders, government contractors, illicit businessmen, and of course the leading members of the machines themselves. . . .
> The bosses were entrepreneurs, not revolutionaries. They provided specific opportunities for individual representatives of deprived groups,

184

but they never questioned the basic distribution of resources in society. Their methods of raising revenue tended toward regressivity. On the whole, the lower classes paid for their own favors. What they got was a *style* of government with which they could feel at home. What the more affluent classes got, though relatively few of them appreciated it, was a form of government which kept the newly enfranchised masses content without threatening the socio-economic status quo.[1]

Today, machine politicians still perform little favors for little men but seldom address themselves to the larger problems facing ordinary citizens. Party regulars take "the existing socio-economic structure . . . as given," Dahl notes. They assume "that the physical and economic features of the city are determined by forces beyond their control."[2]

These same politicians, however, are quite ready to serve those "forces beyond their control." When Chicago's late Mayor Daley took office, he immediately contacted the city's most prominent businessmen, asking them "to list the things they thought most needed doing." The intrinsic worth of a proposal impressed him less than the influential credentials of the people whose proposal it was.[3]

Since their primary concern is to maintain their own positions of influence within society's established order, party politicians, like most churchmen, union leaders and college administrators, generally take a conservative approach, showing little sympathy for new and potentially disruptive demands and little taste for the kind of dialogue and confrontation that one associates with the democratic process.[4] "The man who raises new issues," observed Walter Lippmann more than a half-century ago, "has been distasteful to politicians."[5]

"The rigidity of the two-party system is, I believe, disastrous," added Lippmann. "It ignores issues without settling them, dulls and wastes the energies of active groups, and chokes off the protests which should find a civilized expression in public life."[6] That scathing judgment has stood the test of time. Today the two parties are

---

1. Alan A. Altshuler, *Community Control: The Black Demand for Participation in Large American Cities* (New York: Pegasus, 1970), pp. 74–75.

2. Robert Dahl, *Who Governs?* (New Haven: Yale University Press, 1961), p. 94.

3. Edward Banfield, *Political Influence* (New York: Free Press, 1961), p. 251. For a critical study of the Daley administration see Milton R. Rakove, *Don't Make No Waves—Don't Back No Losers* (Bloomington, Ind.: Indiana University Press, 1976).

4. Michael Parenti, "Power and Pluralism: A View from the Bottom," *Journal of Politics*, 32, August 1970, pp. 501–530.

5. Walter Lippmann, *A Preface to Politics* (Ann Arbor: University of Michigan Press, 1962), p. 195. Originally published in 1914.

6. *Ibid.*, p. 197.

still more ready to blur than clarify political issues. Electoral contests, supposedly providing democratic heterodoxy, have generated
a competition for orthodoxy. In politics, as in economics, competition is rarely a safeguard against monopoly and seldom a guarantee
that the competitors will offer the consumer a substantive choice.

This is not to say there are no differences between (and within)
the major parties or that one party is not preferred by some people
over the other. Generally the racial minorities, union workers,
lower-income urban groups and more liberally oriented professionals support the Democratic party, while the White Protestant, rural,
upper-income groups, big and small businessmen and the more conservative elements of the electorate tend to make their home in the
Republican party.[7] These differences are sometimes reflected in the
voting records of Democratic and Republican legislators, albeit
within a narrow range of policy alternatives.

When magnified by partisan rhetoric, the differences between
the parties appear worrisome enough to induce many citizens to
vote—if not *for* then *against* someone. While there is no great hope
that the party of their choice will do much for them, there persists
the fear that the other party might make things even worse. This les-
ser-of-two-evils approach is perhaps the most important inducement
to voter participation.[8] It is not quite accurate to characterize the
Republicans and Democrats as Tweedledee and Tweedledum. Were
they exactly alike in image and posture, they would have even more
difficulty than they do in maintaining the appearances of choice.
Therefore, it is preferable that the parties be fraternal rather than
identical twins.

From the perspective of those who advocate a fundamental
change in our national priorities, the question is not, "Are there differences between the parties?" but, "Do the differences make a difference?" For the similarities between the parties in organization,
funding, ideological commitment and policy loom so large as frequently to obscure the differences. The Democratic and Republican
parties are both committed to the preservation of the private corporate economy; the use of subsidies, deficit spending and tax allow-
ances for the bolstering of business profits; the funneling of public

---

7. The delegates to the 1976 Republican national convention were mostly White
middle-aged men, more than half of whom earned over $35,000 a year; Preston
Gralla, "Republicans: A Dying Breed," *Valley Advocate* (Amherst, Mass.), September
1, 1976, p. 9.

8. See Murray Levin, *The Alienated Voter* (New York: Holt, Rinehart and Winston,
1960), pp. 37–39. A similar sentiment was expressed by many low-income voters in
Newark and New Haven when explaining their somewhat reluctant preference for the
Democratic party. See my "Power and Pluralism: A View from the Bottom," p. 515.

resources through private conduits, including whole new industries developed at public expense; the concoction of domestic programs that act as palliatives for the less fortunate segments of the population; the use of repression against opponents of the existing class structure; the defense of the multinational corporate empire and intervention against social revolutionary elements abroad. In short, Republicans and Democrats are dedicated to strikingly similar definitions of the public interest, at great cost to the life chances of underprivileged people at home and abroad.

Disagreements between the two parties focus principally on which of them is better qualified to achieve commonly shared goals within a narrow range of means. For instance, Democrats seek to ensure profit growth, limit unemployment and induce economic recovery by increasing consumer spending and government purchases. The Republican approach is to maintain profit growth and to stabilize budgets by limiting wages and cutting nonmilitary spending, especially social services like food stamps and Medicaid. Yet even this pattern is not a fixed one, for Republicans frequently accept greater deficit spending in order to maintain corporate profits—as did Presidents Nixon and Ford, while Democrats advocate cutbacks in human services in order to limit spending—as did President Carter.

The similarities between the parties do not prevent them from competing vigorously for the prizes of office, expending huge sums in the doing. The very absence of significant disagreement on fundamentals makes it all the more necessary to stress the personalized, stylistic features that differentiate oneself from one's opponent. As with industrial producers, the merchants of the political system have preferred to limit their competition to techniques of packaging and brand image. With campaign buttons and bumper stickers, television commercials and radio spots, sound trucks and billboards, with every gimmick and ballyhoo devoid of meaningful content, the candidate sells his image as he would a soap product to a public conditioned to such bombardments.[9] His family and his looks; his experience in office and devotion to public service; his sincerity, sagacity and fighting spirit; his military record, patriotism and ethnic background; his determination to limit taxes, stop inflation, improve wages and create new jobs by attracting industry into the area; his desire to help the worker, farmer, and business person, the young

---

9. See Joe McGinnis, *The Selling of the President 1968* (New York: Simon and Schuster, 1970). For an earlier collection of case studies of mass-media merchandising of political issues and candidates, see Stanley Kelley, Jr., *Professional Public Relations and Political Power* (Baltimore: Johns Hopkins Press, 1956).

and old, the rich and poor and especially those in between; his eagerness to fight poverty but curb welfare spending while ending government waste and corruption and making the streets and the world itself safe by strengthening our laws, our courts and our defenses abroad, bringing us lasting peace and prosperity with honor and so forth—such are the inevitable appeals which like so many autumn leaves, or barn droppings, cover the land each November.

THE TWO-PARTY MONOPOLY

The two major parties cooperate in various stratagems to maintain their monopoly over electoral politics and discourage the growth of radically oriented third parties. "Each views with suspicion the third party movements in America," writes one Washington journalist. "Each in effect is committed to the preservation of the other as its chief competitor."[10] Republicans and Democrats understand that neither will go "too far"; neither will move beyond a narrow range of goals and means; neither has much appetite for the risks of social change; each helps to make the world safe for the other.

All fifty states have laws, written and enforced by Republican and Democratic officials, regulating party representation on the ballot. Frequently the provisions are exacting enough to keep smaller parties from participating. In order to win a place on the ballot, minor parties are required to gather a large number of signatures on nominating petitions, an expensive, time-consuming task. In some states they must pay exorbitant filing fees ($5,000 in Louisiana for an independent candidate) and observe exacting deadlines when collecting and filing nominating petitions. In Pennsylvania third-party candidates for statewide office had to obtain the signatures of 36,000 registered voters within a three-week period; while in Maryland independent candidates were required to collect 51,000 signatures in a short period of time. Sometimes a 5 percent requirement for signatures of registered voters has been interpreted to mean 5 percent of voters from every district within the state—an impossible task for a third party whose base might be confined to a few urban areas.

Persons who sign nominating petitions for unpopular third parties sometimes find their names publicized by town clerks in an effort to embarrass them into withdrawing their names, as happened in Vermont in regard to Communist party petitions. In some states

---

10. Douglass Cater, *Power in Washington* (New York: Random House, 1964), p. 180.

voters who are registered with the major parties are not allowed to sign or circulate minor-party nominating petitions. Petitions are often thrown out on technicalities arising from ambiguities in election laws, compelling the minor party to pursue costly court battles which, whether won or lost, usually are decided *after* the election. Sometimes during primary time, minor parties are raided by large numbers of voters from the major-party organizations who take over the third-party ticket—as was done in 1947 by the Democrats against the American Labor party in New York.

According to one survey, half the nation's thirteen-year-olds believe it is against the law to start a third political party—an indication of how institutionalized the two-party system has become.[11] In a sense, they are right: the law is used as a hurdle and a discouragement against new parties. Of the sparse funds available to minor parties, a large portion is spent not on raising issues and campaigning but on legal fees and other problems connected with trying to gain access to the ballot.

The system of representation itself limits the opportunities of third parties. The single-member district elections used throughout most of the United States tend to magnify the strength of the major parties and the weakness of the smaller ones, since the party that polls a plurality of the vote, be it 40, 50 or 60 percent, wins 100 percent of a district's representation with the election of its candidate, while smaller parties, regardless of their vote, receive zero representation. This is in contrast to a system of *proportional representation*, which provides a party with legislative seats roughly in accordance with the percentage of votes it wins, assuring minor parties of some parliamentary presence. Duverger notes that under the winner-take-all system "the party placed third or fourth is underrepresented compared with the others: its percentage of seats is lower than its percentage of votes, and the disparity remains constantly greater than for its rivals. By its very definition proportional representation eliminates this disparity for all parties: the party that was at the greatest disadvantage before is the one to benefit most from the reform."[12]

---

11. See the *Progressive*, March 1977, p. 14.
12. Maurice Duverger, *Political Parties* (New York: Wiley and Sons, 1955), p. 248, and the discussion on pp. 245–255; E. E. Schattschneider, *Party Government* (New York: Holt, Rinehart and Winston, 1960), pp. 74–84. Not long after World War II, Benjamin Davis and Peter Cacchione, Communists elected to the City Council in New York, lost their seats when the city shifted from proportional representation to single-member districts. The change was explicitly intended to get rid of the Communists and discourage the growth of other dissident parties. Proposals were introduced to abolish proportional representation in local elections in Cambridge, Massachusetts, in 1972 after victories by a few radically oriented candidates.

The winner-take-all, single-member-district system deprives the minority parties not only of representation but eventually of voters too, since not many citizens wish to "waste" their ballots on a party that seems incapable of achieving legislative representation. Some political scientists argue that proportional representation is undesirable because it encourages the proliferation of "splinter parties" and leads to legislative stalemate and instability. In contrast, the present two-party system muffles rather than sharpens ideological differences and allows for the development of a consensus politics devoid of fragmentation and polarization. But one might question why the present forms of "stability" and "consensus" are to be treated as sacred. Stability is often just another word for "keeping things as they are." Whose stability and whose consensus are we talking about? And one might wonder whether stalemate and fragmentation—with their consequent ill effects on the public interest—do not characterize the *present* political system in many policy areas. Above all, the muting effects of the two-party system so thoroughly limit the arena of political choice and dialogue as to manufacture a "stability" and "consensus" that fail to represent the needs of the populace.

If, despite rigged rules and official harassments, radical groups continue to prove viable, then authorities are likely to resort to more violently coercive measures. Almost every radical group that has ever managed to gain some grass-roots organizational strength has become the object of official violence. The case of the American Socialist party is instructive. By 1918 the Socialist party held 1,200 offices in 340 cities including seventy-nine mayors in twenty-four different states, thirty-two legislators and a member of Congress.[13] In 1919, after having increased its vote dramatically in various locales, the Socialists suffered the combined attacks of state, local and federal authorities. Their headquarters in numerous cities were sacked by police, their funds confiscated, their leaders jailed, their immigrant members deported, their newspapers denied mailing privileges and their elected candidates denied their seats in various state legislatures and in Congress. Within a few years, the party was finished as a viable political force. While confining themselves to legal and peaceful forms of political competition, the Socialists discovered that their opponents were burdened by no similar compunctions. The guiding principle of the establishment was (and still is): *When change threatens to rule, then the rules are changed.*

A more recent example is the case of the radical judge, Justin Ravitz, who was elected to Detroit's criminal court in 1972. Ravitz

---

13. James Weinstein, *The Decline of American Socialism* (New York: Monthly Review Press, 1967).

"FROBUSH, THIS PLACE ISN'T BIG ENOUGH
FOR ANY THREE-PARTY SYSTEM."

had long been active in Detroit as a crusading lawyer and had won a good deal of popular support from the Black community, the peace movement and some labor unions. The day after his election, the Detroit Bar Association called for the elimination of popularly-elected judges and for the appointment of all judges by the governor. A spokesman for the bar admitted that this proposal was designed to prevent people like Ravitz from gaining office.[14]

The weeding out of political deviants is carried on *within* as well as outside the major parties. It begins long before the election campaign and involves social forces that extend beyond the party system. First, with few exceptions, acceptable candidates must be born or educated into the middle or upper class, displaying the linguistic and social styles of bourgeois personages. This requirement effectively limits the selection to business and professional people. Then they must express opinions of a kind that win the support of essentially conservative community leaders, party bosses and other estab-

14. Margaret Borys, "Detroit Judge Is a Radical," *Guardian*, December 13, 1972, p. 6.

lished interests. Finally aspiring candidates must have large sums of money of their own or access to those who do. As one senator remarked: "The fundamental problem is that the ability to raise money starts the screening-out process. If you can't get the money, you don't get the nomination."[15] On election day "the voters will have their choice between *two* such carefully chosen candidates. But the real election in which the candidates compete for the backing of business and of its representatives in the parties and the press, has already occurred."[16]

Money is the lifeblood of electoral politics, helping to determine the availability of manpower, organization, mobility and media visibility. Without money, the politician's days are numbered. Commenting on the plight of reformers in Congress, Representative Charles Vanik observed: "As things are now, the public-interest members here have no reward except personal satisfaction. In the long run most of them face defeat by the big-money people. Many of the best men who come here lose after one or two terms."[17]

The Democratic presidential candidate in 1972, Senator George McGovern, found himself abandoned in the early stages of his campaign by wealthy liberal financiers who opposed his proposals for tax reform and income redistribution.[18] McGovern quickly retreated from these positions, placing an advertisement in the *Wall Street Journal* to assure its readers of his faith in the private-enterprise system. In subsequent speeches he informed businessmen that if he were elected, profits would "be bigger than they are now under the Nixon Administration." McGovern eventually did receive some support from wealthy donors, although hardly as much as Nixon.

Radical candidates face great difficulties. Besides coping with severe money problems, they must try to develop a plausible image among a citizenry conditioned for more than a century to hate and fear "anarchists," "socialists," "communists," and "leftists." They find themselves dependent for exposure on mass media that are owned by the conservative interests they are attacking. They see that, along with the misrepresentations disseminated by a hostile press, the sheer paucity of information and haphazard reportage can make any meaningful campaign dialogue nearly impossible. The

---

15. Charles Mathias of Maryland, quoted in Richard Harris, "Annals of Politics: A Fundamental Hoax," *New Yorker*, August 7, 1971, p. 54.
16. John Coleman, "Elections Under Capitalism, Part 2," *Workers' Power*, September 1–14, 1972, p. 11.
17. Quoted in Harris, "Annals of Politics," p. 59.
18. "McGovern's Views Alarm Big Donors on Wall Street," *New York Times*, July 3, 1972.

dissenters compete not only against well-financed opponents but also against the media's many frivolous and stupefying distractions. Hoping to "educate the public to the issues," they discover that the media allow little opportunity for the expositions needed to make their position understandable to voters who might be willing to listen.

A mass electorate makes it impossible for a candidate to appeal directly to the voters. If the media do not cover a third party's campaign, most people remain unaware of its existence. Television gives complete day-by-day coverage to the major-party nominating conventions, and prime-time exposure to the major presidential candidates, inviting them to numerous "Meet the Press" and "Face the Nation" appearances, and offering more than a sufficient amount of gossipy coverage of the charms and foibles of their family members. During the 1976 campaign the networks gave Jimmy Carter and Gerald Ford ten to fifteen minutes of prime-time coverage every evening, while the Socialist Worker party presidential candidate, Peter Camejo, received less than two minutes' exposure in his entire twenty-four-month campaign. "The media do not simply reflect the credibility of a candidate; to a great extent, they create credibility."[19] By withholding coverage from third-party candidates while bestowing it lavishly on Democratic and Republican nominees, the media perpetuate major-party electoral success and minor-party failure.[20]

> It is ironic that while more and more Americans are withdrawing their allegiance from the major parties—and the polls show the number of independents at around 40 percent and growing—the major parties have steadfastly continued to enjoy unchallengeable preeminence in American politics. It is not necessarily because they are valued and respected, but rather because of the biases built into the system.[21]

On those infrequent occasions when progressive dissenters win office, they are often relegated to obscure legislative tasks and receive little cooperation from legislative leaders or bureaucratic

19. Jim McClellan and David E. Anderson, "The Making of the Also-Rans," *Progressive*, January 1977, p. 28, and *passim*.

20. When the Socialist Worker party candidate for president, Peter Camejo, was accorded a half-hour on nationwide television at 1:30 A.M. (the "Tomorrow Show"), his party headquarters was deluged by thousands of pieces of mail from people requesting more information, sending small donations, and asking questions like, "Why haven't I heard about you before?"

21. McClellan and Anderson, "The Making of the Also-Rans," p. 29.

heads. To achieve some effectiveness in a legislative institution whose forces can easily undercut him, the newly arrived representative frequently decides that "for now" he must make his peace with the powers that be, holding his fire until some future day when he can attack from higher ground. To get along he decides to go along; thus begins the insidious process that lets a person believe he is still opposing the ongoing arrangements when in fact he has become a functional part of them. There are less subtle instances of cooptation, as when reformers are bought off with promotions and favors by those who hold the key to their advancement. Once having won election, they may reverse their stands on fundamental issues and make common cause with established powers, to the dismay of their supporters. Those few reformers who persist in making a nuisance of themselves may subsequently find themselves redistricted out of existence, as happened during the 1970–1972 period in New York City to three of the more outspokenly liberal Democratic congressmen and five of the more liberal Democratic state legislators.

In sum, of the various functions a political party might serve—(1) selecting candidates and waging election campaigns, (2) articulating and debating major issues, (3) formulating coherent and distinct programs, (4) implementing a national program when in office—our parties fulfill only the first with any devotion or success.[22] The parties are loose conglomerations of local factions organized around one common purpose: the pursuit of office. For this reason, American parties have been characterized as "nonideological." And indeed they are—in the sense that their profound ideological commitment to capitalism at home and abroad and to the ongoing class structure is seldom made an explicit issue. The parties have a conservative effect on the consciousness of the electorate and on the performance of representative government. They operate from a commonly shared ideological perspective which is best served by the avoidance of iconoclastic politico-economic views and by the suppression or cooptation of dissenters. In their common effort to blur and pass over fundamental issues, the parties prevent class divisions from sharpening and serve a valuable function of maintaining a noisy, apolitical politics, distracting us from the real problems and narrowing the scope of participation while giving an appearance of popular government.

---

22. Party organizations—although not necessarily party labels—are becoming less important even in regard to this function, as the mass media assume an increasingly influential role in campaigns.

DEMOCRATIC COMPETITION: DOES IT EXIST?

According to democratic theory, electoral competition keeps political leaders accountable to their constituents: politicians who wish to remain in office must respond to voter preferences in order to avoid being replaced by their rivals in the next election. But do the conditions of electoral competition actually exist? As noted earlier, a host of political, legal and economic forces so limit the range of alternatives as to raise serious questions about the meaning of popular participation.

Furthermore, with so much of electoral politics reduced to an issueless publicity contest, the advantages go to the incumbent. Obviously, the man who has won office already has built some kind of winning combination of money, organization and influence. In addition, he can use the resources of office to promote his own reelection, catering to the needs of important financial groups and performing favors that win him the backing of special interests. He gets irrigation projects, bridges, harbors, post offices and various other government "pork barrel" projects for his home district, carries on a correspondence with thousands of voters and enjoys an access to the local newspapers and radio and television stations that helps establish him as a "brand name." He has at his disposal almost a quarter of a million dollars each year for staff and office expenses, "a major portion of which is used to help the home folks and keep his name in front of them in a favorable way."[23] The most important task facing any candidate for public office is getting his name known to the voters, and here the incumbent usually has a decisive advantage over the challenger.

Over the last two decades there has been a noticeable breakup of one-party regions: Republicans are now winning victories in Mississippi and Democrats get elected in Maine. Yet one-party dominance is still the rule in a good many locales throughout the rural Northeast, Midwest and South and in many cities. In 1970 one out of every ten representatives was elected to Congress with *no opposition in either the primary or the general election.* In some states, state and local officeholders often are elected to uncontested seats. One-party rule, considered the peculiar disease of "communist tyranny," is not an uncommon condition of American politics.

---

23. Milton Gwirtzman, "The Bloated Branch," *New York Times Magazine*, November 10, 1974, p. 102.

The trend in Congress over the last century has been for members to serve for longer periods and to suffer fewer defeats by challengers. In the 1870s about 50 percent of the members of each Congress were newcomers. By the 1970s from 90 to 96 percent of incumbents who sought office were reelected.[24] Death and voluntary retirement seem to be the important factors behind the turnover in representative assemblies. In this respect, legislative bodies bear a closer resemblance to the nonelective judiciary than we would imagine. One study of municipal governments found that upwards of half the city councilmen anticipated their own voluntary retirement after one term and about one-fourth held nonelective appointments to fill unexpired terms. Many of the councilmen admitted that they paid little heed to constituent complaints. They entered and left office "not at the whim of the electorate, but according to self-defined schedules," a procession of like-minded persons of similar social background.[25]

The prevalence of victorious incumbents is both a cause and an effect of low voter participation. As voters become increasingly discouraged about the possibility of effecting meaningful change through the ballot box, they are less likely to mobilize or respond to reformist electoral movements, thus increasing the unassailability of the incumbents. As the incumbents show themselves unbeatable, their would-be challengers become fewer in number and weaker in spirit. This is not an iron law of politics and the cycle has sometimes been dramatically reversed; but the reversals are usually the exceptions. The predominant situation is one of officeholders who are largely unresponsive to voters and voters who are cynical about officeholders.

NONVOTING AS A RATIONAL RESPONSE

Much has been written about the deficiencies of ordinary voters, their prejudices, lack of information and low civic involvement. More should be said about the deficiencies of the electoral-representative system that serves them. It has long been presumed that since the present political system represents the best of all worlds, those who show an unwillingness to vote must be manifesting some failing

---

24. David Leuthold, *Electioneering in a Democracy* (New York: Wiley and Sons, 1968), p. 127; also the study by Americans for Democratic Action, UPI report, *Collegian* (Amherst, Mass.), November 14, 1977.

25. Kenneth Prewitt, "Political Ambitions, Volunteerism, and Electoral Accountability," *American Political Science Review*, 64, March 1970, p. 10. Prewitt presents data on eighty-two municipal governments.

in themselves. Seldom is nonparticipation treated as a justifiable reaction to a politics that is meaningless in its electoral content and
disappointing in its policy results.

In the United States during the nineteenth century, the small-
town democratic system "was quite adequate, both in partisan organization and dissemination of political information, to the task of
mobilizing voters," according to Walter Dean Burnham.[26] But by
the turn of the century, most of the political means for making important decisions had been captured by powerful industrial elites.
Business interests perfected the arts of pressure politics, wielding a
heavy influence over state legislatures, party organizations, governors and congressmen. At the same time, the judiciary extended its
property-serving controls over the national and state legislatures,
imposing limitations on taxation powers and on regulatory efforts in
the fields of commerce and labor. "Confronted with a narrowed
scope of effective democratic options an increasingly large propor-
tion of the eligible adult population either left, failed to enter or—as
was the case with the Southern Negro . . . was systematically excluded from the American voting universe."[27] Much of the blame for
the diminishing popular participation, Burnham concludes, must
rest with "the political system itself."

The percentage of nonvoters has climbed to impressive levels,
running as high as 60 to 65 percent in congressional and guberna-
torial contests and 40 to 46 percent in recent presidential elections.
Since 1952 an increasingly larger percentage of those who come of
voting age have failed to go to the polls.[28] In the 1978 off-year elections roughly two-thirds of the eligible electorate stayed home. In
the presidential primaries of some states, the participation rate may
be as low as 15 to 20 percent of the registered voters. In many local
elections, voter participation is so low as to make it difficult to speak
of "popular" representation in any real sense. Observing that in a
municipality of 13,000 residents, an average of 810 voters elected
the city council, Prewitt comments:

> Such figures sharply question the validity of thinking that "mass elec-
> torates" hold elected officials accountable. For these councilmen, even
> if serving in relatively sizable cities, there are no "mass electorates";
> rather there are the councilman's business associates, his friends at

---

26. Walter Dean Burnham, "The Changing Shape of the American Political Universe," *American Political Science Review*, 59, March 1965, p. 22; also Burnham's
Critical Elections and the Mainsprings of American Politics (New York: Norton, 1970).
27. Burnham, "The Changing Shape. . ." p. 26.
28. *New York Times*, January 22, 1979.

church, his acquaintances in the Rotary Club, and so forth which provide him the electoral support he needs to gain office.[29]

The political significance of low participation becomes apparent when we consider that nonvoters are disproportionately concentrated among the rural poor, the urban slum dwellers, the young, the elderly, the low-income and nonunion workers and the racial minorities. The entire voting process is dominated by middle-class styles and conditions which tend to discourage lower-class participation.[30] Among the reasons poor Whites in one city gave for not voting were the humiliating treatment they had received from poll attendants in previous elections, the intimidating nature of voting machines, the belief that they were not entitled to vote because they had failed to pay their poll tax (a misapprehension encouraged by unsympathetic town clerks), the feeling that they lacked the education and information giving one the right to participate in the electoral process, and the conviction that elections are a farce and all politicians are ultimately out to "line their own pockets."[31] Residency requirements and the registration of voters at obscure locations and inconvenient hours during the political off-season discriminate against the less established community elements, specifically the poor, the unemployed and transient laborers.[32]

Many of the procedural discouragements to voting have been removed in the last two decades: the poll tax was outlawed as a voting requirement; polling-place racial discrimination has lessened; linguistic, literacy and residency requirements were eased; stringent registration requirements were discarded; and young persons between 18 and 21 were enfranchised. The conventional wisdom of the 1960s predicted that these reforms would increase election-day turnout, but the trend toward declining voter participation continues.[33] Difficult electoral procedures may discourage voting, but an easing of these conditions does not guarantee an increased turnout. For be-

---

29. Prewitt, "Political Ambitions, Volunteerism, and Electoral Accountability," p. 9.

30. Penn Kimball, *The Disconnected* (New York: Columbia University Press, 1972); Rudolph O. de la Garza, "Voting Patterns in 'Bi-Cultural El Paso': A Contextual Analysis of Chicano Voting Behavior," *Aztlan*, 5, 1974, p. 242; and U.S. Census report on young voters, *Washington Post*, June 3, 1979.

31. Opinions reported by campaign workers in Burlington, Vermont. I am indebted to Cheryl Smalley for gathering the information.

32. Steven J. Rosenstone and Raymond E. Wolfinger, "The Effect of Registration Laws on Voter Turnout," *American Political Science Review*, 72, March 1978, pp. 22–45; Kimball, *The Disconnected*, p. 15.

33. Curtis Gans, "The Cause: The Empty Voting Booths," *Washington Monthly*, October 1978, p. 28.

hind much of the nonvoting is a growing, and mostly justified, belief that the promises of politicians are simply part of a grand deception.

In addition, the entire social milieu of the poor militates against participation. Working long hours for low pay, deprived of the kind of services and material security that the well-to-do take for granted, made to feel personally incapable of acting effectively and living in fear of officialdom, low-income people frequently are reluctant to make political commitments of any kind. As Kimball describes it:

> Tenements, rooming houses, and housing projects—the dormitories of the ghetto electorate—provide . . . a shifting, changing human environment instead of the social reinforcements that encourage political involvement in more stable neighborhoods. And the immediate struggle for subsistence drains the reservoirs of emotional energy available for the distant and complex realms of politics. . . . Elections come and go, and the life of poverty goes on pretty much as before, neither dramatically better nor dramatically worse. The posturing of candidates and the promises of parties are simply irrelevant to the daily grind of marginal existence.[34]

Lower-strata groups are skeptical that any one candidate can change things. Their suspicions might be summarized as follows:

1. The reform-minded candidate is still a politician and therefore is as deceptive as any other.
2. Even if he is sincere, the reformer is eventually "bought off" by the powers that be.
3. Even if he is not bought off, the reformer can do little against those who run things.

The conviction is that politics cannot deliver anything significant.[35]

It has been argued that if nonvoters tend to be among the less informed, less educated and more apathetic, then it is just as well they do not exercise their franchise. Since they are likely to be swayed by prejudice and demagogy, their activation would constitute a potential threat to our democratic system.[36] Behind this reasoning lurks the dubious presumption that the better-educated, upper-

---

34. Kimball, *The Disconnected*, p. 17.
35. Michael Parenti, "Power and Pluralism: A View From the Bottom," p. 515; Kimball, *The Disconnected*, pp. 61–62.
36. A typical example of this view is Seymour M. Lipset, *Political Man* (Garden City, N.Y.: Doubleday, 1960), pp. 215–219.

income people who vote are more rational, less compelled by narrow self-interests, and less bound by racial and class prejudices, an
impression which itself is one of those comfortable prejudices that
upper- and middle-class people (including social scientists) have of
themselves. As Kimball reminds us:

> The level of information of the most informed voters is not very high
> by objective standards. The influence of ethnic background, family up-
> bringing, and party inheritance is enormous in comparison to the flow
> of political debate. The choices in a given situation are rarely clearcut,
> and the decision to vote for particular candidates can be highly irra-
> tional, *even at the highest levels of education and experience.*[37]

Some writers argue that low voter turnout in the United States is
symptomatic of a "politics of happiness": people do not bother to
participate because they are fairly content with the way things are
going.[38] But the 40 to 50 million adult Americans outside the voting
universe are not among the more contented but among the less affluent and more alienated, displaying an unusual concentration of socially deprived characteristics.[39] The "politics of happiness" may be
nothing more than a cover for the politics of discouragement. The
nonparticipation of many people often represents a feeling of powerlessness, a conviction that it is useless to vote or demonstrate, useless
to invest precious time, energy and hope, risking insult, eviction, arrest, loss of job and police assault—useless because nothing changes.
For many ordinary citizens, nonparticipation is not the result of
contentment or apathy or lack of civic virtue but an understandably
negative response to the political realities they experience.[40]

---

37. Kimball, *The Disconnected*, p. 63. Italics added. Occasionally there is an
admission by the well-to-do that voting should be limited not to protect democracy but
to protect themselves. A letter to the *New York Times* (December 6, 1971) offered
these revealing words: "If . . . everybody voted, I'm afraid we'd be in for a gigantic upheaval of American society—and we comfortable readers of the *Times* would certainly
stand to lose much at the hands of the poor, faceless, previously quiet throngs.
Wouldn't it be best to let sleeping dogs lie?"

38. Heinz Eulau, "The Politics of Happiness," *Antioch Review*, 16, 1956, pp.
259–264; Lipset, *Political Man*, pp. 179–219.

39. Burnham, "The Changing Shape of the American Political Universe," p. 27.

40. A similar conclusion can be drawn from Studs Terkel, *Division Street: America*
(New York: Pantheon, 1967); Kimball, *The Disconnected*; Levin, *The Alienated
Voter*; Harold V. Savitch, "Powerlessness in an Urban Ghetto: The Case of Political
Biases and Differential Access in New York City," *Polity*, 5, Fall 1972, pp. 17–56;
Parenti, "Power and Pluralism"; Lewis Lipsitz, "On Political Belief: The Grievances
of the Poor," in Philip Green and Sanford Levinson (eds.), *Power and Community*
(New York: Pantheon, 1969), pp. 142–172.

With that in mind, we might question those public-opinion surveys which report that underprivileged persons are more apathetic than better-educated, upper-income citizens. If by *apathy* we mean the absence of affect and awareness, then the poor, the elderly, the young, the racial minorities and the industrial workers who have repeatedly voiced their outrage against oppressive social conditions can hardly be described as "apathetic." Apathy should not be confused with antipathy and alienation. Nor is it clear that these dissident groups are "less informed." What impresses the investigators who actually take the trouble to talk to low-income people is the extent to which they have a rather precise notion of what afflicts them. Certainly they have a better sense of the difficulties that beset their lives than the many middle-class officials who do not even recognize the legitimacy of their complaints.[41]

Finally, among the "rational nonvoters" should be counted those in some Western states who are disqualified from participating in the election of special district governing boards which administer land and water resources and most other services and functions of municipal government. In many of these districts voting is limited to property owners who may cast one vote for each dollar's worth of land they possess in the district, in effect giving control to a few big corporations and rich individuals. Where this is the case, voter turnout is as low as 8 percent, and most district supervisors run unopposed or are appointed by the existing governing board rather than elected.[42]

VOTING AS AN IRRATIONAL RESPONSE

Civic leaders and educators usually characterize nonvoters as "slackers" and seldom as people who might be justifiably cynical about the electoral system. Conversely, they portray voters as conscientious citizens performing their civic responsibilities. Certainly many voters seem to agree, especially those who report that they vote primarily because of a "sense of citizenship duty"; often they believe their vote makes no difference and have little regard for the outcome of the election. Thus in the 1956 presidential campaign, 58 percent of those who described themselves as "not much interested"

---

41. See the citations in the previous footnote.
42. Merrill R. Goodall and James B. Jamieson, "Property Qualification Voting in Rural California's Water Districts," *Land Economics*, 1, August 1974, pp. 292–294.

in the campaign voted anyway. Of those who "didn't care at all" about who won the election, 52 percent voted. Only 13 percent of the people with a "low sense of citizenship duty" voted, as opposed to 85 percent who had a "high" sense. The crucial variable in predicting turnout was "sense of citizenship duty"and not interest in substantive issues.[43] For many citizens, then, the vote seems to be more an exercise of civic virtue than civic power. This raises the interesting question of who really is the deadwood of democracy: the "apathetic" or the "civic minded," those who see no reason to vote or those who vote with no reason?

There are, of course, other inducements to voting besides a sense of civic obligation. The tendency to vote for the lesser, or lesser known, of two evils has already been noted. The location of undesirable traits in one party suggests the relative absence of these traits in the other and sometimes becomes enough reason for partisan choice. Thus the suspicion that Democrats might favor Blacks and labor unions leads some middle-class Whites to assume that the Republican party is devoted to their interests, a conclusion that may have no basis in the actual performance of Republican officeholders. Similarly, the identification of Republicans as "the party of big business" suggests to some working-class voters that, in contrast, the Democrats are *not* for business but for the "little man," a conclusion that may be equally unfounded. Like the masks worn in Greek drama, the party label gives distinct identities to otherwise indistinguishable and often undistinguished political actors, identifying some as villains and others as heroes. By acting as instigators of partisan spirit and partisan anxiety, the parties encourage participation, stabilize electoral loyalties and build reservoirs of trust and mistrust that survive the performances of particular candidates.

Recent data indicate that the events of the past decade have weakened party affiliations. Citizens are more inclined to cross party lines, identify themselves as "independents," and look with distrust on both political parties,[44] yet they continue to vote for major party candidates, even if in split-ticket fashion. They are "independent" within the confines of the two-party monopoly.

Some people vote because it is "the only thing the ordinary person can do."[45] Not to exercise one's franchise is to consign oneself to

---

43. Angus Campbell *et al.*, *The American Voter* (New York: Wiley and Sons, 1960), pp. 103–106.

44. Norman H. Nie, Sidney Verba and John R. Petrocik, *The Changing American Voter* (Cambridge, Mass.: Harvard University Press, 1976).

45. Robert Lane, *Political Ideology* (New York: Free Press, 1962), p. 166; Gabriel Almond and Sidney Verba, *The Civic Culture* (Boston: Little, Brown, 1963), p. 131.

total political impotence, an uncomfortable condition for those who have been taught they are self-governing. The need to *feel* effective can lead to the mistaken notion that one *is* effective. A faith in the efficacy of voting also allows one to avoid the bother of other kinds of participation. Voting not only induces a feeling of efficacy, it often *results* from such a feeling. Persons with a high sense of political efficacy are the more likely to vote. High efficacy is related to a citizen's educational and class level: better-educated people of comfortable income who feel most efficacious in general also tend to feel more politically efficacious than lower-income persons.[46] But while many studies relate sense of political efficacy to voting, there is almost nothing relating sense of political efficacy to actual efficacy. In fact there may be little relationship between the two.[47]

The argument is sometimes made that if deprived groups have been unable to win their demands from the political system, it is because they are numerically weak compared to White middle-class America. In a system that responds to the democratic power of numbers, a minority poor cannot hope to have its way. The representative principle works well enough, but the poor are not numerous enough. Therefore, the deficiency is in the limited numbers of persons advocating change and not in the representative system, which operates according to majoritarian principles. What is curious about this argument is that it is never applied to more select minority interests—for instance, oilmen. Now oilmen are far less numerous than the poor, yet the deficiency of their numbers, or of the numbers of other tiny minorities like bankers, industrialists and millionaire investors, does not result in any lack of government responsiveness to their wants. On most important matters government policy is determined less by the majoritarian principle and more by the economic strength of private interests. The fact that government does little for the minority poor does not mean that it is devoted to the interests of the great bulk of belabored "middle Americans" nor that it operates according to majoritarian principles.

To summarize some of the observations offered in this chapter: important structural and material factors so predetermine the range of electoral issues and choices as to raise a serious question about the representative quality of the political system. Mass politics requires mass resources. Being enormously expensive affairs, elections are

46. See Robert R. Alford and Harry M. Scoble, "Sources of Local Political Involvement," *American Political Science Review*, 62, December 1968, pp. 1192–1206.

47. See Alan Wertheimer, "In Defense of Compulsory Voting," in J. Roland Pennock and John Chapman (eds.), *NOMOS XVI: Participation in Politics* (New York: Lieber-Atherton, 1975).

best utilized by those interests endowed with the resources necessary to take advantage of them. Politics has always been largely "a rich man's game." Ironically enough, the one institutional arrangement that is ostensibly designed to register the will of the many serves to legitimize the rule of the privileged few. The way people respond to political reality depends on the way that reality is presented to them. If people have become apathetic and cynical, including many of those who vote, it is at least partly because the electoral system and the major-party organizations resist the kind of creative involvement that democracy is supposed to nurture. It is one thing to say that people tend to be uninvolved, ill-informed and given to impoverished and stereotyped notions about political life. It is quite another to maintain a system that propagates these tendencies with every known distraction and discouragement. Elections, then, might better be considered a symbol of democratic governance than a guarantee of it, and voting often seems to be less an exercise than a surrender of sovereignty.

12

Who Governs?
Leaders
and Lobbyists

It was Tocqueville who once said that the wealthy have little interest in governing the working people, they simply want to use them.[1] Yet members of the propertied class seldom have been slow in assuming the burdens of public office. The political party, said Secretary of State Seward in 1865, using an image that fit his class experience, is "a joint stock association, in which those who contribute most direct the action and management of the concern."[2] The same might be said of government itself.

"THE PEOPLE WHO OWN THE COUNTRY OUGHT TO GOVERN IT"

While the less glorious tasks of vote herding have fallen to persons of modest class and ethnic origins, the top state and federal offices and party leadership positions, to this day, have remained largely in the hands of White, Protestant, middle-aged, upper-income males of conventional political opinion, drawn from the top ranks of corporate management, from the prominent law and banking firms of

---

1. Alexis de Tocqueville, *Democracy in America*, vol. 2 (New York: Vintage, 1945), p. 171.
2. Quoted in Matthew Josephson, *The Politicos, 1865–1896* (New York: Harcourt, Brace, 1938), p. 13.

"WELL, SOME PEACE IS GOOD FOR THE ECONOMY, BUT NOT TOO MUCH PEACE."

Wall Street, and less frequently, from the military, the elite universities, the foundations and the scientific establishment.

From the beginning of the American Republic to modern times, the great majority of those who have occupied the top political offices of the nation—including the presidency and vice-presidency, the cabinet and Supreme Court—have been from wealthy families (the upper 5 or 6 percent of the population), and most of the remainder have been from well-off, middle-class origins (moderately successful businessmen, commercial farmers and professionals).[3] Of

---

3. C. Wright Mills, *The Power Elite* (New York: Oxford University Press, 1956), pp. 400–402; G. William Domhoff, *Who Rules America?* (Englewood Cliffs, N.J.: Prentice-Hall, 1967), especially chapters 3 and 4; Domhoff, *The Higher Circles* (New

those who went to college, more than one-third attended the elite Ivy League schools. Since World War II, almost all the top executive positions have been occupied by bankers, industrialists and military men, in that order of frequency. The men who ran the nation's defense establishment between 1940 and 1967, according to Richard Barnet, "were so like one another in occupation, religion, style and social status that, apart from a few Washington lawyers, Texans, and mavericks, it was possible to locate the offices of all of them within fifteen city blocks in New York, Boston and Detroit."[4]

The wealthy and well-born carry into public life many of the same class values, interests and presumptions that shape their business and law careers. Be they of "old families" or newly arrived, "reform-minded" or conservative, the rich are not known to advocate the demolition of the economic system under which they prosper. Likewise, political leaders of relatively modest class origins (who gain wealth and power later in life), such as Lyndon Johnson, Richard Nixon and Spiro Agnew, are unlikely to retain a strong identity with the low and humble throughout their ascension. One of the preconditions of the rise of such persons is their willingness to accommodate themselves at a fairly early point in their careers to the interests of those privileged circles whose ranks they aspire to join.

Government and business elites are linked by organizational, financial and social ties, and move easily between public and private leadership posts. To avoid the appearance of "conflict of interests," well-to-do persons who assume government posts place their assets into trusts administered by others. But they still have an interest in the general profitability of big business and must retain the good will of corporate America if they are someday to return to private positions of affluence and power.[5] They still operate from a commonly shared corporate-class perspective.

One of the more important elite coordinating mechanisms has been the Council on Foreign Relations, a private advisory group that plays an unofficial but crucial role in shaping American foreign and domestic policy. It is composed of international bankers, corporate heads, military chiefs, cabinet members, White House advisors, prominent members of Congress, top bureaucrats, and a se-

York: Vintage, 1970); Domhoff, *The Powers That Be* (New York: Vintage, 1979); John C. Donovan, *The Cold Warriors* (Lexington, Mass.: D. C. Heath, 1973); Martin Weil, *A Pretty Good Club: The Founding Fathers of the U.S. Foreign Service* (New York: W. W. Norton, 1978); John Schmidhauser, *The Supreme Court* (New York: Holt, Rinehart and Winston, 1960).

    4. Richard Barnet, *Roots of War* (New York: Atheneum, 1972), pp. 48–49.

    5. "Conflicts of Interest," editorial in the *Progressive*, March 1977, p. 8.

lect number of publishers, news commentators and academics. In one year the major oil companies had thirty of their top executives on the council. Its members included the Rockefeller brothers, DuPonts and Morgans and various acolytes of theirs like Henry Kissinger and Elliot Richardson. President Ford appointed fourteen council members to positions in his administration. Of more recent prominence has been the Trilateral Commission, a private assemblage composed of business and political leaders from the major capitalist countries, initiated by David Rockefeller for the purpose of coordinating policies and protecting multinational corporate interests in a changing world. Its members include President Jimmy Carter, Vice-President Mondale and at one time or another fifteen other top members of the Carter administration.[6]

Not every member of the ruling class is born rich, but most are. Not all wealthy persons are engaged in ruling, some preferring to concentrate on making money or living a life of ease. "The ruling class contains what could be called the politicized members of the upper class," writes Alan Wolfe.

> They are all either businessmen or descendants of businessmen. They are born to power and grow up in an atmosphere that cultivates power. . . . They are chairmen, directors, trustees, vice-presidents, consultants, partners, secretaries, advisers, presidents, members and relatives. They, in other words, are the "they" that people (with acute perception) blame for their troubles. And the blame is deserved, for they have taken the responsibility of shaping the society in their interest. They are conscious of that responsibility. . . . For amusement, they read books (often written with support from their foundations) which "prove" that no ruling class exists in the United States.[7]

The policies they pursue in office frequently are connected directly to the corporate interests they represent in their private lives. Thus the decision-makers involved in the U.S. armed intervention against the worker-student uprising in the Dominican Republic in 1965 consisted of Abe Fortas, A. A. Berle, Jr., Ellsworth Bunker, Averell Harriman and a half-dozen others who were stockholders, directors or counsels for large sugar companies that depended on Dominican sugar and molasses for their operations. "Even without these direct economic interests, it would be difficult for these gentle-

---

6. Every member of the National Security Council—the nation's highest official policy-making body—came from the Trilateral Commission, including council head Zbigniew Brzezinski, a protegé of David Rockefeller.

7. Alan Wolfe, *The Seamy Side of Democracy* (New York: McKay, 1973), pp. 66–67.

men in their 'neutral' decision-making roles to escape the assumptions, inclinations and priorities inculcated by their economic and social milieu."[8]

Within the lower echelons of government, recruitment is less selective in regard to class background, but public employees are subjected to "security" checks to weed out the "risks." However, the concept of "security risk" is an elastic one, easily stretched to include anyone whose political opinions depart from the prevailing consensus.[9]

CAMPAIGN CONTRIBUTIONS: WHAT MONEY CAN BUY

The way campaigns are funded is a reflection of the way wealth is distributed in the society. A small number of big donors pay the bulk of campaign expenses.[10] Thus almost 90 percent of the money contributed to presidential candidates now comes from corporations and business people and their families. In 1972 ninety-five wealthy individuals donated $47.5 million to the Nixon reelection campaign. In 1976, when Jimmy Carter spent $35 million to get elected president, a good part of this sum came from rich contributors and from banking and oil firms, the rest from federal matching funds.[11] In the 1978 contests House and Senate candidates spent almost $150 million on their primary and election campaigns.[12] (The arch-conservative Senator Jesse Helms [R.-N.C.] held the record, lavishing $7.5 million to beat a Democratic opponent who spent only $300,000.) Electoral spending figures confirm the maxim that the better financed candidate usually wins: thus in 1978 the bigger spender won 82 percent of the House races and 85 percent of the Senate contests.[13]

8. Fred Goff and Michael Locker, *The Violence of Domination: U.S. Power and the Dominican Republic* (New York: North American Congress on Latin America, n.d.), quoted in James Petras, "U.S. Business and Foreign Policy," *New Politics*, 6, Fall 1967, p. 76.

9. In 1976 the Civil Service Commission eliminated all political loyalty questions on standard application forms. However, the Commission noted it would continue to conduct field investigations into the loyalty of applicants for sensitive jobs; *New York Times*, September 9, 1976.

10. An excellent study is David Nichols, *Financing Elections: The Politics of an American Ruling Class* (New York: Franklin Watts, 1974); Herbert Alexander, *Money in Politics* (Washington, D.C.: Public Affairs Press, 1972); Herbert Alexander, *Financing Politics* (Washington, D.C.: Congressional Quarterly Press, 1976); G. William Domhoff, *Fat Cats and Democrats* (Englewood Cliffs, N.J.: Prentice-Hall, 1972).

11. *New York Times*, November 18, 1976; *Workers World*, November 19, 1976.

12. *New York Times*, January 18, 1979.

13. *Ibid.*

Republicans generally receive more from big corporate donors than do Democrats, although Democratic lawmakers with strategic committee positions are generously funded by business, the tendency being for corporations to back the incumbents, getting favors from those already in power, regardless of party label.[14] Thus the dairy lobby contributed over $2 million in recent years to both Democrats and Republicans who were members of House and Senate agricultural committees. These committees helped vote the dairy industry federal milk price supports netting them some $500 million.[15] A bill to halt runaway hospital costs would have saved Americans more than $25 billion over a five-year period, but the powerful American Medical Association (AMA) lobby succeeded in having it gutted. In two elections the AMA poured more than $3.2 million into the campaign coffers of Democrats and Republicans who were on committees dealing with medical and hospital proposals.[16] Similarly, banking, real estate, oil and gas, private utilities and other special interests contribute huge sums to candidates at all levels of government to help ensure that the taxing, spending and regulatory laws are written in ways that are pleasing to industry.[17]

While politicians insist that campaign contributions do not influence them, few are inclined to go against those who support them financially. A former assistant to two prominent Democratic senators made the following observation:

> Any member of Congress who says donations don't influence him is lying. All of them are corrupt. The only question is the degree of corruption. One reason members of Congress insist that money doesn't influence them is that they . . . often become convinced of the rightness of their backers' causes without admitting it even to themselves. In time, they come to really believe that the guy who gives the big dough is the best guy and that helping him is in the public interest. But campaign money *has* to influence even the most incorruptible men here, because most people don't give away large sums of money for nothing.[18]

---

14. In the 1976 and 1978 elections business gave easily as much to Democrats as to Republicans—because there were so many more Democratic than Republican incumbents.

15. *New York Times*, January 11, 1973; Common Cause Report (Washington, D.C., 1978).

16. Common Cause Report (Washington, D.C., 1978).

17. Tim Wheeler, "$100 Million for Right-Wing Campaigns," *Daily World*, October 3, 1978.

18. Quoted in Richard Harris, "Annals of Politics: A Fundamental Hoax," *New Yorker*, August 7, 1971, p. 54. In the words of Senator Russell Long: "When you are talking in terms of large campaign contributions. . . the distinction between a campaign contribution and a bribe is almost a hair's line difference."

The bipartisan influence of big-business contributors is so pronounced as to move one Democratic senator to remind his party colleagues that they were neglecting to keep up appearances as "the party of the people." In a speech on the Senate floor urging that the scientific patents of the $25 billion space program not be given away to private corporations but applied for public benefit, Russell Long made these candid remarks:

> Many of these [corporate] people have much influence. I, like others, have importuned some of them for campaign contributions for my party and myself. Nevertheless, we owe it to the people, now and then, to save one or two votes for them. This is one such instance. If any Senator should suspect that he might lose his campaign contributors by voting with me today, I might assure him that I have been able to obtain contributions from some of those people, even though they knew I voted for the public interest as I see it on such issues as this. We Democrats can trade on the dubious assumption that we are protector of the public interest only so long if we permit things like these patent giveaways.[19]

The funds spent by labor unions to influence legislators on issues like minimum-wage laws, union shops, human services and consumer protection seem paltry when matched against the spending power of business. Senator Long observed: "Labor contributions have been greatly exaggerated. It would be my guess that about 95 percent of campaign funds at the congressional level are derived from businessmen."[20] By the end of the 1970s, business was outspending labor by a ten-to-one margin.[21] To juxtapose Big Labor with Big Business in the manner of some American government textbooks is to overlook the fact that spending and lobbying are dominated by business groups. This is not to discount organized labor as an interest group, but to indicate the insufficiency of its political strength, especially when measured against the needs of the working class it attempts to represent.

Federal laws that sought to limit the sums candidates could spend and individuals could contribute have always been easily circumvented by such devices as dummy campaign committees or contributions made in the name of friends and relatives. In 1976 the Supreme Court removed most of the limits on campaign spending by (a) allowing an individual to expend any amount in an "indepen-

---

19. *Congressional Record*, vol. 112, part 9, June 2, 1966.
20. Quoted in Mark J. Green, James Fallows and David R. Zwick, *Who Runs Congress?* (New York: Bantam Books, 1972), pp. 12–13.
21. Wheeler, "$100 Million for Right-Wing Campaigns."

dent" effort to elect or defeat any candidate and (b) allowing candidates themselves to spend as much as they desired of their personal or family fortunes on their own campaigns, a decision greatly favoring the wealthy. The Court reasoned that limitations on spending were an infringement of the First Amendment right to free speech.[22] In addition, the Court upheld the use of public money to match funds of presidential candidates who raise a minimum of $100,000 from each of at least twenty states.

Under the 1974 amendments to the Federal Election Campaign Act, the government pays the costs of the Democratic and Republican conventions and provides matching funds of many millions for "major" party candidates. The same law denies assistance to parties that polled less than 5 percent of the presidential vote in the preceding election, effectively depriving all dissenting third parties of public funds.[23]

The 1974 law, backed by a number of court decisions and Federal Election Commission rulings, allows corporations to form political action committees (PACs) that can solicit contributions from stockholders and from all company employees—from managers on down. PAC operating expenses now can be paid out of corporate funds. The result has been an explosion of corporate PACs—some 776 in 1978—and a dramatic increase in corporation campaign contributions, especially to conservatives in both parties.[24]

The career of Nelson Rockefeller provides us with an impressive example of the use of money in politics. The Rockefeller family spent $10 to $12 million on Nelson's campaign for governor of New York and another $12 million on his tries for the presidency in 1964 and 1968.[25] Rockefeller spent large sums to surround himself with a highly paid staff of lawyers, intellectuals, writers and public-relations experts. He promoted himself through two costly commissions on "national goals" and "critical choices" designed to keep him in the public eye as a national statesman. At the time he was being considered for appointment to the vice-presidency, it was discovered that he had been buying not only political celebrity but political security. Rockefeller admitted to having given nearly $1.8 million in gifts and loans to eighteen public officials since 1957, including

22. *New York Times,* January 31, 1976.
23. Robert Walters, "Millions for Third Parties (Nice Work if They Can Get It)," *Ramparts,* July 1975, pp. 13–16; *New York Times,* January 31, 1976.
24. Randall Rothenberg, "The PACs Go To Market On the Hill," *Nation,* November 18, 1978, pp. 536–539; *Washington Post,* July 20, 1979.
25. Herbert Alexander, *Financing the 1968 Election* (Lexington, Mass.; D. C. Heath, 1971).

$50,000 to Henry Kissinger (who had worked for Rockefeller for fifteen years) three days before Kissinger became special advisor to President Nixon, and $625,000 to the chairman of the Port Authority of New York. (David Rockefeller's Chase Manhattan Bank has large bond holdings in the Port Authority.) Various associates received outright cash gifts from Rockefeller or had loans settled while they held state jobs—despite the fact that New York law prohibits public employees from accepting any gift larger than $25. Judson Morhouse received $100,000, was later convicted of bribery charges in a liquor-licensing case, then had his sentence commuted by Governor Rockefeller. At a Senate hearing, Rockefeller insisted that these gifts were simply manifestations of his affection and esteem for the recipients. "Sharing has always been part of my upbringing," he told the senators, none of whom doubled over with laughter.[26]

Neither the House nor Senate committees investigating his nomination to the vice-presidency questioned Rockefeller about the influence he gained from the gifts. No one wondered aloud whether a "gift" to officials in public agencies that make decisions affecting one's private fortune might not better be called by its more forthright name, a "bribe." Coming to Rockefeller's support, Representative Shirley Chisholm (D.-N.Y.) made the revealing comment: "Who among us politicians in the House, indeed, in government today, is pure and above reproach?"[27] Who indeed? With only a few gingerly objections, Congress confirmed Nelson Rockefeller as vice-president.

Rockefeller had been labeled an "Eastern liberal" by ultraconservative members of his party. Yet in almost fourteen years as governor of New York, he greatly increased the tax burden on low- and middle-income people while failing to impose a single new tax on big business. During his administration, manufacturing properties were exempt from taxation in New York. He put a sales tax on the consumer, then increased it. He quadrupled the cigarette tax, tripled the gasoline tax and extended the state income tax to include low-paid working people who had been previously exempted. He vetoed a $1.50 minimum-wage bill as "inflationary." He slashed welfare for mothers with children to 67 cents a day, and ordered anyone earning more than $4,500 a year to be denied Medicaid assistance. As the recession deepened in New York, Rockefeller responded with heavy cuts in human services. As vice-president he supported all of President Ford's conservative policies, including the high military

---

26. *Newsweek*, October 21, 1974; *New York Times*, October 7, 1974.
27. *Guardian*, December 11, 1974.

budget and the vetoes of social legislation. Rockefeller supported U.S. global interventionist policies and for years was a hawk on Vietnam, albeit not an honestly outspoken one like Barry Goldwater.

LOBBYISTS AND THEIR SPECIAL INTERESTS

Lobbyists are persons hired by organized interest groups to influence legislative and administrative policies. Some political scientists see lobbying as essentially a "communication process." They argue that the officeholder's perception of a particular policy is influenced solely or primarily by the information reaching him. The lobbyist's role is one of providing that information. By this view, the techniques of the "modern" lobbyist consist mostly of disseminating data and "expert" information and making public appearances before legislative committees rather than the obsolete tactics of secret deals and bribes.[28] The students of lobbying who propagate this image of the influence system overestimate the changes that have occurred within it. *The development of new lobbying techniques does not mean that the older, cruder ones have been discarded.* Along with the slick brochures, expert testimonies and technical reports, corporate lobbyists still have the slush fund, the kickback, the stock award, the high-paying job offer in private industry, the lavish parties and prostitutes, the meals, transportation, housing and vacation accommodations and the many other hustling enticements of money.

From the lowliest city councilman to the White House itself, officeholders accept money and favors from lobbyists in return for favored treatment. "Members of the House Banking and Currency Committee," complained its former chairman, the late Wright Patman (D.-Tex.), "have been offered huge blocks of bank stocks free of charge and directorships on bank boards. Freshmen members have been approached within hours of their arrival in Washington and offered quick and immediate loans. In one instance that was reported to me, the bank told the member, " 'Just write a check, we

---

28. Lester Milbrath, *The Washington Lobbyists* (Chicago: Rand McNally, 1963), p. 185 and *passim*. See also Douglass Cater's comparison of the "new" with the "old" NAM in his *Power in Washington* (New York: Random House, 1964), p. 208. For a good critique of the Milbrath view of lobbying, see Ernest Yanarella, "The Military-Industrial Complex, Lobbying and the ABM Decision: Some Notes on the Politics of Explanation," unpublished monograph.

29. Quoted in Cirino, *Don't Blame the People*, p. 144.

will honor it.' "[29] "Everyone has a price," Howard Hughes once told an associate who later recalled that the billionaire handed out about $400,000 yearly to "councilmen and county supervisors, tax assessors, sheriffs, state senators and assemblymen, district attorneys, governors, congressmen and senators, judges—yes, and vice-presidents and presidents, too."[30]

Many large corporations have a special division dedicated to performing favors for officeholders. The services include everything from free Caribbean trips on private jet planes to loans, private contacts and illegal gifts. An employee at ITT's congressional-liaison section publicly complained about the way congressmen continually called her office for favors "on a big scale." This situation "shocked" her, she said, even though "very little in Washington would shock me."[31]

The case of Claude Wild, Jr., is instructive. As a vice-president for Gulf Oil and a lobbyist, Wild had the full-time job of passing out, over a twelve-year period, about $4.1 million of Gulf's money to more than one hundred U.S. senators and representatives, eighteen governors and scores of judges and local politicians; included on his gift list were Lyndon Johnson, Richard Nixon, Gerald Ford and Jimmy Carter (when he was governor of Georgia).[32] Other oil companies also contributed millions in illegal gifts to officeholders in return for special protections and tax favors.[33]

In addition to the sums distributed at home, the multinationals have paid out many millions in bribes and contributions to reactionary governments, militarists and conservative leaders in countries like South Korea, Bolivia, Iran (under the Shah), Taiwan, Japan

30. Howard Kohn, "The Hughes-Nixon-Lansky Connection: The Secret Alliances of the CIA from World War II to Watergate," *Rolling Stone*, May 20, 1976, p. 44. Hughes contributed heavily to Nixon's campaigns, and, according to his close aides, Robert Maheu and John Meier, sought to have the Vietnam war prolonged until he had made sufficient profits on his helicopter program; *New York Times*, April 9, 1975. Hughes has been romanticized as a "cowboy capitalist"; I have a better name for him.
31. Quoted in the *New York Times*, March 31, 1972. For a fascinating eyewitness account of corruption and special influence in Washington by a former lobbyist, see Robert Winter-Berger, *The Washington Pay-Off* (New York: Dell, 1972); also Lawrence Gilson, *Money and Secrecy* (New York: Praeger, 1972); and *New York Times*, April 28, 1975.
32. Since the contributions were illegal, the money was first laundered by Gulf through a Caribbean subsidiary and then a Canadian bank. See the *Wall Street Journal*, November 17, 1975; *Philadelphia Evening Bulletin*, November 12, 1975; *Washington Post*, June 24, 1979.
33. Over a ten-year period, forty-five senators and representatives received a total of $8 million in illegal payments from four oil companies, according to SEC investigators; see Jack Anderson and Les Whitten's column, *Washington Post*, March 22, 1976; and *New York Times*, September 9, 1976.

and Italy.[34] The international influence system works both ways: there also are about 15,000 persons employed as foreign lobbyists, spending $100 million a year to influence U.S. lawmakers and other public officials.[35]

The big-time Washington lobbyists are usually attorneys or business people who have proven themselves articulate representatives of their firms, or ex-legislators or former bureaucrats with good connections. Lobbyists have been known to draft legislation, write speeches for House and Senate members, plant stories in the press, launch well-financed letter and telephone pressure campaigns, and make sumptuous campaign contributions and bribes on behalf of their powerful clientele. Whatever their varied backgrounds, the one common resource lobbyists should have at their command in order to be effective is money. Money buys what one House aide called that "basic ingredient of all lobbying"—*accessibility* to the officeholder[36] and, with that, the opportunity to shape his or her judgments with arguments of the lobbyist's own choosing. Accessibility, however, involves not merely winning an audience with a congressman—since even ordinary citizens sometimes can get to see their representatives and senators—but winning his or her active support. In one of his more revealing moments, Woodrow Wilson pointed out:

> Suppose you go to Washington and try to get at your Government. You will always find that while you are politely listened to, the men really consulted are the men who have the big stake—the big bankers, the big manufacturers, and the big masters of commerce. . . . The masters of the Government of the United States are the combined capitalists and manufacturers of the United States.[37]

It is, then, something more than "information flow" that determines influence, the decisive factor being not just the message but the messenger. Even if information does play a crucial role in shaping the officeholder's awareness of the problem, the ability to transmit and disseminate information to decision-makers, to cultivate liaisons and propagate one's cause, itself presumes access to organiza-

---

34. *New York Times*, February 5, 1976; *Workers World*, March 5, 1976; Anthony Sampson, "How the Oil Companies Help the Arabs Keep Prices High," *New York*, September 22, 1975, p. 48; "Profits of Crime," *Nation*, June 30, 1979, p. 772.

35. Russell Warren Howe and Sarah Hays Trott, *The Power Peddlers* (Garden City, N.Y.: Doubleday, 1977).

36. Quoted in Harris, "Annals of Politics," p. 55. Winter-Berger emphasizes this in *The Washington Pay-Off*.

37. Quoted in D. Gilbarg, "United States Imperialism" in Bill Slate (ed.), *Power to the People* (New York: Tower, 1970), p. 67.

tion, expertise, time, labor and material supplies—things that money can buy. In addition, the mere possession of great wealth and the control of industry and production give corporate interests an advantage unknown to ordinary working citizens, for business's claims are paraded as the "needs of the economy" and, as it were, of the nation itself. Having the advantage of pursuing their interests within the framework of a capitalist system, capitalists can predetermine and control the range of solutions.[38]

The business-dominated pressure system found in Washington exercises a similar sway over state and local governments. The idea (popular among political scientists in the 1950s) that strong party leadership would be an effective bulwark against special interests appears to be without foundation. Many state legislatures have strong party systems, with individual legislators voting as their party leaders want, but these leaders, in turn, are heavily influenced by business lobbyists. The influence exercised on state legislatures by big-money interests "is so widespread in this country it appears endemic."[39] The state legislatures are "the willing instrumentalities of an array of private corporate entities."[40] While most of the public has no idea what their state representatives are doing, the banks, loan companies, gambling interests, big franchise holders, insurance firms, utilities, manufacturers, oil and gas companies and Farm Bureau lobbyists carry on a regular liaison with them, showering them with campaign contributions, legal retainers, liquor, paid vacations, free entertainment, special-term "loans" and investment tips. Subservience to business is so pervasive as to make it almost impossible to tell the lawmakers from the lobbyists. State legislators usually work only part-time at their tasks, devoting the better part of their days to their private law practices, insurance firms, realty agencies and other enterprises, which often benefit from their legislative efforts. About half the New York legislators are attorneys who service businesses with direct interests in state laws. A sizable number of the legislators are trustees or directors of banks.[41]

Surveying the organized pressure groups in America, E. E. Schattschneider notes: "*The system is very small.* The range of orga-

---

38. For a discussion of how power is used not only to *pursue* interests but to *define* them, see my *Power and the Powerless* (New York: St. Martin's Press, 1978).
39. Martin Waldron, "Shadow on the Alamo," *New York Times Book Review*, July 10, 1972, p. 2.
40. "The Sick State of the State Legislatures," *Newsweek*, April 19, 1965, p. 31; *Boston Globe*, September 8, 1976.
41. *Times-Union* (Albany, N.Y.), January 19, 1974. This same story quotes a prominent banking official as saying: "I don't buy legislators dinners, I buy legislators."

nized, identifiable, known groups is amazingly narrow; there is nothing remotely universal about it."[42] The pressure system, he concludes, is largely dominated by business groups, the majority of citizens belonging to no organization that is effectively engaged in pressure politics. Almost all organized groups, even nonbusiness ones such as community, religious, educational and professional associations, "reflect an upper-class tendency,"[43] not surprisingly, since ordinary working people rarely have the time, money or expectation level that would enable them to participate.

The pressure system is "small" and "narrow" only in that it represents a highly select portion of the public. In relation to government itself, the system is a vast operation. "Most of the office space in Washington that is not occupied by government workers is occupied by special-interest lobbyists, who put in millions of hours each year trying to get special legislation enacted for the benefit of their clients," writes Richard Harris. "And they succeed on a scale that is undreamed of by most ordinary citizens."[44] A favorable adjustment in rates for interstate carriers, a special tax benefit for a family oil trust, a high-interest bond issue for big investors, a special charter for a bank, a tariff protection for auto producers, the leasing of some public lands to a lumber company, emergency funding for a faltering aeronautics plant, a lenient occupational health code for employers, a postal subsidy for advertising firms, a soil bank for agribusiness, the easing of safety standards for a food processor, the easing of pollution controls for a chemical company, an investment guarantee to a housing developer, a lease guarantee to a construction contractor—all these hundreds of bills and their thousands of special amendments and the tens of thousands of administrative rulings which mean so much to particular interests and arouse the sympathetic efforts of legislators and bureaucrats will go largely unnoticed by a public that pays the monetary and human costs, and has not the organization, information and means to make its case—or even to discover that it has a case.

Public-interest groups, professing to speak for the great unorganized populace, make many demands for reform but have few of the resources that could move officeholders in a reformist direction. In any case, most public-interest groups accept the capitalist system as a given, hence the kinds of "within-the-system" changes they advo-

42. E. E. Schattschneider, *The Semi-Sovereign People* (New York: Holt, Rinehart and Winston, 1960), p. 31. Italics in the original.
43. *Ibid.*, pp. 33–34, and the studies cited therein.
44. Harris, "Annals of Politics," p. 56.

cate are usually of a cosmetic nature or, at best, offer only marginal improvements: thus the advocacy of seat belts and pollution devices for automobiles rather than a nonprofit, publicly owned mass-transportation system; better labeling of commercial products rather than an attack on the waste and abuses of commercialized consumerism; the elimination of no-deposit throwaway beverage bottles rather than the modification of the profit system and its war against the environment; public exposure of lobbying spending rather than an end to the concentration and use of private wealth for public power. When public-interest groups actually take stands on the bigger issues, their inability to bring about fundamental changes becomes more glaringly apparent. It is not merely political timidity that limits them to marginal struggles, it is also the relative sparsity of power resources available to them within the existing politico-economic system.

Pressure-group activities are directed not only at officeholders but encompass entire segments of the public itself. Grant McConnell offers one description of this "grass-roots lobbying":

> The electric companies, organized in the National Electric Light Association, had not only directly influenced Congressmen and Senators on a large scale, but had also conducted a massive campaign to control the substance of teaching in the nation's schools. Teachers in high schools and grammar schools were inundated with materials. . . . Each pamphlet included carefully planted disparagement of public ownership of utilities. The Association took very active, if inconspicuous, measures to insure that textbooks that were doctrinally impure on this issue were withdrawn from use and that more favorable substitutes were produced and used. College professors . . . were given supplemental incomes by the Association and, in return, not infrequently taught about the utility industry with greater sympathy than before. . . . Public libraries, ministers, and civic leaders of all kinds were subjected to the propagandistic efforts of the electric companies.[45]

The purpose of grass-roots lobbying is to build a climate of opinion favorable to the corporate giants rather than to push a particular piece of legislation. The steel, oil and electronics companies do not advertise for public support on behalf of the latest tax depreciation bill—if anything, they would prefer that citizens not trouble themselves with thoughts on the subject—but they do "educate" the public, telling of the many jobs the companies create, the progress and

---

45. Grant McConnell, *Private Power and American Democracy* (New York: Knopf, 1966), p. 19.

services they provide, the loving care they supposedly give to the environment, etc. This kind of "institutional advertising" attempts to place the desires of the giant firms above politics and above controversy—a goal that is itself highly political.

In 1976 progressive groups in various states were able to place referenda on the ballot pertaining to nuclear safety, graduated state income tax, public ownership of utilities, rent control, environmental protection and other such issues. In response the business community launched a multimillion-dollar media blitz, with slick, full-page ads and radio and TV commercials, to defeat most of these initiatives. In states like Oregon, Washington, Colorado, Ohio, California and Massachusetts, opinion polls showed that the defeated referenda had been supported by large margins in the early stages of the campaign, only to be rejected by the voters after massive propaganda assaults were launched by the corporations. Once more citizen groups learned a painful truth about the power of money: corporate interests will spend heavily from profits extracted from the working and consuming public to defeat proposals of benefit to workers and consumers.[46]

CORRUPTION AS AN
AMERICAN WAY OF LIFE

In recent years there have been reports on corruption involving federal, state and local officials in every state of the Union. In Congress, "Corruption is so endemic that it's scandalous. Even the honest men are corrupted—usually by and for the major economic-interest groups and the wealthy individuals who together largely dominate campaign financing."[47] "In some states—Louisiana, for instance—scandals are so prolific that exposure of them has absolutely no impact," reports one observer.[48] A Republican member of the Illinois state legislature estimated that one-third of his legislative colleagues accepted payoffs.[49] In a six-year period, the number of

46. Corporations spent $2 million to defeat referenda in Massachusetts; nuclear interests spent close to $47 million throughout the country; California agribusiness spent almost $2 million; see "Referenda Lessons," *Progressive*, March 1977, p. 11; *Boston Globe*, November 4, 1976; *Guardian*, November 17, 1976.

47. George Agree, director of the National Committee for an Effective Congress, quoted in Harris, "Annals of Politics," p. 62.

48. Waldron, "Shadow on the Alamo," p. 2. See also Peter Cowen, "Graft Held Fact of Life in Boston," *Boston Globe*, October 2, 1972.

49. Paul Simon, "The Illinois State Legislature," *Harper's*, September 1964, p. 74.

public officials convicted in federal courts included a vice-president, three cabinet officers, three governors, thirty-four state legislators, twenty judges, five state attorneys general, twenty-eight mayors, eleven district attorneys and 170 police officers—and this included only those unlucky or clumsy enough to get caught.[50] In New York City alone, half the Police Department was reported by the Knapp Commission to be accepting payoffs. Widespread corruption has been found in the police forces of Chicago, Philadelphia, Indianapolis, Cleveland, Houston, Denver, and numerous smaller cities, involving such practices as protecting narcotics dealers and gamblers, accepting bribes, burglarizing stores (or covering up burglaries), looting parking meters, shaking down prostitutes and intimidating witnesses who attempted to testify against police crime.[51] Meanwhile FBI leaders have used Bureau funds for personal purposes; and FBI agents, supervisors and inspectors considered it "accepted procedure" to fabricate information from nonexistent "paid informers" and then pocket the money officially reported as having been paid to the "informers."[52]

On a still grander scale, the Nixon administration was implicated in major scandals involving the sale of wheat, an out-of-court settlement with ITT, price supports for dairy producers, corruption in the Federal Housing Administration, stock market manipulations, and political espionage—the Watergate affair. And Vice-President Spiro Agnew resigned from office because of charges of bribery, extortion and corruption.[53] A Senate investigation revealed that just among employees of the General Services Administration (the agency that handles the supplies and maintenance contracts for much of the rest of the government) annual theft amounts to $66 million, and that fraud, theft and waste throughout the government might be costing the taxpayers as much as $25 billion annually.[54]

Campaigning for president in 1976, Jimmy Carter made a plea for honesty in government at a $100-a-plate dinner in Miami, while

---

50. For revealing accounts of corruption in states like West Virginia, Maryland and New Jersey, see the articles by John Rothchild, Mary Walton, Thomas B. Edsall and Michael Rappeport published together under the title "Revenue Sharing with the Rich and the Crooked," *Washington Monthly*, February 1972, pp. 8–38; also *Guardian*, August 31, 1977.

51. *Time*, May 6, 1974; *New York Times*, March 11, 1974.

52. *New York Times*, January 15, 1978, and December 6, 1978. The FBI has strenuously resisted court orders to surrender informer files—one reason might be the Bureau's fear of disclosure of bogus informers.

53. Agnew pleaded guilty to income-tax evasion, was fined $10,000 and given three years' probation. In return for his guilty plea and resignation from the vice-presidency, the Justice Department dropped the other charges.

54. Common Cause Bulletin (Washington, D.C., 1979).

beside him on the dais sat a mayor recently imprisoned for tax evasion, a couple of Florida state senators who had just pleaded guilty to conflict of interest, a commissioner facing trial for bribery, and three other commissioners charged with fraud.[55] After becoming president, Carter, the Democrat, dismissed a Republican U.S. attorney, David Marston, who was prosecuting powerful Democratic politicians in Philadelphia for such crimes as bribery, mail fraud and obstruction of justice.[56] And Carter's close assistant, Bert Lance, had to resign as director of the Office of Management and Budget because of allegedly shady and dishonest banking practices.

Corruption in America is so widespread that, as Lincoln Steffens pointed out long ago, throwing the rascals out only means bringing more rascals in. Through all this, the public looks on with growing cynicism, uttering jokes about the habits of politicians and sometimes failing to appreciate how the corrupt officeholder is part of the same individuated acquisitive system that includes the plundering corporate manager, the lying advertiser, the rent-gouging landlord, the price-fixing merchant, the cheating lawyer, the fee-gouging doctor[57] and, at a more modest level, the pilfering auto mechanic and television repairman.

Rather than being an outrageous violation of the rules of the game, corruption is the name of the game. It is not so much a matter of showing that some officeholders pilfer as of showing that almost all of them—and their private-interest cohorts—do it routinely; not so much a matter of finding a few bad apples as noting that the barrel itself is rotten. Besides denouncing corruption we should understand the politico-economic system that makes it ubiquitous. The public sector is engaged in close and continual intercourse with the private sector. The competition for government contracts, subsidies and other favors is an important part of the overall corporate struggle for profit and growth. The temptation for corporate interests to use large sums of money to win decisions that bring in vastly larger sums is irresistible; indeed, it is less a temptation than a necessary and even prudent practice—one that promises grand rewards and relatively few risks, especially since those who would be the

---

55. *Workers World*, May 7, 1976.

56. *New York Times*, January 22, 1978.

57. Doctors have cheated the government out of "a billion dollars a year and all their patients much more," reported health officials, by falsifying health-insurance claims, padding bills, participating in kickbacks and overcharging for often unnecessary laboratory tests by as much as 100 to 400 percent; *Seattle Post-Intelligencer*, August 1, 1976; *New York Times*, January 11, 1973.

guardians of the law, themselves have their palms out, or are in other ways beholden to the corrupting powers.

The temptations encountered by the politician are, of course, strong. Politicians too face a competitive market, and their campaign expenses are burdensome. To avoid yielding to the special interests, to refuse to give to the haves, is to turn oneself into a have-not and seriously lower one's chances of political survival. Even the nonelected official, who has no campaign expenses, finds it difficult not to yield to the illegal wants of special interests, especially when everyone else seems to be doing the same, when the whistleblower is penalized rather than lionized, and when there are rewards if one cooperates.

In sum, if the powers and resources of the social order itself are used for the maximization of private greed and gain, and if the operational ethic is "looking out for number one," then corruption will be chronic rather than occasional, a systemic product rather than an outgrowth of the politician's flawed character.

13

Congress: The Pocketing of Power

As noted earlier, the framers fashioned a Constitution with the intent of deflecting what they feared to be a tempestuous popular will. In order to guard against democratic "excesses" and ensure that the more prudent elements (that is, themselves and other men of their class and convictions) held the reins of government, the framers separated the functions of state into executive, legislative and judicial branches and installed a system of checks and balances. These measures were designed to forestall popular action and make fundamental changes in the economic and social order most unlikely. They understood what some theorists today seem to have forgotten: in a society in which private wealth is gathered into the hands of a few, the *diffusion* of power among the various segments of government does not necessarily mean the *democratization* of power but more likely the opposite. Confrontations between concentrated private wealth and fractured public power, between big business and little government, do not usually yield democratic results. Fragmented power is more readily pocketed by specialized, well-organized, entrenched private interests and is thereby less responsive to the mass public.

Looking specifically at the United States Congress, one is struck by how effectively the diffusion of power has led to undemocratic results. The deficiencies of Congress have been documented by journalists, political scientists and congressmen themselves.[1] Without

---

1. The best of recent works is Mark J. Green, James M. Fallows and David R. Zwick, *Who Runs Congress?* (New York: Bantam Books/Grossman, 1972); also Joseph

224

planning to cover everything that might be said about the legislative branch, let us consider some of the more important points.

RULE BY SPECIAL INTEREST

For many years power in Congress rested with the twenty or so standing committees in each house which determine the destiny of all bills—rewriting some, giving affirmative action to a few and burying most. These committees have been dominated by chairpersons who rose to their positions by seniority—that is, by being repeatedly reelected, usually from more conservative districts or states not known for their two-party competition or high electoral participation. The commitment to seniority has been a pervasive unwritten norm of Congress, determining not only the choosing of chairpersons but the assigning of members to committees and the selection of subcommittee chairpersons.[2] However, seniority is readily ignored by senior members when it is in their interest to do so. Former Senator Joseph Clark notes that during one session of the Senate the seniority rule was violated when filling vacancies in eight important standing committees, to the advantage of conservative senators and to the disadvantage of the already underrepresented liberals.[3]

The party with a majority, be it in the House or Senate, is the one that controls the chairmanships of that house. Since World War II, except for brief interludes, control of Congress has been in the hands of the Democrats or, more specifically, the senior members of the Democratic party, who for a long time were mostly Southern conservatives. Some of the aging Southern committee chairpersons in both the House and the Senate have been succeeded by non-Southerners who generally have been less conservative. In the House, chairmanships have been moving away from rural districts toward somewhat less conservative urban and suburban ones.[4]

Seniority has remained the rule in both houses, although the House Democratic Caucus has instituted a number of changes to weaken the hold of committee chairpersons, removing several from

---

S. Clark, *Congress: The Sapless Branch* (New York: Harper & Row, 1964); Joseph S. Clark et al., *The Senate Establishment* (New York: Hill and Wang, 1963); Drew Pearson and Jack Anderson, *The Case Against Congress* (New York: Simon and Schuster, 1968); and Richard Billing, *House Out of Order* (New York: E. P. Dutton, 1965). Dutton, 1965).

2. George Goodwin, "The Seniority System in Congress," *American Political Science Review*, 53, June 1959, p. 412.

3. Clark, *The Senate Establishment*, p. 40 ff.

4. *New York Times*, February 10, 1976.

their positions and expanding the powers of subcommittees.[5] No longer can chairpersons arbitrarily select subcommittee chairpersons, nor can they stack a subcommittee with members of their own choice or cut its budget. Totaling about 385 in the House and Senate, the subcommittees have staffs of their own and fixed legislative jurisdictions. Advancement within the subcommittees, as within the full committees, is still mostly by seniority.

Some of the power taken from the committees was slated to shift to the elected leadership of the House—the speaker's office—which supposedly would have been in a position to initiate and respond to broad policy initiatives. But that part of the Democratic Caucus reforms was never completed, since many House members preferred the system of divided authority offered by subcommittees. Thus, the committee system in Congress has been replaced by "the subcommittee system," in which every organized interest has, in the words of one congressman, "a port of entry into Congress."[6] What is missing is a countervailing central leadership to support issues that affect interests other than the privileged ones. "More than mere specialization, the subcommittee permits development of tight little cadres of special interest legislators and gives them great leverage."[7] In agriculture, for instance, cotton, corn, wheat, peanut, tobacco and rice producers compete for federal support programs; each interest is represented on the various subcommittees of the Senate and House Agricultural Committees by senators and representatives ready to do battle on their behalf. The fragmentation of power within the subcommittees simplifies the lobbyist's task of controlling legislation. *It offers the special-interest group its own special-interest subcommittee.* To atomize power in this way is *not* to democratize it.[8] The separate structures of power tend to monopolize decisions in specific areas for the benefit of specific groups. Into the interstices of these substructures fall the interests of large segments of the unorganized public.

Whether Congress is organized under a committee system, a subcommittee system or a strong centralized leadership—and it has en-

---

5. The Democratic Caucus is the meeting of all House Democrats. Its function is to discuss strategies and issues; it is composed of the majority party of the House and therefore can shape the rules under which the House operates.

6. Representative David Obey (D.–Wisc.) quoted in the *New York Times*, November 13, 1978.

7. Douglass Cater, *Power in Washington* (New York: Random House, 1964), p. 158. The subcommittee system has been a long time developing. The House Democratic Caucus reforms did not create it but advanced and legitimized it.

8. See Grant McConnell, *Private Power and American Democracy* (New York: Knopf, 1966), p. 193 and *passim*.

"SORRY, I DON'T CATER TO SPECIAL INTERESTS!"

joyed all three in its history—it seems unchanging in its dedication to maintaining the corporate-enterprise system. Whatever the struggles that occur between liberals and conservatives, Democrats and Republicans, each Congress reproduces an array of grants, subsidies, leases, franchises, in-kind supports, direct services, noncompetitive contracts, guaranteed investments, loss compensations and other forms of government largesse to big business. And each Congress sustains the same (or an increasingly inequitable) system of tax deductions for capital gains and unrealized capital gains, accelerated depreciation, investment credits, business expenses, tax-free income and corporate foreign royalties. At the same time, Congress continues to vote billions of dollars for bloated military budgets and billions for right-wing dictatorships throughout the Third World, while providing inefficient and insufficient social services at home. What has failed to appear on Congress's agenda is any notion of major structural changes in class and power, of moving the economy toward nonprofit forms of production for social use rather than production for corporate profit. As an integral part and product of the existing politico-economic system, Congress is not likely to initiate a transformation of that system. Thus it tends to treat the economic problems of society either as being without solution or as worthy of little more than the spending programs of the past.

On those occasions when public opinion is aroused about some issue like auto safety, pollution or unsafe foods, Congress is likely to respond by producing legislation that gives every appearance of dealing with the problem but which is usually wanting in substance: thus we are treated to a lobbyist registration act that does little to control lobbying practices, a campaign financing act that makes campaign funding ever more dependent on big-business contributions, an occupational safety act and a civil rights act that are seldom enforced, a public housing act that creates profits for speculators and developers rather than houses for the poor and an environmental protection act that fails to protect the environment.

The unorganized public, composed of ordinary working people, exercises an influence over Congress that is seldom deep or durable. Given the demands made on his or her time by job and family, and the superficial and often misleading coverage of events by the media, the average wage earner has little opportunity to give sustained, informed attention to more than a few broad issues, if that. But throughout the legislative process, the organized interests remain actively engaged in shaping the substantive details of legislation. Thus the final bill usually will be sufficiently diluted or transformed to accommodate powerful groups.

Sometimes, even in the face of an aroused public and sustained media exposure, Congress will make no positive response. After several years of intensive and massive public demonstrations against the Vietnam intervention and with polls indicating that a majority of the people favored withdrawal from Vietnam, Congress was still voting huge appropriations for the war by lopsided majorities, and large numbers of senators and representatives—a majority in the House—still adhered to a "hawk" position.[9] In April 1973, in the

---

9. See Garrison Nelson's excellent analysis: "Nixon's Silent House of Hawks," *Progressive*, August 1970, pp. 13-20.

face of a nationwide meat boycott, demonstrations and a deluge of letters and telephone calls protesting inflation, Congress voted down all proposals for price freezes and price rollbacks. Opposing the proposals were "cattlemen, banking and business interests and food merchants."[10] In 1977 and 1978, despite a long period of pressure by labor, consumer and public-interest groups, Congress succumbed to a strong display of corporate lobbying and voted to deregulate the price of natural gas (at an anticipated $30 billion cost to consumers); shortly afterward, it voted down a proposed consumer protection agency.

Congress is inclined to remove itself from scrutiny whenever the public gets too interested in its affairs. The Senate Armed Services Committee responded to the public's growing concern about military spending by increasing its percentage of secret hearings from 56 percent to 79 percent. The House Appropriations Committee held 92 percent of its meetings behind closed doors one year. Most other committees held at least one-third of their sessions in secret.[11] Business interests enjoy a ready access to committee reports while newspersons and public-interest advocates are kept in the dark. "The thing that really makes me mad is the dual standard," complained a Senate committee staff member. "It's perfectly acceptable to turn over information about what's going on in committee to the auto industry or the utilities but not to the public."[12]

Sometimes secrecy envelops the entire lawmaking process: a bill cutting corporate taxes by $7.3 billion was (a) drawn up by the House Ways and Means Committee in three days of secret sessions, (b) passed by the House under a closed rule after only one hour of debate with (c) about thirty members of the House present for the (d) non-roll-call vote.[13] Under such conditions even the highly motivated muckraker, experienced journalist, or academic specialist has difficulty ascertaining what is going on.

The addiction to secrecy is nowhere more evident than in Congress's efforts to keep the Central Intelligence Agency free from public scrutiny. Despite disclosures of widespread, covert, unlawful and dangerous activities by the CIA, Congress rejected moves to publicize the Agency's budget.[14] When Representative Michael Harrington (D.–Mass.) released classified information on the CIA's role in

10. The Associated Press report carried in the *Schenectady Gazette*, April 17, 1973.
11. See the *Washington Monthly*, September 1972, p. 17.
12. Green *et al.*, *Who Runs Congress?*, p. 56.
13. See the observations of Thomas H. Stanton reported in the *Washington Monthly*, April 1972, p. 18.
14. *New York Times*, October 2, 1975.

the overthrow of a democratic government in Chile, the House Armed Services Committee voted to deny him further access to classified materials about the Agency.[15] The House Select Committee on Intelligence wrote a report that was highly critical of CIA activities, but the House voted to withhold it from the public until it had been censored by the president, who could delete any information that might "adversely affect . . . intelligence activities."[16] Neither Congress nor the president indicated what items in the report were damaging to national security. Apparently exposure of CIA crimes and abuses weakened the Agency's effectiveness and thereby posed a danger to our security. By this view, intelligence agencies should be free to do pretty much anything they want without being subjected to public scrutiny—a state of affairs which itself poses serious dangers to our security.

Many congressmen allow their offices to be used as bases of operation for lobbying activities. One influential lobbyist, Nathan Voloshen, regularly worked out of Speaker John McCormack's office, paying McCormack a substantial "rent" along with a percentage of the take in return for use of the speaker's name and influence on behalf of Voloshen's business clients.[17] According to Winter-Berger, the lobbyist's main job is to circumvent existing laws and get preferential treatment "for clients who have no legal rights to them." To achieve this the lobbyist pays cash to "one or more members of Congress—the more influential they are, the fewer he needs," who make the contacts with the executive agency handling the matter. "Most lobbying is underground, because more than opinions are exchanged. Money is exchanged: money for favors, money for deals, money for government contracts, money for government jobs."[18] It is "a very common occurrence" for congressmen to telephone or

15. *New York Times*, June 20, 1975. The secret testimony of then-CIA Director William Colby, which Harrington made public, directly contradicted previous public testimony by former CIA Director Richard Helms and public statements by Henry Kissinger and other officials who had repeatedly lied to Congress and the public about the Agency's involvement in Chile.

16. *New York Times*, January 30 and February 2, 1976. The Select Committee that wrote the report, under the chairmanship of Representative Otis Pike (D.-N.Y.) did not think it was harmful to national security and had voted to make it public. The report was eventually leaked to the press; see *New York Times*, March 30, 1976, and September 19, 1976.

17. See Robert Winter-Berger, *The Washington Pay-Off* (New York: Dell, 1972). Winter-Berger was a lobbyist who worked closely with Voloshen and McCormack. He offers a good deal of astonishing eyewitness testimony in his book. Voloshen was eventually convicted of fraud and given a suspended sentence. At his trial, McCormack professed to be ignorant of Voloshen's doings and everyone believed him.

18. *Ibid.*, pp. 14, 38.

write the Justice Department on behalf of business interests, according to former Attorney General Richard Kleindienst, who added: "We have a responsibility to permit that kind of thing to occur."[19]

The humorist Will Rogers once observed: "Congress is the best money can buy." The average senator or representative is an influence peddler, doing favors not only for ordinary folks back home but for special folks with special demands. Thus Representative Daniel Flood (D.–Pa.), a senior member of the House Defense Appropriations Subcommittee, which exercises a crucial influence over the military budget, goaded the Pentagon into buying tens of millions of dollars worth of anthracite, which it neither needed nor wanted. Flood thereby satisfied coal producers in his district who happened to be campaign contributors and close associates of his.[20] Often the client does not live in the congressman's district or even in the United States. Representatives John Murphy (D.–N.Y.) and Charles Wilson (D.–Tex.) were fervent spokesmen for former Nicaraguan dictator Somoza. Murphy used his office to facilitate business deals between Somoza and various domestic and foreign companies that contributed to Murphy's campaigns. And Wilson was a major stockholder in a Texas-based company with interests in prerevolutionary Nicaragua.[21]

Frequently members of Congress act without benefit of prodding by any pressure group, either because they are so well attuned to its interests or see the world in the same way as does the pressure group, or because they have lucrative holdings of their own in the same industry. Thus Representative Clarence Brown of Ohio owned a broadcasting station and sat on the House subcommittee that regulated broadcasting. The late Representative Robert Watkins of Pennsylvania was chairperson of a trucking firm whose profits depended on rules passed by Watkins's Commerce Committee. Certain members, like former Senator James Eastland (D.–Miss.), are owners of large farm holdings and sit on committees that shape the farm subsidy programs that directly enrich them. The late Senator Robert Kerr (D.–Okla.) exercised direct control over legislation affecting gas, uranium, oil and other natural resources. By 1960 he owned numerous oil wells, 25 percent of America's uranium mines and 75 percent of the world's richest helium pool. Much of his wealth was accumulated after he was elected to the Senate. Senator Jacob Javits

---

19. Quoted in Martin Gellen, "ITT: The Tentacles of Power," *Guardian*, March 29, 1972, p. 3.

20. *Boston Globe*, February 23, 1978.

21. *Guardian*, December 6, 1978.

(R.–N.Y.), who owns stock in Citibank and was a member of a law firm that did millions of dollars of business for the bank, has been a strong and persistent advocate for banking interests, enough to make him known as "the Senator from Wall Street."[22] What is called "conflict of interest" in regard to the judiciary is defined as "expertise" in Congress. What we have are persons who use their public mandate to legislate for their private interests. That they seldom see any conflict in these roles itself shows how readily they define the public good in terms compatible with their own fortunes.

Plutocracy—rule *by* the rich *for* the rich—prevails in Congress. Nearly half the U.S. Senate is made up of millionaires or near-millionaires. At least thirty-six senators have investments in banking and other financial institutions; more than a third of the senators make money every time the military budget increases, for they have interests in firms that rank among the top defense contractors. Almost half of all Senate members are either on boards of federal banks or among the stockholders. Over 150 House members have substantial investments in real estate and retail business, and over a hundred have interests in banking and savings and loan associations, including many who sit on the House Banking Committee and Ways and Means Committee, both of which deal with banking legislation.[23] Most members of Congress are corporate lawyers, bankers, business people and agribusiness farmers, roughly in that order, with an additional scattering of doctors, teachers, journalists and other professionals. The great bulk of the American population belongs to occupations and income levels that have no direct representation in Congress.[24]

Congressmen pilfer from the public treasure. Among their bad habits, the most common are:

1. Junketing—traveling for fun at government expense under the guise of conducting overseas committee investigations
2. Having relatives on the payroll and pocketing their salaries
3. Taking salary kickbacks from staff members

---

22. Charles McCollum, "Jacob Javits: The Senator from Wall Street," *Village Voice*, August 29, 1974, pp. 3, 27–28.

23. Members of Congress are now required to disclose their financial holdings. But many file "incomplete, misleading or useless" statements, according to the *Congressional Quarterly*, September 2, 1978. More thorough disclosures would very likely reveal more extensive financial holdings.

24. Millionaire representatives are a phenomenon found at the state level as well. In a poor state like West Virginia, an estimated half of the state legislators are millionaires, many of them coal mine owners, while almost none are environmentalists. Jean Callahan, "Cancer Valley," *Mother Jones*, August 1978, p. 40.

4. Keeping unspent travel allocations for personal use
5. Double billing—charging both the government and a private client for the same expense
6. Using their franking privilege for mailing campaign literature[25]
7. Using committee staff workers for personal campaign purposes[26]
8. Keeping persons on the staff payroll whose major function is to perform sexual favors[27]

Venality takes more serious forms. In the last decade about twenty-five members of Congress or their aides have been indicted or convicted of bribery, influence peddling, extortion, mail fraud or other such crimes. And those were only the few unlucky enough to get caught. From 1975 to 1976 at least nineteen senators were implicated in a multimillion-dollar corporate slush fund, including then-Senate minority leader Hugh Scott (R.–Pa.). Officials of Gulf Oil testified that Scott had accepted and actively solicited illegal contributions from Gulf of $10,000 a year. These charges were widely publicized in the press, but instead of moving to clean house, half the members of the Senate Ethics Committee declined to reply to inquiries about the Scott case, and the other half observed that an investigation would be "premature." The committee had not investigated a senator's ethics in almost ten years. Scott, a millionaire, suddenly decided to retire from the Senate in 1976.[28] The Ethics Committee finally initiated an investigation of Scott and two dozen other senators which it decided to drop a short time later without calling any corporate witnesses (including Gulf lobbyists who were willing to name names). The committee refused to open Scott's financial papers or turn them over to the Internal Revenue Service.[29]

The House Ethics Committee has behaved no differently from its opposite number in the Senate. When a member of the Korean CIA, testifying before the committee, named thirty congressmen to whom

25. Right-wing Congressman Larry McDonald (R.–Ga.) set something of a record in his first six months in office by inserting 140 speeches into the Congressional Record, which were then turned into government reprints, charged off to the government and sent out on computerized mailing lists to constituents and prospective donors. Al Aronowitz, "America's Ten Craziest Congressmen," *Gallery*, November 1978, p. 101.

26. Green *et al.*, *Who Runs Congress?*, pp.131–159; and "Ethics on Capitol Hill," *Progressive*, August 1977, pp. 8–10.

27. *New York Times*, May 26, 1976; *New York Post*, June 14, 1976.

28. *Progressive*, March 1976, p. 11.

29. *Boston Globe*, September 22, 1976. The chairman of the Ethics Committee was Howard Cannon (D.-Nev.), who himself was said to be the recipient of illegal gifts from Northrup Corporation. See *The American Sentinel*, July 1, 1975, p. 3.

he had given almost $1 million in bribes in exchange for votes in Congress in support of his government, the Ethics Committee responded by indicting only two excongressmen.[30]

THE LEGISLATIVE LABYRINTH

As intended by the framers of the Constitution, the very structure of Congress has a conservative effect on what the legislators do. The staggered terms of the Senate—with only one-third elected every two years—makes a sweeping turnover less likely, and is designed to blunt any mass sentiment for a thorough change. The division of the Congress into two separate houses (bicameralism) makes legislative action all the more difficult, giving an advantage to those who desire to prevent reforms. With bicameralism, lobbyists have more opportunities to exert pressure and more places to set up roadblocks; legislation that gets through one house can often be buried or mutilated in the other house.

A typical bill before Congress might go the following route: after being introduced into, say, the House of Representatives, it is (1) committed to a committee, where it is most likely summarily ignored, pigeonholed or gutted by the chairperson, or (2) parceled out to various subcommittees for extensive hearings, where it might then meet its demise or (3) reported out of subcommittee to full committee, greatly diluted or completely rewritten to suit influential lobbyists and their clients, some of whom sit on the committees as members of Congress. In the unlikely event that it is reported out of the full committee, the bill (4) goes to the Rules Committee, where it might be buried forever or subjected to further mutilation or replaced entirely by a bill of the Rules Committee's own preference. Upon reaching the floor of the House (5) it might be further amended during debate or voted down or referred back to committee for further study. If passed, *it must repeat essentially the same process in the Senate*, assuming the Senate has time for it.

If the bill does not make it through both houses before the next congressional election, it must be reintroduced and the entire process begun anew. Not surprisingly, the House and Senate frequently fail to pass the same version of a bill; differences then have to be ironed out in ad hoc conference committees composed of several

---

30. An earlier probe had disclosed that 115 congressmen had taken bribes from South Korean agents. Executive officials, including Henry Kissinger, were implicated as well. *New York Times*, July 11, 1977; *Workers World*, June 2, 1978.

senior members from each house. More than one conference committee has rewritten a bill to better suit special interests. The bill that survives the legislative labyrinth and escapes an executive veto to become an *act* of Congress, and the law of the land, may be only an *authorization* act—that is, it simply brings some program into existence. Congress then must vote *appropriations* to finance the authorized policy; hence, *the entire legislative process must be repeated for the appropriations bill.* Not infrequently legislation authorizing the government to spend a certain amount for a particular program is passed, but no appropriations are subsequently voted to finance it. Congress's task is made no easier by the duplication of bills and overlapping committee jurisdictions. In one session seventy bills were introduced to change the date of Veterans Day back to the traditional November 11. There are twenty-two House committees and subcommittees dealing—none of them very successfully—with the problems of the aged.[31]

Bills which benefit special corporate interests seldom get caught in the congressional labyrinth; generally when the big companies want action, they get it. But legislation designed to serve the politically weak, the low income and the unorganized is treated with painfully slow deliberation, if at all. Without pause, Congress voted $6.75 million for a market news service to furnish timely reports on major agricultural commodities to enable agribusiness to better determine when to sell and how to price its products. But this same Congress debated at great length the passage of a minor pilot project supplying breakfast in school for hungry children, a program that would reach only a tiny number of the millions of malnourished American children.[32] In almost everything Congress does, the pattern remains the same. Multibillion-dollar tax breaks for big business are passed in a matter of days with little debate, while reform bills languish in committee. Multibillion-dollar defense bills are passed in a matter of hours, while pitifully inadequate welfare measures are haggled over with that kind of ungracious stinginess the haves so frequently display toward the have-nots.[33]

---

31. For studies on the legislative process see Richard Fenno, Jr., *Congressmen in Committees* (Boston: Little, Brown, 1973); Roger Davidson and Walter Oleszek, *Congress Against Itself* (Bloomington: Indiana University Press, 1977); Morris Fiorina, *Congress: Keystone of the Washington Establishment* (New Haven: Yale University Press, 1977).

32. *Hunger, U.S.A.*, a report by the Citizens' Board of Inquiry into Hunger and Malnutrition in the United States (Boston: Beacon Press, 1968), p. 80.

33. A further instance: while voting for the largest military budget in history, in 1978 the House slashed $800 million from the Health, Education and Welfare Department budget, including $225 million to remove architectural barriers for the handicapped. *New York Times*, June 23, 1978.

For all their activity, 100 senators and 435 representatives cannot produce an integrated national program. The subcommittee system with its fragmented power works against a coherent nationally-oriented program. In addition, members of Congress have neither the time nor the staff to inform themselves in any comprehensive way about the myriad problems of the nation or the vast undertakings of the executive branch. The Defense Department has more people preparing its budget than Congress has for all its functions combined. For most of its technical information and legislative initiatives Congress relies on the executive departments or on lobbyists from private industry, who often write the bills that friendly congressmen later introduce as legislation.

More than ever, Congress is awash with special-interest money, a situation that helps create special-interest legislators. Congress "is at best a collection of well-intentioned people who have fallen back on a service role while making a great deal of noise about larger issues."[34] A congressman spends the bulk of his time performing minor ombudsman services for constituents, making calls to public agencies on behalf of private interests and answering the huge quantity of mail he receives. In the time left for legislative tasks, he devotes himself to several specialized subcommittees, trying to build up some expertise in limited areas, in effect making himself that much more of a special-interest lawmaker who defines legislation in terms of distinct "problems" (e.g., tariffs, defense contracts, taxes, forestry) and who focuses little attention on the interrelatedness and *systemic* nature of politico-economic problems. On matters outside his domain he defers to his other special-interest colleagues.

With its fragmented pockets of special power, Congress is not just bicameral, it is almost "multicameral." These various special-interest congressional factions achieve working majorities through various trade-offs and mutual accommodations, a "logrolling" process that is not the same as compromise. Rather than checking one another as in compromise situations, and thus blunting the selfish demands of each—possibly with some benefit to the general public—interest groups end up supporting one another's claims, at the expense of those who are without power in the pressure system. Thus the oil lobby will back farm supports in exchange for agribusiness support of oil leases. In both cases the ordinary consumers and taxpayers bear the costs. *Logrolling is the method by which the vari-*

---

34. Sanford Ungar, "Bleak House: Frustration on Capitol Hill," *Atlantic*, July 1977, p. 38. Ungar was referring to the House, but his description might be applied to the Senate as well.

ous haves reconcile their differences, usually at the expense of the have-nots. The net effect is not a *check* on competing claims but a *compounding* of claims against the interests of the unorganized public.

This array of special interests has led some political scientists to the mistaken conclusion that Congress is a pluralistic arena, composed of shifting fluid coalitions that vary greatly from issue to issue, offering no discernible pattern of class and ideological cleavage. But a recent study has found fairly consistent liberal-conservative ideological divisions in such issue areas as domestic spending, foreign policy, race and civil liberties.[35] The conflicts between the "special interest" legislators and the "public interest" ones are not resolved by log-rolling but by a show of strength—with the results commonly favoring the conservatives who represent the business community, the medical association and the suburban well-to-do, rather than the liberals who sometimes represent blue-collar workers, racial minorities and consumer groups. Even when liberal forces "win," the legislative outcome is usually so piecemeal and ambiguous as to have little effect in redistributing the costs and benefits of politico-economic life.[36]

CONGRESS: A PRODUCT OF ITS ENVIRONMENT

While Congress is a body supposedly dedicated to a government of laws, not of men, its procedures "are founded all too much on unwritten, unspoken, and largely unnoticed informal agreements among men."[37] The norms and customs that are so much a part of life in the House and Senate are generally conservative in their effect. The emphasis on elaborate forms of courtesy and on avoiding public remarks that might be construed as personally critical of colleagues discourages a good deal of discussion of things that are deserving of criticism. "The Senate is . . . the biggest mutual admiration society in history," observes a congressional intern. "How heated can debate get when every four seconds you're referring to your so-called rival as 'the honored gentleman from Illinois'? And

---

35. See the excellent study by Jerrold E. Schneider, *Ideological Coalitions in Congress* (Westport, Conn.: Greenwood Press, 1979).

36. Much of the evidence presented earlier on the outputs of the politico-economic system supports this point. See especially chapters 5 and 7.

37. Clark, *The Senate Establishment*, p. 15. Clark was describing the Senate, but his observation applies to both houses.

that's not just a game; it's the whole spirit of the place."[38] The tendency to minimize differences usually works to the advantage of those who prefer to avoid the confrontations needed to effect change.

In addition, there are various parliamentary devices, from time-consuming quorum calls to filibusters, which make it easier for entrenched interests to thwart action. The rule of unlimited debate in the Senate allows a small but determined number of senators to filibuster a bill to death or kill it by exercising the *threat* of filibuster. Over the years the filibuster has been used extensively by Southern senators against civil rights bills and to a lesser degree by conservatives against measures deemed harmful to big business. On still rarer occasions liberals have resorted to the filibuster on behalf of one or another "public interest" issue.

The freshman legislator is socialized into a world of cronyism that makes the mobilization of legislative majorities around broad issue-oriented programs difficult to achieve. He learns not to give too much attention to issue politics—since issues can be divisive—but to develop personal loyalties to senior members, defer to their judgments, avoid exacerbating debates and become a reliable member of the club. The longer he stays in Congress the more his commitment to issues seems to blur.[39] He soon realizes that opportunities for choice committee assignments and other favors are extended to him by leaders in accordance with his willingness to go along with things. In recent years this pattern has changed somewhat as junior members have manifested a marked inclination to challenge the seniority system and carve out a piece of the action for themselves through the subcommittee system.

Members of Congress now may have greater "independence," but it is independence from their party leadership and from older colleagues, not from the moneyed lobbyists and well-organized pressure groups that work so effectively on the Hill and back home. In addition, lawmakers are restrained by a host of forces that threaten to make it too costly for them to embark upon a preferred course of action. Hence, they often act in a way contrary to their own political proclivities, operating in a state of anticipatory response to larger influences. The "law of anticipatory response," as Schneider

---

38. Quoted in Melvin Eli, "Most Interns Find D.C. Insulated and Elitist," *Valley Advocate* (Amherst, Mass.), September 15, 1976.
39. This is a conclusion offered to me by one close student of Congress, Garrison Nelson.

notes, works with persistent effect,[40] and, I would add, in a society of concentrated wealth and power, it works largely with conservative effect, teaching caution to the maverick. Congressmen anticipate the powerful interest groups, the president, the other chamber, certain executive officials and agencies, state and local political and governmental groups, the electorate and the press. "All of these will constrain what congressmen believe worth an investment of time and effort and what they believe must be written off as desirable but infeasible."[41]

In recent years many members of Congress have been finding their jobs to be more demanding and less rewarding. The work load has greatly increased; special-interest groups are more numerous and more demanding; and in the post-Watergate era—in the wake of financial scandals in Congress and unsolved crises in the economy—congressmen have lost much of their previous prestige and status and are, more than ever, objects of suspicion in the public eye. In addition the erosion of the seniority system has diminished the rewards of political longevity. One result is that record numbers of lawmakers are voluntarily retiring, at the rate of almost one in ten in recent years. Congress is less often a place where one settles in for life.[42]

Although the legislative branch is inhabited by special interests, it is not quite accurate to call it "unrepresentative." In a way, Congress is precisely and faithfully representative of the power distributions of the wider society in that "power goes to those . . . legislators who service powerful interests, while isolation goes to those who merely represent powerless people."[43] And as long as Congress reflects the distribution of economic power in the wider society, it is not likely to change much even if liberals in both houses manage to gain control of the major committees, and even if the cloture rule is changed to enable the Senate to rid itself of the filibuster, and even if the Rules Committee is deprived of all its arbitrary powers, and even if seniority is done away with. For what remains is the entire system of organized corporate power with its hold over the economic life of the nation and the material resources of the society, its control of the media and mass propaganda, its dominance of most cultural

40. Schneider, *Ideological Coalitions in Congress*, p. 8.
41. *Ibid.*
42. *New York Times*, March 27, 1978, and November 13, 1978.
43. Ralph Nader, "Making Congress Work," *New Republic*, August 21–28, 1971, p. 19.

and social institutions, its organized pressure groups, high-paid lobbyists and influence-peddling lawyers, big money contributions and
bribes—all of which operate with such telling effect on legislators,
including many of the professedly liberal ones.

To be sure, a representative system *should* be a pressure system,
enabling constituents to influence their lawmakers. But what is usually missing from the lawmaker's own view is any real appreciation
of the one-sidedness of the pressure system. For many in Congress, as
in the state legislatures, the existing pressure system *is* the representative system; that is to say, those groups having the money, organization, visibility and expertise to *take* an interest in legislative affairs
are presumed to be the only ones that *have* an actual interest. The
muted levels of society are left pretty much out of the picture.

14

The President: Guardian of the System

Because the American presidency is such a highly elevated office we tend to forget that its occupants operate within the same system of power and interest as other politicians. Our task is to take a nonworshipful look at the presidency and the political forces which give it shape and direction.

THE CORPORATE POLITICIAN

The president, we are told, plays many roles. He is not only chief executive, he is "chief legislator," commander-in-chief, head of state and leader of his party. Seldom mentioned is his role as guardian and spokesman of business. Far from being an opponent of the special interests, the president is the embodiment of the executive-centered political system that serves them, playing an active part in defending American corporate interests at home and abroad.

As authoritative figures whose opinions are widely publicized, presidents do their share to indoctrinate the American people into the dominant business ideology, publicly praising industrialists for their allegedly great contributions to American life. "You men . . . are the leaders of this community," President Johnson once announced to a group of corporation heads, "and through your in-

dustries the leaders of the United States."[1] Every modern president
has had occasion to warn the citizenry of the dangers of radicalism,
the regimentations of socialism and the tyrannies of communism. All
have accepted and praised the "free enterprise system" and denounced its alternatives. President Carter proclaimed himself "an
engineer, a planner and a businessman," who understood "the value
of a strong system of free enterprise" with its "minimal intrusion of
government in our free economic system."[2] One writer's description
of President Ford could easily apply to any number of other
presidents:

> [He] follows the judgment of the major international oil companies on
> oil problems in the same way that he amiably heeds the advice of other
> big businesses on the problems that interest them. . . . He is . . . a solid
> believer in the business ideology of rugged individualism, free markets
> and price competition—virtues that exist more clearly in his mind than
> they do in the practices of the international oil industry.[3]

---

1. From the *Public Papers of the Presidents, Lyndon B. Johnson, 1963-1964*, vol. 2,
pp. 1, 147–151, reprinted in Marvin Gettleman and David Mermelstein (eds.), *The
Failure of American Liberalism* (New York: Vintage, 1971), pp. 124–128.
2. Carter's acceptance speech at the 1976 Democratic National Convention; *Seattle
Post-Intelligencer*, July 16, 1976.
3. William Shannon, *New York Times*, July 22, 1975.

Whether Democrat or Republican, liberal or conservative, the president tends to treat capitalist interests as synonymous with the nation's well-being.[4] He will describe the overseas investments of giant corporations as *"United States* investments abroad," part of *"America's* interests in the world," to be defended at all costs—or certainly at great cost. He will speak of "our" oil in the Middle East and "our" markets in Latin America and "our" raw materials in Southeast Asia (to be defended by *our* sons) when what he is referring to are the holdings of a small, powerful segment of the population. Presidents have presented their multibillion-dollar spending programs on behalf of private industry as necessary for *"America's* growing needs" and have greeted the expansion of big business and big profits as manifestations of "a healthy *national* economy" and as good for the *"national* interest."

At the Constitutional Convention, the wealthy planter Charles Pinckney proposed that no one qualify for the presidency who was not worth at least $100,000—a most handsome sum for 1787. While the proposal was never written into the Constitution, it seemingly has been followed in practice. The men who have occupied the highest office, with a few notable exceptions, have come from the highest income brackets. Many enter the White House after an extended period of professional and personal ties with banking and business firms. Since World War II, most presidential candidates on the Democratic and Republican tickets have been millionaires either at the time they first campaigned for the office or by the time they departed from it. In addition, presidents have drawn their top advisors and administrators primarily from industry and banking and have relied heavily on the judgments of corporate leaders.

Like other politicians, the men who run for president must procure vast sums from the rich in order to pay their campaign costs. Big contributors disclaim any intention of trying to buy influence with their gifts, insisting that they give freely because they "believe" in the candidate and think he will make the best president—certainly the best money can buy. They believe he will pursue policies that are beneficial to the national interest. That they view the national interest as something often indistinguishable from their own financial interests does not make their support hypocritical but all the more sincere. Their campaign contributions are not merely for a better personal deal but for a better America. And their image of a

---

4. Consider for instance Carter's relationship with David Rockefeller's Trilateral Commission. See Christopher Lydon, "Jimmy Carter Revealed: He's a Rockefeller Republican," *Atlantic*, July 1977, pp. 50–59.

better America is a product of their own class experiences and life values.

If it should happen, however, that after the election the big contributor finds himself or his firm burdened by a problem that only the White House can handle, he sees no reason why he shouldn't be allowed to exercise his democratic rights like any other citizen and ask his elected representative, who in this case happens to be his friend, the president of the United States, for a little help. Big interests have big problems, often national and international in scope, which require the attention of no one less than the president. Thus the Business Roundtable, a coalition of executive heads of 160 major firms, headed by the chairman of DuPont, not only buys hundreds of congressional votes each year but also enjoys regular access to the White House regardless of who its occupant happens to be.[5] Large donors to President Nixon's campaign, including certain insurance moguls, dairymen, bankers, carpet manufacturers, coal mine owners, railroad tycoons, hamburger restaurant-chain owners and managers of giant conglomerates like ITT, benefited many times over from White House intercessions on their behalf. In the case of ITT, the Nixon administration helped settle a multibillion-dollar antitrust suit against that corporation in return for a promised $400,000 donation.[6]

There is a view—made popular about the time Harry Truman was president—that the greatness of the office lends greatness to its occupants; even those persons of mediocre talent and stature supposedly grow in response to the presidency's great responsibilities and powers. Closer examination shows that most White House occupants have been just as readily corrupted as ennobled by the power of the office, inclined toward self-righteous assertion, compelled to demonstrate their macho toughness and decisiveness, intolerant of, and irritated by, public criticism and not above using their power in unlawful ways against political opponents. Thus at least six presidents employed illegal FBI wiretaps to gather incriminating information on rival political figures. The White House tapes, which recorded the private Oval Office conversations of President Nixon, revealed him to be a petty, vindictive, bigoted man who

---

5. See the *Guardian's* discussion, February 23, 1977, of a *Business Week* report on the Roundtable.

6. *New York Times*, June 15, 1973; also Anthony Sampson, *The Sovereign State of I.T.T.* (New York: Stein and Day, 1973). For other evidence of White House efforts on behalf of campaign donors see James Ridgeway, "Republican Campaign Contributions," *Village Voice*, October 20, 1972, p. 13 ff.; Ben A. Franklin, "Milk Aide Says a Lawyer for Nixon Sought Funds," *New York Times*, January 11, 1973.

manifested a shallowness of spirit and mind which the majestic office could cloak but not transform.[7]

THE DUAL PRESIDENCY

Presidents have made a show of concern for public causes, using slogans and images intended to enhance their popular appeal; thus Teddy Roosevelt had his "Square Deal," Woodrow Wilson his "New Freedom," Franklin Roosevelt his "New Deal," Harry Truman his "Fair Deal," John Kennedy his "New Frontier," and Lyndon Johnson his "Great Society." Behind the fine sounding labels one discovers much the same record of service to the powerful and neglect of the needy. Consider John Kennedy, a liberal president widely celebrated for his devotion to the underdog. In foreign affairs, Kennedy spoke of international peace and self-determination for all peoples, yet he invaded Cuba after Castro nationalized the holdings of U.S. corporations. He drastically increased military expenditures, instituted new counterinsurgency programs throughout the Third World and set up aid programs in underdeveloped nations that mostly benefited American investors.

In domestic matters Kennedy presented himself as a champion of civil rights, yet did little to create new job opportunities for Black people. And he refrained from taking legal action to support antidiscrimination cases or to prevent repeated atrocities against civil rights organizers in the South. Kennedy talked as if he were the special friend of the working people, yet he imposed wage restraints on unions at a time when the worker's buying power was stagnant or declining, and he strongly opposed introduction of the 35-hour week. He also instituted tax programs and deficit-spending policies that carried business profit rates to all-time highs without reducing unemployment. The image of Kennedy as antibusiness was undeserved: "In fact, in every significant area—wage policy, tax policy, international trade and finance, federal spending—the president showed a keen understanding and ready response to the essential corporate program."[8] With his youth, vigor, intelligence and public

---

7. In 1973, official audits revealed that Nixon had spent $10 million of the taxpayer's money on improvements for his private estates and that he had made illegal tax deductions of around a half-million dollars. Nixon's former White House counsel, John Dean, testified that on occasion the president had requested the Internal Revenue Service to stop auditing the incomes of close friends. *New York Times,* June 21 and 25, 1973, April 4, 1974; also June 22, 1973, for other reports of intervention on behalf of White House friends.

8. Bernard Nossiter, *The Mythmakers* (Boston: Beacon Press, 1964), p. 40.

utterances, Kennedy gave every appearance of being the active liberal, while actually he worked cautiously within the special-interest system instead of attempting to challenge or change it.[9]

Conservative presidents, such as Richard Nixon and Gerald Ford, manifested the same tendency to *talk* for the people and *work* for the corporate elites. Both of them voiced their support for environmental protection while opening new forest lands for commercial exploitation and opposing the regulation of strip mining. Both gave lip service to the problems of the Vietnam veteran, the plight of the elderly and the needs of the poor, yet opposed extending benefits and services to these groups and even supported cutbacks. And both Nixon and Ford pursued tax policies that benefited upper-income brackets and massive spending programs that served the giant corporations. While reviling the "big spenders" in Congress, Ford spent so freely on big business and the military that he created a record $65 billion deficit in fiscal 1975. Ford vetoed bills for school lunches, child day care and child nutrition programs. And he vetoed bills providing water sewer grants, disaster aid, rehabilitation for the physically and mentally handicapped and a minimum wage increase.[10]

President Carter supplied the same admixture of liberal rhetoric and conservative policy. He promised to cut the bloated military budget by some $5 billion and instead increased it $10 billion to a record $126 billion. He promised to "reduce the commerce in arms sales," but arms sales under his administration rose to new levels. He pledged to reduce the size of U.S. forces in South Korea but three years later there were more U.S. troops in that country than when he took office. While he talked of helping the needy, Carter proposed cutbacks in summer youth jobs, Comprehensive Employment and Training Act public service jobs, subsidized housing, school milk funds, child nutrition programs and disability benefits. After campaigning as a friend of labor, he went on, once in office, to oppose most of the AFL-CIO legislative program. And like his predecessors, he continued to dole out multibillion-dollar credits and subsidies to big business.[11]

---

9. See Ian McMahan, "The Kennedy Myth," *New Politics*, 3, Winter 1964, pp. 40–48; Richard Walton, *Cold War and Counter-Revolution: The Foreign Policy of John F. Kennedy* (Baltimore: Penguin Books, 1972); Bruce Miroff, *Pragmatic Illusions* (New York: McKay, 1976). For a treatment of the disparity between Lyndon Johnson's liberal rhetoric and his conservative policies, see Gettleman and Mermelstein, *The Failure of American Liberalism*; and Robert Sherrill, *The Accidental President* (New York: Grossman, 1967), chapters 3, 5 and 6.

10. See for instance, *New York Times*, September 11 and October 8, 1975.

11. *New York Times*, February 25, 1977 and January 15, 1978; Michael Klare, "Arms Sales Unlimited," *Progressive*, December 1977, pp. 9–11.

If presidents tend to speak one way and act another, it is less likely due to some inborn flaw shared by the varied personalities who occupy the office than to something in the nature of the office itself. Like any public officeholder, elected or otherwise, the president plays a dual role in that he must satisfy the major interests of corporate America and at the same time make a show of serving the people. He differs from other politicians in that the demands, expectations and functions of his office are greater and therefore the contradictions deeper. More than any other officeholder, he deals with the overall crises of capitalism, for he is the national executive, but he is also the only nationally elected leader (along with the vice-president, of course), and hence the most popular, the focus of mass attention and mass demand. So the president, even more than other politicians, is caught in the contradiction of wanting to represent "all the people" but finding that he must first tend to the needs of those who control the wealth, land, resources, technology, industry and jobs of the nation.

Although he may try, the president discovers he cannot belong to both the corporations and the people. Occasionally he may be instrumental in getting Congress to allocate monies and services for the needy, but whatever his intentions, he comes no closer to solving the deep structural problems of the politico-economy. So, like any politician, he fills the air with promises to "fight" inflation, unemployment and poverty and finds he has not the means of achieving these laudable ends, for he cannot both serve capitalism as capitalism needs to be served and at the same time drastically transform it. He cannot come up with a solution because he is part of the problem, or part of the system that creates the problem.

While congressmen are the captives of the special interests, the president, elected by the entire country, tends to be less vulnerable to the moneyed pressure groups and more responsive to the needs of the unorganized public—at least this is what political scientists taught after years of observing presidents like Roosevelt, Truman and Kennedy tussling with conservatives in Congress. As we have seen, our various presidents resemble the average pressure politician to a greater extent than we were taught to believe. Nevertheless, the president is more likely to see the ramifications that issues have for the overall system than the average member of Congress, who is concerned primarily with the problems of his district or state. Since the problems of the *nation* are his concern, the president is drawn to a broader perspective and is somewhat less likely to act as a special-interest politician. And when he does represent special interests he is less likely to be recognized as doing so, for he can define his policies on behalf of oil companies, banks, military contractors and aerospace technologists as necessary for the security and well-being of the nation itself.

Here then we can begin to see why the presidency is often considered a "progressive office." The growth of capitalism from a diverse array of small, local producers to national and multinational conglomerates has come at a cost to smaller firms and has necessitated increasingly active controls by the federal government. The government has helped secure markets for the bigger corporations by subsidizing them at the expense of smaller interests and by imposing regulations that limit the latter's opportunity to compete successfully. Presidents have been instrumental in thus "rationalizing" the economy, a process that began at least as early as Theodore Roosevelt.[12] In representing the more powerful, advanced, Eastern financial and industrial interests, the president has played a "progressive" role, so to speak, updating the economy and getting businessmen to accept a modern, state-regulated, state-supported capitalism.

In keeping with this task, the president reconciles conflicts between major producer interests, attempting to keep particular companies in line with the overall needs of the corporate economy: hence he might oppose tariff protections for particular firms in order to avoid having foreign countries retaliate by closing their markets to American multinationals in general. Or he might do battle with an industry like steel to hold prices down in order to ease the inflationary effects on other producer interests. When engaged in such conflicts the president takes on an appearance of opposing the special interests on behalf of the common interest. In fact, he might be better described as protecting the common interests of the special interests.

Finally, as the only elected officeholder accountable to a national constituency, and as the focus of popular expectation and constant attention from the media, the president does feel the pressure more than anyone else to solve the nation's problems.[13] It is his task, if anyone's, to ameliorate the hardships of the populace and discourage the tendency toward disruption, protest and troublesome rebellion. There are limits to how inequitable and oppressive the politico-economic system can be. Those who work too single-mindedly for the privileged classes run the risk of undermining the system. So bil-

---

12. See the discussion on the Progressive Era in chapter 5.
13. During President Carter's first months in office he received more than 20,000 telephone calls a day. On Dial-a-President Day, more than nine million people called the White House. See Richard Pious, *The American Presidency* (New York: Basic Books, 1979).

lions are spent on social programs to blunt the discontent that the underprivileged feel, wedding them to the system—by means of the dole. Here too, the president has been the key force in that process of reform which consists of giving a little to the many in order to keep a lot for the few. Again, his is a "progressive" role, but one intended to sustain rather than transform the existing system.

The success any group enjoys in winning the intervention of the president has less to do with the justice of its cause than with whether it occupies a high or low place in the class structure. If a large group of migrant workers and a small group of aerospace executives both sought the president's assistance, it would not be too difficult to predict which of them would be more likely to win it. Witness these events of April 1971:

(1) Some 80,000 to 90,000 migrant farm workers in Florida, out of work for much of the season because of crop failures and explicitly exempted from unemployment compensation, were left without means of feeding themselves and their families. Welfare agencies supplied some surplus foods that were "almost pure starch, usually unpalatable, and cause diarrhea to children." Faced with the prospect of seeing their children starve, the workers demonstrated in large numbers outside President Nixon's Key Biscayne vacation residence in Florida. The peaceful gathering was an attempt to attract public attention to their plight and to get the White House to intercede. The workers succeeded in attracting the attention only of the police, who dispersed them, charging their lines with swinging clubs. The demonstration was reported in a few small-circulation radical newspapers and ignored by most of the establishment news media.

There was no evidence that the farm workers' message ever intruded upon the president's attention, although information about their condition did reach several lower-level federal agencies. Subsequent appeals to Washington brought no response. Eventually the Florida farm counties were declared disaster areas only because of the crop losses sustained by the commercial farms. The government emergency relief money ended up in the hands of the big growers who worked with state agencies in distributing it. Since the migrant workers had no state residence, they did not qualify for relief and were "summarily left out of the decisions."[14]

(2) During the very week the farm workers were being clubbed in Key Biscayne, leaders of the aerospace industry placed a few tele-

---

14. Tom Foltz, "Florida Farmworkers Face Disaster," *Guardian*, April 3, 1971, p. 4.

phone calls to the right people in Washington and, without benefit
of demonstration or agitation, were invited to meet quietly with the
president to discuss their companies' job problems. Later that same
day the White House announced a $42 million authorization to the
aerospace industry to relocate, retrain and in other ways assist its
top administrators, scientists and technicians. The spending plan,
an industry creation, was accepted by the government without prior
study.[15]

Contrasting the treatment accorded the farm workers with that
provided the aerospace industrialists (or big farm owners, or big
dairymen, or representatives of U.S. Steel, ITT, etc.), we might ask:
is the president responding to a "national interest" or a "special interest" when he helps the giant firms? Much depends upon how the
labels are applied. Those who believe the national interest necessitates taking every possible measure to maintain the profits and
strength of the industrial and military establishment, of which the
aerospace industry is a part, might say the president is not responding to a special interest but to the needs of national security. Certainly almost every president in modern times might have agreed
and acted accordingly. Industry is said to be the muscle and sinews
of the nation. In contrast, a regional group of farm workers represents a marginal interest. Without making light of the suffering of
the migrant families, it is enough to say that a president's first responsibility is to tend to our industrial economy. In fact, the argument goes, when workers act to disrupt and weaken the sinews of industry, as have striking coal miners, railroad operators and steel
workers, the president may see fit to deal summarily with them.

Other people would argue that the national interest is not served
when giant industries receive favored treatment at the expense of the
taxpayers, consumers and workers and to the lasting neglect of millions like the farm workers. That the corporations have holdings
which are national and often multinational in scope does not mean

15. *New York Times*, April 2, 1971. It would take an exceptional flight of the imagination by any president to visualize the sufferings of the poor: the president lives rent-
free in a 132-room mansion called the White House, set on an 18-acre estate, with a $2
million maintenance budget and a domestic staff of 83, including six butlers; a well-
stocked wine cellar; a private movie room; a gymnasium; tennis courts; a bowling
alley and a heated outdoor swimming pool. In addition, he has the free services of a
private physician, a dozen chauffeured limousines, numerous helicopters and jets, including Air Force One—which costs $2,000 an hour to fly—access to country retreats,
a $50,000 yearly expense allowance—and for the few things he must pay for himself, a
$200,000 annual salary. Journalists and political scientists have described the pres-
idency as a "man-killing job." Yet presidents live well and generally live long, at least
as long as the average American male and certainly longer and better than the average
migrant worker.

they represent the interests of the nation's populace. The "national interest" or "public interest" should encompass the ordinary public rather than the big commercial farm owners, corporate elites and their well-paid technicians and managers. Contrary to an established myth, the public monies distributed to these favored few do not "trickle down" to the mass of working people at the bottom—as the hungry farm workers can testify.

Whichever position one takes, it becomes clear that there is no *neutral* way of defining the "national interest." Whichever policy the president pursues, he is helping some class interests rather than others, and it is a matter of historical record that presidents have usually chosen a definition of the national interest that serves the giant conglomerates. It is also clear, whether we consider it essential or deplorable, that the president, as the most powerful officeholder in the land, is most readily available to the most powerful interests in the land and rather inaccessible to us lesser mortals.

THE PRESIDENT VERSUS CONGRESS: WHO HAS THE POWER?

Since the turn of the century, the burdens of government have grown enormously at the municipal, state and federal levels and in the executive, legislative and judicial branches. But as industrial capitalism expanded at home and abroad, the task of serving and protecting its vast interests and dealing with the problems it has caused has fallen disproportionately on that level of government which is national and international in scope—the federal—and on that branch which is suited for carrying out the necessary technical, organizational and military tasks—the executive.[16] The powers of the executive have increased so much that today there is no such thing as a "weak" president, for even Eisenhower, who preferred to exercise as little initiative as possible in most affairs, found himself proposing huge budgets and participating in decisions of far greater scope than anything handled by a "strong" president a half century before. If there has been an expansion of presidential powers it has been less due to the aggrandizing impulses of White House occupants than to an accretion in the governing functions of the office. When individual presidents have gathered power to themselves, this

---

16. Today the federal government spends more in one day (about a billion dollars) than it spent in the first sixty years of its existence.

was less a cause of, than a response to, the growing demands placed on the office.[17]

The growth of the powers of the presidency has been so great as to have occasioned a *relative* decline in the powers of Congress (even though the scope of legislative activity itself has greatly increased over the years). This is especially true in international affairs. Congressional influence over foreign policy has been exercised largely by withholding funds, passing resolutions, ratifying treaties, confirming ambassadors and other such means; but in recent times presidents increasingly have bypassed Congress or confronted it with *faits accomplis*, making covert military commitments, ignoring legislative amendments in international matters, circumventing the Senate's power to ratify treaties by resorting to "executive agreements," and placing White House policymakers beyond the reach of congressional interrogation by claiming "executive privilege" for them. Although "executive privilege" is nowhere mentioned in the Constitution, it has been used to withhold information on everything from undeclared wars to illegal campaign funds and burglaries. In 1976 Ford invoked it when refusing to supply a House committee with information on the CIA.[18] The net effect of the growth in presidential power has been to move important policy decisions increasingly out of public view and into the secrecy of the executive office.

The legislative branch is often no better informed than the public it represents. For a number of years Congress unknowingly funded CIA operations in Laos and Thailand that were in violation of congressional prohibitions. Most of the members of the Senate who were questioned by Senator William Proxmire (D.-Wisc.) had never heard of the automated battlefield program for which they had voted secret appropriations.[19] Congress ordered a halt to further expansion of a controversial naval base on an island in the Indian

---

17. For an interesting discussion of presidential power see Pious, *The American Presidency*.

18. "Executive privilege" was given a legal peg by the Nixon-appointed Supreme Court, which, while ruling that the concept did not apply to criminal cases (the release of the White House tapes in the Watergate affair), did declare that a "presumptive privilege" for withholding information belonged to the president. See *U.S. v. Nixon* 418 U.S. 683 (1974). Most certainly "presumptive," since it has no existence in the Constitution or in any law.

19. Paul Dickson and John Rothchild, "The Electronic Battlefield: Wiring Down the War," *Washington Monthly*, May 1971, pp. 6–14. If the Pentagon Papers reveal anything, it is the secretive, unaccountable nature of executive policy. See the latter portion of Richard J. Barnet's *Roots of War* (New York: Atheneum, 1972) for an account of the ways public opinion is manipulated by officialdom; also John C. Donovan, *The Cold Warriors: A Policy Elite* (Lexington, Mass.: D. C. Heath, 1973).

Ocean, only to discover subsequently that construction was continuing and air activities had steadily increased at the base.[20] A report from two House Foreign Affairs subcommittees[21] complained of the "unwillingness of the executive branch to acknowledge major decisions and to subject them to public scrutiny and discussion."[22]

In many instances, whether in foreign or domestic matters, it is not that the president acts without Congress but that he commands levers of power which leave the legislature no option but to move in a direction predetermined by him. The executive branch's control of crucial information, its system of management and budgeting and its vast network of specialized administrators and staff workers enable it to play a greater role in shaping the legislative agenda than the understaffed, overworked and often ill-informed legislators. Approximately 80 percent of the major laws enacted have originated in the executive branch.

Congress itself has been compliant about the usurpation of its power. Since 1790, the legislature has granted each president, and a widening list of executive agencies, confidential funds for which no detailed invoices are required. The statute that created the CIA permitted it to expend billions without regard to the provisions of law regulating government spending and without the knowledge of Congress.[23] Congress has preferred to pass on to the president the task of handling crises and making troublesome and unpopular policy choices on behalf of the corporate system at home and abroad.

The peculiar danger of executive power is that it executes. Presidents have repeatedly engaged in acts of warfare, for instance, without congressional knowledge or approval because they have had at their command the military forces to do so. If the executive branch proposes, it just as often disposes, having the final word on what and how things get done, acting with the force of state, exercising daily initiatives of its own on a scale so massive and detailed, so secretive and closely linked to its military and security forces as to be held unaccountable more often than not. Indeed, the growth of the presidency has been a growth in its unaccountable and unilateral powers. The crimes of Richard Nixon, then, were not an anomaly

---

20. UPI dispatch in *Workers World*, January 2, 1976.

21. The House Foreign Affairs Committee is now the House International Relations Committee.

22. The subcommittees' statement is quoted in Graham Hovey, "Making Foreign Policy," *New York Times*, January 22, 1973, p. 31. Yet, as noted in the previous two chapters, Congress seems willing enough to go along with most of the executive's secret practices and has a number of its own.

23. Louis Fisher, *Presidential Spending Power* (Princeton, N.J.: Princeton University Press, 1975).

but a fulfillment of the growing capacity for abuse and evil that inheres in the office.

In the post-Watergate era, Congress felt the need to limit the expansive nature of the executive branch. To cite a few instances:

1. After seeing Nixon repeatedly impound funds appropriated by a Democratic Congress for domestic programs, Congress passed the Impoundment Control Act of 1974, requiring the president to get congressional permission to defer spending appropriations—and the deferral cannot extend beyond the end of the year.

2. Congress now has budget committees with staffs that can more effectively study the president's budget, a longer budgetary review period and better coordinating procedures within both houses—all designed to give Congress greater control over federal spending.

3. The Foreign Military Sales Act was amended to enable Congress, by concurrent resolution, to prevent any major arms sales to other nations; the president is also required to give the legislature advance notice on sales.

4. In forty years, three presidents declared states of "national emergency"—to win support for war, to break strikes, to freeze wages and to stop bank failures. Under the National Emergencies Act of 1976, all powers held by the executive as a result of past emergencies were terminated as of 1978, and all future emergencies declared by the president must end on the date specified in a presidential proclamation or in a legislative concurrent resolution, whichever date is earlier.[24]

Many of the restrictions imposed by Congress exist more in form than in substance. Thus the president can still grant himself emergency powers, even if only for a specified time. And there still exist some 470 statutes which extend potentially dictatorial emergency powers to the president, allowing him to seize properties, institute martial law, control all transportation and restrict travel.[25] Congress now requires that the president send it a copy of any secret agreement made with other governments. But if the president de-

24. For a good discussion of these points see Harvey G. Zeidenstein, "The Reassertion of Congressional Power: New Curbs on the President," *Political Science Quarterly*, 93, Fall 1978, pp. 393–409.

25. See the joint statement by Senators Church and Mathias for the Senate Committee on the Termination of the National Emergency, quoted in the *Guardian*, January 23, 1974.

cides that public disclosure might harm "national security," he can submit the text to the confidential review of only the Senate Foreign Relations Committee and the House International Relations Committee; in effect, still keeping the agreement secret.[26]

Under the guise of limiting presidential power, Congress sometimes inadvertently expands it. Thus the War Powers Resolution, placing the president under obligation to seek congressional approval within sixty days for any war he has launched, actually expands his warmaking powers, since the Constitution does not grant the president power to engage in warfare without *prior* congressional approval.[27]

Commanding the kind of media exposure that most politicians can only dream of, the president is able to direct attention to his program, be it for defense spending, taxes, wage controls, foreign trade, oil imports or international conflicts; and once he succeeds in defining his program as crucial to the "national interest" and himself as the key purveyor of that interest, Congress usually votes the necessary funds and enabling powers, contenting itself with making marginal modifications and inserting special amendments for special friends of its own. This is particularly the case if the president is not attempting anything of a radically deviant nature but much less true if he is hoping to initiate a program of a seemingly progressive kind.

One recalls that liberals frequently complained about the way Congress managed to thwart the desires of liberal presidents like Truman and Kennedy. They concluded from this that Congress had too much power and that the president needed more. But having witnessed a conservative president like Richard Nixon regularly effect his will over a Democratic Congress, some of these same liberals then concluded that the president had too much power and Congress not enough. Actually, there is something more to these respective complaints than partisan inconsistency. In the first situation liberals are talking about the president's insufficient ability to effect

---

26. See Zeidenstein, "The Reassertion of Congressional Power . . . "
27. Not all the restrictions Congress imposes on the president are to be considered for the better. It is one thing when the legislature limits presidential powers in order to assert its own constitutional responsibilities and curb executive abuses, but Congress has also shown itself hostile toward the president when he tries to bring the immense federal bureaucracy, which is infiltrated by special interests and subjected to powerful centrifugal forces, under tighter White House control. Attempts by Nixon, and later by Carter, to make federal departments and agencies more accountable to White House staff members, who in turn are directly accountable to the president, have been treated by Congress as usurpation. As the elected chief executive, the president should be able to exercise control over his nonelected executive branch.

measures that might benefit the many millions toward the bottom of the social ladder. And in the second instance they are talking about the president's seemingly limitless ability to make overseas military commitments and to thwart social-welfare legislation at home.

What underlies the ostensibly inconsistent liberal complaint is the fact that *the relative powers of the executive and legislative branches depend in part on the interests being served,* and that regardless of who is in what office, the political system operates more efficiently to realize conservative goals than reformist ones, both the executive and legislative branches being more responsive to the corporate powers than to economically deprived social groups. Thus the president tends to be more powerful than Congress when he assumes a conservative stance, and less powerful when he wants to push in a progressive direction. This is a reflection of not only wider politico-economic forces but of the way the Constitution structures things. As the framers intended in 1787, the system of separation of powers and checks and balances is designed to give the high ground to those who would resist social change, be they presidents or congressmen. Neither the executive nor the legislature can single-handedly initiate reform, which means that conservatives need to control only one or the other branch to thwart domestic actions (or in the case of Congress, key committees in one or the other house) while liberals must control both houses and both branches.

Small wonder that conservative and liberal presidents have different kinds of experiences with Congress. Since a conservative president generally wants very little from Congress in the way of liberal domestic legislation and, with a few well placed allies in the legislature, can often squelch what little Congress attempts to produce in that direction, he is less beholden to that body than a liberal president. Should Congress insist upon passing bills that incur his displeasure, the conservative president need control only one-third plus one of either the House or the Senate to sustain his vetoes. If bills are passed over his veto, he can still undermine legislative intent by delaying enforcement under various pretexts relating to timing, efficiency and other operational contingencies. The Supreme Court has long been aware that its decisions have the force of law only if other agencies of government choose to carry them out. In recent years Congress has been coming to the same realization, developing a new appreciation of the executive's power to command in a direct and palpable way the people, materials and programs needed for carrying out decisions.

The techniques of veto, decoy and delay used by a conservative president to dismantle or hamstring already weak domestic programs are of little help to a liberal president who might claim an interest in social change, for the immense social problems he faces cannot be solved by executive sleight-of-hand. What minor efforts liberal presidents make in the field of "social reform" legislation are frequently thwarted or greatly diluted by entrenched conservative powers in Congress. It is in these confrontations that the Congress gives every appearance of being able to frustrate presidential initiatives.

CHANGE FROM THE TOP?

The ability of even a well-intentioned executive to generate policies for the benefit of relatively powerless constituents is, to say the least, quite limited. Not only presidents but mayors and governors have complained of the difficulties of moving in new directions. The Black mayor of Gary, Indiana, Richard Hatcher, one of the more dedicated and socially conscious persons to achieve public office, offered this observation:

> I am mayor of a city of roughly 90,000 Black people but we do not control the possibilities of jobs for them, or money for their schools, or state-funded social services. These things are in the hands of the U.S. Steel Corporation, and the County Department of Welfare, the State of Indiana. . . . For not a moment do I fool myself that Black political control of Gary or of Cleveland or of any other city in and of itself can solve the problems of the wretched of this nation. The resources are not available to the cities to do the job that needs doing.[28]

Hatcher's statement is not unique. "The speeches of mayors and governors," writes Richard Goodwin, "are filled with exculpatory claims that the problems are too big, that there is not enough power or enough money to cope with them, and our commentators sympathize, readily agreeing that this city or that state is really ungovernable."[29]

When presidents, governors and mayors contend that the problems they confront are of a magnitude far greater than the resources they command, we can suspect them of telling the truth. Most of the resources are preempted by vested interests. The executive leader

28. From a speech delivered by Hatcher to an NAACP meeting, reprinted in the *Old Mole* (Boston), October 5, 1968.
29. Richard Goodwin, "Reflections: Sources of the Public Unhappiness," *New Yorker*, January 4, 1969, p. 41.

who begins his term with the promise of getting things moving is less likely to change the political-corporate-class system than be absorbed by it. Once in office, he finds himself staggered by the vast array of entrenched powers working within and without government. He is confronted with a recalcitrant legislature and an intractable bureaucracy. He is constantly distracted by issues and operational problems that seem to take him from his intended course, and he is unable to move in certain directions without incurring the hostility of those who control the economy and its institutional auxiliaries. So he begins to talk about being "realistic" and working with what is at hand, now tacking against the wind, now taking one step back in the often unrealized hope of taking two steps forward, until his public begins to complain that his administration bears a dismaying resemblance to the less dynamic, less energetic ones that came before. In the hope of maintaining his efficacy, he begins to settle for the *appearance* of efficacy, until appearances are all he is left struggling with. It is this tugging and hauling and whirling about in a tight circle of options and ploys that is celebrated by some as "the give-and-take of democratic group-interest politics." To less enchanted observers the failure of reform-minded leaders to deliver on their promises is another demonstration of the impossibility of working for major changes within a politico-economic system structured to resist change.

15

The Politics
of Bureaucracy

As everyone complains, bureaucracy is beset by iner-
tia, evasion and unaccountability, but there are reasons why bureaucrats behave as they do, and many of these reasons are profoundly
political, being less a peculiarity of bureaucrats than a reflection of
the wider system of power and interest in which they operate.

GOVERNMENT BY SECRECY
AND DECEPTION

The first line of defense for any bureaucracy, Max Weber once
wrote, is the withholding of information. Actually, it is the first line
of defense of any person in authority who wishes to keep as much beyond public criticism as possible. Officials who lie or who resort to
secrecy do so not only to maintain a free hand in the pursuit of their
interests (or the interests they serve) but because they distrust the
public's ability to judge correctly. These two sentiments strengthen
each other, as when officeholders do their best to keep the public ignorant and then use this ignorance as justification for not inviting
public criticism.

Chief executives have repeatedly misled Congress and the public
about U.S. overseas interventions and then claimed a special knowledge or expertise in foreign affairs. Thus, past administrations have
lied to the American public about the U.S. role in overthrowing
popular governments in countries like Guatemala, Iran, Indonesia,

259

the Dominican Republic and Chile. Over the years different presidents and their aides have lied about the extent of U.S. covert intervention in Indochina, much of Latin America, Cuba, Angola, Portugal, Jamaica and East Timor. The government lied about the CIA's use of U-2 spy planes over the Soviet Union until the Russians produced a live American U-2 pilot who had been shot down over their territory. And the government repeatedly lied to keep secret some 3,630 B-52 raids that took place in Cambodia from 1969 to 1970.[1]

After a review of its secret files, the Defense Department declassified 710 documents and destroyed 355,300. A director of the CIA destroyed all tape recordings of his calls over a six-year period. President Ford vetoed a bill that would have made government-held information more accessible to the public. Senate investigators estimated that the United States has as many as 400 to 600 secret agreements with other countries which the White House refused to deliver to Congress, including aid agreements with the fascist government of Chile and trade agreements with the Soviet Union.[2]

The White House and various executive agencies frequently cooperate more closely with private business than with Congress, especially when it comes to keeping things secret. Government regulation of prices charged by utilities and gas companies and government leasing of offshore drilling tracts to oil companies are based on data supplied by the interested corporations; this information is not available to Congress or the public. The Social Security Administration (SSA) has declined to publicize its report on Medicare operations and its related Blue Cross program, despite growing public criticism of rising costs and curtailed benefits.[3] While the Internal Revenue Service freely hands out tax records to agencies like the FBI, it refused to disclose to Congress its highly questionable ruling on a capital gains tax allowing ITT to take over a big Hartford insurance company.[4] And in the departments of Agriculture, Interior, Commerce and Defense, the doings of government and industry are frequently known only to select groups of bureaucrats and corporate

---

1. See David Wise, *The Politics of Lying* (New York: Random House, 1973) for numerous examples of government deception and secrecy; also *New York Times*, October 18, 1974, March 2 and 26, 1976; *Guardian*, September 29, 1976.
2. *Charlotte* (N.C.) *Observer*, July 11, 1975.
3. But the SSA does make available to private groups the files it keeps on citizens, as does the Veteran's Administration, according to a GAO investigation. *New York Times*, July 20, 1978.
4. *New York Times*, February 26, 1974.

leaders, leaving the rest of us to guess whether these policies are economically or socially beneficial.[5]

The government has repressed information concerning health and safety problems. As early as 1954 the Food and Drug Administration was warned that the cyclamates put in many drinks and foods were linked to cancer. Yet five years later the FDA listed the cyclamates as safe, and it was not until 1969 that it removed them from beverages. (It still allows them in certain foods.) The Atomic Energy Commission, and now the Nuclear Regulatory Commission, repeatedly suppressed information about the highly hazardous features of nuclear reactors. Although a study commissioned by the Department of Health, Education and Welfare showed that herbicides used in heavy amounts as defoliants in Vietnam and as weed killer in the United States produced birth deformities at low-exposure levels, for years this information was suppressed. Meanwhile, one-eighth of the acreage in South Vietnam was sprayed with these chemicals, and a drastic increase in deformed births was reported. Investigations into these and other incidents caused two Stanford University scientists to report:

> We believe, as a result of our studies, that . . . the executive decision-making process too often sacrifices the safety and welfare of the public to the short-term interests of the government bureaucracy and the large industrial interest to which it has become allied. . . . In these cases, where the facts and the best expert advice did not support the current administration policy, the primary interest of the Executive in the facts was to suppress them—even while stressing in public that its policies had a sound technical foundation.[6]

Those public servants who defy the code of secrecy to inform a congressman or reporter that something is wrong risk punishment by their superiors. One such "whistleblower," Andrew Susce, an IRS agent, uncovered a multimillion-dollar tax fraud perpetrated by mobsters and politicians, and was fired for his persistence in the case.[7] When a weapons-cost analyst, Ernest Fitzgerald, testified that a Lockheed cargo plane cost $2 billion more than contracted, the Air Force abolished his job. Once fired, dissidents find few em-

---

5. James Ridgeway, "How Government and Industry Keep Secrets from the People," *New Republic*, August 21 and 28, 1971, pp. 17–19.
6. The Stanford report was released in early 1971; its authors were Dr. Frank von Hippel and Dr. Joel Primack.
7. For Susce's story see John Hayes, *Lonely Fighter* (Secaucus, N. J.: Lyle Stuart, 1979).

ployment opportunities in government or in industries dealing with government contracts.[8]

To prevent other federal employees from "committing truth," the government sought greater power to control and punish disclosures—even disclosures of unclassified materials. It argued in several court cases that government information is government property, therefore when whistleblowers take and release such information they are guilty of theft. In effect, the government claims the power to make anything it does an official secret.[9] Former Attorney-General Bell denounced Justice Department personnel who leaked information to the press regarding FBI wrongdoings as having violated their oath "to uphold the law."[10] Thus, leaking information about crimes is itself treated as a crime, and "upholding the law" means collaborating in the cover-up or at least looking the other way.

It is senseless to urge people to work for change within the system when they cannot find out what the system is doing. This is not to say that government does not communicate with the public; indeed the public is subjected to a continual barrage of propaganda from official sources. Many millions of dollars are spent yearly by federal agencies and departments, of which the Pentagon is the most prolific, in the form of hundreds of magazine articles and motion pictures, thousands of radio scripts and tens of thousands of press releases and planted news stories.[11]

BUREAUCRATIC ACTION AND INACTION

The rulings of bureaucratic agencies are published daily in the *Congressional Federal Register*, a volume as imposing in size as the *Congressional Record* itself. Many of these rulings are as significant as major pieces of legislation, and in the absence of precise guidelines from Congress, they often take the place of legislation. In 1972, for instance, without a single law being passed and without a word of public debate, the Price Commission approved more than $2 billion in rate increases for 110 telephone, gas and electric com-

---

8. Helen Dudar, "The Price of Blowing the Whistle," *New York Times Magazine*, October 30, 1977, for a number of such cases, including Fitzgerald's; also Alexander Cockburn and James Ridgeway, "Scientist J. Anthony Morris—He Fought the Flu Shots and the U.S. Fired Him," *Boston Globe*, March 13, 1977.

9. *New York Times*, July 12, 1978; also Morton Halperin's Op-ed in *New York Times*, August 8, 1978.

10. *New York Times*, May 18, 1977.

11. See J. William Fulbright, *The Pentagon Propaganda Machine* (New York: Vintage, 1971).

panies, thereby imposing upon the public by administrative fiat an expenditure far greater than what is contained in most of the bills passed by Congress.[12] Even when legislation does exist, it usually allows for leeway in application. Which laws are applied fully and which are ignored, what interpretations are made to suit what interests, what supplementary regulations are formulated—these matters, of keen concern to lobbyists, are almost unknown to the general public.

To treat public administration as a "neutral" and "nonpartisan" function is grossly misleading.[13] The political process does not end with the passage of a bill but continues with equal or even greater intensity at the administrative level, albeit in more covert fashion. The administrative process becomes part of the pressure-group process and frequently has the effect of changing or subverting the intent of the law. Succumbing to business pressures, administrators will ignore statutory deadlines and delay carrying out the law. Thus, a congressional act requiring commercial fishermen to use certain netting techniques to protect endangered species like porpoises remained unenforced because fishing interests found it too costly and burdensome.[14] The Federal Reclamation Act, intended to shield small farmers from the concentrated wealth and speculations of agribusiness, declares that waters from federal dams cannot be supplied to farms exceeding 160 acres per person or to absentee-owned farms. But the law has gone unenforced for decades, as corporations like Standard Oil, Purex and Southern Pacific Railroad accumulated vast holdings and were subsidized by the taxpayer-funded water projects.[15]

The Resource Conservation and Recovery Act, the first comprehensive law governing the disposal of garbage and toxic wastes, was supposed to clean up industrial dumping and prevent tragedies like the one at Love Canal in Niagara Falls. But at every turn industrial

---

12. See the report by Senator Lee Metcalf in *Ramparts*, November 1972, p. 24.

13. The myth of administrative "neutrality" is encouraged by such things as the Hatch Act, a law prohibiting political activities by federal employees, presumably to preserve them from corrupt or biased influence. The act accomplishes no such thing. What it does is prevent millions of Americans from organizing in the defense of their own beliefs and interests, while leaving them fully exposed to the politics of bureaucracy. The constitutionality of the act was upheld by the Supreme Court in 1973 by a 6–3 decision, in *U.S. Civil Service Commission* v. *National Association of Letter Carriers*.

14. See the comments by environmental lawyer James Moorman reported in the *New York Times*, February 12, 1974.

15. Kathy Keilch, "Agribusiness Skirts U.S. Water Law," *Guardian*, February 8, 1978.

lobbyists stymied the Environmental Protection Agency (EPA), requiring the agency to spend much of its time and limited resources responding to industry's complaints, both directly and through Congress and the courts. Meanwhile the law remained unenforced and industry continues to produce 34 million tons of dangerous wastes every year.[16]

Often agencies are not sufficiently equipped to handle the enormous tasks that confront them. Though it is supposed to regulate a $400 million industry called campaign financing, the Federal Election Commission does not have a single certified public accountant on its auditing staff.[17] With 10,000 employees, EPA may take fifteen years to assess the safety of all pesticides, let alone control and restrict their use. Meanwhile the chemical industry pours about 1,000 new potentially toxic chemicals into the environment each year—seemingly at a faster rate than they can be monitored and controlled.[18]

People who bemoan the "inaction" within municipal, state and federal administrations and who insist that things don't get done because that's simply the nature of the bureaucratic beast, seem to forget that only certain kinds of things don't get done—other things are accomplished all too well. A law establishing a "community development" program for the ghetto, passed by a reluctant Congress in response to the urgings of liberal spokesmen and the pressure of demonstrations and urban riots, is legally the same as a law enacted to develop a multibillion-dollar, high-profit weapons system, the latter supported by giant industrial contractors, well-placed persons within the military, scientific and university establishments and numerous congressmen whose patriotism is matched only by their desire to bring the defense bacon home to their districts and keep their campaign coffers filled by appreciative donors. If anything, the weapons program is of vastly greater administrative complexity than the smaller, modestly funded ghetto program. Yet the latter is more likely to suffer from inaction and ineffectiveness, the important difference between the two programs being not bureaucratic but political. *The effectiveness of the law depends on the power of the groups supporting it.* Laws that serve powerful interests are like-

---

16. Newsletter of Environmental Action, Washington, D.C., 1979.
17. *Washington Post*, April 30, 1979.
18. *New York Times*, December 12, 1977. EPA must also review the safety of most other toxic substances; *New York Times*, October 30, 1977. The law provides a loophole for industry, requiring EPA to consider compliance costs and available substitute chemicals before restricting a substance. See Dennis Schaal, "EPA Shuts Eyes to Environmental Peril," *Guardian*, September 20, 1978; Richard Lyons, "Chemicals in Search of a Solution," *New York Times*, December 25, 1977.

ly to enjoy a vigorous life while laws that have only the powerless to nurture them are often stillborn.

Years after passage of a law making some 13 million children eligible for medical examinations and treatment, Congress discovered that almost 85 percent of the youngsters had been left unexamined, causing, in the words of a House subcommittee report, "unnecessary crippling, retardation, or even death of thousands of children." The report blamed HEW for its laxity in properly enforcing the programs and for failing to penalize laggard states.[19] The question is whether such a performance of nonenforcement is tolerated when the client interests are not powerless children but powerful industrialists, military contractors, oil companies or bankers.

Bureaucracies grow and grow, mostly in response to the needs of big business and the military, but also because bureaucrats themselves, in order to justify their existence and advance their careers, spawn new programs and consume more funds. In time, the sheer vastness of the bureaucracy lends itself to waste and duplication. The National Science Foundation made a study of automotive fuel and another of mass transportation only to discover that the Army and the Department of Transportation had already conducted similar studies. There are thirteen different advisory committees on cancer, four on air pollution and three on alcoholism. Seventeen agencies deal with "consumer concerns," none of them effectively. And there are five water-research agencies.

With all the waste and duplication, important public needs such as antitrust enforcement, occupational safety, transportation safety, community health, consumer protection (including regulation of cosmetics and drugs), environmental protection and welfare services remain improperly regulated or completely neglected. Millions of people staff the gargantuan federal bureaucracy, but relatively few perform the services most needed by ordinary citizens. Service goes to those who have the power to command it. The size of an agency, in any case, is a less significant determinant of its performance than the political influences bearing upon it. With a limited budget of only $3 million in 1949, the Food and Drug Administration proceeded against thousands of violators. In 1976, with a $200-million budget, FDA did not take court action against a single major drug company.[20]

With the right political support bureaucracies are capable of carrying out policies of momentous scope. "The feat of landing men

19. UPI dispatch in the *Collegian* (Amherst, Mass.), October 8, 1976.
20. Paul Murphy and Rene Care Murphy, "Consumer Beware," *Village Voice*, April 12, 1976, p. 12.

on the moon," Duane Lockard reminds us, "was not only a scientific achievement but a bureaucratic one as well."[21] The same might be said of the Vietnam war, the U.S. counterinsurgency effort in Latin America, the exploits of the Internal Revenue Service, and the farm, highway, housing and defense programs. These endeavors represent

---

21. Duane Lockard, *The Perverted Priorities of American Politics* (New York: Macmillan, 1971), p. 282.

the mobilization and coordination of stupendous amounts of energy, skill and material resources by complex, centralized systems of command—i.e., bureaucracies. What is impressive about the federal housing program, for instance, is not how little has been done but how much, yet with so little benefit to low-income people: how many public agencies established, billions spent, millions of work hours expended, millions of tons of materials utilized, and hundreds of thousands of structures built and subsidized at such profit to realty speculators, manufacturers, big merchants, banks and public officials and at such cost to the taxpayers—a stupendous bureaucratic effort. Bureaucracy's failure to serve the unorganized and needy public has led some observers to the mistaken notion that it serves no one. But as we have seen in previous chapters, for some groups the government has been anything but idle.[22]

The same can be said of Congress. As already noted, the complaint that Congress can't get things done is incorect. While unable to accomplish certain things, especially in regard to low-income housing, hunger, medical care, unemployment and mass transportation, Congress is capable of extraordinary achievements. The space, defense, highway, agricultural and tax programs are not only bureaucratic feats, they are legislative ones. The question is not, "Why can't administrators and legislators act?" but, "Why are they able to act so forcefully and successfully in some ways and not at all in other ways?" The first question invites us to throw up our hands in befuddlement; the second requires that we investigate the realities of power and interest.

Why are reform-minded administrative bodies rarely able to operate with any effectiveness? Consider the fate of the agency set up to regulate some area of industry on behalf of consumers, workers or the environment. In its youth, the agency may possess a zeal for reform, but before long the public concern that gave it impetus begins to fade. The business-owned news media either turn their attention to more topical events or present an unsympathethic or superficial picture of the agency's doings. The president, if he was originally sympathetic to the agency's mission, is now occupied with more pressing matters, as are its few articulate but not very influential friends in Congress. But the industry that is supposed to be brought under control remains keenly interested and by now is well alerted and ready to oppose government intrusions. First, it may decide to challenge the agency's jurisdiction or even the legality of its exis-

22. See Orion F. White, Jr., "The Dialectical Organization: An Alternative to Bureaucracy," *Public Administration Review*, 19, January–February 1969, pp. 32–41.

tence in court, thus preventing any serious regulatory actions until a legal determination is made.[23] If the agency survives this attack, there begins a series of encounters between its investigators and representatives from the industry. The industry is able to counter the agency's moves with a barrage of arguments and technical information, not all truthful but sufficiently impressive to win the respectful attention of the agency's investigators. The investigators begin to develop a new appreciation of industry's side of the story and of the problems it faces in maintaining profitable operations. Indeed, for extended periods it is the only side administrators may be exposed to, and in time they begin to adopt industry's perspective.[24]

If the agency persists in making unfavorable rulings, businessmen appeal to their elected representatives, or to a higher administrative official or, if they have the pull, to the president himself. In its youthful days, after World War I, the Federal Trade Commission moved vigorously against big business, but representatives of industry prevailed upon the president to replace "some of the commissioners by others more sympathetic with business practices: this resulted in the dismissal of many complaints which had been made against corporations."[25]

Frequently members of Congress demand to know why an agency is bothering their constituents. Administrators who are more interested in building congressional support than in making congressional enemies are likely to apply the law in ways that satisfy influential legislators. "If the bureaucrats are to escape criticism, unfavorable publicity, or a cut in their appropriations, they must be discreet in their relations with the legislative body."[26] Some administrative bodies, like the Army Corps of Engineers, so successfully cultivate support among powerful congressmen and big-business clientele as to become relatively free of supervisory control from department heads or the White House. "Fierce rivalries for funds and functions go on ceaselessly among the departments and between the agencies. A cunning bureau chief learns to negotiate alliances on Capitol Hill

---

23. See the discussion in Grant McConnell, *Private Power and American Democracy* (New York: Knopf, 1966), p. 288.

24. For instance, a report by the National Academy of Sciences found that EPA "is inevitably dependent" on the industries it regulates for much of the information it uses in decision-making, and that such information is easily withheld or distorted to serve industry's ends; *New York Times*, March 22, 1977; also *Washington Post*, August 24, 1979.

25. Edwin Sutherland, *White Collar Crime* (New York: Holt, Rinehart and Winston, 1949), p. 232.

26. E. Pendleton Herring, "The Balance of Social Forces in the Administration of the Food and Drug Law," *Social Forces*, 13, March 1935, p. 364.

[Congress] that bypass the central authority of the White House."[27] In the executive branch, as in Congress, the fragmentation of power is hardly indicative of its democratization. Rather it represents little more than a distribution among entrenched special interests.

Administrators are immobilized not only by "bureaucratic infighting" but by pressures bearing upon them from the wider politico-economic system. Given a desire to survive and advance, the bureaucrat tends to equivocate in the face of controversial decisions, moving away from dangerous areas and toward positions favored by the strongest of the pressures working on him. With time, the reform-minded agency loses its crusading spirit and settles down to standard operations, increasingly serving the needs of the industry it is supposed to regulate. The more public-spirited staff members either grow weary of the struggle and make their peace with the corporations, or leave, to be replaced by personnel who are "acceptable to, if not indeed the nominees of, the industry."[28]

Frequently administrative personnel are drawn from the very industry they are charged with regulating, their business background being taken as proof of their "expertise." They often return to higher positions in the same industry after serving their terms in office. Likewise, many career administrators eventually leave government service to accept higher-paying jobs in companies whose interests they favored while in office.[29] This promise of a lucrative post with a private firm can exercise a considerable influence on the judgments of the ambitious public administrator.

THE ANARCHY OF REGULATION

Most administrative bodies fall under the command of department heads and the president. But the independent regulatory commissions operate outside the executive branch, making quasi-judicial rulings that can be appealed only to the courts.[30] Congress created

27. Douglass Cater, *Power in Washington* (New York: Random House, 1964), pp. 10–11.

28. McConnell, *Private Power and American Democracy*, p. 288; also see Francis E. Rourke (ed.), *Bureaucratic Power in National Politics* (Boston: Little, Brown, 1965).

29. To cite one of many examples: Dr. Joseph Sadusk of the FDA prevented a synthetic antibiotic from being recalled off the market, and even ruled against precautionary wording on the label, despite evidence that the drug caused blood toxicity and even death. Soon after, Sadusk left the FDA and became vice-president of a pharmaceutical firm that realized high profits from the drug. Milton Silverman and Phillip Lee, *Pills, Profits and Politics* (Berkeley, Calif.: University of California Press, 1974).

30. The major independent regulatory commissions are the Civil Aeronautics Board, Federal Communications Commission, Federal Power Commission, Federal

the regulatory commissions to be independent of the normal administrative departments in the hope of keeping them free of the politics that permeated other executive bodies. The hope was an unrealistic one. For all the reasons discussed in this chapter, they are no more independent of special influences and they perform much the same as the regular departmental agencies—the niceties of structure counting for less than the realities of power and interest. The regulatory agencies "set up to protect the consumer from giant companies have become instead agents of the industries, granting fixed prices favorable to them, granting them monopolies, costing the public an estimated 16 to 24 billion a year more for what it buys."[31] Industry needs to be regulated, but for whose benefit?

As long as production is for the purpose of private profit rather than social use, regulation for the public interest is an improbable goal. On those rare occasions when government agencies succeed in enforcing a regulation on behalf of the unorganized citizenry, the accomplishment requires enormous time and effort and usually has only a minimal effect, if any, on the political economy. Thus it took the Federal Trade Commission twelve years of court orders and negotiations to get the manufacturers of Geritol, a vitamin and iron preparation, to stop claiming that their product fights something called "tired blood."[32] It took the FTC ten years to stop Crowell Collier from conducting fraudulent door-to-door encyclopedia sales, and another sixteen years to get the makers of Carter's Little Liver Pills to stop selling their laxative as an effective treatment for sluggish liver function.[33] And an antitrust action begun during the Johnson administration against IBM, charging it with monopolizing the computer business, dragged on for a decade and will not be settled until a Supreme Court decision sometime in the late 1980s—or twenty years after the suit was begun.

Trade Commission, Interstate Commerce Commission, National Labor Relations Board, Securities and Exchange Commission, Consumer Product Safety Commission. While the commissions report directly to Congress, their personnel are appointed by the president, with Senate confirmation. See Louis Kohlmeier, *The Regulators: Watchdog Agencies and the Public Interest* (New York: Harper & Row, 1969). Kohlmeier finds that regulation has resulted in diminished competition, producer-controlled markets, restricted consumer choice and higher prices.

31. ABC news commentator Howard K. Smith, quoted in the *New York Post*, August 6, 1976. A two-year congressional investigation concluded that regulatory agencies are committed "to the special interests of regulated industry and lack . . . sufficient concern for underrepresented interests" of the public. *New York Times*, October 3, 1976.

32. *New York Times*, July 5, 1969.

33. Philip A. Hart, "Swindling and Knavery, Inc.," *Playboy*, August 1972, p. 160.

Administrators run into difficulties with the powers that be if they show themselves to be insufficiently understanding of "the needs of industry." Consider John O'Leary, a career government administrator who was appointed director of the Bureau of Mines in 1968. Press reports and protests were being directed at the unsafe conditions in the mines and the failure of the bureau to enforce safety regulations—in the wake of an underground explosion that had taken the lives of seventy-eight miners. Encouraged by the public concern, O'Leary ordered the bureau's inspectors to make unannounced spot checks of safety conditions, a step involving an element of surprise that had been rarely tried before, although required by law. In one month, O'Leary's men made 600 spot checks, almost four times the number for the entire previous year, and ordered workers out of more than 200 unsafe mines. O'Leary urged his inspectors to still greater efforts and publicly charged that the coal mining industry was "designed for production economy and not for human economy, and there's going to have to be a change of attitudes on that."[34] The change came—but it was not the one hoped for. The mine companies made known to the White House their strong desire to be rid of the troublesome bureau director. After lasting only four months, O'Leary was removed from office. His successor, a former CIA employee, reestablished more cooperative relations with the mine owners, making personal appearances at corporate gatherings, riding in company planes and avoiding confrontations.[35]

People like O'Leary are the exception. In most instances public bureaucrats are, and must be, faithful servants of private industry. For instance, the GAO discovered that the Federal Power Commission violated its own regulations and granted natural gas producers repeated and unjustified price-rise extensions, costing customers several billion dollars in a three-year period.[36] The probusiness bias affects all departments: the Defense Department came to the rescue of large commercial farms that were hurt by the farmworkers' grape boycott by increasing its orders for grapes by 350 percent. Several

34. *New York Times*, February 17, 1969; "Mine Safety Case Hit," *Christian Science Monitor*, April 8, 1970.

35. Jack Anderson, "Mine Officials Got Free Air Travel," *Times-Union* (Albany, N.Y.), June 17, 1973. The more recently organized Mine Enforcement Safety Administration has proven itself no better, having tolerated widespread safety violations "by issuing only wrist-slapping fines." *Guardian*, December 29, 1976.

36. *New York Times*, September 15, 1974. The same kind of problem exists on the state level. A consumer-activist group charged that the Department of Public Utilities in Massachusetts was allowing the telephone company to overcharge Massachusetts residents $100 million a year; *The Boston Globe*, September 29, 1976.

years later the Pentagon tried to break the lettuce boycott by increasing its orders for nonunion lettuce.[37] A meat company faced with labor conflicts was awarded the bulk of the federal school lunch program's beef contract. And a trucking company that was losing sales because of a strike was bailed out by a $1.6-million government contract, illegally extended beyond the expiration date.[38]

And so it goes. The Highway Safety Bureau and the entire Department of Transportation defer to the oil-highway-automotive combine; the Agriculture Department promotes the policies and products of giant farming corporations; the Interstate Commerce Commission continues its long devotion to the trucking and railroad companies; the Federal Communications Commission serves the monopolistic interests of the telephone and telegraph companies and the networks; the Federal Aviation Administration makes air travel a safe business venture for airlines but not a safe travel venture for passengers; the Securities and Exchange Commission regulates the stock market mostly for the benefit of the large investors and to the detriment of small ones; the Federal Power Commission pursues a permissive policy on behalf of the private utilities; the Army Corps of Engineers continues to mutilate the natural environment on behalf of agricultural corporations, utilities, and land developers; various bureaus within the Department of Interior serve the oil, gas, mining and timber companies;[39] and one need not speculate on the

---

37. The 16-million pounds of scab grapes bought by the Pentagon in 1969 were shipped to Vietnam, where the bulk of them rotted on the docks. The Pentagon's largest lettuce contract went to the nonunion producer Bud Antle, an affiliate of Dow Chemical, the company that made napalm for the government. See About Face! (U.S. Servicemen's Fund Newsletter), December 1972.

38. Workers World, October 25, 1974.

39. There is an ample literature documenting how administrative bodies serve the interests of the industries they are supposed to regulate. See Kohlmeier, The Regulators; Anthony Lewis, "To Regulate the Regulators," New York Times Magazine, February 22, 1959; Bernard Schwartz, The Professor and the Commissions (New York: Knopf, 1958); Walter S. Adams and Horace Gray, Monopoly in America (New York: Macmillian, 1955); The Ralph Nader Study Group Report, The Interstate Commerce Omission: The Public Interest and the ICC (New York: Grossman, 1970), Robert C. Fellmeth, project director; James Ridgeway, "The Antipopulists," Ramparts, December 1971, pp.6–8; Richard Ney, The Wall Street Jungle (New York: Grove Press, 1970); Jack Anderson," 'Safe Air Travel'—It could be a Myth," Colorado Springs Sun, April 20, 1977; Michael Parfit, "The Army Corps of Engineers: Flooding America in Order to Save It," New Times, November 12, 1976, pp. 25–37; John Baskin, "A Close-Up On the Corps," Ibid., pp. 39–44; Robert Engler, Politics of Oil (Chicago: The University of Chicago Press, 1976); Henning Sjostrom and Robert Nilsson, Thalidomide and the Power of the Drug Companies (New York: Basic Books, 1973).

many billions distributed every year by the Department of Defense to pay the profits and costs of favored manufacturers.[40]

Government today is an "anarchy of regulation," with hundreds of administrative units independent of the president (although most of them are not supposed to be) and independent of their departments and each other. Congressional oversight of these agencies, a Senate report concluded, is scant and sporadic, largely because members of Congress fear reprisals from the powerful economic interests who are regulated, and congressional committees are often "stacked with members who share similar backgrounds and values with the agencies they are charged with overseeing."[41] This "iron triangle" of bureaucratic unit, congressional committee and corporate interest—with the latter as the triangle's base—can withstand attacks by public advocacy groups, press exposés and attempts by the president to make the agency serve wider social goals.[42]

So tightly bound are the public bureaucrats to the private interests that it is often difficult to tell the regulators from the regulated. More than half the appointees to regulatory jobs are persons who previously were employed by the regulated industry.[43] In 1972 the undersecretary of agriculture, responsible for enforcing meat inspection, was a former state inspector with close ties to the meat industry, who had actively opposed the very federal meat-inspection laws he now was to enforce. In 1976 the secretary of the interior was Stanley Hathaway, former governor of Wyoming, who had consistently opposed conservation programs that were now under his jurisdiction. A deputy assistant secretary in charge of water development had previously served as a paid lobbyist against water-pollution legislation. An MIT professor with close ties to the nuclear industry was chosen for the Nuclear Regulatory Commission, a position that involved him in the licensing of new nuclear plants and the development of regulations and research. Before his appointment as chief counsel for the Food and Drug Administration, Peter Hutt defended drug companies for a leading Washington law firm.[44] A sixty-three-

---

40. See the section in chapter 6 entitled "The Pentagon: Billions for Big Brother."
41. Unanimously approved report by the Senate Government Operations Committee; *New York Times*, February 10, 1977.
42. Frederic V. Malek, *Washington's Hidden Tragedy: The Failure to Make Government Work* (New York: Free Press, 1978).
43. *New York Times*, October 3, 1976.
44. The above examples are from the *New York Times*, April 28, 1975, and October 3, 1976; *I.F. Stone's Weekly*, January 27, 1969; Lockard, *Perverted Priorities of American Politics*, p. 280; *Valley Advocate* (Amherst, Mass.), June 29, 1977; Murphy and Murphy, "Consumer Beware," p. 13.

person National Industrial Pollution Control Council (with salaries and expenses of $475,000 a year paid by the government) was set up to advise the president on pollution reforms. All the members were businessmen from industries that, according to Senator Lee Metcalf, "contribute most to environmental pollution."

Federal housing programs have been supervised by conservative businessmen who were openly hostile to low-income public housing. The occupational safety program has been administered by business and government officials who were originally opposed to occupational safety legislation. Energy programs have been administered by former oil company executives who are unenthusiastic about, if not openly hostile, to the development of alternative energy sources. The head of the Arms Control and Disarmament Agency was a former executive from the defense industry and an advocate of stronger military power. The ACDA staff, in general, was "dominated by military men, conservatives and Wall Street types."[45]

The opportunities for corruption within the executive branch are plentiful. Officials have received illegal favors and gratuities from companies under their jurisdiction. In 1978 it was revealed that the General Services Administration, which acts as the procurement agency for the federal government, was in the throes of widespread corruption, involving many millions of dollars in bribes, kickbacks and payments for services never rendered. Officials in the FDA and FPC, in violation of federal rules, have owned stock in the companies they were supposed to be regulating, and others have received illegal favors and gratuities from firms under their jurisdiction.[46]

It is not enough to bemoan the fact that government agencies end up serving interests they are supposed to regulate;[47] rather we should understand how this situation is an inescapable outcome of the politico-economic realities in which the administrators operate. Most agencies have the inherently contradictory function of both regulating a particular industry—supposedly for the public interest—and promoting the industry's economic health and viability. But to promote the interests of the industry in a profit system is often to violate the interests of consumers and workers. Administrators

45. Sidney Lens, "The Doomsday Strategy," *Progressive*, February 1976, p. 28.
46. For such instances see *New York Times*, March 1 and November 16, 1975, September 15, 1974, and January 20, 1976; *Christian Science Monitor*, September 1, 1978; *Boston Globe*, October 11, 1976.
47. See *New York Times*, October 3, 1967, for a report on federal regulatory commissions.

find they cannot serve the people and serve the corporations too. Before long the needs of the major producer interests take precedence over the more diffuse demands of the public. Thus one hears that the goal of keeping the environment free of poisonous, life-damaging industrial effusions must be weighed against "industry's need to maintain production."

The special interests occupy a special position above the public interest. Indeed, in a capitalist society the special interests *are the systemic interest*, controlling the economic life of the society. Hence, regulation of the capitalist economy on anything but its own terms eventually does not work, not merely because industrialists employ shrewd lobbyists who can manipulate timid and compliant bureaucrats, but because industry *is* the economic system and sooner or later government must meet that system on its own terms or change to another. And when meeting the system on its own terms, regulation becomes little more than a way to rig prices at artificially high levels, control markets for the benefit of large producers, secure high profits, evade safety and environmental standards, limit the ability of consumer, labor and public advocacy groups to defend their interests and allow private corporations more direct and covert access to public authority.

Small wonder that reorganization schemes to eliminate the bureaucratic morass and allow for more responsible decision-making seldom work. Every newly-elected president who promises to clean up "the bureaucratic mess in Washington" ends up creating a still bigger bureaucracy under one or another reorganization plan. Bureaucracy is less a cause than an effect of special-interest politics. As long as private powers exist and grow, so will the bureaucratic units that serve and protect them and are in turn protected by them. The problems of the economy, affecting all dimensions of society, cannot be solved merely by redrawing bureaucratic lines, for corporate capitalism continues to recreate the conditions that defy rational regulation.

President Carter's creation of a Department of Energy (DOE) provides an apt illustration. The reorganization plan was heralded as a bold new effort to both streamline the bureaucracy and solve the energy crisis by bringing the many scattered agencies that deal with energy under one jurisdiction. It did neither, growing into a $10 billion-a-year cabinet-level department that contributes almost nothing to conservation or energy production. For behind DOE's new bureaucratic charts there stand the same old private interests, the oil companies, bankers and investors, who control the resources of energy and who continue to exercise their will over DOE and the nation, while accountable to neither.[48]

To begin to be effective, regulation would require monitoring and enforcement units that are almost as vast and varied as the industrial and commercial forces to be regulated—an unrealistic expectation. Short of that, regulation is destined to be haphazard, spotty and of limited effect. What would be needed to change things is not an endless proliferation of regulatory units but a change in the conditions that demand so much regulation—that is, a different method of ownership and a different purpose for production. Until fundamental systemic changes are made in the economic order, it seems regulation will continue to fail where it is most needed.

PUBLIC AUTHORITY IN PRIVATE HANDS

The ultimate submergence of public power to private interest comes when government gives, along with its funds and services, its very *authority* to business. Grant McConnell has documented how state authority is taken over by private groups in such areas as agriculture, grazing, medicine, industry and trade.[49] Thus Western ranches not only enjoy the use of federal land and water, they also have been granted the public authority that goes with the task of administering such resources. Control of land and water has been handed over to local "home-rule" boards dominated by the large ranchers, who thereby successfully transform their economic power "into a working approximation of publicly sanctioned authority."[50] Large agricultural producers exercise a similar authority in the administration of farm programs. "Agriculture has become neither public nor private enterprise. It is a system of self-government in which each leading farm interest controls a segment of agriculture through a delegation of national sovereignty. Agriculture has emerged as a largely self-governing federal estate," enjoying a power that has extended "through a line unbroken by personality or party in the White House."[51]

One congressional committee, investigating relations between government and industry, complained of a "virtual abdication of

48. Janet Marinelli, "Energy Shortage at DOE," *Environmental Action*, November 4, 1978, pp. 12–14.
49. See McConnell, *Private Power and American Democracy*. Another interesting work that picks up on McConnell's analysis and offers some additional evidence is Theodore Lowi, *The End of Liberalism*, 2nd ed., (New York: W. W. Norton, 1979).
50. McConnell, *Private Power and American Democracy*, p. 210.
51. Lowi, *The End of Liberalism*.

administrative responsibility" on the part of officials in the Department of Commerce, their actions in many instances being "but the automatic approval of decisions already made outside the Government in business and industry."[52] In every significant line of industry, advisory committees staffed by representatives of leading firms work closely with government agencies, making most of the important recommendations. In trying to assess their roles, it is "difficult to determine where the distinction between advice and the making of policy lies."[53] There are 3,200 committees and boards advising the executive branch and Congress, costing the government many millions a year to finance. The most influential are composed exclusively of big businessmen and deal with banking, chemicals, communications, pollution control, commercial farming, natural gas, oil, utilities, railroads, taxation, etc. They meet regularly with administrative leaders to formulate policies. Their reports become the basis for administrative actions and new legislation. These business advisors have unparalleled occasion to monopolize informational inputs, defining "industry's needs" from the vantage point of their own interests. With the coercive power of the state backing their decisions, they secure advantages over smaller competitors, workers and consumers of a kind less easily gained in open competition.

When the government first began to gather information for legislation on water pollution, it consulted the Advisory Council on Federal Reports, a private body which describes itself as the official business consultant to the Budget Bureau; it also considers itself responsible only to the business community. The Advisory Council, in cooperation with the Budget Bureau, set up a committee on pollution, which included representatives of DuPont, the Manufacturing Chemists Association and the American Paper Institute. The committee opposed the policy advocated by Congress, which was to set up an inventory on water pollutants.[54] In deference to industry's wishes, the government decided that the inventory would be provided by companies only on a voluntary basis, in effect approving industry's claim that the toxic wastes it unleashed into the public waters were a trade secret and a property right. The meetings of these business advisory committees are not open to the press or public.

---

52. From a congressional report cited in McConnell, *Private Power and American Democracy*, p. 271.
53. McConnell, *Private Power and American Democracy*, p. 275.
54. Robert W. Dietsch, "The Invisible Bureaucracy," *New Republic*, February 20, 1971, p. 19.

In many state and municipal governments, as in the federal government, business associations, dominated by the biggest firms in the area, are accorded the power to nominate their own personnel to licensing boards, production boards and other administrative bodies. The transfer of public authority to private hands frequently comes at the initiative of large companies. But sometimes the government will make the first overtures, organizing private associations, then handing them the powers of the state, thereby supposedly moving toward "voluntaristic" and "decentralized" forms of policymaking. In fact, these measures transfer public power to favored producers without their being held democratically accountable for the sovereign authority they exercise.

There exists, then, unbeknownst to most Americans, a large number of private decision-makers who exercise public authority without having to answer to the public and who determine official policy while considering their first interest and obligation to be their private businesses. They belong to what I would call the "public-private authority." Included in this category are the various quasi-public corporations, institutions, foundations, boards, councils, "authorities" and associations, one of the most powerful being the Federal Reserve Board. The "Fed," as it is called, determines the interest rate and the money supply. Although its decisions affect the entire economy, the Fed is beholden to the banks and is run mostly by bankers. The Fed's members are appointed to staggered fourteen-year terms by the president, who can make only two appointments during his four-year term. Once appointed, the board members answer to no one. The Fed operates without even the pretense of democratic accountability, working in total secrecy, refusing to have Congress or the White House audit its books. The five regional members of its most powerful policy committee are selected not by the president but by bankers from the various regions. The bankers pick their own people to sit on a public agency and make public policy that is backed by the powers of government but is not accountable to government. In the words of one investigator, the Fed is "an intensely arrogant government agency, one that is mired in secrecy, often inept, responsible to no one . . . and dedicated to helping powerful, entrenched interests rather than the public."[55]

Another public-private entity is the Port Authority of New York, a "public corporation" created by interstate compact for the purpose of running the bridges and tunnels between New York and New Jer-

---

55. Lee Berton, "Don't Bank on It," *Penthouse*, October 1976, p. 56; also "What Is the Federal Reserve?" *Dollars and Sense*, March 1976, p. 14.

sey and the various metropolitan airports. Its bonds are sold to large financial institutions and rich individuals. It is answerable to none of the governing bodies in the region—not to the mayors, nor the city councils, nor the state legislators, nor the governors of New York and New Jersey, nor the U.S. Congress—but it can condemn property and construct tax-exempt developments. The profits from its commercial ventures ($12 million annually from the JFK Airport restaurants alone) are distributed as *tax-free returns to private investors*. Millions in surpluses which could be used to salvage New York's decaying mass-transit system are kept in reserve by the Port Authority, "not for the people of New York City, but for bondholders. Thus does public authority and private power come together in a massive fusion of wealth that leaves the ordinary taxpaying New Yorkers as its victim."[56]

There are numerous "public authorities" at the federal, state and local levels carrying out a widely varied range of activities. They all have several things in common: they are authorized by state legislatures or Congress to function outside the regular structure of government, and because of their autonomous corporate attributes, they are seldom subjected to public scrutiny and accountability. In 1972 the public authorities in New York State alone had an outstanding debt (bonds owned by banks and rich investors) of $8.9 billion, more than twice the state's debt. To meet their obligations, the public authorities float new bond issues, none of which are passed upon by the voters, and thus make demands on future tax revenues. They are creatures that have the best of both worlds, feeding off the state treasure while accountable only to themselves.[57]

The public-private authority extends overseas. When the Peruvian generals nationalized the holdings of private American oil companies, the president sent a special envoy to protest the move and negotiate for reacquisition. The U.S. Information Agency publishes, at the taxpayers' expense, pamphlets extolling the benefits of private oil exploration for distribution in Ecuador. Agents of ITT and the CIA jointly consider ways of preventing a democratically elected Socialist from taking office in Chile. The private interests do not merely benefit from public policy; they often *make* policy, selecting the key officials, using public funds or channeling funds of their own

---

56. When the Port Authority had trouble renting space in its ugly World Trade Center, a predicament that could have meant a loss for its bondholders, then-Governor Rockefeller came to the rescue by renting fifty-eight floors for state government offices. One of the biggest Port Authority bondholders is the Rockefeller-controlled Chase Manhattan Bank.

57. *New York Times*, December 27, 1972.

through public agents, directing World Bank loans and foreign aid investments, offering recommendations that are treated as policy guidelines—in sum, pursuing their interests abroad with all the formal authority and might of the United States government behind them.

The corporate interests exert an influence that cuts across particular administrative departments. Within a government whose power is highly fragmented, they form cohesive, though sometimes overlapping, blocs around major producer interests like oil, steel, banking, drugs, transportation and armaments; these blocs are composed of bureaucrats at all levels, regulatory commissioners, senior congressmen, lobbyists, newspaper publishers, trade associations and business firms, operating with all the autonomy and unaccountability of princely states within the American polity.

GOVERNMENT "MEDDLING"

If government is capitalism's provider and protector at home and abroad, and if government and business are so intermingled as to be often indistinguishable, then why are businessmen so critical of "government meddling in the economy"? There are a number of explanations. First, as previously noted, businessmen are not opposed to government activity as long as it is favorable to them. Since the beginning of the Republic, state intervention in the economy usually has been at the behest of leading producers. "Whether we like it or not, the federal government is a partner in every business in the country," announced Lammot duPont Copeland, president of Du-Pont Chemicals. "As businessmen we need the understanding and cooperation of government in our effort to throw the economic machine into high gear."[58] When business leaders denounce government "meddling" they are referring to those infrequent occasions when public agencies attempt to impose environmental protections, antitrust laws or worker and consumer safety regulations. When business criticizes "excessive government spending" it has in mind programs which appear to benefit lower-income people. The business community has always been fearful that government might become unduly responsive to popular sentiments, arousing mass expectations and eventually succumbing to demands that could seriously

---

58. Quoted in David Bazelon, "Big Business and the Democrats," in Marvin Gettleman and David Mermelstein (eds.) *The Failure of American Liberalism* (New York: Vintage, 1971), pp. 145–146.

challenge the existing distribution of income and wealth and perhaps even upset the class structure. The business critique is not against existing arrangements of government, most of which have served industry well, but against government activities that might mobilize new constituencies, introducing unsettling elements into policy areas now firmly under control of entrenched business groups.

Business Week once made this very point: "There's a tremendous social and economic difference between welfare pump priming and military pump priming. . . . Military spending doesn't really alter the structure of the economy. It goes through the regular channels. As far as a businessman is concerned, a munitions order from the government is much like an order from a private customer." But spending for public works and social welfare "makes new channels of its own. It creates new institutions. *It redistributes income.* It shifts demand from one industry to another. It changes the whole economic pattern. . . ."[59] The money spent is not as readily channeled into the existing corporate profit system. To the extent it is used for nonprofit purposes, social welfare spending is a potential menace to private enterprise.

The hostility that businesses feel toward government regulation may or may not be genuine, McConnell notes, depending on who is getting regulated for what. The railroads are quite happy with regulation by the ICC; the securities trade is pleased with the services of the SEC; and the oil industry is at home with the National Petroleum Council. "Few industries . . . however, approve of any aggressive operation by the Antitrust Division, although this agency is the true protector of the avowed ideology."[60]

Second, attacks on government officials are a means of bringing them closer into line with industry's desires. Despite the controls exercised in the selection and advancement of government personnel, some public servants forget their commitment to the business community and entertain sympathies toward a wider constituency. Pressure must be applied to remind them of the vulnerabilities of their agencies and careers. Third, many of the complaints lodged

---

59. *Business Week*, February 12, 1949, quoted in Harry Braverman, *Labor and Monopoly Capital* (New York: Monthly Review Press, 1974), p. 286*fn*. (Italics are mine).

60. McConnell, *Private Power and American Democracy*, p. 295. The question then is not do we need more or less regulation, but what kind? Selective preferences for regulation exist also among public advocacy groups, with many calling for *more* government services for the needy and *more* health, safety and environmental regulations, and *less* regulatory protections and services for big business.

against government are from firms least favored by government policies. Business is not without its interior divisions: policies frequently benefit the wealthier firms at the expense of smaller ones. The howls of pain emanating from these weaker competitors are more likely to be heard by us than the quiet satisfaction of the giant victors. Small businesses usually have good cause to complain of government meddling, since most regulations are written to suit the corporate giants and are often excessively burdensome for the smaller enterprise. Many government agencies more vigorously pursue their enforcement efforts against small companies because—unlike the big firms—they have less influence in Congress and cannot afford to defend themselves in drawn-out litigation.[61]

Finally, I would suggest that much of the verbal opposition to government is a manifestation of the businessman's adherence to the business ideology, his belief in the virtues of rugged individualism, private enterprise and private competition.[62] That he might violate this creed in his own corporate affairs does not mean his devotion to it is consciously hypocritical. One should not underestimate the human capacity to indulge in selective perceptions and rationales. These rationales are no less sincerely felt because they are self-serving; quite the contrary, it is a creed's congruity with a favorable self-image and self-interest that makes it so compelling. Many businessmen, including those who have benefited in almost every way from government contracts, subsidies and tax laws, *believe* the advantages they enjoy are the result of their own self-reliance, efforts and talents in a highly competitive "private" market. They believe that everyone *except* them goes running to the government for a handout.

---

61. Ann Crittenden, "Big Burden for Small Business: Government Rules," *New York Times*, July 2, 1977.

62. See Francis X. Sutton *et al.*, *The American Business Creed* (New York: Schocken Books, 1962).

16

The Supremely Political Court

All three branches of government are sworn to uphold the Constitution, but the Supreme Court alone has the power of reviewing the constitutionality of actions taken by the other two branches, at least in regard to cases brought before it. While there is nothing in the Constitution giving the Court this function the proceedings of the Constitutional Convention reveal that many of the delegates expected the federal judiciary to overturn laws it deemed inconsistent with the Constitution.[1] Of even greater significance than its power of judicial review is the Court's power to interpret the intent and scope of laws as they are applied in actual situations. This power of judicial *interpretation* is also limited to cases brought before the Court by contesting interests. Our main concern here is with trying to understand the *political* role the Court has played over the years.

WHO JUDGES?

Some Americans like to think of the Constitution as a vital force, having an animation of its own. At the same time they expect Supreme Court justices to be above the normal prejudices of other per-

---

1. Max Farrand, *The Framing of the Constitution of the United States* (New Haven: Yale University Press, 1913), pp. 156-157. See Chief Justice John Marshall's argument for judicial review in the landmark case of *Marbury* v. *Madison*.

sons. Thus they envision "a living Constitution" and an insentient Court. But a moment's reflection should remind us that it is the other way around. The Supreme Court is deeply engaged in the political process. If the Constitution is, as they say, an "elastic instrument," then much of the stretching has been done by the nine persons who sit on the Court, and the directions in which they pull are largely determined by their own ideological predilections.

Some Supreme Court justices have insisted otherwise, contending that the Court is involved in judgments that allow little room for personal prejudice. Justice Roberts provided the classic utterance of this viewpoint:

> When an act of Congress is appropriately challenged in the Courts as not conforming to the constitutional mandate the judiciary branch of the government has only one duty—to lay the Article of the Constitution which is invoked beside the statute which is challenged and to decide whether the latter squares with the former. All that the Court does, or can do, is to announce its considered judgment upon the question.[2]

This image of the Constitution as a measuring stick and the justice as measurer has been challenged by critics of the Court and even by some justices. No less a member than Chief Justice Hughes pointedly observed, "We are under a constitution but the constitution is what the judges say it is."[3]

By class background, professional training and political selection, Supreme Court justices over the generations have more commonly identified with the landed interests rather than the landless, the slave owners rather than the slaves, the industrialists rather than the workers, the exponents of Herbert Spencer rather than the proponents of Karl Marx, the established social elites rather than the unemployed Blacks, underpaid migrants or illiterate immigrants. Approximately a century ago Justice Miller, a Lincoln appointee to the Court, made note of the class biases of the judiciary:

> It is vain to contend with judges who have been at the bar, the advocates for forty years of railroad companies, and all the forms of associated capital, when they are called upon to decide cases where such interests are in contest. All their training, all their feelings are from the start in favor of those who need no such influence.[4]

---

2. *United States* v. *Butler*, 297 U.S. 1 (1936).
3. Dexter Perkins, *Charles Evans Hughes* (Boston: Little, Brown, 1956), p. 16.
4. Quoted in Felix Frankfurter, *Mr. Justice Holmes and the Supreme Court* (New York: Atheneum, 1965), p. 54.

Nor is the situation much different today. One study shows that the people who enjoy life tenure on federal courts, whether appointed by Democratic or Republican presidents, are drawn preponderantly from highly privileged backgrounds.[5] Another study finds that the American Bar Association's quasiofficial Federal Judiciary Committee, whose task is to pass on the qualifications of prospective judges, favors those whose orientation is strongly conservative and supportive of corporate interests.[6] Few mavericks, reformers or populists are appointed to the federal bench. As one U.S. District Court judge puts it: "Who are we after all? The average judge, if he ever was a youth, is no longer. If he was ever a firebrand, he is not discernibly an ember now. If he ever wanted to lick the Establishment, he has long since joined it."[7]

PLAYING WITH THE CONSTITUTION

There is an old saying that the devil himself can quote the Bible for his own purposes. The Constitution is not unlike the Bible in this respect, and over the generations, Supreme Court justices have shown an infernal agility in finding constitutional justifications for the continuation of almost every inequity and iniquity, be it slavery or segregation, child labor or the sixteen-hour workday, state sedition laws or federal assaults on the First Amendment.

Regarding the Court's decisions in economic affairs, Justice Felix Frankfurter once observed:

> The raw material of modern government is business. Taxation, utility regulation, agricultural control, labor relations, housing, banking and finance, control of the security market—all our major domestic issues— all phases of a single central problem, namely, the interplay of economic enterprise and government. These are the issues which for more than a generation have dominated the calendar of the Court.[8]

Throughout most of its history the Court was a bastion of conservative economics. If the federal government wanted to establish

---

5. Sheldon Goldman, "Johnson and Nixon Appointees to the Lower Federal Courts: Some Socio-Political Perspectives," *Journal of Politics*, 34, August 1972, pp. 934-942.
6. See Joel B. Grossman, *Lawyers and Judges: The ABA and the Politics of Judicial Selection* (New York: Wiley, 1965).
7. Marvin E. Frankel, "An Opinion by One of Those Softheaded Judges," *New York Times Magazine*, May 13, 1973, p. 41.
8. Frankfurter, *Mr. Justice Holmes*, p. 41.

national banks, or give away half the country to private speculators, or subsidize industries, or set up commissions and boards that fixed prices and interest rates on behalf of manufacturers, railroads and banks, or send Marines to secure corporate investments in Central America, then such activities were as perfectly acceptable to the majority of the Court as to the majority of the business community. But if the federal or state governments sought to limit workday hours, or outlaw child labor, or establish minimum wages, or guarantee the rights of collective bargaining, or in other ways impose some kind of limitation on the privileges of business, then the Court ruled that government could not tamper with the natural processes of the private market nor interfere with the principle of laissez-faire by depriving owner and worker of "liberty of contract" and "substantive due process."[9] Whether the Court judged the government to be improperly interfering with the economy depended less on some constitutional principle than on which social class benefited.

The concept of "substantive due process" illustrates as well as any other judicial doctrine the way the Court manufactures new constitutional meanings under the guise of interpreting old ones. By about 1890, after years of pressure from corporate lawyers and American Bar Association spokesmen, the Court decided that due process referred not only to procedural matters, such as safeguards against arbitrary arrest, right to counsel and a fair and speedy public trial, but to the *substance* of the legislation—that is, not only to the way the law had been made and applied but to its very content.[10] Having determined that there was such a thing as "substantive due process," which ordinarily might have been considered a contradiction in terms, the Court then could review every kind of legislation passed by the states that was brought before it by business plaintiffs. When Congress enacted social-welfare legislation outlawing child labor, the Court would find it to be a violation of "substantive due process" under the Fifth Amendment and an unconstitutional usurpation of the reserved powers of the states under the Tenth Amendment.[11] When the states passed social-welfare legisla-

---

9. See for instance *Allgeyer* v. *Louisiana*, 165 U.S. 578 (1897); *Lochner* v. *New York*, 198 U.S. 45 (1905); and *Adair* v. *United States*, 208 U.S. 161 (1908).

10. See Arthur A. North, S. J., *The Supreme Court, Judicial Process and Judicial Politics* (New York: Appleton-Century-Crofts, 1966), pp. 40-43.

11. See *Hammer* v. *Dagenhart*, 247 U.S. 251 (1918). The Tenth Amendment reads: "The powers not delegated to the United States by this Constitution, nor prohibited by it to the States, are reserved to the States respectively or to the people." See also *Carter* v. *Carter Coal Co.*, 298 U.S. 238 (1936).

tion, the Court would find it in violation of "substantive due process" under the Fourteenth Amendment.[12] Thus while prohibiting Congress from supposedly encroaching on the reserved powers of the states, the Court prevented the states from using their reserved powers.

The Fourteenth Amendment, adopted in 1868 ostensibly to establish full citizenship for Blacks, says, "No State shall make or enforce any law which shall abridge the privileges or immunities of citizens of the United States; nor shall any State deprive any person of life, liberty, or property, without due process of law; nor deny to any person within its jurisdiction the equal protection of the laws." The Court decided that the word "person" included corporations and that the Fourteenth Amendment was intended to protect business conglomerations from the vexatious regulations of the states.

In regard to Blacks, the Court handed down a series of decisions in the latter half of the nineteenth century and the early twentieth, most notably *Plessy* v. *Ferguson*,[13] which, in effect, turned the Fourteenth Amendment on its head and denied Blacks equal protection. The *Plessy* decision enunciated the "separate but equal" doctrine, which said that the forceful separation of Blacks from Whites did not impute inferiority as long as facilities were more or less equal (which they rarely were). The doctrine gave constitutional legitimation to the racist practice of segregation.

Perhaps encouraged by the loose construction given to the word "person" or more likely convinced that they really were persons despite the treatment accorded them by a male-dominated society, feminist advocates began to argue that the Fourteenth Amendment and the Fifth Amendment applied to women and that the voting restrictions imposed on them by state and federal governments should be abolished. A test case reached the Supreme Court in 1894 and the justices decided that they could not give such a daring reading to the Constitution.[14] The Court seemingly had made up its mind that "privileges and immunities of citizens" and "equal protection of the laws" applied to corporate institutions and not to women and Blacks.

For more than a century, into the New Deal era, the Supreme Court was the bastion of laissez-faire capitalism, striking down reforms produced by the state legislatures and Congress, and limiting

---

12. *Morehead* v. *New York*, 298 U.S. 587 (1936).
13. 163 U.S. 537 (1896).
14. *Minor* v. *Happersett*, 88 U.S. 162 (1894).

government's ability to regulate the economy. The Court served this capitalist interest almost too well—to the point of making necessary changes impossible. An increasingly centralized economy demanded an increasingly centralized regulation of business and labor. The Great Depression of the 1930s made clear to many liberal policy-makers that only the federal government could revive a stagnant economy, creating new investment opportunities and subsidizing business on a grand scale. At the same time the government had to implement long-overdue reforms, designed to give a small share of the bounty to workers and create an appearance of social justice. Justice Louis Brandeis expressed this liberal position clearly:

> There will come a revolt of the people against the capitalists, unless the aspirations of the people are given some adequate legal expression. . . . Whatever and however strong our convictions against the extension of governmental function may be, we shall inevitably be swept farther toward socialism unless we can curb the excesses of our financial magnates.[15]

Capitalism had to be reformed and updated, if only to prevent socialism. As Joan Roelofs noted, robber barons and naked exploitation had to be replaced by a more covert, technocratic form of rule, one that made some gesture at including well-organized and highly agitated working-class elements.[16] From 1937 onward, under pressure from the White House, the Supreme Court began to accept the constitutionality of New Deal legislation, recognizing collective bargaining and central regulation of certain industrial conditions, and accepting social welfare legislation designed to take the edge off popular unrest and defuse potentially revolutionary American movements.[17] Thus the Court joined governing elements in the executive and legislative branches that were seeking to mitigate some of the worst effects of economic depression and corporate power. At the same time the Court continued to hand down decisions that excluded from the Bill of Rights persons who agitated and organized against capitalism.

---

15. Louis D. Brandeis, *Business: A Profession* (Boston: Small, Maynard, 1933), p. 330, cited in Joan Roelofs, "The Supreme Court and Corporate Capitalism: An Iconoclastic View of the Warren Court in the Shadow of Critical Theory," paper presented at the Northeastern Political Science Association meeting, November 1978.

16. Roelofs, "The Supreme Court and Corporate Capitalism . . ."

17. See my discussion of the New Deal in chapter 5.

NIBBLING AWAY AT
THE FIRST AMENDMENT

While opposing restrictions on economic power, the Court seldom has opposed restraints on free speech. The same conservatism that feared experimentation in economics also feared expression of the radical ideas which espoused such changes.[18] The First Amendment says, "Congress shall make no law . . . abridging the freedom of speech, or of the press." This would seem to leave little room for doubt as to the freedom of *all* speech.[19] Yet ever since the Alien and Sedition Acts of 1798, Congress and the state legislatures have found repeated occasion to pass laws penalizing the expression of heretical ideas. Over the years many who expressed opposition to government policy and to the established politico-economic system were deemed guilty of "subversion" or "sedition."[20] During the First World War, Congress passed the Espionage Act, under which almost two thousand successful prosecutions were carried out against persons, usually socialists, who expressed opposition to the war. One individual, who in private conversation in a relative's home voiced his opposition to U.S. intervention, opining that it was a rich man's war, was fined $5,000 and sentenced to twenty years in prison.[21] The American socialist leader Eugene V. Debs was imprisoned during the war for enunciating similar opinions from a public platform. While in prison Debs ran for president on the Socialist party ticket and received almost a million votes.

The High Court's attitude toward the First Amendment was best expressed by Justice Holmes in the famous *Schenck* case. Schenck was charged with attempting to cause insubordination among U.S. military forces and obstructing recruitment, both violations of the Espionage Act of 1917. What he had done was distribute a leaflet that condemned the war as a wrong against humanity perpetrated by Wall Street; it also urged people to exercise their right to oppose

---

18. See Frankfurter's comments in *Mr. Justice Holmes*, p. 85.

19. Even the staunchest proponents of free speech allow that libel and slander might be restricted by law, although here too such speech when directed against public figures has been treated as protected under the First Amendment. See *New York Times Co. v. Sullivan*, 376 U.S. 254 (1964), and *Time, Inc. v. Hill*, 385 U.S. 374 (1967).

20. *Sedition* is defined in Webster's Dictionary as "excitement of discontent against the government or resistance to lawful authority."

21. Hearings before a Subcommittee of the Senate Judiciary Committee, *Amnesty and Pardon for Political Prisoners* (Washington, D.C.: Government Printing Office, 1927), p. 54. See also Charles Goodell, *Political Prisoners in America* (New York: Random House, 1973), chapter 4.

the draft but confined itself to advocating peaceful measures, such as a petition for the repeal of the draft law. The leaflet, Holmes contended, had the intention of influencing persons to obstruct the draft. The function of speech, especially of political advocacy, is to induce actions. In ordinary times such speech is amply protected by the First Amendment, but "the question in every case," Holmes reasoned, "is whether the words used are used in such circumstances and are of such a nature as to create a clear and present danger that they will bring about the substantive evils that Congress has a right to prevent."[22] Holmes never established why obstruction of the draft was a substantive evil except to assume that prosecution of the war was a substantive good (the very idea that Schenck was trying to challenge), and therefore actions hampering the war effort were evil and Congress could stop them.

Free speech, Holmes argued, "does not protect a man in falsely shouting fire in a crowded theatre and causing a panic." Maybe so, but the analogy is a farfetched one: Schenck was not in a theater but was seeking a forum in order to voice political ideas and urge opposition to policies Holmes treated as above challenge. "When a nation is at war," Holmes continued, "many things that might be said in time of peace are such a hindrance to its efforts that their utterance will not be endured so long as men fight and that no Court could regard them as protected by any constitutional right." Behind the tempered prose Holmes was summoning the same argument paraded by every ruler who has sought to abrogate a people's freedom: these are not normal times; there is a grave menace within or just outside our gates; extraordinary measures are necessary and the democratic rules must be suspended for our nation's security. At no time was it established that Schenck had actually obstructed anything. He was convicted of *conspiracy* to obstruct.[23] The allegedly wrongful *intent* of his action, regardless of its success, constituted sufficient reason to

---

22. *Schenck* v. *United States*, 249 U.S. 47 (1919); also Holmes's decision in *Debs* v. *United States*, 249 U.S. 211 (1919).

23. Under the law, "conspiracy" is an agreement by two or more people to commit an unlawful act, or to commit a lawful act by unlawful means. In some cases, likemindedness or working for a common purpose, even without actual planning sessions or cooperative actions has been treated as sufficient evidence of conspiracy. Thus, some antiwar demonstrators brought to trial for conspiracy to incite riot had not met each other until the time of the trial. The conspiracy doctrine was described by Judge Learned Hand as the prosecutor's "darling"; it can make a crime out of the most amorphous political rally and out of the thoughts in people's heads even when these are expressed openly and promulgated by lawful means. See Jessica Mitford, *The Trial of Dr. Spock* (New York: Knopf, 1969); also Thomas I. Emerson, *The System of Freedom of Expression* (New York: Vintage, 1971).

declare his leaflet a "clear and present danger" to the survival of the Republic.[24]

More than once the Court treated the allegedly pernicious quality of an idea as certain evidence of its lethal efficacy and as justification for its suppression. This was especially true if the purveyors of the idea were thought to be radicals and revolutionaries. In 1940 Congress passed the Smith Act, making it a felony to teach and advocate the violent overthrow of the government. Soon after, a group of socialists were convicted under the act and sent to prison. Ten years later the Justice Department indicted the top leadership of the Communist party on charges of conspiring to organize to teach and advocate the violent overthrow of the government, specifically by forming the Communist party and teaching its members the ideas of Marxism-Leninism. The defendants were convicted but took their case to the Supreme Court.

In a 6 to 2 decision in *Dennis et al.* v. *United States*,[25] the Court upheld the Smith Act and the convictions. In several concurring opinions, the majority, led by Chief Justice Vinson, argued that even though there did not seem to be a clear and present danger of a communist coup, the government need not wait for one. The potential "gravity" of such a danger was sufficient grounds for protective action. In any case, there was no freedom under the Constitution for those who conspired to propagate revolutionary movements. Free speech was not an absolute value but one of many competing ones. The priorities placed on these values was a legislative matter best settled by Congress—as had been done by passage of the Smith Act.

Justices Black and Douglas dissented, arguing that the defendants had not been charged with any acts nor even with saying anything about violent revolution. They were indicted for conspiring to reorganize the Communist party and at some future time publish things which would teach and advocate revolution, including the classic writings of Marx, Engels and Lenin. The First Amendment was designed to protect the very views we might find offensive and dangerous. Safe and orthodox ideas rarely needed the protection of the Constitution; heretical ones did. It was one thing to argue against communist beliefs, but another to repress and imprison those who held them.

---

24. Holmes was considered one of the more liberal justices of his day. And in subsequent cases he did place himself against the Court's majority and on the side of the First Amendment, earning the title of the "Great Dissenter." See his dissents in *Abrams* v. *United States*, 250 U.S. 616 (1919), and *Gitlow* v. *New York*, 268 U.S. 652 (1925).
25. 341 U.S. 494 (1951).

Six years after Dennis and the other top leaders of the Communist party were jailed, fourteen more party leaders were convicted under the same Smith Act. This time a majority of the Court made a distinction between "advocacy of abstract doctrine and advocacy directed at promoting unlawful action" and decided that the Smith Act had intended to outlaw only the latter.[26] Thus, without declaring the act unconstitutional, the Court overthrew the conviction, arguing that the law had not been applied correctly. Justice Black, concurring in the decision, did enter a "dissent in part," along with Justice Douglas, expressing the opinion that the Smith Act itself should be declared a violation of the First Amendment. "I believe," Black stated unequivocally, "that the First Amendment forbids Congress to punish people for talking about public affairs, whether or not such discussion incites to action, legal or illegal."

Needless to say, Black's postulate remains the minority opinion among the directors, trustees and owners of our public and private institutions and even among some who fancy themselves to be civil libertarians. They argue that revolutionaries should not be allowed to take advantage of the very liberties they seek to destroy. Revolutionary advocacy constitutes an abuse of freedom by urging us to violate the democratic rules of the game.[27] Hence, the argument goes, in order to preserve our political freedom, we may find it necessary to deprive some people of theirs. Several rejoinders might be made to this position.

First, as a point of historical fact, the threat of revolution in the United States has never been as real or as harmful to "our liberties" as the measures allegedly taken to protect us from revolutionary ideas. History repeatedly demonstrates the expansive quality of repression: first, revolutionary advocacy is suppressed, then proponents of unpopular doctrines, then "inciting" words, then "irresponsible" news reports and public utterances that are not "balanced" or "constructive," then any kind of dissent which those in power might find intolerable.

Second, the suppression is conducted by political elites who, in protecting us from what they consider "harmful" thoughts, deprive

26. *Yates et al.* v. *United States*, 354 (1957).

27. For samples of this kind of thinking see the Vinson and Jackson opinions in the *Dennis* case; also Sidney Hook, *Political Power and Personal Freedom* (New York: Criterion Books, 1959); Carl A. Auerbach, "The Communist Control Act of 1954: A Proposed Legal-Political Theory of Free Speech," *The University of Chicago Law Review*, 23, Winter 1956, reprinted in Samuel Hendel (ed.), *Basic Issues of American Democracy*, 8th ed. (Englewood Cliffs, N.J.: Prentice-Hall, 1976), pp.59–63.

us of the opportunity of hearing and debating revolutionary advocates, and try to make up our minds for us. An exchange is forbidden because the advocate has been silenced.

Third, it is a debatable point whether socialist, communist and other radical revolutionaries are dedicated to the destruction of freedom. Most revolutionaries would argue that freedom is one of the things lacking in the *present* society. The millions who are crushed by poverty and hunger and the millions more who are stupefied by the business-owned mass media are hardly free. The constructing of new social alternatives and new modes of communal organization can bring an *increase* in freedom, including freedom from poverty and hunger, freedom to share in making the decisions that govern one's work conditions, education, community and life, freedom to experiment with new forms of social organization and production. Admittedly some freedoms enjoyed today would be lost in a revolutionary society—for instance, the freedom to exploit other people and get rich from their labor, the freedom to squander human and natural resources and treat the environment as a septic tank, the freedom to monopolize information and the freedom to exercise unaccountable power. In many countries throughout the world, successful social revolutionary movements have brought a net increase in the freedom of individuals, revolutionaries argue, by advancing the conditions necessary for the preservation of health and human life, by providing jobs and education for the unemployed and illiterate, by using economic resources for social development rather than for corporate profit and by overthrowing repressive reactionary regimes and ending foreign exploitation and involving large sectors of the populace in the task of socialist reconstruction. Revolutions can extend a number of real freedoms without destroying those that never existed for the common people. The repression in America is here and now, while the hope for a better life lies ahead. The argument can be debated but not if it is suppressed.

Far from being a bulwark against government suppression, the Court has usually gone along with it. When the Southern states imposed the tyranny of racial segregation on Black people and other non-Whites after Emancipation, the Court, as noted, obligingly formulated the doctrine of "separate but equal" to give constitutional justification to segregation. And when the U.S. government decided to uproot 112,000 law-abiding Japanese-Americans from the West Coast at the onset of World War II, forcing them to relinquish their homes, businesses, farms and other possessions and herding them into concentration camps for the duration of the war on the incredible notion that they might pose a threat to our West Coast defenses, the Supreme Court found that, given the exigencies of war, the government was acting within the limits of the Constitution.[28]

THE COURT TODAY

The Supreme Court's record in the area of personal liberties is gravely wanting, yet it is not totally devoid of merit. "Let us give the Court its due; it is little enough," Robert Dahl reminds us.[29] Over the years the Court has extended the protection of the First Amendment and other portions of the Bill of Rights to cover not only the federal government but state government (via the Fourteenth Amendment). Attempts by the states to censor publications,[30] deny individuals the right to peaceful assembly[31] and weaken the separation between church and state[32] were overturned. During the 1960s, the Court under Chief Justice Earl Warren took some important steps to safeguard the individual's rights in criminal justice proceedings, including the right of a poor person to benefit of counsel in state criminal trials,[33] and of an arrested person to have a lawyer at the onset of police interrogation.[34]

In some states, less than a third of the population elected more than half the legislators; the Warren Court ruled that malapportioned district lines had to be redrawn in accordance with population distribution, so that voters in the overpopulated districts were not denied equal protection under the law.[35] The Court also gave indication of taking the disestablishment clause in the First Amend-

---

28. *Hirabayashi* v. *United States*, 320 U.S. 81 (1943), *Korematsu* v. *United States*, 323 U.S. 214 (1944) and *Ex parte Endo*, 323 U.S. 283 (1944). These decisions were rendered by the "liberal" Stone Court. As with many other shady aspects of American history, students are taught little about this. For a long time the Japanese-Americans had been an object of resentment because of their successful farming and social mobility on the West Coast. The relocaton left many of them destitute, and almost all their land was grabbed by agribusiness firms.
29. Robert A. Dahl, "Decision-Making in a Democracy: The Role of the Supreme Court as a National Policy-Maker," *Journal of Public Law*, 6, no. 2, 1958, p. 292.
30. *Near* v. *Minnesota*, 283 U.S. 697 (1931).
31. *DeJonge* v. *Oregon*, 299 U.S. 353 (1937).
32. *McCollum* v. *Board of Education*, 333 U.S. 203 (1948).
33. See *Gideon* v. *Wainwright*, 372 U.S. 335 (1963).
34. *Escobedo* v. *Illinois*, 378 U.S. 478 (1964) and *Miranda* v. *Arizona*, 384 U.S. 436 (1966).
35. See *Baker* v. *Carr*, 369 U.S. 186 (1962), and *Reynolds* v. *Sims*, 377 U.S. 533 (1964). A similar decision was made in regard to congressional districts in *Wesberry* v. *Sanders*, 376 U.S. 1 (1964).

ment seriously by ruling that prayers in the public school were a violation of the separation of church and state.[36]

The Warren Court handed down a number of decisions aimed at abolishing racial segregation. The most widely celebrated was *Brown* v. *Board of Education*,[37] which unanimously ruled that "separate educational facilities are inherently unequal" because of the inescapable imputation of inferiority cast upon the segregated minority group, an imputation that is all the greater when it has the sanction of law. This decision overruled the "separate but equal" doctrine enunciated in 1896 in the *Plessy* case.

The direction the Court takes depends partly on the political composition of its majority. Refortified with four Nixon-appointed justices and a Ford-appointed one, the Court under Chief Justice Burger took a decidedly conservative turn. In the area of criminal justice, for instance, the Burger Court decided that it was no longer necessary to have a unanimous jury verdict for conviction—a decision that abolished the need for having a jury agree that the prosecution has proven guilt beyond a reasonable doubt.[38] In another decision, the Burger Court ruled that police may stop and frisk people almost of their own discretion, thus making it easier for them to intimidate dissenters, demonstrators, Blacks and other "troublesome" elements.[39]

The *Miranda* decision, which forbade the use of police torture in obtaining confessions, was weakened by the Burger Court, as was the right of Black defendants to have prospective jurors questioned about their possible racial prejudices.[40] In a 7 to 2 decision, the justices declared the death penalty to be constitutional and not in violation of the Eighth Amendment's prohibition against "cruel and unusual punishment."[41] They also handed down a decision denying reporters a right to confidential news sources;[42] and by a 5 to 4 vote

---

36. See *Engles* v. *Vitale*, 370 U.S. 421 (1962), and *School District of Abington* v. *Schempp*, 374 U.S. 203 (1963). The First Amendment reads: "Congress shall make no law respecting an establishment of religion, or prohibiting the free exercise thereof."

37. 347 U.S. 483 (1954). See also the decision nullifying state prohibitions against interracial marriage: *Loving* v. *Virginia*, 388 U.S. 1 (1967).

38. *Johnson* v. *Louisiana*, 32 L. Ed. 2d 152 (1972) and *Apodaca* v. *Oregon*, 32 L. Ed. 2d 184 (1972).

39. In this instance, *Adams* v. *Williams*, the Burger Court was expanding on a policy set down by the Warren Court in *Terry* v. *Ohio*, 392 U.S. 1 (1968); see also *United States* v. *Robinson*, 414 U.S. 218 (1973).

40. *Michigan* v. *Mosley*, 46 L. Ed. 2d 313 (1975), and *Ristaino* v. *Ross*, 47 L. Ed. 258 (1976).

41. *Gregg* v. *Georgia*, 428 U.S. 153 (1976).

42. *United States* v. *Caldwell*, 33 L. Ed. 626 (1927).

296 / Democracy for the Few

they refused to impose any limitation on Army surveillance of lawful civilian political activity. In a passionate dissent Justice Douglas called the latter decision "a cancer in our body politic. . . . The Bill of Rights was designed to keep agents of Government and official eavesdroppers away from assemblies of people."[43]

The Court ruled that military posts may ban speeches and demonstrations of a "partisan" political nature and prohibit distribution of political literature—thus denying American soldiers the First Amendment rights they are supposedly prepared to defend with their lives.[44] While it was all right for the Army to spy secretly on civilian political activity, it apparently was wrong for civilians to bring political ideas openly to the Army. Both decisions were consistent with the Court's determination to keep the military and society free from socialist and other radical political ideas.

In most decisions involving disputes between workers and owners, the Burger Court has sided with the owners. Thus it ruled that workers do not have the right to strike over safety issues if there are contract provisions for arbitration.[45] This decision denies miners the right to walk off the job in the face of dangerous work conditions deliberately covered up by management; it requires that they enter the mines and risk being killed during the weeks it takes to settle the issue by arbitration.

The Burger Court's dedication to social inequality was manifested with exceptional clarity in its decision to prevent school districts with low property values from having as much money spent on education as those with higher property values. The Court decided that a state may constitutionally vary the quality of education in accordance with the amount of taxable wealth located in its districts. The Court seemed to be saying there could be any degree of inequality short of absolute deprivation; as long as the Chicano children had *some* kind of school to go to, this would satisfy the equal-protection clause of the Fourteenth Amendment. The decision hardly lived up to the principles enunciated in the 1954 *Brown* case, Justice Marshall pointed out in a dissent.[46]

In keeping with its support of social inequality and its defense of privilege, the Burger Court decided that the principle of "one-person, one-vote" need not be observed in elections for special-purpose governmental bodies like water districts. Since the expenses of the

---

43. *Laird* v. *Tatum*, 408 U.S. 1 (1972).
44. *Greer* v. *Spock*, 47 L. Ed. 2d 505 (1976).
45. *Gateway Coal Co.* v. *United Mine Workers*, 414 U.S. 368 (1974).
46. *San Antonio Independent School District* v. *Rodriguez*, 36 L. Ed. 2d 16 (1973).

water district are met by the landowners, the majority reasoned, then landowners alone should have the vote.[47] In his dissent Justice Douglas pointed out that four corporations owned nearly 85 percent of the acres in the district while 189 landowners had less than 3 percent. Small owners, tenant farmers and sharecroppers all should have a say, he argued, because irrigation, water usage and flood control "implicate the entire community." The ballot, he pointed out in a companion case, is restricted to the wealthy few who can violate "our environmental ethics" and in other ways do their will.[48]

In two other cases, the justices held that indigents who could not afford court fees had no right to their day in court.[49] While not directly overruling certain Warren Court decisions the Burger Court sometimes did its best to erode them. Finding no way to contravene the constitutionality of the earlier reapportionment cases, for instance, it decided that the "one-person, one-vote" rule should be applied less rigorously to state legislative districts than to congressional districts. In allowing for a population deviation as wide as 16.4 percent, the Court reasoned that state districts have indigenous qualities that ought sometimes to be preserved.[50]

The Burger Court handed down several decisions that showed little sympathy for the rights of children. In one case, a junior high school student was pinioned to a table by school officials and then beaten with a paddle enough to leave him bedridden for a week; in another a child was struck so fiercely as to lose temporarily the use of his arm; but the Court ruled that the Eighth Amendment prohibiting the infliction of cruel and unusual punishment did not protect school children from corporal punishment no matter how severe.[51]

In most criminal cases, the Burger Court has favored the prosecution over the defendant. In First Amendment cases, the Burger Court has favored the interests of restrictive authority over those of free speech, free press and independent thinking.[52] On environmental and discrimination cases, the Burger Court's record has been mixed, as is true of its decisions regarding abortion and separation of

---

47. *Salyer Land Co.* v. *Tulare Lake Basin Water Storage District*, 35 L. Ed. 2d 675 (1973).

48. *Associated Enterprise, Inc.* v. *Toltec Watershed Improvement District*, 35 L. Ed. 2d 675 (1973).

49. *Ortwein* v. *Schwab*, 35 L. Ed. 2d 572 (1973). Also *United States* v. *Kraus*, 34 L. Ed. 2d 626 (1973).

50. *Mahan* v. *Howell*, 35 L. Ed. 2d 320 (1973).

51. *Ingraham* v. *Wright*, 430 U.S. 651 (1977).

52. See for instance *Zurcher* v. *Stanford Daily*, 436 U.S. (1978). For a critique of the Burger Court see Leonard Levy, *The Nixon Court and Criminal Justice* (New York: Harper & Row, 1975); also the report in the *New York Times*, July 6, 1978.

church and state. Most mixed of all was the landmark *Bakke* case, in which the Court by a 5 to 4 vote, with opinions by six of the justices, affirmed the constitutionality of college admission programs that give special consideration to racial minorities to help remedy past discrimination against them; in the same decision the Court ruled 5 to 4 that Bakke, a White applicant, should be admitted to the University of California Medical College because the school's affirmative-action program was inflexibly biased against White applicants like him.[53] The "two-sided ruling aroused some confusion and controversy," the *New York Times* noted,[54] but its net effect was to weaken, albeit not abolish, affirmative action.

INFLUENCE OF THE COURT

It is easier to describe the blatantly political role played by the Court than to measure its actual political influence. But a few rough generalizations can be drawn. First, as a nonelective branch occupied by persons of elitist class background, the Court has exercised a preponderantly conservative influence. On matters of social welfare legislation, the Court wielded a strategic minority veto for years. Laws on workmen's compensation, child labor, unionization and other reform legislation of a kind that had been enacted in European countries a generation before were delayed ten to twenty-five years by the Court. It prevented Congress from instituting income taxes, a decision that took eighteen years and a constitutional amendment to circumvent.

But we should remember that the Court's ability to impose its will on the nation is far from boundless. Presidents usually get the opportunity to appoint two or more members to the Court and thus exert an influence over its makeup. Furthermore, the Court cannot make rulings at will but must wait until a case is brought to it either on appeal from a lower court or, far less frequently, as a case of original jurisdiction. And the Court agrees to hear only a small portion of the cases on its docket, thus leaving the final work to the lower courts in most instances.

Members of the Court have been aware that the efficacy of their decisions depends on the willingness of other agencies of government to carry them out. A Court that runs glaringly against the tide risks being attacked. Its appellate jurisdiction might be circumscribed by

---

53. *Regents of the University of California* v. *Bakke*, 57 L. Ed. 2d 750 (1978).
54. *New York Times*, June 29, 1978.

Congress, its decisions ignored and itself subjected to ridicule and hostility. Some members of the Court, such as Justices Harlan and Frankfurter, were so impressed by the limitations of its power and its vulnerability to the other branches as to counsel a doctrine of "judicial restraint," especially when the Court tried to move in innovative ways.[55]

The Court is always operating in a climate of opinion shaped by political forces larger than itself. Its willingness to depart from the casuistry of *Plessy* v. *Ferguson* and take the Fourteenth Amendment seriously in *Brown* v. *Board of Education* depended in part on the changing climate of opinion concerning race relations and segregation between 1896 and 1954. Responding to the widespread agitation by women's groups and to the changing climate of opinion regarding the social roles of women, the conservative "Burger Court has contributed more to the development of U.S. women's legal equality and constitutional freedom than any previous judicial body,"[56] including the previous Warren Court which, while more liberal in its makeup, operated in more conservative times regarding women's rights.

At the same time the Court is not purely a dependent entity. That it had to deny women protection under the Fourteenth Amendment for almost a century and had to accept segregation for more than fifty years is not certain. The arguments used on the eve of the *Brown* decision in 1954—that the Court should not push people, that hearts and minds had to change first, that you can't legislate morality, and that there would be vehement and violent opposition—were the same arguments used during the days of the *Plessy* case. In fact there was vehement and often violent opposition to the *Brown* decision. But there also was an acceleration of opinion in support of the Court's ruling, in part activated by that very ruling. (Just as there was an increase in *segregationist* practices after the *Plessy* case, from 1896 to 1914, probably in part encouraged by *Plessy* and decisions like it.) Hence, some of the Court's decisions have an important feedback effect. By playing a crucial role in defining what is legitimate and constitutional, the Court gives encouraging

---

55. For instance, see the dissents by Frankfurter and Harlan respectively in the apportionment cases: *Baker* v. *Carr*, 369 U.S. 186 (1962), and *Reynolds* v. *Sims*, 377 U.S. 533 (1964).

56. Leslie Friedman Goldstein, "Sex and the Burger Court: Recent Judicial Policy Making toward Women," in Marian Palley and Michael Preston (eds.), *Race, Sex and Public Policy* (Lexington, Mass.: D.C. Heath, 1979). Citing numerous cases, Goldstein adds that there also have been "major rejections" of the legal demands of women's rights by the Burger Court.

cues to large sectors of the public. Unable to pass a civil rights act for seventy years, the Congress enacted three in the decade after the *Brown* case. And Blacks throughout the nation pressed harder in an attempt to make desegregation a reality. Organizing efforts for civil rights increased in both the North and the South, along with "Freedom Riders," sit-ins and mass demonstrations. The political consciousness of a generation was joined, and who is to say that the Warren Court did not play a part in that?[57] The Supreme Court, then, probably has a real effect on political consciousness and public policy, albeit in limited ways and for limited durations.

One caveat should be given: progressive people have relied too heavily on the Supreme Court and on courts in general. For anyone engaged in the struggle for justice, the courts may occasionally be a necessary evil, but they are not the friends of progressive and socialist causes. With the exception of a brief ten-year span under Chief Justice Warren, the Supreme Court has been the most conservative branch of government. The Court, like the very laws and Constitution it interprets, is limited to a frame of reference that accepts and defends existing class and property relations.

---

57. For studies on the effects of High Court decisions see Theodore Becker (ed.), *The Impact of Supreme Court Decisions: Empirical Studies* (New York: Oxford University Press, 1969).

17

Democracy
for the Few

The United States is said to be a pluralistic society, and indeed a glance at the social map of this country reveals a vast agglomeration of regional, occupational and ethnic groups and state, local and national governing agencies. If by pluralism we mean this multiplicity of private and public groups, then the United States is pluralistic. But then so is any society of size and complexity, including allegedly "totalitarian" ones like the Soviet Union with its multiplicity of regional, occupational and ethnic groups and its party, administrative, industrial and military factions all jostling for position and power.[1]

But the proponents of pluralism presume to be saying something about how *power* is distributed and how *democracy* works. Specifically, pluralism means that

1. Power is shared among representative sectors of the population.

1. See, for instance, Donald R. Kelly, "Interest Groups in the USSR: The Impact of Political Sensitivity on Group Influence," *Journal of Politics*, 34, August 1972, pp. 860–888; also H. Gordon Skilling and Franklyn Griffiths (eds.), *Interest Groups in Soviet Politics* (Princeton, N.J.: Princeton University Press, 1971). By the simple definition of pluralism offered above, even Nazi Germany might qualify as pluralistic. The Nazi state was a loose, often chaotic composite of fiercely competing groups. See Heinz Höne, *The Order of the Death's Head* (New York: Coward, McCann, and Geoghegan, 1970).

2. The shaping of public policy involves inputs from a wide range of competing social groups.
3. No one group enjoys permanent dominance or suffers permanent defeat.
4. The distribution of benefits is roughly equitable or certainly not consistently exploitative.

Thus Ralf Dahrendorf writes: "Instead of a battlefield, the scene of group conflict has become a kind of market in which relatively autonomous forces contend according to certain rules of the game, by virtue of which nobody is a permanent winner or loser."[2] If there are elites in our society, the pluralists say, they are numerous and specialized, and they are checked in their demands by other elites. No group can press its advantages "too far" and any group that is interested in an issue can find a way within the political system to make its influence felt.[3] Business elites have the capacity to utilize the services of the government to further their interests, but, the pluralists argue, such interests are themselves varied and conflicting. The government does many different things for many different people; it is not controlled by a monolithic corporate elite that gets what it wants on every question. Government stands above any one particular influence but responds to many. Power in America "is plural and fluid. . . . " Not only is there "Big Government but also Big Business, Big Labor, Big Distribution, the Big Press, the Big Church and the Big Army."[4]

PLURALISM FOR THE FEW

The evidence offered in the preceding chapters leaves us little reason to conclude that the United States is a "pluralistic democracy" as

2. Ralf Dahrendorf, *Class and Class Conflict in Industrial Society* (Stanford, Calif.: Stanford University Press, 1959), p. 67.
3. One of the earliest pluralist statements is in Earl Latham, *The Group Basis of Politics* (Ithaca: Cornell University Press, 1952). See also Arnold M. Rose, *The Power Structure* (New York: Oxford University Press, 1967); Robert Dahl, *Who Governs?* (New Haven: Yale University Press, 1961); Edward Banfield, *Political Influence* (New York: Free Press, 1961); Nelson Polsby, *Community Power and Political Theory* (New Haven: Yale University Press, 1963). The criticisms of pluralism are many: the best collection of critiques can be found in Charles A. McCoy and John Playford (eds.), *Apolitical Politics* (New York: Crowell, 1967); see also Marvin Surkin and Alan Wolfe (eds.), *An End to Political Science: The Caucus Papers* (New York: Basic Books, 1970).
4. Max Lerner, *America as a Civilization* (New York: Simon and Schuster, 1957), pp. 398 and 406.

conceived by the pluralists. To summarize and expand upon some of the points previously made:

(1) Public policies, whether formulated by conservatives or liberals, Republicans or Democrats, fairly consistently favor the large corporate interests at a substantial cost to millions of workers, small farmers, small producers, consumers, taxpayers, the elderly and the poor. Benefits distributed to lower-income groups have proven gravely inadequate to their needs and have failed to reach millions who might qualify for assistance. Government efforts in crucial areas of social need have rarely fulfilled even the minimal expectations of reform-minded advocates. There are more people living in poverty today than there were ten years ago, more substandard housing, inflation and unemployment, more chronic insecurity, immiserization and social pathology, more crime, suicide and alcoholism, more environmental devastation and pollution, more deficiencies in our schools, hospitals and transportation systems, more military dictatorships throughout the world feeding on the largesse and power of the Pentagon, more people—from South Africa to Greece to the Philippines to Brazil to Mississippi—suffering the oppression of an American-backed status quo, more profits going to the giant corporations and more corporate influence over the institutions of society, more glut in the private commodity market and more scarcity and want in public services. Cities are on the verge of bankruptcy, and governors in almost every state are cutting back on assistance programs for low-income families, the elderly, the handicapped and the retarded. And in the midst of all this, presidents and other politicians mouth platitudes, urging us to regain "faith in ourselves" and in "our institutions."

(2) To think of government as nothing more than a broker or referee amidst a vast array of competing groups (these groups presumably representing all the important and "countervailing" interests of the populace) is to forget that government best serves those who can best serve themselves. That is not to say that political leaders are indifferent to popular sentiments. When those sentiments are aroused to a certain intensity, leaders will respond, either by making minor concessions or by evoking images of change and democratic responsiveness that are lacking in substance. Leaders are always "responding" to the public, but so often it is with distracting irrelevancies, dilatory and discouraging tactics, facile reassurances, unfulfilled promises, outright lies or token programs that offer nothing more than a cosmetic application to a deep social problem. The overall performance of our political system even in times of so-called social reform might best be characterized as giving *symbolic*

allocations to public sentiment and *substantive* allocations to power-ful private interests.

Indeed, one might better think of ours as a dual political system. First, there is the symbolic political system centering around elec-toral and representative activities including party conflicts, voter turnout, political personalities, public pronouncements, official role-playing and certain ambiguous presentations of some of the public issues which bestir presidents, governors, mayors and their respec-tive legislatures. Then there is the substantive political system, in-volving multibillion-dollar contracts, tax write-offs, protections, re-bates, grants, loss compensations, subsidies, leases, giveaways and the whole vast process of budgeting, legislating, advising, regulat-ing, protecting and servicing major producer interests, now bending or ignoring the law on behalf of the powerful, now applying it with full punitive vigor against heretics and "troublemakers." The sym-bolic system is highly visible, taught in the schools, dissected by academicians, gossiped about by newsmen. The substantive system is seldom heard of or accounted for.

(3) Far from the fluid interplay envisioned by the pluralists, the political efficacy of groups and individuals is largely determined by the resources of power available to them, of which wealth is the most crucial. Not everyone with money chooses to use it to exert po-litical influence, and not everyone with money need bother to do so. But when they so desire, those who control the wealth of society en-joy a persistent and pervasive political advantage. Instead of being just another of many interests in the influence system, corporate business occupies a particularly strategic position. On the major is-sues which determine much of the development of society itself, business gets its way with Congress, the president, the courts and the bureaucracy because there exists no alternative way of organizing the economy within the existing capitalist structure. Because busi-ness controls the very economy of the nation, government perforce enters into a unique and intimate relationship with it. The health of the capitalist economy is treated by policymakers as a necessary con-dition for the health of the nation, and since it happens that the economy is in the hands of big companies, then presumably govern-ment's service to the public is best accomplished by service to these companies. The goals of business (rapid growth, high profits and se-cure markets) become the goals of government, and the "national in-terest" becomes identified with the dominant propertied interests. Since policymakers must operate in and through the private econ-omy, it is not long before they are operating *for* it.

(4) The pluralists make much of the fact that wealthy interests do not always operate with clear and deliberate purpose.[5] To be sure, elites, like everyone else, make mistakes and suffer confusions as to what might be the most advantageous tactics in any particular situation. But if they are not omniscient and infallible, neither are they habitual laggards and imbeciles. If they do not always calculate rationally in the pursuit of their class interests, they do so often and successfully enough.

It is also true that the business community is not monolithic and unanimous on all issues. The socialist economist Paul Sweezy has pointed out some of the fissures within the business world: there are regional differences (Eastern versus Southwestern capital), ideological ones (reactionary versus liberal capitalism) and corporate ones (Ford versus General Motors)—all of which add an element of conflict and indeterminacy to economic and political policies. But these are the conflicts of haves versus haves and they seldom include the interests of the unorganized public. Nor, as Sweezy reminds us, should we exaggerate the depths of these divisions:

> Capitalists can and do fight among themselves to further individual or group interests, and they differ over the best way of coping with the problems which arise from their class position; but overshadowing all these divisions is their common interest in preserving and strengthening a system which guarantees their wealth and privileges. In the event of a real threat to the system, there are no longer class differences—only class traitors, and they are few and far between.[6]

(5) If American government is not ruled by one cohesive, conspiratorial elite, there is ample evidence of continual collusion between various corporate and governmental elites in every area of the political economy. Though there is no one grand power elite, there are many fairly large ones. And these elites often conspire with and seldom restrain each other. A look at the politico-economic system shows that many of the stronger ones tend to predominate in their particular spheres of activity more or less unmolested by other elites and unchecked by government.[7]

---

5. Dahl, *Who Governs?*, p. 272. Also see Robert A. Dahl, *Modern Political Analysis* (Englewood Cliffs, N.J.: Prentice-Hall, 1970).
6. Paul Sweezy, *The Present as History* (New York: Monthly Review Press, 1970), p. 138.
7. See Peter Bachrach, *The Theory of Democratic Elitism* (Boston: Little, Brown, 1967), p. 37.

As we have seen, corporations are not merely beyond the reach of government; they incorporate public authority in their own undertakings. Government does play a crucial role in redirecting sectors of the corporate economy that tend to become disruptive of the system as a whole: hence Teddy Roosevelt's occasional trust-busting, Franklin Roosevelt's opposition to holding companies and John Kennedy's attempt to force steel companies to hold back their prices. But such actions are usually limited in their range and are in-duced by a desire to protect the business economy *in toto*.

Most elitist conflicts, we noted, are resolved not by compromise but by logrolling and involve more *collusion* than competition. These mutually satisfying arrangements among "competitors" leave out the interests of broad, unorganized sectors of the public and are usually harmful to public interests—as when the costs of collusion are passed on to the public in the form of higher prices, higher taxes, environmental devastation and inflation. The demands of the have-nots may be heard occasionally as a clamor outside the gate, and now and then morsels are tossed to the unfortunates—especially if private suppliers can make money on such programs. But generally speaking, pluralist group politics engages the interests of extremely limited portions of the population and only within a field of political options largely shaped by the interests of corporate capitalism.

Interest group politics is tiered or structured according to the scope and power of the contenders. Big interests, like the oil com-panies, banks and defense industry, operate in the most important arena, extracting hundreds of billions of dollars from private markets and the public treasure, affecting the well-being of whole communities and regions, and exercising control over the most im-portant units of the federal government. In contrast, consumer groups, labor unions and public interest advocates move in a more limited space, registering their complaints against some of the worst, or more visible, symptoms of the corporate system, and occa-sionally winning a new law or regulation that proves largely ineffec-tual in treating the endlessly proliferating ill effects of capitalism. Finally, the weakest interests, like welfare mothers and slum dwel-lers, are shunted to the very margins of political life, reminding us of their existence with an occasional demonstration in front of city hall, making a claim on the shrinking "nonessential" and often non-existent human services budget.

It is worth repeating that *the diffusion of power does not neces-sarily mean the democratization of power.* A wide array of corpo-rate groups is not indicative of a wide sharing of power in any demo-cratic sense, for the sharing occurs among propertied interests that are becoming increasingly less competitive and more concentrated and collusive in both economic ownership and political influence. Decision-making power is "divided" in that it is parceled out to special public-private interest groups—quasiautonomous, entrenched coteries that use public authority for private purposes of low visibility. The fragmentation of power is the pocketing of power, a way of insulating portions of the political process from the tides of popular sentiment. This purpose was embodied in the constitutional structure by the framers in 1787 and has prevailed ever since.

THE MYTH OF THE MIXED ECONOMY

The continued growth of government activity in the economy has led some observers to the mistaken notion that we are gradually moving toward a "post-capitalist" society, one that is neither capitalist nor socialist but a "mixed economy."[8] Proponents of this view avoid any consideration of what government does and whom it benefits when mixing itself with the economy. They fail to differentiate between federal regulation *of* business and federal regulation *for* business, and they assume that the power of government is neutral and socially beneficent.[9]

Both liberal and conservative theorists have treated the increasingly socialized *costs* of the public sector as evidence of increasingly socialized *benefits*, with liberals generally approving and conservatives disapproving of this trend. Conservatives attack the "welfare state" and liberals defend it; few in either camp question whether we really have one. In reality, government involvement in the economy represents not a growth in socialism (as that term is normally understood by socialists) but a growth in state supported capitalism, *not the communization of private wealth but the privatization of the commonwealth.* This development has brought a great deal of government planning, but it is not of the kind intended by socialism, which emphasizes the subordination of private profit and the reallocation of resources for new social priorities. As several English socialists have pointed out, in criticism of the policies of the British Labour party:

> Planning now means better forecasting, better coordination of investment and expansion decisions, a more purposeful control over demand.

8. See, for instance, Dahrendorf, *Class and Class Conflict in Industrial Society.*
9. Gabriel Kolko, *The Triumph of Conservatism* (Chicago: Quadrangle Books, 1967), p. 286.

This enables the more technologically equipped and organized units in the private sector to pursue their goals more efficiently, more "rationally." It also means more control over unions and over labor's power to bargain freely about wages. This involves another important transition. For in the course of this rationalization of capitalism, the gap between private industry and the State is narrowed.[10]

In Western industrial nations today, including the United States, government economic planning revolves around "the preservation and regulation of capitalism, not its demise."[11] The outcome is a more centralized blend of capitalist public-private powers. Under the notion of "rational planning" and the guise of insulating decision-making from selfish interest groups and corrupt politicians, corporate-political elites will push for tighter control over the political economy while bypassing the public, the trade unions and the Congress. "Herein lies the fallacy of the liberal hope that planning can achieve social justice."[12] For it is state planning *for* and *by* the corporate elites. Its function is not social welfare or reform but the maintenance of capital profitability at home and abroad.

Given the near monopoly they enjoy over society's productive capacity, the giant corporations remain the sole conduit for most public expenditures. Whether it be for schools or school lunches, sewers or space ships, submarines or airplanes, harbors or highways, government relies almost exclusively on private contractors and suppliers. These suppliers may be heavily subsidized or entirely funded from the public treasure, but they remain "private" in that a profit—usually a most generous risk-free one—accrues to them for whatever services they perform. The government is not a *producer* in competition with business, such rivalry not being appreciated in a capitalist economy, but a titanic *purchaser* or *consumer* of business products. Bound by this consumer role, government is dependent on business. This can be seen clearly during wars and cold wars, when intensified public spending brings greater governmental reliance on private industry. While some people bemoan the growth of government "interference" in business affairs, the reality is that business management has moved more deeply into public affairs with each

---

10. Stuart Hall, Raymond Williams and Edward Thompson, "The May Day Manifesto," excerpted in Carl Oglesby (ed.), *The New Left Reader* (New York: Grove Press, 1969), p. 115.

11. Stanley Aronowitz, "Modernizing Capitalism," *Social Policy*, May/June 1975, p. 20.

12. Aronowitz, "Modernizing Capitalism," p. 24. See also S. M. Miller, "Planning: Can It Make a Difference in Capitalist America?" *Social Policy*, September/October 1975, pp. 12–22.

new national mobilization, keeping public spending closely in line with industry's own profit interests.[13]

The commitment by government to expend its wealth primarily through private conduits in ways that do not compete with, and only serve to bolster, the private profit system marks one of the key differences between socialism and state-supported capitalism. Whether the difference is thought to be desirable or not, it first should be understood. The "mixed economy" as found in the United States has very little to do with socialism. Increases in spending may represent a growth in the public sector of the economy but not in the *publicly owned, public-serving* sector. The distinction between the "public" and "private," then, is a misleading one, since *the growth of the public sector represents little more than an increase in the risk-free, high-profit market of the private sector.* Sometimes the government will exercise direct ownership of a particular service, either to assist private industry—as with certain port facilities and technological research and training institutions—or to perform services which private capital no longer finds profitable to provide—as with nationalized coal mines in Great Britain or the bus and subway lines in many American cities. Private capital relinquishes its franchise and moves on to greener pastures, while the ownership, risks and losses are passed on to the public.[14]

There is the anticipation, common among some radicals, that as the problems of the economy deepen, modern capitalism will succumb to its own internal contradictions; as the economic "substructure" gives way, the "superstructure" of the capitalist state will be carried down with it and the opportunity for a humane, anti-imperialist, democratic, socialist society will be at hand. One difficulty with this position is that it underestimates the extent to which the political system can act with independent effect to preserve the capitalist class. The political system is more than a front for the economic interests it serves; it is the single most important force that corpo-

---

13. See Walter LaFeber, *The New Empire: An Interpretation of American Expansion, 1860–1898* (Ithaca, N.Y.: Cornell University Press, 1963) for evidence of the growing interdependence of government and business as each expanded its activities. Also see Paul Koistinen, "The 'Industrial-Military Complex' in Historical Perspective: The Inter War Years," in Irwin Unger (ed.), *Beyond Liberalism: The New Left Views American History* (Waltham, Mass.: Xerox College Publishing, 1971), pp. 227–239; and David Horowitz (ed.), *Corporations and the Cold War* (New York: Monthly Review Press, 1969).

14. Public ownership in this context is often only on paper. In the case of transit systems that are passed from private to public hands (discussed in chapter 7), the takeover really represents nothing more than a change from private stocks to public bonds— owned by the same wealthy class and banks that had owned the stocks. In addition the bonds are tax-free and offer a return guaranteed by the public treasure.

rate America has at its command. The power to use the police and the military, the power of eminent domain, the power to tax, spend and legislate, to use public funds for private profit, the power of limitless credit, the power to mobilize highly emotive symbols of loyalty and legitimacy—such resources of the state give corporate America a durability it could never provide for itself through the economy alone. The resilience of capitalism cannot be measured in isolated economic terms. Behind the corporation there stands the organized power of the state; "the stability and future of the economy is grounded, in the last analysis, on the power of the state to act to preserve it."[15] To maintain themselves, the corporations can call on the resources of the state to rationalize and subsidize their performance, maintain their profit levels, socialize costs by taxing the many and keep the malcontents under control through generous applications of official violence.

In sum, the merging of the public and private sectors is not merely a result of the growing complexity of. technological society or a transition toward socialism; it is in large part the outcome of the realities of power and capitalist class interest.

REFORM WITHIN THE SYSTEM?

It is not quite accurate to presume that non-elites never win victories. The last century of intensive struggle between labor and management, continuing to this day and involving such groups as farm workers, hospital workers, teachers and white-collar employees, brought notable advances in the working conditions of millions. But change, if not impossible within state-supported capitalism, is always limited by the overall imperatives of that system and is usually of a cosmetic or marginal nature. In most instances the acceptable changes prove to be supportive and even profitable to the larger capitalist interests. Hence, as already noted, most of 'the regulatory "reforms" benefited the giant producers at the expense of smaller producers and consumers.

Sometimes elites will initially oppose even these kinds of changes, not realizing the gains available to them. The auto industry was against safety features in automobiles until it realized that they could be installed as high-priced accessories which the customer was legally required to buy. And doctors vigorously opposed Medicare and Medicaid as steps toward "socialism" until they discovered gold

---

15. Kolko, *The Triumph of Conservatism*, p. 302.

in those programs. For with public funding available, the doctors and the hospitals now were able to double and triple their fees, charging their patients amounts they would not have dared impose had the patient been the sole payer. The result is that medical expenses zoomed upward without a commensurate improvement in medical care—although certainly some elderly people now have assistance they would not have had earlier. *To pour more money into a service without a change in the market relations enjoyed by the suppliers is merely to make more public funds available to the suppliers without guaranteeing an improvement in the service.*

It is somewhat ironic to credit capitalism with the ability to reform itself through gradual improvements when (a) most of the reforms have been vehemently resisted by capitalist elites, (b) most of the problems needing reform have been caused or intensified by capitalism and (c) most of the actual programs end up primarily benefiting the capitalist producers.

Conservatives complain that we have thrown billions at our socioeconomic problems with no results. From this correct observation they mistakenly conclude that since little can be done about these problems within the *present* system, then the problems are insoluble. For the elites who own this country, if wiping out widespread poverty and starvation entails changing the entire system and jeopardizing elite class positions, then better to have poverty and starvation.

Some of the more liberal elites believe our problems can be solved within the present system of state-supported capitalism, it being principally a matter of changing our "warped priorities." To be sure, the priorities are warped: upper-income Americans spend over $2 billion a year on jewelry— more than is spent on housing for the poor—and no less than $3 billion on pleasure boating—a half billion more than what the fifty states spend on welfare. Over the years greater sums have been budgeted by the government for the development of the Navy's submarine-rescue vehicle than for occupational safety, public libraries and day care centers combined. The Pentagon stores more ammunition in its dumps ($10.4 billion worth) than the costs of all natural resource programs including pollution control, conservation, community development, housing, occupational safety and mass transportation. The total expenses of the legislative and judiciary branches and all the regulatory commissions combined constitute little more than one-half of 1 percent of the Pentagon's budget. More public monies are given away every year to the creditor class, the top 1 percent of the population, in interest payments on public bonds, than are spent in five years on services to the bottom 20 percent.

The government has any number of policy options which might be pursued: it could end its costly overseas military interventions, drastically cut its military expenditures, phase out its expensive space programs,[16] eliminate the multibillion-dollar tax loopholes for corporations and rich individuals, increase taxes on industrial profits, cut taxes for lower- and middle-income groups, prosecute industries for pollution and for widespread monopolistic practices, end multibillion-dollar giveaways and legislate a guaranteed minimum income well above the poverty level. Government also could distribute to almost 2 million poor farmers the billions now received by rich agricultural producers, and it could engage in a concerted effort at conservation and enter directly into nonprofit production and ownership in the areas of health, housing, education and mass transportation.

Such measures have been urged, but in almost every instance government has pursued policies of an opposite kind. It is not enough to scold those who resist change as if they did so out of obstinance or ill-will; it is necessary to understand the dynamics of power that make these policies persist in the face of all appeals and human needs to the contrary. Those who bemoan the "warped priorities" of our society assume that the present politico-economic system could produce a whole different set of effects. But the question is, *Why* have new and more humane priorities not been pursued? And the answer is twofold: First, because the realities of power do not allow for fundamental reform, and second, because the present politico-economic system could not sustain itself if such reforms were initiated. Let us take each of these in turn:

(1) Quite simply, those who have the interest in fundamental change have not the power, while those who have the power have not the interest. It is not that decision-makers have been unable to figure out the technical steps for change; it is that they oppose the things that change entails. The first intent of most officeholders is not to fight for social change but to survive and prosper. Given this, they are inclined to respond positively not to group *needs* but to group *demands*, to those who have the resources to command their attention. In political life as in economic life, needs do not become marketable demands until they are backed by "buying power" or "exchange power," for only then is it in the "producer's" interest to respond. The problem for many unorganized citizens and workers is that they have few political resources of their own to exchange. For the politician, as for most people, the compelling quality of any ar-

---

16. The space shuttle program and the B-1 bomber together cost more than the entire Vietnam war.

gument is determined less by its logic and evidence than by the strength of its advocates. And the advocate is strong if the resources he controls are desired and needed by the politician. The wants of the unorganized public seldom become demands—that is, they seldom become imperatives to which political officials find it in their own interest to respond, especially if the changes needed would put the official on a collision course with those who control the resources of the society and who see little wrong with the world as it is.

(2) Most of the demands for fundamental change in our priorities are impossible to effect within the present system if that system is to maintain itself. The reason our labor, skills, technology and natural resources are not used for social need and egalitarian redistribution is that they are used for corporate gain. The corporations cannot build low-rent houses and feed the poor because their interest is not in social reconstruction but in private profit. For the state to maintain whatever "prosperity" it can, it must do so within the ongoing system of corporate investments. To maintain investment, it must guarantee high-profit yields. To make fundamental changes in our priorities, the state would have to effect major redistributions in income and taxation, cut business subsidies, end deficit spending and interest payments to the rich, redirect capital investments toward nonprofit or low-profit goals and impose severe and sometimes crippling penalties for pollution and monopolistic practices. But if the state did all this, the investment incentives would be greatly diminished, the risks for private capital would be too high, many companies could not survive and unemployment would reach disastrous heights. State-supported capitalism cannot exist without state support, without passing its immense costs and inefficiencies on to the public. The only way the state could redirect the wealth of society toward egalitarian goals would be to exercise total control over capital investments and capital return, but that would mean, in effect, public ownership of the means of production—a giant step toward *socialism*.

It is understandable then why appeals to fair play and exhortations for change do not bring the fundamental reallocations needed: quite simply, the problem of change is no easier for the haves than for the have-nots. Contrary to the admonitions of liberal critics, it is neither stupidity nor opaqueness which prevents those who control the property and the institutions of this society from satisfying the demand for change. To be sure, elites suffer their share of self-righteous stubbornness, but more often than not, meaningful changes are not embarked upon because they would literally threaten the survival of privileged interests; like most other social groups the elites show little inclination to commit class suicide.

What is being argued here is that, contrary to the view of liberal critics, the nation's immense social problems are not irrational off-shoots of a basically rational system, to be solved by replacing the existing corporate and political decision-makers with persons who would be better intentioned and more socially aware. Rather, the problems are rational outcomes of a basically irrational system, a system structured not for the satisfaction of human need but the multiplication of human greed. Within the imperatives of that system, well-intentioned reform-minded persons end up having either to obey the economic imperatives of that system or be removed from positions of responsibility. The reforms they manage to effect are the kind the system will allow, ones which do not tamper with the basic interests of class privilege, power and property.[17] As long as liberals proceed with an incorrect diagnosis, they will never come up with solutions. As long as we look for solutions within the very system that causes the problems, we will continue to produce cosmetic, Band-Aid programs. The end result is shameful public poverty and shameless private wealth.

QUESTIONING THE STATUS QUO

Defenders of the status quo argue that protest is a thing of the past and that today people are in a conservative mood. They point to students who are struggling for grades instead of for revolution and to the backlash against the Equal Rights Amendment (ERA), busing, abortion and gay rights. Yet there is also much evidence to the contrary. In colleges today there is probably more critical analysis of the capitalist system than during the more activist antiwar days of the 1960s. Campuses throughout the country have witnessed rallies, demonstrations, strikes, sit-ins and arrests over such issues as university investment in firms doing business with South Africa, the firing of radical professors, cuts in minority studies and women's studies and questions of governance, admissions, living conditions and tuition.[18]

---

17. It is not that state-supported capitalism is the cause of every social ill in modern society but that capitalism and the capitalist state have no fundamental commitment to remedying social ills, despite their command over vast resources that might be directed toward such ends. And, from the evidence of past chapters, it might be argued that state-supported capitalism has been doing much to create and intensify the very conditions which breed social ills both at home and abroad.

18. For example, at the University of California, Santa Cruz, in 1978, 419 students protesting university investments in South Africa were arrested—the largest demonstration action that campus had seen in years.

In 1976 tens of thousands massed for a people's bicentennial demonstration in Philadelphia, demanding an end to American imperialism and capitalism—an event that was ignored by the business-owned press. Religious groups, Catholic and Protestant, modernist and fundamentalist—including Southern Baptists and Evangelicals like Billy Graham—are raising their voices against military spending and the arms race. Recent years have brought large demonstrations in major cities against oppression in South Africa, Ireland, Chile and a half dozen other lands. Environmentalist and public interest groups continue to disseminate their views to increasingly sympathetic audiences. And there have been large demonstrations and mass acts of civil disobedience against nuclear power throughout the nation.

Repeatedly pronounced dead and buried, labor militancy continues to erupt in the form of wildcat strikes against cutbacks, layoffs and unsafe working conditions. In recent years there has been a sharp increase in strikes, with major walkouts by steel workers, coal miners, truck drivers, farm workers, teachers, and newspaper, hospital and utility workers. These struggles are largely ignored by the media, but one thing is certain: it is grossly misleading to portray workers as complacent flagwavers who are enamored of the status quo.[19] Even if they are attached to certain traditional symbols and values from the political realm, their unhappiness with economic conditions may well lead them to question these attachments. Since the political and economic spheres are so closely intertwined, economic discontent may eventually give rise to discontent with the political system that supports and protects a corporate economy.

Political consciousness changes sometimes visibly and noisily, sometimes deeply and quietly. The transition in Black consciousness offers an interesting case in point. It is probably no accident that in the latter half of the twentieth century the first challenges to the established ideology and to the image of "America the beautiful" came from Black people. Forcibly brought to this country centuries ago as chattels for the sole purpose of economic exploitation, Blacks, after the Emancipation and over the generations, continued to suffer every exploitation, discrimination and violence to body and spirit that White America was capable of inflicting. By the 1960s Blacks

---

19. Andrew Levison, *The Working-Class Majority* (New York: Penguin Books, 1975), offers much evidence to debunk the Archie Bunker stereotype of workers. For excellent studies of radicalism and militancy in the American labor movement, see Jeremy Brecher, *Strike* (New York: Fawcett, 1974); and Richard O. Boyer and Herbert M. Morais, *Labor's Untold Story* (New York: United Electrical, Radio and Machine Workers, 1972).

were saying publicly what many of them had always felt privately: that there was little justice for Black people in White America, that Blacks did not share equally in the progress our country was allegedly enjoying and that they must develop their own identities and consciousness and mobilize against White bosses, unions, landlords, merchants, police, government officials and the White power system in general.

As the Black protest grew, other groups began getting the message, and Chicano, Native American, Puerto Rican and women's liberation groups voiced similar indictments about the roles and social conditions imposed upon them. And just as the Black protest started with demands for integration into the established system only to develop serious questions about the desirability of that goal ("Who wants to integrate into a burning house?"), so did the other protest groups begin to wonder whether piecemeal entry into the established structure would bring them any closer to a resolution of widespread social ills. When a Black becomes a corporation vice-president or a woman becomes a Navy pilot it is a net loss for all oppressed people, they argued, since corporate executives and Navy officers, whether White males or Black females, serve the interest of those in power and not those in need.[20]

Today many Black leaders reject total integration as an unrealistic and even undesirable goal. Integration, they point out, usually means the selective absorption of talented Blacks into White-dominated institutions, with little substantive return to the Black masses. No ethnic group in the United States ever wanted total integration, Nathan Wright, Jr., notes: "All have asked simply for desegregation. Desegregation involves some integration as a means to an end but not as an end in itself."[21] Desegregation is an important step forward, leading to the removal of legal and de facto barriers that loom as instruments of racial insult and oppression. Ultimately, though, the betterment of the Black people will come, radical Blacks say, not through piecemeal absorption into the White establishment but

---

20. For discussions of how the Black liberation struggle is tied to the class struggle, see the writings of James Boggs and Grace Boggs; see also Julius Lester, "The Current State of Black America," *New Politics*, 10 June 1973, pp. 4–13. For an earlier statement see my "Assimilation and Counter-Assimilation: From Civil Rights to Black Radicalism," in Philip Green and Sanford Levison (eds.), *Power and Community* (New York: Pantheon, 1969), pp. 173–194. For statements on how the liberation of women is tied to the liberation of the working class, see Rosalyn Boxandall *et al.* (eds.), *America's Working Women: A Documentary History—1600 to the Present* (New York: Random House, 1976).

21. Nathan Wright, Jr., "The Crisis Which Bred Black Power," in Floyd D. Barbow (ed.), *The Black Power Revolt* (Boston: Sargent, Porter, 1968), p. 117.

through an upheaval of the entire exploitative politico-economic system and the deliverance of the resources of power into the hands of the poor and the working people of all races—what we call social revolution. Within the Black community today there is also a growing identification with the anti-imperialist struggles of the Third World, especially those in Africa, and with this a deeper indictment of the corporate system at home.

Millions of Americans, of course, are still committed to the acquisitive, competitive values discussed in chapter 3. Millions still live with a fear of equality and a scarcity psychology that pits each against the other. Much of this sentiment is reinforced by the simple fact that the system obliges us to compete in order to survive and in order to live with any modicum of comfort and security. But despite these powerful conditioning forces, despite the secret actions and manipulations used by the state to maintain the status quo and despite elitist control over most of the resources of power and over the institutions and information of this society, the American people are not indifferent to the exploitative and unjust features of the existing system. As noted in chapter 3, opinion surveys show that Americans have far more progressive positions than the leaders of both parties. The opinion polls show the marked decline in "faith" that the public, including many "middle Americans," feels for its political and economic institutions, a development troublesome enough to evoke alarmed comments from business leaders and their counterparts in government. Ordinary Americans are not as oblivious to their own needs as are their leaders. They justly feel victimized as wage earners, tenants, home owners, taxpayers, commuters and consumers, and they are far more open to progressive solutions than is supposed.

Why then have we been left with the feeling that the nation is in a conservative mood? First, because political, business and media representatives have been telling us so. When 150 students took over a building at Columbia University in 1968, the media treated it as an event of momentous significance and gave it national coverage. Today, larger and equally militant campus demonstrations go unreported. Having decided that protests are passé, the media treat activism as nonexistent, thereby influencing how we see our times and ourselves.[22]

Political interests seek to engineer appearances as well as realities, for appearances tend to become realities. People do not act on

---

22. John Magney, "Mountains, Molehills and Media Hypes," *Working Papers*, May/June 1979.

what is real but on what they believe to be real. There is a self-ful-
filling dimension to power. If the ruling elites can convince everyone
that everyone else has lost interest in progressive struggles then many
of us will lapse into a disheartened quietude—which is what the ruling elites want.

Second, much of the progressive sentiment reflected in opinion
polls is "soft," or in other words, diffused, unorganized and not always embraced with firmness. Therefore, it seldom has the same impact on policies as do the big money and organized pressure of corporate America. Opinion polls show that people do not want natural
gas prices deregulated nor the military budget expanded, yet Congress—listening to different drummers in the lobbies of Capitol
Hill—votes for these things. The majority of Americans are for
legalized abortion but a well-financed and well-organized minority
is turning the lawmakers around.

Finally, it is not that Americans are conservative but that conservatives have been gaining greater visibility, spending unusually
large sums to back conservative candidates and conservative issues,
channeling popular discontent into things like tax rebellions and the
antifeminist and antiabortion movements, all the while ignoring the
questions of class oppression and the nature of the corporate
political economy, and the questions of who gets what, when and
how.[23]

UPWARD FROM CAPITALISM

More than half a century ago the great sociologist Max Weber
wrote: "The question is: How are freedom and democracy in the
long run at all possible under the domination of highly developed
capitalism?"[24] That question is still with us. And the answer suggested in this book is that freedom and democracy have at best a ten-
uous, marginal existence in capitalist society.

---

23. Proposition 13 in California offers a good example of how popular resistance to
an oppressive tax structure is directed by conservatives toward their own ends.
Responding to a campaign heavily financed and led by wealthy businessmen, California voters approved Proposition 13, an amendment to their state constitution, which
limits property taxes to only 1 percent of the cash value of the holding and requires a
two-thirds vote of the state legislature or any pertinent local legislature in order to increase any tax in the state. The biggest beneficiaries of Proposition 13, however, have
been the corporations and banks and the biggest losers the ordinary citizens who eventually must learn to do without essential services.

24. H. H. Gerth and C. Wright Mills (eds.), *From Max Weber: Essays in Sociology*
(New York: Oxford University Press, 1958).

How can we speak of most government policies as being products of the democratic will? What democratic will demanded that Washington be honeycombed with high-paid lobbyists and corporate lawyers who would spend their time raiding the public treasure on behalf of rich clients? When was the public consulted on tideland oil leases, Alaskan oil leases, bloated defense contracts, agribusiness subsidies and tax write-offs? When did the American people insist on having unsafe, overpriced drugs and foods circulate unrestricted and an FDA that protects rather than punishes the companies marketing such products? When did they urge the government to help the gas, electric and telephone companies to overcharge the public? When did the voice of the people clamor for a multibillion-dollar space program that fattened corporate contractors and satisfied the curiosity of some astronomers and scientists while leaving the rest of us still more burdened by taxes and deprived of necessary services here on earth? What democratic will decreed that we destroy the Cambodian countryside between 1969 and 1971 in a bombing campaign conducted without the consent or even the knowledge of Congress and the public? And what large sector of public opinion demanded that the government intervene secretly in Laos with U.S. Marines in 1969 or financially sustain a war of Portuguese colonial oppression in Africa or subvert progressive governments in Chile, Indonesia and elsewhere?

Far from giving their assent, ordinary people have had to struggle to find out what is going on. And to the extent that a popular will has been registered, it has been demonstrably in the opposite direction, against the worst abuses and most blatant privileges of plutocracy, against the spoliation of the environment and the plunder of the treasury, against the use of government power to serve corporate conglomerates and against military intervention in other countries.

The political system will belong to the people only when the resources of power belong to them, enabling them to effect their democratic will at all levels of private and public institutional life. This will entail a struggle of momentous scope against the corporate elites that now control our labor and our politics. The purpose will be not to replace those at the top with others but to demonstrate that we do not need anyone *on top*, that there is no immutable need for gargantuan government and stratified, bureaucratized, authoritarian institutions and that those involved in the life activities of an institution and affected by its actions should have command of its resources. In a democratic socialist system, the factories, mills, mines, offices, educational institutions, newspapers, hospitals, and so on will not be privately owned for private gain but will be controlled by and for their clients and workers. That is the goal toward which our efforts should be directed.

What is important under socialism is not only whether something is publicly owned and financed but the *purpose* or goals toward which production is directed and the way priorities are set and decisions made. The commitment is, or should be, to communal, collective and responsible decision-making and toward the elimination of poverty and pollution, the end of imperialism, the equalization of life chances, the bettering of the lives of millions of needy working people.[25] Once the wealth, labor and creative energies of people are liberated from the irrational social purposes of a capitalist system, the potentialities for human advancement and individual initiative will be greatly increased, as has happened in a number of Third World countries that have liberated themselves from imperialism. Under the present system we are taught passivity, consumerism, spectatorism, isolation and incompetence. Our energies often are directed into overly specialized and mindless tasks for the production of a glut of gadgets and gimmicks that no one really asked for. We are taught that the controlling decisions over our lives must remain in the hands of those "above" us, those who claim to know better—or else "there will be chaos." There are people who insist that worker control of factories is "impracticable," yet worker-control systems have been set up in several countries with workers devising their own job assignments, rotating their tasks, teaching each other new skills, setting their own work paces, making managerial decisions, controlling budgets and production schedules and the like.[26] The results have been remarkable for worker morale and production efficiency, but in capitalist nations such innovations are potentially dangerous to the owning class, for once workers realize they do not need management to command them, they may begin to question why the profits must go to the corporate owners, who contribute nothing to production.

---

25. In the view of many socialists, especially those identified with the radical movement in America, public ownership of the means of production for the purpose of building an authoritarian, hierarchical society with substantial income inequalities, dominated by a bureaucratic elite as in the USSR, is not socialism, or, at best, it is a tragically misshaped form of socialism, one that might provide a fairly decent minimum standard of social services for all its citizens, including free education and good medical care, but which denies them the opportunities for personal initiative and cooperative control over the conditions of work, study, community and environment and over the products of their minds and their labor and over the larger policies of their nation.

26. David Jenkins, *Job Power: Blue and White Collar Democracy* (New York: Penguin, 1974).

There are people who cannot imagine an alternative university system and are frightened at the prospect of changing the present structure,which gives nearly total power to successful businessmen who serve as oligarchic trustees while the rest of us remain powerless dependents. Yet there already exist such democratically organized institutions of learning. There are people who cannot imagine that hospitals can be organized in any way that would diminish the elitist, authoritarian, money-making role of the head doctors and trustees, and allow staff and patients to play a real part in decision-making, openly criticizing mistakes and collectively working for improvements. Yet such hospitals, and quite good ones, exist in other parts of the world.[27] What a pathetic failure of the political imagination that some of our professional people cannot, or dare not, imagine more sensible, efficient and democratic ways of organizing our social, political and economic institutions. Out of a fear that their class and professional privileges might be challenged, some people resist all equalizing changes and commit themselves to living unexamined lives.

But those of us who have some feeling for social justice and liberation must educate ourselves about the nature of the politico-economic system we live in. (My hope is that this book has been a step in that direction.) We must liberate our political imaginations and learn about alternative forms of social organization and alternative social values. We must confront and engage our peers in the kind of dialogue that heightens our awareness and helps us free ourselves and each other from the elitist, hierarchical values that imprison us, including the bigotry toward working-class people and the sexism, racism and fear of equality we have all been taught. We must, in our places of work and community, organize politically, learn to work cooperatively, engage in direct action, demonstrations, strikes, boycotts and in every way work against the manifold inhumanities of capitalism.

Finally, through the use of what limited political resources we have, we must make the effort to educate both ourselves and others regarding the unjust and undemocratic features of state-supported capitalism and the possibilities for an alternative anti-imperialist, antiracist, antisexist, democratic socialism. This last point is an important one. The wasteful, destructive effects of corporatism within our nation, the pressures of competition between capitalist nations, the growing discontent and oppression of the populace, the con-

---

27. See Joshua Horne, *Away with All Pests* (New York: Monthly Review Press, 1971) for a discussion of medical practices in China.

ROTHCO

ALIVE AND WELL

tinual productive growth within socialist nations, the new revolutionary victories against Western imperialism in the Third World,
all these things make objective conditions increasingly unfavorable
for capitalism. Yet people will not discard the system that oppresses
them until they see the feasibility of an alternative one. It is not that
they think society *should* be this way but that it *must* be. It is not
that they don't want things to change, but they don't believe things
can change—or they fear that whatever changes might occur would
more likely be for the worse.

What is needed is widespread organizing not only around particular issues but for a socialist movement that sees both the desirability of an alternative system and the *possibility* and indeed the great *necessity* for an alternative. Throughout the world and at home, forces for change are being unleashed. There is much evidence—some of it presented in the pages above and in chapter 3—indicating that Americans are well ahead of the existing political elites in their willingness to embrace new alternatives, including public ownership of the major corporations and worker control of production. With time and struggle, as the possibility and necessity for progressive change become more evident and the longing for a better social life grows stronger, people will become increasingly intolerant of the monumental injustices of the existing capitalist system and will move toward a profoundly revolutionary solution. We can be hopeful the day will come, as it came in social orders of the past, when those who seem invincible will be shaken from their pinnacles and a new, humane and truly democratic society will begin to emerge.

About the Author

Michael Parenti received his Ph.D. from Yale University and has taught political and social science at various colleges and universities. In addition he has been a guest lecturer on campuses throughout the country. He has written articles for numerous academic journals and popular periodicals. Among his books are *The Anti-Communist Impulse, Trends and Tragedies in American Foreign Policy* (a book of edited readings) and *Power and the Powerless*. The latter, published by St. Martin's Press, is a study of how power, class and social institutions shape political consciousness.

Index

National Educational Television (NET), 169
National Emergencies Act (1976), 254
National income (1940), 74–75
National Industrial Pollution Control Council, 274
National interest and policy identified with dominant propertied interests, 65, 304
National Labor Relations Board, 4, 36
National Petroleum Council, 281
National Recovery Act (NRA), 71
Native Americans, 105, 146, 316
Nazi Germany, as pluralistic society, 301
Nazi war criminals, 153
Near v. *Minnesota*, 294
Needs, productivity, bigness and, 18–22
Nelson, Garrison, 228, 238
Nelson, Jack, 145
Nevins, Allan, 68
New Deal, 65, 70–75, 287–288
Newfield, Jack, 36, 107, 128, 130
Newhouse (firm), 169
Newland, Carl, 137–138
Newman, Bill, 128
Newspapers. *See* Press, the
New York City
  fiscal crisis of, 107
  taxes paid by, 87
New York City Police Department (NYPD), 221
New York Times v. *Sullivan*, 289
Ney, Richard, 272
Nichols, David, 209
Nie, Norman H., 202
Nillson, Robert, 272
Nixon, Richard M., 41, 47, 80, 130, 192, 207, 213, 215
  Congress vs., 253, 255
  contributions to campaigns of, 209, 214
  deficit spending and, 187
  as dual president, 246, 249
  and executive privilege, 252
  personal characteristics of, 244–245
  Supreme Court and, 295
  and Watergate, 156–158, 221, 239
No-growth capitalism, as contradiction in terms, 13
Nonproductive areas, 17–18
  See also Bureaucracy; Defense, Department of; Unemployment compensation; Welfare programs
Nonvoting, as rational response, 196–201
North, Arthur A., 286

Nossiter, Bernard, 245
Nuclear industry, 117–118
Nuclear power, 116–118, 171, 220
Nuclear Regulatory Commission (NRC), 117, 261, 273

Obey, David, 226
O'Brien, Mary Win, 112
Occupational safety, 111–112
  Supreme Court and, 296
Ortwein v. *Schwab*, 297
Officeholders, 11
  and campaign contributions, 209–214
  corruption of, 220–223
  lobbyists and, 214–220
  who are the, 205, 209
  See also Bureaucracy; Congress; Elections; Presidents; Supreme Court
Oglesby, Carl, 308
O'Leary, John, 271
Oleszek, Walter, 235
Olney, Richard, 67
Olsen, David, 8
One-person, one-vote rule, 296–297
O'Toole, George, 154
Overtime work, 26
Ownership, separation of management from, as myth, 10–11
Oyle, Irving, 109

Pacific Railroad, 263
Page, Joseph A., 112
Pahlevi, Mohammed Riza (Shah of Iran), 174, 215
Pakistan, 84
Palley, Marian, 299
Palmer raids, 148
Palmore, Erdman, 26
Panama, 18
Paraguay, 174
Parfit, Michael, 272
Parker, Richard, 8, 99
Patman, Wright, 214
Patterson, E. F., 78
Patterson, Tim, 178
Pearson, Drew, 225
Penalties (criminal), 130–133
Penn Central Railroad, 11
Pennock, J. Roland, 203
Pentagon. *See* Defense, Department of
Pentagon Papers, 157
People's Republic of China, 82
Perkins, Dexter, 284
Perlo, Victor, 28